Palgrave Macmillan Studies in Family and Intimate Life

Titles include:

Graham Allan, Graham Crow and Sheila Hawker
STEPFAMILIES

Harriet Becher
FAMILY PRACTICES IN SOUTH ASIAN MUSLIM FAMILIES
Parenting in a Multi-Faith Britain

Elisa Rose Birch, Anh T. Le and Paul W. Miller
HOUSEHOLD DIVISIONS OF LABOUR
Teamwork, Gender and Time

Deborah Chambers
SOCIAL MEDIA AND PERSONAL RELATIONSHIPS
Online Intimacies and Networked Friendship

Robbie Duschinsky and Leon Antonio Rocha (*editors*)
FOUCAULT, THE FAMILY AND POLITICS

Jacqui Gabb
RESEARCHING INTIMACY IN FAMILIES

Stephen Hicks
LESBIAN, GAY AND QUEER PARENTING
Families, Intimacies, Genealogies

Clare Holdsworth
FAMILY AND INTIMATE MOBILITIES

Rachel Hurdley
HOME, MATERIALITY, MEMORY AND BELONGING
Keeping Culture

Peter Jackson (*editor*)
CHANGING FAMILIES, CHANGING FOOD

Riitta Jallinoja and Eric Widmer (*editors*)
FAMILIES AND KINSHIP IN CONTEMPORARY EUROPE
Rules and Practices of Relatedness

Lynn Jamieson, Ruth Lewis and Roona Simpson (*editors*)
RESEARCHING FAMILIES AND RELATIONSHIPS
Reflections on Process

David Morgan
RETHINKING FAMILY PRACTICES

Eriikka Oinonen
FAMILIES IN CONVERGING EUROPE
A Comparison of Forms, Structures and Ideals

Róisín Ryan-Flood
LESBIAN MOTHERHOOD
Gender, Families and Sexual Citizenship

Sally Sales
ADOPTION, FAMILY AND THE PARADOX OF ORIGINS
A Foucauldian History

Tam Sanger
TRANS PEOPLE'S PARTNERSHIPS
Towards an Ethics of Intimacy

Elizabeth B. Silva
TECHNOLOGY, CULTURE, FAMILY
Influences on Home Life

Lisa Smyth
THE DEMANDS OF MOTHERHOOD
Agents, Roles and Recognitions

Palgrave Macmillan Studies in Family and Intimate Life
Series Standing Order ISBN 978–0–230–51748–6 hardback
978–0–230–24924–0 paperback
(*outside North America only*)

You can receive future titles in this series as they are published by placing a standing order. Please contact your bookseller or, in case of difficulty, write to us at the address below with your name and address, the title of the series and the ISBN quoted above.

Customer Services Department, Macmillan Distribution Ltd, Houndmills, Basingstoke, Hampshire RG21 6XS, England

Home, Materiality, Memory and Belonging

Keeping Culture

Rachel Hurdley
Cardiff University, UK

palgrave
macmillan

First published 2013 by
PALGRAVE MACMILLAN

Palgrave Macmillan in the UK is an imprint of Macmillan Publishers Limited, registered in England, company number 785998, of Houndmills, Basingstoke, Hampshire RG21 6XS.

Palgrave Macmillan in the US is a division of St Martin's Press LLC, 175 Fifth Avenue, New York, NY 10010.

Palgrave Macmillan is the global academic imprint of the above companies and has companies and representatives throughout the world.

Palgrave® and Macmillan® are registered trademarks in the United States, the United Kingdom, Europe and other countries.

ISBN 978–0–230–23028–6

This book is printed on paper suitable for recycling and made from fully managed and sustained forest sources. Logging, pulping and manufacturing processes are expected to conform to the environmental regulations of the country of origin.

A catalogue record for this book is available from the British Library.

A catalog record for this book is available from the Library of Congress.

Cyflwyniad

Diolch o galon i fy nghariad Trefor,
y gŵr gorau yn y byd

The Other

There are nights that are so still
that I can hear the small owl calling
far off and a fox barking
miles away. It is then that I lie
in the lean hours awake listening
to the swell born somewhere in the Atlantic
rising and falling, rising and falling
wave on wave on the long shore
by the village that is without light
and companionless. And the thought comes
of that other being who is awake, too,
letting our prayers break on him,
not like this for a few hours,
but for days, years, for eternity.

R. S. Thomas (2003 [1988])

Contents

Illustrations

Foreword

Rendering the familiar strange is a frequent characterisation of the craft of the sociologist or social anthropologist and by now the literature is full of memorable examples of this practice. Some of the more obvious examples come, although in different ways, from the writings of Simmel, Goffman and Garfinkel among others. But it can be argued that a much wider body of research and theorising is directed to showing that something which might seem highly individual or personal in fact demonstrates patterns and regularities. Paradoxically, perhaps, demonstrating that an individual set of practices is not as unique as the practitioner might consider in fact demonstrates the oddness of that social behaviour seen more generally.

In this book, Rachel Hurdley provides a clear demonstration of this process of making the familiar seem unfamiliar. Discussed in simple, straightforward descriptive terms, her topic is one which will be recognised by most of her readers: mantelpieces. Her concerns include what we put on mantelpieces and in what order, how and when these items are changed and how these changing displays reflect wider social relationships and personal life. Her exploration takes on issues of memory (individual, shared and collective), identity and the meaning of home. These and other topics such as the nature of gifts and heirlooms receive fresh insights when seen from the vantage point of the taken-for-granted mantelpiece. There are also questions to do with their very existence (in times when heating no longer focuses upon a single fireplace) and their positioning. How and why do mantelpieces survive when faced with competition from, say, flatscreen televisions?

In part this study, using qualitative techniques, allows individuals themselves to describe and talk about their practices. These voices are direct and vivid, although one assumes that these respondents were somewhat surprised that their everyday decisions could possibly be of interest. But Rachel goes beyond this to provide, in addition, a variety of histories (including but not confined to Mass Observation reports) which deal not simply with what is reported or recorded but how this reporting is conducted. The relational histories that arise when considering the provenance of objects displayed, the 'storying of objects', are not simply resources to provide more detailed descriptive accounts but are topics in their own right for further interrogation. Put more simply, she is not simply concerned with what is displayed but with how people account for these displays.

All this would be enough for one full and critical account of a hitherto unexplored area of domestic life. But Rachel goes further. She recognises that her sample probably provides an over-representation of white, middle-class and UK-based respondents. One way of making the familiar strange is to attempt to see these everyday practices through other eyes and so she provides accounts of respondents outside the limits of her initial sample. These eyes may be American or Chinese or, at an even further remove, those of refugees or asylum seekers. Through a series of moves towards the end of the book, the author takes us away from the objects, the photographs, the bills on display to consider wider social practices, wider divisions of class, gender and nationality and to consider some of the largest questions of all: human responsibilities and human connectedness.

David Morgan

Series Editors' Preface

The remit of the *Palgrave Macmillan Studies in Family and Intimate Life* series is to publish major texts, monographs and edited collections focusing broadly on the sociological exploration of intimate relationships and family organisation. As editors we think such a series is timely. Expectations, commitments and practices have changed significantly in intimate relationship and family life in recent decades. This is very apparent in patterns of family formation and dissolution, demonstrated by trends in cohabitation, marriage and divorce. Changes in household living patterns over the last 20 years have also been marked, with more people living alone, adult children living longer in the parental home and more 'non-family' households being formed. Furthermore, there have been important shifts in the ways people construct intimate relationships. There are few comfortable certainties about the best ways of being a family man or woman, with once conventional gender roles no longer being widely accepted. The normative connection between sexual relationships and marriage or marriage-like relationships is also less powerful than it once was. Not only is greater sexual experimentation accepted, but it is now accepted at an earlier age. Moreover, heterosexuality is no longer the only mode of sexual relationship given legitimacy. In Britain as elsewhere, gay male and lesbian partnerships are now socially and legally endorsed to a degree hardly imaginable in the mid-20th century. Increases in lone-parent families, the rapid growth of different types of stepfamily, the de-stigmatisation of births outside marriage and the rise in couples 'living-apart-together' (LATs) all provide further examples of the ways that 'being a couple', 'being a parent' and 'being a family' have diversified in recent years.

The fact that change in family life and intimate relationships has been so pervasive has resulted in renewed research interest from sociologists and other scholars. Increasing amounts of public funding have been directed to family research in recent years, in terms of both individual projects and the creation of family research centres of different hues. This research activity has been accompanied by the publication of some very important and influential books exploring different aspects of shifting family experience, in Britain and elsewhere. The *Palgrave Macmillan Studies in Family and Intimate Life* series hopes to add to this list of influential research-based texts, thereby contributing to existing knowledge and informing current debates. Our main audience consists of academics and advanced students, though we intend that the books in the series will be accessible to a more general readership who wish to understand better the changing nature of contemporary family life and personal relationships.

We see the remit of the series as wide. The concept of 'family and intimate life' will be interpreted in a broad fashion. While the focus of the series will clearly be sociological, we take family and intimacy as being inclusive rather than exclusive. The series will cover a range of topics concerned with family practices and experiences, including, for example, partnership; marriage; parenting; domestic arrangements; kinship; demographic change; intergenerational ties; life course transitions; step-families; gay and lesbian relationships; lone-parent households; and also non-familial intimate relationships such as friendships. We also wish to foster comparative research, as well as research on under-studied populations. The series will include different forms of book. Most will be theoretical or empirical monographs on particular substantive topics, though some may also have a strong methodological focus. In addition, we see edited collections as also falling within the series' remit, as well as translations of significant publications in other languages. Finally we intend that the series has an international appeal, in terms of both topics covered and authorship. Our goal is for the series to provide a forum for family sociologists conducting research in various societies, and not solely in Britain.

Graham Allan, Lynn Jamieson and David Morgan

Acknowledgements

First of all, thanks are due to the participants in the study, who invited me into their homes, gave me their words, photos, mantelpieces and other materials. A special thank you to Deb, whose story is in the Epilogue. Thanks to Philippa Grand, who first showed interest in a book about mantelpieces, and her colleagues; also, thanks to David Morgan for our conversations and his generous feedback on drafts of this book.

Mike Biddulph, whose sketches are at the end of the main text and book cover, made fine interpretations of my chaotic drawings and ramblings – thanks, Mike, for your patience and general brilliance.

Most of the fieldwork and some of the writing for the book was funded by the Economic and Social Research Council. Its earliest beginnings were in a master's dissertation (2001; Award No. K00429923410), which led to a doctoral thesis, *Dismantling Mantelpieces: Consumption as Spectacle and Shaper of Self in the Home* (2001–2006; Award No. R42200134124), and finally a post-doctoral award, *Dismantling Mantelpieces: Bringing Culture Home* (2008–2009; Award No. PTA-026-27-1575).

The bulk of the writing and the second stage of fieldwork were completed during my time as *The Sociological Review* Fellow 2009–2010. The film series *Making Wales, Remembering Home*, which I made with asylum seekers, radically challenging my thinking about things and identity relations, was funded by Beacon for Wales/Goleufa Cymru and co-produced with the Welsh Refugee Council. Mass Observation (MO) material is reproduced with permission of Curtis Brown Group Ltd, London, on behalf of The Trustees of the Mass Observation Archive (to whom I am very grateful for keeping MO alive and well, especially Dorothy Sheridan and Jessica Scantlebury).

Thank you to all these organisations.

Chapter 7 was first published as 'Objecting Relations: The Problem of the Gift' (2007) in *The Sociological Review* 55: 1: 124–143; it has been a little altered for the book. Some of the material on narrative appeared in *Sociology* 40: 4: 717–313 in 'Dismantling Mantelpieces: Narrating Identities and Materialising Culture in the Home'; this has been much revised. Wiley-Blackwell and Sage publishers gave permission for use of these. Many thanks to Gunjana Thomas for permission to use his father's poem *The Other* as a preface.

Thank you to my mentors, Paul Atkinson, Sara Delamont and Joanna Latimer in Cardiff School of Social Sciences (SOCSI); also to Rebecca Leach and Rolland Munro at *The Sociological Review* for their wise words, patient listening and encouragement. Also, thanks to my colleagues and friends in both SOCSI and the Cardiff School of Planning and Geography: in particular, Mike Biddulph, Sophie Donaldson, Katy Greenland, Joan Haran, William Housley, Mike Levi, Mike Maguire, Nerys Owens and Karen Parkhill, who at various times have endured cups of tea, lunch and dog walks with me, and provided timely support and insight. Many thanks to Ruth Westgate, the Cardiff ancient historian, who suggested several sources for the Cretan/Athenian house/hearth and read over Chapter 1.

Thanks, too, to Caro Baggaley, Helen Baxter, Chrissie (the Duchess), Jane Darke, Jay Kynch, Em Morgan, Kate Pahl and Laurie Taylor, who in various excellent ways have been good friends. *Diolch*, Smith family and their little cottage, Bronfelin.

Ma, Dad, Daniel and co., Adrian, Chrissie, dearest La, A.C. U.S., Delyth and other members of my family who have put up with me, looked after me when I've been ill, gone fishing and provided doses of common sense – thank you.

Finally, at home, thank you, my lovely Trev – also to Idris, Boris, Jim, Mostyn, Betsy, Eric (RIP) and the hens and ducks who put up with us humans in their space.

Prologue

Diane and Derek

Diane: All that's on my breakfast bar is my mugs for the kitchen and the, oh, I got a little coffee pan.

Derek: It comes in handy for everything though, doesn't it?

Diane: Oh well, they stick things on it, but I don't, I mean if I got cards or anything, it goes on there [the top of the gas fire in the back sitting room].

Derek: We use it more as a, like a mantelpiece than what we do as a breakfast bar.

Diane: Well this isn't a mantelpiece.

Derek: It's somewhere to put stuff. It's never used as a breakfast –

Diane [to me]: – yes, but for what you meant in your letter, I would have said I use the gas fire.

RH: The gas fire, yes.

Diane: Yes, because if I've got a letter or anything, say I write and it goes to post – I put it down there.

Derek: Or leave it where you –

Diane: – yes I put it on there, you know. A birthday card – the gas fire's hardly ever used because of the central heating. So I put birthday cards on there and on the television.

RH: Ah yes, because you've got things on the TV as well.

Diane: On the telly as well, yes. So I would say that if I had to finish filling [the questionnaire] in, I would put the gas fire and the telly and the breakfast bar.

RH [to Derek]: And what made you think of the breakfast bar as being the mantelpiece?

Derek: Simply to – it would take words to that effect to – we always put stuff on there (Figures P.1 and P.2).

Figure P.1   Derek's 'mantelpiece'

Figure P.2   Diane's 'mantelpiece'

Karen

So I picked a frame up in TKMaxx, and it was just, cos it sort of blended in and it was nice colours. But I haven't actually got a picture to go in it – cos I think I want a really nice picture. And I can't decide what it's going to be at the moment, you know, cos yes, it is the focal point and I want something quite nice to go there, and I haven't sort of – I'm quite fussy. I wouldn't put anything in. I'm a bit like that with things like, I wouldn't put anything in just for it to go, obviously a picture in. Oh, I won't have a picture in until I find the perfect one, and then I'll put that in – I think.

[*She eventually put the photograph frame (still empty) in a bedroom drawer*] (Figure P.3)

Figure P.3   Karen's focal point

Introduction: Dismantling Mantelpieces

> Thus the minuscule, a narrow gate, opens up an entire world. The details of a thing can be the sign of a new world which, like all worlds, contains the attributes of greatness.
>
> (Bachelard 1994 [1958]: 155)

Why mantelpieces matter: a short story

One winter's night, a few years ago, I was sitting in front of some programme or other on the television, too lazy or tired to do anything else. Yawning as yet another advert break interrupted my entertainment, I glanced idly to the left, at the mantelpiece above the unlit gas fire. I had seen it ten thousand times – without really seeing it – but on that night, I looked at it as if for the first time.

I looked at the symmetrical display and thought, 'Why have I done that?' I stared at the vase of flowers in the very centre of the arrangement and recalled how I had decided always to have fresh flowers in the middle of the mantelpiece. More often than not, these were weedish types from the garden or park – I could not buy *myself* flowers. And the photographs – my grandparents' wartime wedding picture – placed there following my grandfather's death; one of my mother, laughing, that she disliked, as she disliked all photos of herself. She had always – it seemed like always – insisted on keeping an ancient French fertility goddess on her mantelpiece. Funny it was *her* mantelpiece, as if my stepfather did not figure in this focal point. And like my mother, I displayed holiday souvenirs of a particular sort – such as the reproduction Nefertiti head. Her mother, on the other hand, had gladly ripped the old fireplace from her terraced house, and replaced it with a neat electric fire, atop which had sat, as far back as I could remember, a china clog, a small plate and a piece of Blue John stone.

That black stone Nefertiti head was like a million others on sale at every marketplace and tourist shop I had visited with my father in Egypt. He bought one, and I got two as gifts for my brother and mother. I knew where the heads were in those other three houses: on my mother's mantelpiece, the top of my father's gas fire and my brother's bookshelf. His young family were somewhat cramped, renovating their first house. And when I happened to notice that souvenir on my mantelpiece, I remembered all those others, scattered about the British Isles. Somehow, it joined up my absent, divorced, dispersed family. I remembered the holiday, then thought yet again that I now found the head a little tacky; but I had to have a souvenir, and it was too good to throw away. It was, moreover, so intimately bound up with some duty to keep my family together, on my mantelpiece and in my memory, that to hand it to a charity shop seemed like a betrayal.

Then there was that frightening face carved from a branch, a present from a brother-in-law. I knew it would be heresy to get rid of it, but had turned its face to the wall, leaving on show the unworked wood. It was turned back if he visited. Matching this, on the other side of the vase, was the carved wooden head of a Fijian man. My paternal grandfather had made this for my maternal great-grandfather, after visiting us in Fiji when I was a baby. Or so I remembered. In turn, I had inherited the ornament when Great-Grandad died. It was my most precious object, which my mother had grudgingly allowed me to take, somewhat annoyed that I had removed it – *my* heir-loom – from her lounge. What family history and identity I had invested in that small carving: of my childhood in the South Pacific, of craftsman-ship and unity. I have fondly retold that tale on many occasions, even on a national radio programme – which was when my mother and grandmother heard it. Sitting in front of Granny's electric fire, looking at the clog, the plate, the stone, I was told very firmly that this was an impossible mem-ory: the two men had never met; they never knew each other; how could I think that? The wooden head was bought by my mother as a gift for her grandfather. A beautiful but cheap souvenir, one of many: how come I had remembered it differently, and how would I rework that brutal change into my family story?

The twin to the Nefertiti head was a pottery palm-reader hand, which I had bought as a gift for my stepfather. But somehow, it had ended up on my mantelpiece, because I liked it, and felt doubtful whether he would. It made more sense for me to keep it, surely. But I was uncertain it really belonged there – it made the display look a bit ... *bodily*, bodied, embodied; whatever the word might be that describes an assemblage of heads, family photos, that hand, and the collection of masks, animal ornaments and pho-tographs of people around the room. But they were all there for a reason, or at least, I had a reason for them all to be there, although they cluttered up the small sitting room. I hung on to these things because people had given them to me, or I liked them (sometimes I even liked the gifts). They brought certain people, places and times into the here and now; even events such as my grandparents' wedding. They had always to be kept out, on show, so I could remember them. But honestly, how often did I actually look at them? And my (now former) mother-in-law's clumsy question – 'Do you dust?' had made me wonder whether their absence might be a relief, from the burden of memory, the very weightiness, the thinginess of things. Without them, would I recall those particular memories and stories? What would I remember?

There was the other sort of stuff on the mantelpiece too: the fluff of cards – I am remembering them as birthday cards, for it was winter, and too early for Christmas – and probably postcards or pretty letter cards. I know some cards stayed rather longer than others: pictures I liked, or invitations to weddings, even though I was well aware when these would be. Another kind of thing was tucked in between the 'official' display: the reminders, the boring odds and ends of vet appointments, a letter and the key for the friend who was coming later.

And then (for it is surprising how many thoughts one can have in an advert break) I looked at the mantelpiece itself, above the nasty gas fire that I was too poor to replace, and which I kept despite the new central heating – 'just in case', as my father said. This was a 1930s ex-local authority house, with fireplaces still in the sitting room and two of the bedrooms. Someone had, at some point, removed the kitchen fireplace and filled it in, but had left this quite inconvenient, high mantelpiece in the sitting room. The shape of the room and positioning of the aerial socket meant that the television had to go in the alcove beside the chimney breast, and the need for two sofas, so everyone could sit down, meant that we always looked side-on at the television screen. The combination of two doors, the window and the fireplace dictated the positioning of the furniture. It would have made sense, in terms of how the room was used, to put the television under the mantelpiece, and remove the obsolete gas fire, but that just seemed wrong. These days, we might have hung a flatscreen above the mantel, as my current neighbours have done, even though that means craning the neck at an awkward angle. It would make so much more sense to get rid of the mantelpiece and hearth altogether, and put the television at the right height in the middle of the wall for everyone to watch in comfort. My brother, now settled in the renovated house, did just that, hanging the screen above the radiator. A few months later, feeling a lack of something, he put a shelf between the two, for the digital photo frame (which doubles as a clock), the Blu-Rays and Playstation (Figure I.1).

Why did I want the mantelpiece there, in the centre of the room, but barely look at it because we were watching television, reading or chatting? It was not as if there was a fire there anymore. Why did I always have the fresh flowers in the middle, candlesticks at each end and the mirror above (I forgot to mention those)? What were those particular objects doing up there – the disliked gift, the present I had failed to hand over to my stepfather, the heads, the wedding photograph, my poor mother's picture, with the various cards and oddments between or behind all of this? Why was it only

Figure I.1   The flatscreen shelf

me, rather than my husband or the two long-term lodgers, who did all this? Who had put those ideas in my head, and when, exactly, was I going to dust? By what process had I selected these particular objects from those I owned, which filled the dresser, sat in front of the books, dodged the condensation on the windowsill and even stood on the floor by the hearth (a wooden pig from an ex-boyfriend, rather chewed by the dog, but I didn't quite like to throw it out)?

The awful symmetry, the mirror, the candles – I knew them all from somewhere, but where precisely, I could not place. It was a shelf above a redundant fire; out of place, really, inconvenient. I had attached such importance and pride to what was on there; yet still I used it as a storage space. Did I want others to look at the 'official', the permanent, the *real* display, but ignore the mundane ephemera and the dust? It was the central point of the room – the house – the first thing people saw when coming in from the tiny hallway, but when we were in there, I scarcely saw it. Without it, what would the room be like? And where would we pose for our customary (slightly ironic) snapshots in our smart clothes before nights out: in front of the television, or against the door?

I was putting certain things, in a particular order, on the mantelpiece and on other surfaces around the house, and I wanted that mantelpiece in my living room; but I could explain neither the origin nor the purpose of what I was doing: uncertain certainties. I knew that it had something to do with comfort and tradition, design and convention, what others thought of me, and what I thought about myself, my family, friends and the past. Something that had been invisible – in the very centre of the living room – had become visible, and more than that, loud. To ignore it would have been rude.

Opening questions

The aim of this book is to shout, 'ISN'T THIS STRANGE? Look at it, it's there, in your living room, or in your mother's or somewhere in your childhood.' Even if it is not a physical presence, it is central to the ideal 'family home', in cultural memory, as an idea. Magazines, shop windows, pubs, country hotels, family albums and grand portraits maintain its power to evoke home, comfort, beauty. There are clocks in the middle, mirrors above, symmetry and, very often, NO FIRE. Once again: NO FIRE. Why are they there? Why do people want them? Why are housebuilders still putting them in? Why does the ever-bigger television jostle for space with it in the living room? Why do some people put coffee cups and bills and TV remotes on them, while others absolutely will not? And why do so many people in conversation with me say, 'Oh, it's a shrine, isn't it?', whereas not one of the study's informants did, and one was offended by her aunt calling hers an 'altar'? There are a few, in seminars and presentations, who put up their hands to point out, quite proudly, that they have a 'real' fire in their house, as if this changed the extra-ordinariness of the mantelpiece in Britain, where 96 per cent of dwellings are centrally heated (Office for National Statistics [ONS] 2011). Why is it a point of pride to have a 'real' fire at home? Most homes have at least one television, the majority with satellite, digital or cable. Around three-quarters of all homes have internet access (ONS 2011), but the gathering-place of the hearth remains in its traditional form and position. Further, what part did it play in the making of the modern United States, and how did it emerge as a symbol of both Western modernity and poor education in 21st-century China, yet promise the essence of classic Englishness to 1960s immigrants settling in the UK? What do people do to build and maintain memory and identity when they have no home, no display spaces and nothing that counts as 'displayable'? Finally, how can one forget painful memories and get rid of unwanted identities if they are so bound up with the 'stuff' of home?

At numerous seminar and conference presentations, as a doctoral candidate and junior researcher, I hoped eagerly for wise theoretical feedback and criticism about my *Dismantling Mantelpieces* research. Instead, almost without exception, members of the audience told me stories of their own mantelpieces, their 'focal point', and those of their friends and neighbours, reminiscing about their childhood homes. Academics brought photos on their mobile phones to show me. At international events, I would be told of similar spaces – not necessarily around the fireplace – in homes in Turkey, Denmark, the Netherlands. Friends took photographs on their travels, sent postcards of archaeological sites I 'might be interested in', mentioned various museum exhibitions and paintings (*Whistler's Mother* was a favourite). A geographer took me aside to tell me I was a geographer; sociologists welcomed me as one of their own; and others called the work anthropology, ethnography, ethnoarchaeology and, most recently, auto-archaeology. The topic seemed to strike deep within the collective memory, to silence critical voices and bestride academic, historical and national boundaries.

The mantelpiece belonged to everyone, and everywhere: it was everymantelpiece. The phrase that resonated throughout these encounters beyond the empirical study was, 'It's a shrine, isn't it?' Popular home interiors publications echo this talk of shrines, altars, household gods, evoking ancient Rome and Greece, reproducing images of 1950s families sitting around the fire (Gold and Ward 1994). Every winter, the mantelpiece, elegantly adorned above a roaring fire, still graces the cover of multiple 'ideal home' style magazines, just as it holds central position in Christmastime shop windows.

Yet these diverse outpourings of nostalgia, of identification with the 'meaningfulness' of mantelpiece displays and the ubiquitous spectacles of 'hearth and home' were counterbalanced by other perspectives emerging from the research. It was as often a shelf of undusted, unlooked-at objects above a cold hearth, towards which the furniture might face, but which took second place to the television. Keys and oddments were dumped there; mug rings might stain its surface; postcards and greetings cards could sit there for months. More often than not there was a clock at its centre, flanked by the symmetry of ornaments, photos and candlesticks with a mirror above, reminiscent of mantelpieces from the 1930s or earlier. Some were bleak plains of air-freshener cans, ashtrays, broken pens, pill bottles or an old apple core. Its very presence was an anachronism: at once a remembrance of times past and a forgotten, or neglected, present. Shelf for storage; dusty showcase of dirt and trash; cheap copy of ten million other mantels: how could this be a 'focal point' of home and family, let alone a presentation – or construction – of self?

Beyond these mantelpiece tales of nostalgia and neglect were those of anxiety, discord, mourning and healing. It was a site of bitter household battles, a place of remembrance for a stillborn child, somewhere to put toys for naughty children to see but not touch, or for newly displaying a candlestick that the just-dumped ex-boyfriend hated. These stories unfolded the extraordinary importance of everyday domestic display practices in the daily reworking of one's place in and beyond family and home, and the usually unspoken work of small things in the making of memory. These stories are biographical, yet connect with greater histories of conflict, damage and loss, of taken-for-granted methods of 'doing' identity. Discussions during lectures I gave for social (public) housing professionals responsible for frontline provision highlighted this. At first, some of them were somewhat sceptical, as a few are at first, about the point of such research (as one of the questionnaire respondents wrote, 'I hope my taxes aren't paying for this'). But after drawing and talking about their own mantelpieces and display areas, the housing officers would start talking about going into tenants' living rooms, looking at what is on display and making judgements based on this. Or they would recall how some tenants, left in temporary accommodation (sometimes for years), do nothing with their houses, leaving them unadorned, often uncleaned, and what that might mean beyond the easy assumption of dirty idleness. Someone remembered how refugees packed, in their one precious suitcase, family photographs. Another recalled how one woman, housed with her daughter in a single room, had made space on the bookshelf for the few photographs and ornaments she had taken with her from the family home, a place of abuse. For one mature student, the wardrobe door in his cramped rented room was the only place he had for pictures and photographs.

The spaces people have or make for display, or do not make, are enmeshed with other losses and absences. Some participants in the study, such as destitute asylum seekers, had no things with which to display memory, and no home of their own to present a face to the world. Identity, belonging, memory and family are the comfortable words associated with the study of home. Prejudice, absence, exclusion, displacement are their forgotten companions. Attending to the absences, the gaps and changes in domestic displays and the stories associated with them is vital to understanding home not simply as a comfortable idea, but rather as a constant process of home-making, in which participation is neither universally equal nor simple. The mantelpiece is a shrine, of sorts, but exactly what enshrined practices unfold when it is made the focal point of sociological study?

Further, this study of the mantelpiece elicits how culture is not some side-kick to the important business of the economy, nor is the study of culture an esoteric byline to macro-socio-economic analyses; Culture is not something that posh people do, while everyone else watches the soccer and gets drunk. As the backdrop to so many photographs and paintings, the mantelpiece provides a shorthand reference to the status of an individual or family in its grandeur or simplicity; in a magazine, shop window or bar, it is a quick-fix, small-scale reference to 'Home'. It is the background to other activities: watching television, working or playing on the computer, chatting in the kitchen or doing homework in a bedroom. This book opens it out, brings it to the foreground, making it the focus for thinking about how culture works and is worked in the often barely-seen business of everyday life. As multiple spaces in the big family house, a strip of shelf in a rented room, held in the memory or built in the imagination, the mantelpiece is a way into understanding how remembering and forgetting, belonging and exclusion work in the everyday making of culture.

Why do shop owners put mantelpieces at the centre of Christmas window displays? Why are there still mantelpieces in pubs and bars? Why do people keep them, or put them back into their centrally heated homes, and why do housebuilders still incorporate them into their (more expensive) homes? What makes one display instantly 'readable' by neighbours as 'middle-class'? Why was a display of china on the mantelpiece the very essence of Britishness for a migrant family, and what makes a mantelpiece American? Thinking about these questions opens up the ways in which domestic material cultures are intertwined with relations between public and private, home and marketplace, memory and history, identity and nationhood, taste and class, difference and equality. The next section introduces founding concepts which were 'good to think': about how to dismantle mantelpieces, and in turn, how they dismantled taken-for-granted assumptions about home, memory and identity.

Deep foundations: making culture

What follows is a highly edited quotation from the beginning of *The Order of Things* (Foucault 1989 [1966]). I was drawn to this, first, by the title, which conveys why a study of mantelpieces, those iconographic yet trivial lines, could possibly matter:

> This book first arose out of a passage in [Jorge Luis] Borges, out of the laughter that shattered, as I read the passage, all the familiar landmarks of my thought—our thought that bears the stamp of our age and our geography—breaking up all the ordered surfaces and all the planes with which we are accustomed to tame the wild profusion of existing things, and continuing long afterwards to disturb and threaten with collapse our age-old distinction between the Same and the Other. This passage quotes a 'certain Chinese encyclopaedia' in which it is written that 'animals are divided into: (a) belonging to the Emperor, (b) embalmed, (c) tame, (d) suckling pigs, (e) sirens, (f) fabulous, (g) stray dogs, (h) included in the present classification, (i) frenzied, (j) innumerable, (k) drawn with a very fine camelhair brush, (l) et cetera, (m) having just broken the water pitcher, (n) that from a long way off look like flies'. In the wonderment of this taxonomy, the thing we apprehend in one great leap, the thing that, by means of the fable, is demonstrated as the exotic charm of another system of thought, is the limitation of our own, the stark impossibility of thinking that [...] Moreover, it is not simply the oddity of unusual juxtapositions that we are faced with here [...] The monstrous quality that runs through Borges's enumeration consists, on the contrary, in the fact that the common ground on which such meetings are possible has been destroyed. What is impossible is not the propinquity of the things listed, but the very site on which their propinquity would be possible.
>
> (Foucault 1989 [1966]: xvi–xviii)

Choosing, discarding, ordering – disposal in its widest sense – is how meaning is made and unmade. The very emplacement of a list, the disruption of a text by this oddly mundane genre of writing, is perhaps the first matter to attend to (Duszat 2012). This unsettling of a norm is followed by further discombobulations, within Foucault's *Preface*, and in its origins and its effects within scholarly debate (Wicks 2003). Treated at 'face value' by some scholars, as a literary joke by others, the doubtful genealogy of Borges's (1975 [1942]) list, itself a response to the notion of an invented language to replace Latin (Wilkins 1668), is a shaky foundation for a Preface to a text. The idea of 'common ground', of 'impossible propinquity', of lists that are 'storied up' to make sense, lines of beauty, lines of engagement, boundaries of what is thinkable, lives that are liveable, showable, tellable: this is why these lines echoed round the book. Therefore, although these deep conceptual foundations were vital to understanding how mantelpieces matter, it was the process of unsettling them that matters as deeply.

Culture and memory as everyday practice

The work of both Pierre Bourdieu and Mary Douglas opened up the ways in which small acts of separation, often buried in habit, put culture – as practice – at the centre of social norms, differences and stratifications. In what is often seen as a key text in post-structuralist interpretations of the house, Bourdieu related the internal structure of Berber houses in Algeria to certain 'homologous oppositions' such as fire and water, male and female, high and low (1977, 1979). He clarified how these internal oppositions of domestic space related to divisions of external public space, although this reading has been contested (de Certeau 1984: 52; Silverstein 2004). The house, as a primary 'structuring structure', is thus the principal site for interiorising practices of distinguishing or associating oneself or social group from others. These distinction practices are so implicit that their origins are forgotten through 'genesis amnesia'. Bourdieu's later study in France positioned consumption practices in social space, with lines of distinction and difference drawn according to categories of cultural, symbolic, economic and social capitals (1984). His elaboration of *habitus* posited that 'the mode of appropriation of cultural goods' is one way in which social relations objectified in things are 'insensibly internalised', calling such study a 'social psychoanalysis'. Close study, therefore, of 'taste' practices can unpack embedded relations of power, including class, gender or family hierarchy and thus of 'symbolic violence' (for example, Werbner 1996; Adkins 2004). Bourdieu's reflexive sociological practice meant he also recognised this 'forgetting' as a flaw of sociologists (1990).

Douglas's work analysing ritual and taboo, which she related to differing attitudes towards domestic dirt and untidiness (2002 [1966]), was another way of thinking about the implicit rules and meanings of everyday actions and assumptions (1973). She argues that dirt is only 'matter out of place' and that boundaries are arbitrary, and therefore cultural. Further, since 'cultural categories are public matters...[and]...if uncleanness is matter out of place, we must approach it through order' (2002: 180). She therefore took a structural approach by observing how patterns are maintained by exclusion or by explanation of ambiguity and anomaly within the pattern. There is no difference between primitive and modern societies, except that primitives have comprehensive patterning systems whereas moderns apply it to 'disjointed separate areas of existence'. Private individuals can have private assumptions, but these are not cultural categories. Douglas also asserts that for binary rituals of categorising space as inside/outside, clean/dirty, familiar/strange, safe/dangerous, 'the laws of nature are dragged in to sanction the moral code'.

Both Douglas and Bourdieu's systematic approaches were influenced by Marcel Mauss's gift theory (1990 [1950]). Based on extensive surveys of archaic and primitive gift societies, his work makes a distinction between societies where the obligation to give, receive and reciprocate gifts is a total social system, and market societies, in which commodities are exchanged for money. Mauss therefore distinguishes between 'inalienable' gifts, inseparable from the person of the giver and demanding reciprocation, and 'alienable' goods. His aim was political, to promote the potential of social democracy to substantiate interpersonal bonds in an analogy with the gift economy. Despite failing to bring about social reform, Mauss's great contribution was in demonstrating how so-called pre-modern societies had economies as complex as modern market systems, thus illuminating the legal, symbolic, moral, aesthetic and interpersonal aspects of both types of social organisation. With close reference to etymology and ancient practice, Mauss emphasises the doubleness of seemingly straightforward exchanges and things: the gift is also poison, just as taboo practices and things are also sacred. The ambiguous properties of gifts and 'givens' were useful in thinking about traditional, enshrined artefacts and practices.

By linking the anthropology of 'culture' with concepts of both political and moral economy, Mauss had opened up the debate in consumption practices, in which the boundaries between 'gift' and 'commodity' have been increasingly blurred (Douglas and Isherwood 1996 [1979]; Miller D. 1987, 1995, 1998). This is particularly interesting in conjunction with the growth in the 'heritage industry', shifting conceptual boundaries between homes, museums and the market economy, as we will see in chapters 7 and 8. Studies of consumption as everyday practice have drawn attention to its political dimensions, and in particular, modes of consuming as active constructions of identity (Bennett and Watson 2002; Highmore 2002; Bennett 2003). While Bourdieu's work on consumption has been extensively criticised for its omissions and flaws, it has been a vital foundation for recent work nuancing and building on notions of class, capital and culture (Atkinson 2012). For example, examining gender and ethnicity in distinction practices, careful elicitations of whiteness and working-class women's *habitus*, and the concept of cultural omnivores reflect the continuing importance of his work, as I discuss later.

Relating materiality and memory

As both an iconic remnant of apparently ancient concepts of hearth and home, and an ordinary yet often obstructive presence in modern living rooms, the mantelpiece is ideal material for reimagining social worlds. This book unfolds how the mantelpiece is accounted for now, in the 21st century, and how the past and the present work (and are worked) in the production of space (Lefebvre 1991 [1974]; de Certeau 1984). It is now commonplace to assert that history is not 'fact' (Crowley 2001), that the history of 'ordinary' people is as valid as scholarly accounts (Charlton *et al.* 2006) and memory, as biographic narrative, is as contingent and multi-dimensional as any other form of telling (Carsten 2007b). Later on in the book, we will start to see how the exclusionary effects of 'ordinariness' quietly operate. Drawing on Appadurai's argument against 'the past [as] a limitless and plastic symbolic resource' (1981: 201), this chapter examines how the past, while malleable, is shaped within particular boundaries.

Considering the house, like all types of building, as a 'memory machine', Douglas writes how as 'institutionalised memory', it 'is capable of anticipating future events' (1993: 268). In her work *How Institutions Think* (1986), she develops Evans-Pritchard's (1949) and Maurice Halbwachs' (1992 [1952]) writing on collective memory, to suggest how present social relations construct the past:

> The mirror, if that's what history is, distorts as much after revision as before... when we look closely at the construction of past time, we find the process has very little to do with the past at all, and everything to do with the present. Institutions create shadowed places where nothing can be seen, and no questions asked. They make other areas show finely discriminated detail, which is closely scrutinised and ordered.
>
> (Douglas 1993: 69)

Since home – of whatever sort – is the first institution we all encounter, scrutiny of how its places of visibility and invisibility, remembering and forgetting are ordered unfolds modes of ordering in/of other institutions. Connecting the home and its materials with other institutionalised or 'characteristic ways of history-making' (Mills 1959: 7) means that the mantelpiece can be viewed as domestic museum, gallery or miniature monument, relating to national or collective, performative memory practices (Connerton 1989; Halbwachs 1992 [1952]; Conlin 2006) including memories of war and trauma, such as the holocaust (Schwarz and Schuman 2005) and public monuments (Low and Lawrence-Zuniga 2003). Quite how everyday, vernacular memorialising, remembering and forgetting connect with 'history' in this vigorously debated field is another matter (Nora 1989; Samuel 1994; Dwyer 2000; Forty and Kuchler 2001; Ricoeur 2006; Hetherington 2008; Connerton 2009; Tolia-Kelly 2010). How mantelpiece displays relate to the 'public' politics of display in museums, and the ways in which they organise things, space, time, human bodies, senses and thinking is of particular interest (Bennett 1995; Macdonald 1998; Hetherington 2003). A crucial element in Douglas's and Bourdieu's work was the way in which they illuminated the often opaque ways in which the past shaped present and future meaning-making practices. Thinking closely about the materialisation of these, through, for example, the display of photographs, gifts or souvenirs, is a way of understanding culture – and memory – as small repeated actions (Turkle 2007; Rose and Tolia-Kelly 2012). This links up with empirical studies recovering everyday ways of remembering the dead, of materialising mourning, loss and absence, from theories about the late modern fear of mortality (Hallam and Hockey 2001; Hockey *et al.* 2010a; Parrott 2010).

'Ordinary', domestic, shared material memory practices, such as the mantelpiece, can be conceived as Bourdieu's (1977) 'nostalgic structures' and/or Williams' 'structures of feeling' (1977). While 'nostalgia' remains a bone of contention among scholars of nationhood, particularly with its links to heritage (Hewison 1987; Wright 2009), such concepts touch on affective dimensions of home: as haunting, dream, image-space, imaginary and psycho-geography (Benjamin 2006 [1932–1934]; Bachelard 1994 [1958]; Marcus 1995; Busch 1999). Bachelard suggested that 'topoanalysis' was as vital to understanding how people make meaning as psychoanalysis. These 'home-makings' resonate with memory as ghost (Carsten 2007b), as disruptive haunting in the city (Hetherington 2008), and reach beyond home as material, to home as 'dwelling' (Heidegger 2010 [1962]; Latimer and Munro 2009) and relational extension (Strathern 2004 [1991]).

The meaning of home

As this book is concerned with 'pasts', a brief overview of the origins of 'the meaning of home' as an area of study will be useful (see also Mallett 2004). It has been an obvious area of research in social anthropology and sociology (see, for example, edited collections by Carsten and Hugh-Jones 1995; Birdwell-Pheasant and Lawrence-Zuniga 1999; Chapman and Hockey 1999b; Cieraad 1999a; Miller 2001a). Until recently, though, the study of housing in Britain has focused primarily on policy, economics and architecture (see post-war studies such as Gale 1949; also Hall 1992; Malpass and Murie 1999). After all, the house in Britain had originally been nothing more than a moveable roof for the fire (Prizeman 1975). However, due in part to an article by Saunders and Williams (1988) which called for a move to perceiving the house as a crucial space of interaction, drawing on Giddens' (1984) conception of *locale*, the 'meaning' of home became a focus for study.

Some sociological and psychological research has attempted to separate the conflations of house, dwelling and home (for example, Benjamin and Stea 1995, especially Brink 1995; Rapaport 1995). 'House' and 'dwelling' have been distinguished as the physical structure of a form built for habitation, although there might not actually be a built form (Oliver 2003). 'Home', on the other hand, is imbued with cultural, social and affective meanings that hold a special place in the individual and popular imagination, memory and everyday life. The definition of home in relation to the individual has been gradually refined from Haywards' (1975) categorisation. Haywards listed five aspects of home: boundaried physical structure; territory, locus in space; self and self-identity; and finally social and cultural unit. Sixsmith's psychological analysis (1986) found 20 different meanings of home that could be grouped into 3 'experiential modes'; personal, social and physical structure. However, these focused on the relation between the individual and the home, and other contributions from transactionalism and phenomenology moved away from this emphasis on the role of home in the life of the individual to look at the effects of social and cultural factors on the experience of home (Kemeny 1991).

Reviews of earlier British housing policies have demonstrated the often flawed social engineering and/or profit motives that directed housebuilding and planning policies such as 1930s suburbia and the move to small kitchens (Oliver *et al.* 1981; Gold and Ward 1994), the loss of the parlour (Attfield 1999), New Towns (Attfield 1995) and the move to domestic electricity (Ravetz and Turkington 1995). These reinterpretations suggest that nothing in the British house should be taken for granted, and are worth sociological/anthropological attention, just as non-Western houses have been scrutinised for decades (Oliver 1975, 2003; Bourdieu 1977; Gell 1998). Amit (1999) called for a similar move to doing anthropology 'at home', and this closing down of the gap between 'us' and 'the other' (Said 2003 [1978]) can be seen in the recent literature (for example, Rapport 2002).

Much research into the domestic interior has concentrated on notions of privacy, privatism and privatisation (Saunders and Williams 1988). Some writers have traced this assumption back to the creation of the private domestic sphere during the urbanisation and industrialisation of Britain in the late 18th and early 19th centuries (Hall 1979; Forty 1986; Hepworth 1999; Davidoff and Hall 2002), arguing that the construction of 'home sweet home' enabled the middle classes to maintain moral distance from the degradation and exploitation of workers. For the first time in Britain, industrialisation meant that the worlds of work and home were geographically separate, and cottage industry ceased, placing the sphere of production firmly outside the dwelling. This literature relates privatism to gender relations and the 'cult of domesticity' in the 19th century (Hepworth 1999). Reiger (1985), for example, refers to a Weberian notion of 'disenchantment' with the invasion of home by experts, 'rationalisation' and technologies relating to household 'chores'.

The culture of domesticity brought new pressures to bear on women regarding their influence on morality and aesthetics. They were expected to regulate not only their own behaviour, but also that of their families and the private aesthetic of the domestic interior, in contrast to that of public art, which remained a masculine domain (Forty 1986; Sparke 1995; Davidoff and Hall 2002). Some scholars have argued that this was consequently translated into an anti-domestic modernist aesthetic in the early 20th century which excluded and subordinated women from 'distinctly unhomey' future- and technology-oriented expert design, which alienated these houses' inhabitants (Rybczynski 1986: 187), but others criticise this as a simplification of the complex relations of self, household and home (Reed 1996; Morley 2000) and specifically of women's appropriation of the modernist aesthetic (Giles 2004; see also Attfield 1995). The dominant 'benign' discourse of home as private sanctuary, as clean, as feminine has come increasingly under scrutiny, seen not only as overly simplistic, but also as masculine and even misogynistic discourse (see Morley 2000: 56–85 for discussion; also Steedman 1982; Matrix 1984; Chapman 1999b; Chapman and Hockey 1999a; Blunt and Varley 2004; Casey and Martens 2007; Macdonald 2007).

The conflation of 'home', 'household' and 'family' is a common practice (Mackintosh 1979), masking tensions that are often pressing upon the wife/mother (in traditional nuclear families in Britain) (Hunt 1995; Chapman 1999b; Morley 2000; see also Berger and Kellner's early microsociology of marriage, 1964). Similarly, the easy elision of self and home has been the focus of critical attention by some, pointing out that this similarly ignores negotiations and conflict between members of the household (for example, Gullestad 1995; Reed 1996; Chapman 1999b), class-based differences or other motivations (Dolan 1999).

Many scholars argue that home is not private, personal and detached from the public realm. Graham Allan (1989) comments that the living room is 'interstitial', a perfected view of the 'real' home, although this still supports the notion that there is 'private' space in the home. Jane Darke and Craig Gurney (2000) focus on the guest–host relationship, and the 'gaze' of the guest, which may be welcomed or spurned depending on the meaning of the house as symbol of economic success, embodied taste or site of family life. They relate this to Erving Goffman's (1959) 'impression management' to avoid 'letting the side down' (Darke and Gurney 2000: 80; see also Osaki 2003). Some writers have similarly scrutinised the more complex constraints on privacy and choice. For example, the position of the kitchen alters the position of the cook as central, visible and also able to observe activities inside and/or outside the house (Hillier and Hanson 1984; Fiske 1992).

David Morgan's work has been fundamental in shifting the ground of sociology of home and family 'from a noun to a verb' (1996, 2011). Families are not structures, but practices and processes, intimately bound up with the 'doing' of gender and other dimensions of identity. In a recent commentary on 'the phenomena' of everyday life as '… nebulous, pervasive and ambiguous: obvious to the point of elusiveness', Susie Scott presents a nuanced review of home both as everyday practice and as a site for constructing identity (Scott 2009: 2; see also Bennett *et al.* 1999; Bennett 2002).

Staging and performing identity

Empirical studies in the power relations of housing design have shown how people have subverted design imperatives, such as open-plan living rooms and flats without entrance halls (Attfield 1995; Hanson 1998; Rosselin 1999). Other work has opened up the 'leaky' home further (Felski 1999–2000: 26), by interpreting relations between architecture and the state (Buchli 1999, 2002). Victor Buchli argues elsewhere that the seeming weightiness of 'spatial logics' of architecture (Hillier and Hanson 1984) can be disrupted by the 'most ephemeral manipulations of material culture' (Buchli 1999: 6). Houses can be 'architectures of exclusion' (Brindley 1999) – for example, for disabled people (Burns 2004). The materiality of home thus becomes potent in scrutinising the nexus between personal and social, public and private constructions of meaning with relation to time, space and identity.

The mantelpiece has been called a 'frame for the fire' and a 'proscenium arch' in popular design books (Wilhide 1994; also Miller D. 1995), highlighting common assumptions that the 'main feature' is the fire. However, the mantelpiece is more than a piece of wood or stone: it furnishes a room, transforms the fire from natural phenomenon to boundaried artefact, offers a surface for display and a central place to stand, look or point at and on which to put things down. Central to my methods of researching mantelpiece display was Erving Goffman's approach to social interaction. In his view, the 'furnished frame' (1971; also 1986 [1974]) is the interpretive apparatus which shapes the staging of everyday life. While he uses the picture frame as a means of explaining how this conceptual frame makes sense of experience, I suggest reversing this relation for the purpose of understanding how the mantelpiece 'works' as a setting for everyday performances of home, family, memory and identity. Goffman argued that 'performance' is not a type of special practice set aside from normal situations, but that all interaction is performed by social actors, who also act as audiences for others. Thus, the 'self' (whatever that is) is 'presented' in everyday life through careful 'impression management' (1959, 1986). Interaction is situated and framed in social settings which have particular expectations, involving gesture, talk, 'face work' and props. The house, like other sites of social interaction, has front-stage and back-stage regions (although these are not necessarily spatially fixed), where different performances take place (see also Osaki 2003). This dramaturgic, mythological defamiliarising of the business of everyday life is allusive of poetic/dramatic representations, offering a sociological method for thinking about family and the 'furniture' of domestic life.

The poetics of home

Morgan argued that homes as 'living spaces defined as such by their inhabitants, may develop a sense of personal identity in even some of the least favourable settings where "home" is represented by little more than a poster stuck to the wall or a few objects on the mantelpiece' (1996: 182). The everyday mantelpiece – and the practices that go on around it – can be framed by an awareness of the poetics of such things and spaces, making visible 'immortal ordinary society' (Garfinkel 1988).

Two books particularly opened up home as a peculiar space: Witold Rybczynski's *Home: A Short History of an Idea* (1986) and Gaston Bachelard's *Poetics of Space* (1994). In Rybczynski's unpacking of nostalgia as a method of dislocating from the present, he argues that domesticity is 'an idea in which technology was a distinctly secondary consideration' (1986: vii). In a detailed history of the chair, its uses, positioning and technology, he explores the idea of home, rather than providing a definite 'answer'. Concentrating on architectural, social and cultural influences upon what are now seen as 'natural' ideas such as privacy, domesticity and comfort, he demonstrates that these taken-for-granted concepts are quite recent (see also Ariès 1993; Cieraad 1999, 1999c). Bachelard conceptualises the house as a space intimately connected with the body and mind, an ongoing reminder of the dream- and past-self. Focusing on the symbolism of the house and its rooms, he elicits the potential of the miniature to open up vast worlds. Bourdieu's (1977: 118) 'mythico-poetic' symbolism of domestic space resonates with this, although his measuring out of the house and its divisions seems unrelated to Bachelard's psycho-geography of home (1994 [1958]; see also Barthes 2000 [1957]).

This approach to understanding the struggle for symbolic meaning, cultural practice, economic domination and social status could therefore be termed poetic, in its attention to the relations between the mythic and the mundane, miniature and monumental. C. Wright Mills, in his call to awaken the 'sociological imagination' made the intersection of biography and history the focus of sociological study, using whatever materials might be available to address the problem at hand (1959). This mode of organising is analogous to the practice of making home with 'a few objects' – biographical materials – on the mantelpiece, enmeshing domestic space with identity. The poetics of home and sociological reimaginings of 'home' are the book's twin concerns.

New moves in 'identity' as relation

Identity studies as an interdisciplinary and cross-disciplinary field has grown over the last decade (see Wetherell and Mohanty 2010; see also Lawler 2008), a manifestation of 'identity' as what Latour might call a 'matter of concern' (2004). A brief review of British research projects from the 'Identities and Social Action' programme, funded by the Economic and Social Research Council, gives a flavour of recent discussions (Wetherell 2009a; see also Hurdley 2010b). Loosely addressing Judith Butler's (2004a) question of how people build 'liveable' lives (Wetherell 2009b), the studies challenge meta-theories of social change – in particular, those pushing the 'individualisation' thesis (for example, Giddens 1991; Beck 1992; Bauman 2001a; Beck and Beck-Gernsheim 2002) – through empirical studies of class and community, ethnicity and migration, and intimate identities. For example, in the field of school 'choice', Reay *et al.* (2007) acknowledge a certain resonance with Giddens's (1991) reflexive individual in a neo-liberal, globalised economy. Yet by showing how white middle-class parents choosing 'bad' schools actually develop and confirm their 'abundance of capital', they argue that the individual is not the primary site for understanding identity, criticising the view of the individual 'self-as-consumer' (Rose 1998) that dominates both social theory and policy. From a different perspective, Heath *et al.* (2009) interrogate subjective aspects of class to address claims by Beck (1992), Beck and Beck-Gernsheim (2002) and Bauman (2001a) that collective class identities are in decline. Their meticulous analysis of survey data 1964–2005 qualifies the 'compulsion on individuals to choose their own biographies' (Heath *et al.*: 38) with a historically informed emphasis on the importance of political debate and development.

Other studies address dominant themes in ethnicity theory, such as Gilroy's (2004) 'conviviality', Hall's (1992) 'new ethnicities' and Billig's (1995) 'banal nationalism'. They emphasise the necessity for close-up empirical scrutiny of spatialised, messy, shifting intersections of histories, race, ethnicity, faith, sexuality and gender within localised social networks. In an ethnography of a Young Offenders' Institution, for example, the researchers are surprised to make out a 'resistant but constrained and deliberately instrumental conviviality' in an 'austere' institution exemplifying Gilroy's 'post-colonial melancholia' (Earle and Phillips 2009). However, equally unforeseen is their finding that ethnicity is not the primary mode for articulating identity, but highly localised (imported) 'postcode pride'. Their argument that 'Muslim' identity offers social solidarity (as well as resistance) within the prison regime is echoed in Gill Valentine and Deborah Sporton's (2009) study of narrative identities among Somali children in Sheffield. They show how active identity construction is always contingent on recognition by wider communities in 'power-laden spaces', since the prioritisation of faith above race, ethnicity, gender and ethno-national categories is due to the importance of continuity and 'emotional salience' in forming subjectivities. The late modern sociological focus on fluid, multiple identities must therefore be inflected by contingency, constancy and emotional investment.

Attention is drawn to the apparent disappearance of class and *habitus*, engaging with Bourdieu's (1986; 1999) thinking on inequality and distinction. The studies make compelling arguments for the persistence of social solidarity, the similarity in narratives of 'intelligibility' across social divisions and the occlusion of class and capital in rhetorics of self-transformation. Beverley Skeggs and Helen Wood (2009), for instance, unfold how the relations between class, culture and self are played out even in the seemingly personal sphere of self-improvement, while television-watching habits are similarly classed and classifying. It is worth noting here that their work presents the television as part of working-class 'domestic architecture', but a 'bad, powerfully corrupting object' for the middle classes (2009; Fiske 1992). This continues Skeggs' central concern with the small processes of classing and devaluing, in which middle-class 'circuits of value' dominate (1997, 2004, 2010, 2011, 2012; also Lawler 2005). In doing so, she engages with Bourdieu's failure to explain how personhood is made by/for those with the 'wrong' capital, or who cannot access defined 'fields of exchange'. She conceives of relations being made and maintained through 'just-talk' and '*the gift of attention over time*'. Of particular interest to this study, she argues that '…their relationships to commodities bore the weight of affective significance…such as inherited jewellery or ornaments as memories of holidays, families, from friends' (2011: 505).

The intersectional, spatialised character of 'identity' – itself a problematic term – has increasingly inflected 'class' with history, ethnicity, gender, age and place (Crompton *et al.* 1991; Savage 2007, 2008, 2010; Bennett *et al.* 2009). Mike Savage's ongoing concern with '…unacknowledged normality of the middle-class', of their values as a 'universal particular' is a central concern in keeping class and *habitus* in the foreground of debates about inequalities (Savage 2003: 536). The affective dimensions of asymmetrical power are present in Bourdieu's notion of 'symbolic violence', where forms of domination 'are made, unmade and remade in and by the interactions between persons' (1977: 184). This has been picked up in critiques of class and gender. Here, it is central to understanding how seemingly small cultural materials and practices can be assembled in a *quiet violence* which maintains power inequalities.

Further, the 'turn' to relationality and extension, conceptions of personhood long espoused by Marilyn Strathern (1988, 1995, 2004) are sensitive to *affect*: intangible, yet 'touching' relations (for example, Latimer 2001; Munro 2004, 2005; Puig 2012). These theories have resonances with writers focusing on heterogeneity, material-semiotics, complexities and mess (such as Latour 1993, 2004, 2005; Law 1994, 1999, 2003, 2004, 2008; Monguilod 2001; Law and Mol 2002; Mol 2003). While some continue to keep 'affect' within interpersonal relations (Wetherell 2012), others, more usefully, focus on networks, relations and circuits of persons, materials and space. Affect can open up new spaces for sociological imaginings/imaginaries (Hetherington 2011; Latimer and Skeggs 2011), but its very elusiveness makes affective strategies in, for example, symbolic violence, hard to pin down.

While moving from theories of production to theories of consumption was an important move in sociology and anthropology, critiques of the consumerist, individualised society (surely a contradiction in terms) as the late modern/postmodern condition (Bauman 2001a, 2001b) fail. Following *agents provocateurs* such as *The System of Objects* (Baudrillard 1996 [1968]) in 'raising the stakes' of everyday consumption to encompass global power relations, works such as Bauman's are crucial to think with, but such readings (and they are *readings*) cannot account for the 'disposal' of meanings as circulating materials (including bodies), rather than the 'see-saw' of production and consumption (Munro 2001: 129; also Strathern 1995; Evans 2012). The notion of 'relational materiality' (Law 1994: 23) – how assemblages of people, things, talk and architecture, among others, work together in performing and ordering the social – is central to this study. What concerns John Law, among others, is 'modes of ordering':

> It is not just a matter of the politics of research (although this is important). It is also a matter of the politics of reality... So it is, for me, a point that is simultaneously a matter of method, politics, ethics and inspiration. Realities are not flat. They are not consistent, coherent and definite. Our research methods necessarily fail. Aporias are ubiquitous. But it is time to move on from the long rearguard action that insists that reality is definite and singular.
>
> (Law 2003: 11)

He proposes a *sociology of verbs* to counter the pretence of a neat *sociology of nouns*, which means '...we are still being constituted in so many syntaxes of hideous purity' (1999: 28; see also Morgan 2011). In that spirit, this is enough of 'the literature' for now; reading, like writing, is a cumulative thinking practice, and as the book progresses, we will see how these various modes of thinking about home work into its fabric. Without the order of Douglas and Bourdieu, there can be neither disorder, nor space for slippage or gaps for doubt to creep in. The ritual of the literature is over; now it is time for the mess. The first aim of the book is to focus in detail on the mantelpiece, to show how thinking through things, rather than skimming their surfaces and moving on, brings forth power, culture and identity relations from the background of everyday life. It is only after I have dealt thoroughly (enough) with this *matter* that I will think through how this might relate to wider current debates about materiality in the concluding chapter.

Designs: the fieldwork and the book

Written sources for the study include archaeological research in Greece and Rome, classical literature, design and architectural histories, the sociology of space and place, materiality, home and family, memory and the everyday. The Mass Observation Archive (Mass Observation 2012) in Sussex was the fundamental documentary source, as we will see in Chapter 2. The Geffrye Museum (Geffrye Museum 2012) in London exhibits reconstructions of period rooms, while historic buildings are rebuilt at the Museum of Welsh Life near Cardiff (St Fagans 2012). Visiting these enabled me to reflect on how visitors (including me) spectated and commented on the displays, often talking about their own homes or childhood memories. I interviewed two museum curators and visited houses and castles open to the public in Britain and the United States, to think about the practice of professional curation. I made pinboard 'postcard collections' of mantelpiece paintings or photographs on sale in galleries and museums, and also participants' photos. Other work included giving lectures and presentations to different academic audiences, during which I often asked them to sketch and talk about their own mantelpieces and home aesthetics. I drew pictures of 'my' mantelpiece – this book. A temporarily final version concludes this text, sketched by Mike Biddulph, a far finer artist than me (see also Hurdley 2012 for a digital rendering). The aim was to keep the textures and multiplicity of mantelpieces, and practices around them – some expert, conscious and reflexive, some happenstance or messy – in the foreground. I did not want to flatten these out to a computer screen of writing and images, ordered into the instant recall of folders and files. There is very little discussion of methodology in the book, since I have written about this extensively elsewhere (Hurdley 2006a, 2006b, 2007a, 2007b, 2013).

The participants include 150 people in Cardiff who answered a questionnaire and drew pencil sketches of their mantelpieces. Of these, 30 people (and other members of these households) agreed to be interviewed in their homes, and half of these took photographs of their mantelpieces every fortnight for a year (2003–2004). Their biographies can be found in the Appendix, or online, together with their 'photo-calendars' and more details about other participants. For ethical reasons, this is a password-protected website, accessible by emailing me (via Hurdley 2012). This link also takes you to my website, where all the digital content relating to the book, including links to external resources such as museum/archive websites are stored. The book also draws on a Master's study I undertook in Oxford in 2001, for which I interviewed 12 people in their homes. The interviews were 'structured' by talk around and about their mantelpieces, or the places they chose as their mantelpiece, such as a window sill or shelf unit, all of which I photographed. These self-selecting participants were, in the main, homeowners who identified themselves as middle-class and white British/Welsh/English.

Two-thirds of them were female. They also tended to be heterosexual, married or in long-term cohabiting relationships, with children. Personal accounts are only one way of making sense of the mantelpiece; the interviews and questionnaires were a partly a process of tracing how everyday practice becomes sedimented into tradition, and how this then pushes out into the making of class, gender, ethnicity and nationhood (Hobsbawm and Ranger 1983). The British mantelpiece has diverse origins, but can be seen as part of a British obsession with the open fire (Muthesius 1979). This is partly, but not entirely due to the climate, as Chapter 1 elaborates. At first, the overwhelmingly 'white middle-class homeowner with family' response to the questionnaires concerned me, but it became clear that the near-absence of 'other' people was, precisely, the point. Therefore, the later interviews and questionnaires are to elicit its narrowness: the thin line.

With the aim, then, of troubling the analysis based upon the initial fieldwork, I decided to interview a selective sample who did not fit into this apparently tidy 'norm'. In 2008–2011, therefore, I interviewed a Muslim researcher working on a project about Muslim homes and families. I also visited two families who have always lived in rented housing, supported by state benefits. In addition, an expatriate Scottish family living in Massachusetts and a native Californian had lengthy recorded conversations with me. I carried out postal questionnaires with five people on two- to four-year secondments from the British civil service, living in rented accommodation around Washington, DC. Also, two Chinese urban planners gave me their accounts of domestic display practices in China, and expert knowledge of housing patterns. I asked four African participants to scrutinise the boundaries of what was considered ordinary domestic display in Britain. As one of them put it: 'It's just what *you* do.' Finally, I made a film series, *Making Wales, Remembering Home*, with asylum seekers and refugees (Hurdley 2012). Originally designed as a public engagement project connected to the *Dismantling Mantelpieces* study, about the mementoes and practices of 'making home', it changed direction completely when it emerged that two of the volunteers were destitute, with another made homeless during filming. While unsettling connections further between memory, identity, home and 'stuff', the ongoing project also brought to the fore my growing discomfort with the theories of identity and culture that had dominated my interpretation of 'the mantelpiece'.

A word here on Britishness and Englishness: the confusion between Britain and England remains a constant of national identity/identities (Langlands 1999; Kumar 2005; McCrone 2008; Skey 2012). Ann Phoenix documents:

> ...a history of shifts in ethnicised identities, often from essentialised, fixed understandings of ethnicities and identities to more open

theorisations and empirical analyses of multiplicity, dynamism, decentring and unconscious processes.

(Phoenix 2010: 314)

Most of the participants for the study lived in Wales, and were asked to ascribe their own 'class' and 'ethnicity'. Some ascribed themselves as 'white' or 'Welsh', others as 'British', 'Caucasian' or – in one case – 'Scouse'. Altogether there were 22 different ascriptions, with many leaving 'ethnicity' blank (Hurdley 2006b). There is certainly one Welsh mantelpiece vernacular – the carved slate mantels in the slate-mining area of north Wales. However, the capital city, Cardiff, on the southern coast at the base of the post-industrial valleys region, is often seen as set apart from the rest of Wales, which is principally rural. Language can divide, with Welsh-medium schools now complicating the question of who is 'really' Welsh. North Wales is often more oriented to Liverpool as its capital, with deep roots connecting it to this city on the coast of north-west England. Roots and routes are complexly intertwined (Clifford 1997), and 'Welshness' is just as multiple and shifting an identity as Englishness, or British Muslim identity. I struggled with using the terms 'British' and 'English' throughout the book, and never resolved the ambiguity of these deeply affective 'nationhood' identities (Ahmed 2004). Similarly, 'class', particularly 'middle-class', was a slippery term (Skeggs 1997; Lawler 2005). While over a third identified themselves as 'middle', there were 15 self-ascriptions altogether, including 'working', and others who distinguished their class of 'upbringing' from current lifestyle. A sizeable minority left the section blank or wrote phrases such as, 'no idea, doesn't matter'. The relations between 'class', gender and ethnicity were to become increasingly fraught during the research and writing process.

The book loosely follows this gradual emergence into new ways of thinking about the relations between identity, home, memory and the 'stuff' with which narratives and other ways of telling are made. As the fieldwork moved between various libraries and the growing body of ever more disparate participants, the boundaries of what counted as 'taken-for-granted practice', in terms of *theirs* as participants, and *mine* as a sociologist, both slid together and widened. Concepts of identity and of identity theory became increasingly unstable and the gaps in cohesive social theory widened. The 'common ground' of understanding between participants and me shifted; tectonic plates grating, frictive force throwing forth sparks. The book is therefore a double narrative, tracing out the fieldwork. First, it is both a genealogy of the 21st-century 'globalised' mantelpiece and an archaeology of everyday homely practices. Second, it is an unfolding of central social theories of materiality, culture and identity towards the edges of current sociological thinking. Therefore, the first overall aim of the book is to keep mantelpieces 'on the move', to unsettle sedimented practices of 'doing' home, memory and identity, and the relations between them. The second is to work out how doing this kind of sociology *matters*.

The book is divided into three parts. The first part considers different mantelpiece 'pasts'; the second looks at mantelpieces and other display spaces 'here' 'now' in Britain, while the third part considers other histories and modes of domestic display practice in Britain, China and the United States. In the final chapter, the recent film project with asylum seekers and refugees opens up other ways of doing and theorising identity and belonging, where loss and hope, precarity and solidity are intertwined. In relating how the research links into the current politics of materiality, identity and culture as process, I conclude with an *idea of home*.

Part I – Pasts: history, archive and memory

'The past is a foreign country, they do things differently there' is the often-repeated sentence from L.P. Hartley's novel, *The Go-Between* (1953). Not only did people do 'things' differently in the past, the past itself is open to being done differently, according to who is writing, seeing or talking about it, and in what form. The fireplace is a particular form, a Π shape in the house that has persisted for centuries in Britain and elsewhere, an iconic figure closely bound up with tradition and memory. The aim of Part I is to make the familiar strange, to displace sedimented ideas of this domestic icon. By examining three 'mantelpiece pasts' – historiography, archive and memory – it unfolds the multiple ways in which the mantelpiece, and different forms of accounting for it, *make* history.

'The historian represents the organised memory of mankind, and that memory, as written history, is enormously malleable', commented C. Wright Mills (1959: 144). Chapter 1 opens up the historiography of the European hearth and the British mantelpiece – how these histories have been written – rather than what that (unknowable) history is. Whereas the first chapter focuses on expert and scholarly methods of producing the historical mantelpiece, Chapter 2 looks at another way of making the past, through the Mass Observation Archive. Initially conceived as a counter to elite versions of social science and history, the Mass Observation project, started in 1937, asked 'ordinary' people to participate in an 'anthropology of ourselves', to make 'museums...of domestic objects' (Madge and Harrisson 1937: 35). This produced hundreds of *Reports* of what volunteers (and their friends, relatives and neighbours) displayed on their mantelpieces (Mass Observation 1937). In 1983, a second collection of *Mantelpiece Reports* was made, prompted by Mass Observation's director's desire to record ordinary homes 'for our historian of the future' and 'a museum curator in years to come' (Mass Observation 1983).

Chapter 3 considers how the mantelpiece is produced as memory, and vice versa, through participants' accounts. Memory, like the mantelpiece, is a cultural process, an interplay of stories of personal memory, fragments of family history, vague yet authoritative cultural tradition and sensory comfort. The ways in which mantelpieces and their displays materialise memory, and memory is deployed to account for the presence (or absence) of mantelpieces in contemporary homes, demonstrate how the mantelpiece is both a strategy and an effect of remembering.

The tangibility and malleability of these different pasts demonstrate how the politics of 'small' history, of 'ordinary' memory, are as vital to understanding culture as monuments, museums and authoritative histories. Moreover, in presenting history, archive and memory as active and open-ended processes, Part I starts to unpick the work that goes into the making of culture.

Part II – Presents – ordering identities, things and home

The anonymity of things, those commonplaces of the mantelpiece, offer comfort to those who look upon them. Just a vase, a candlestick, a stone – nothing to disturb the eye or offend the taste. Receiving gifts and heirlooms is part of the normal calendar of family life for many British people: birthdays and Christmases punctuated by marriages and deaths. Clocks, ornaments, photographs and cards are the taken-for-granted materials that celebrate and commemorate a life. Similarly, the commonplaces of home – the mantelpiece, the television, the kitchen work-surface – are just 'there', the unthought-of surfaces of domestic space. And yet a vase may be deeply enmeshed in an account of identity transformation, or mean 'nothing, really'. Further, why is it that so many women are given ornaments? The persistence of the mantelpiece as a focal point in the main living room on which to keep things – particular sorts of things, at particular times – means it is an intense site for performances of identity, family and taste. Just as C. Wright Mills urged readers 'to feel as if suddenly awakened in a house with which they had only supposed themselves to be familiar' (1959: 8), the aim of Part II is to question the 'stickiness' of the taken-for-granted: telling stories about things, gift practices and the management of domestic space as both site for living and sight for others.

Chapter 4 examines the coalescence of identities, stories and things. Drawing on participants' interview narratives, the first aim is to seize (however tenuously) the moment at which a thing becomes a 'mantelpiece object', and examine how the apparently static mantelpiece tableau has a dramatic history. This is the everyday drama of identity performance through the staging of domestic displays. The second aim is to reflect on the very act of telling stories about things as an 'ordinary' cultural event. In Chapter 5, the focus is on a particular sort of thing, the gift, to open up the messiness of this seemingly simple practice. How do processes of gift receiving, displaying and disposal relate to the ongoing maintenance of different, even competing identities? Chapter 6 problematises two other 'givens': the parts the mantelpiece plays in the ordering of domestic space and time. Its relation to the television and the doorway of the main reception room makes it a central site for understanding the daily negotiations of family and the visitor's gaze. Time – as seasons, rituals and events – is also presented through, for example, clocks, cards, candles and calendars. The purchase and display of such things is also a method for ordering time, in performances of belonging, control and competence. Moreover, such arrangements of time, space and materials are among the first that children look upon, showing them 'how to' organise and make sense of experience. Home is the primary site for learning how to do identity, as display, performance and as contingent, relational process.

Part III – Cultures of 'home': other ways of looking

'The past is a foreign country; they do things differently there' introduces Part I. Its aim is to make the familiar strange: the history-making work around this traditional focal point. This last section returns to that from a different angle, treating the mantelpiece as a foreign body: what is it doing here? Reflecting also on Part II, which focuses on identity relations, it asks again: what is it doing here? What are the wider implications of construing the mantelpiece as a British domestic icon, intimately attached to ongoing constructions of personal identity, family and memory? What deeper cultural 'givens' are its apparent foundations? 'It is perhaps one defining characteristic of our period that it is one in which for the first time the varieties of social worlds it contains are in serious, rapid and obvious interplay', wrote C. Wright Mills over half a century ago (1959). In the 21st century, interactions of these worlds and their effects invite scrutiny, particularly those worlds that seem beguilingly storied and photogenic (even the dust), formed around that simple question: 'What's on your mantelpiece?'

As previous chapters show, domestic display is related to belonging, separation, transformation, ownership and loss. However, while politics of the domestic, the personal and familial opened up, participants rarely moved beyond the boundaries of these worlds. The decision of overwhelmingly 'white middle-class homeowners with partner/children' to participate in the research, and near-absence of 'other' people had been, I realised, the point. I had to go looking for a second group of participants. Further fieldwork, with British expatriates on the East Coast of the United States, Californians, a second-generation British Muslim woman, a poor white working-class Welsh family, white African migrants and visiting Chinese town planners, is not designed to provide an extensive survey of the multicultural mantelpiece. This is not a catalogue. The aim is to elicit the narrowness of the mantelpiece: the thin line of what is made explicit and visible among people who are assumed to share common ground (Foucault 1989) in the ordinary business of family and home. These participants' diverse accounts could easily have been folded into earlier discussions; much of what we talked about and looked at was similar to the first group's accounts. The division is to produce a certain effect, that of illuminating some – some, not all – of the edges of what counts for 'normal' in this commonplace mantelpiece world.

In Part III, two chapters focus on interviews with this second group, so that the 'everyday', 'homely' constructions of history, biography, memory and identity become refracted through other ways of making culture. How we gather people and things about us, how we remember, memorialise, monumentalise – at home, in museums, streets and social media – is political. Reflections in chapters 1, 2 and 6 on the role of the mantelpiece in ordering domestic geographies, bodies and temporalities link here with its part in organising nation, history, recognition and exclusion. National museums and monuments accomplish a particular mode of memory, culture and nationhood. The mantelpiece, Chapter 7 proposes, is another kind of national heritage, if we look at it through the sidelong gaze of those on the margins. While chapters 3, 4 and 5 elicit how moral economies of memory, story and gift are worked into the cultural politics of home, Chapter 8 discusses how the home and the 'market' are also linked in complex ways: consumption is an important practice in accomplishing different identities at home, in the politics of belonging, the making and keeping of nation.

The Conclusion brings in asylum seekers and refugees, to disrupt what 'we' are doing in making 'circuits of value' which render 'the rest' meaningless. By making these different conceptions of personhood, things, space and time visible, I show how these are not value-less, but offer another way of 'doing things'. I pick up on some of the questions, puzzles and loose ends of the book, linking them to current theories of identity and everyday practice as relational, processual and not necessarily cohesive. Taking another step back from the focal point of 'ordinary' practices, I examine the edges of the 'common ground' of seemingly shared cultures of materiality, identity, family and home. Thinking about remembering, forgetting and loss, the discussion proposes other ways of making worlds.

Why do mantelpieces matter? How did things come to play such an important part in our lives? What makes certain things matter, and others not? And, in turn, how do some people matter, and some not? In the end, then, this book is about *who matters*.

Part I
Pasts: History, Archive and Memory

1
Histories of Domestic Fire

> It is part of our condition that the purity for which we strive and sacrifice so much turns out to be hard and dead as a stone when we get it... Purity is the enemy of change, of ambiguity and compromise. Most of us would indeed feel safer if our experience could be hard-set and fixed in form.
>
> (Mary Douglas 2002 [1966]: 162–163)

Introduction: writing history

This chapter examines scholarly and expert writing about four developmental phases of domestic fire in Europe: the hearth, fireplace, mantelpiece and, finally, objects displayed on mantels. The first problem is material 'evidence': what has survived and, just as importantly, what has not. Stone and wood, rich and poor, male and female: what now can be seen of them? Second, I will stress how points of view re-emerge and transform, to demonstrate how 'coherent', taken-for-granted explanations fall apart under sustained scrutiny. This is not a 'timeline' of the mantelpiece, but a messy assemblage of diverse traces (Law 2004; Savage 2007). This 'throwing together' re-orders seemingly coherent historic narratives to highlight the gaps between them, where different interpretations become visible.

The 'hearth' has certainly been a focus for anthropological attention. For example, Janet Carsten's absorbing ethnography of a Malayan fishing village, *The Heat of the Hearth* (1997), analyses eating/cooking practices, kinship/familial and gender relations in connection with the division of work and space, among other topics. Although I discuss the social history of the hearth, there are two significant differences from work such as Carsten's. First, the end point of this historiographical survey is the 'cold of the mantelpiece' in the houses where there is no longer, or never has been, a cooking hearth. That distinction elicits the second: despite connections between such ethnographic studies of long-established kinship/family societies, centred geographically around the village, house and hearth, and social histories of traditional European/American life around the cooking fire, there has been no critical examination of the similarities and differences between *there/then* and the 'social life' of the contemporary mantelshelf above the fireless fireplace. If the house is a primary 'structuring structure' (Bourdieu 1977), it is so completely implicated in ongoing processes of meaning-making (and thus, power) that every aspect of its historiography and current, specific manifestations invites analysis. Nostalgic discourses of 'family, hearth, shrine, tradition' and the peculiar ways in which these interplay with counter-rhetorics such as individualism, taste and modernity deserve close attention. The cold mantelpiece, both detached from and attached to the 'hearth', is an ideal location for producing critical understandings of how these discourses make history, home and identity.

The historiography of architecture is complex and approached from many different perspectives, such as the global (Fletcher 1989), continental (Pevsner 1963 [1943]) or period-specific (Long 1993; Fernie 2002). Architecture can be included in a more general historical survey of a 'civilisation' (Boardman *et al.* 1988); a country (Foster 2004); the everyday life of an historical period (Quennell and Quennell 1937); an artistic movement (Greensted 2010); or colonialisation (Herman 2005). Public or larger domestic buildings and large-scale architectural trends have often been the focus of architectural publications, although cultural, regional specificity and vernacular or smaller domestic structures have had more attention recently. Buildings of a particular region, such as northern New England (Garvin 2002), houses of a region (Johnson 1993) or a type or period in that region might be the focus (Gowans 1986). Perhaps the writer or editor will draw together global vernacular domestic forms (Oliver 2003), the 'ordinary' British house (Barfoot 1963) or the history of a single Chinese family home (Berliner 2003). Studies of building and design technologies can focus on a single person (Fazion and Snadon 2006), a specific technique (Peterson 2000), the use of a material (Reinberger 2003) or a particular form, such as the grid, manifested in the brick (Higgins 2009).

Frequently, the development of the fireplace is incorporated into these studies, mentioned only in passing, pictured as part of a room or used to illustrate a particular point about the principal subject. The exterior might be the writer's main concern, particularly in works on historical architecture, accompanied by photographs, sketches and architectural drawings. Historical interior architecture is easily portrayed for extant buildings such as palaces, grand houses and public buildings, but drawings and descriptions of ruined or much-altered interiors must be reconstructed through the expertise of archaeologists and historians, and (this is the nub) through conjecture. The deployment of con-jecture (from the Latin verb *conicere*, to 'throw together') makes reading treacherous for the researcher. While the writer might take care to point out that, by their very nature, domestic interiors, particularly of the less wealthy, are poorly recorded, and materials such as wood, pottery and fabric are prone to perish, it is all too easy then to 'throw something together' that makes sense as a coherent narrative.

The next section will focus on modern texts about hearths in ancient Greece and Rome. This is not an assertion that the Roman/Greek hearth and associated cults or displays are the foundation stones for all current practices. As Goffman (1986) argued, myth and folklore are key referents in social performances. While there are many origins of the 'hearth' myth, I have selected this thread precisely because it is embedded in the cosmology for western European and American architecture.

Hearths, ancient and modern

When authors write about something as solid and unambiguous – it seems – as the domestic hearth, it is tempting to attribute the same substantive qualities to the text. By contrasting 19th-, 20th- and 21st-century writing about the hearth, we can see how Victorian certainty dissolves into present ambiguity. In tandem, parallel views of contemporaneous texts show how these are simply accounts – versions – of the hearth. Between the criss-crossing beams of light they throw upon the past, we may glimpse a shadow of something that might have been.

Authority and authorship

The canonical Latin dictionary by Lewis and Short (1879; see Perseus 2012) is still in common use. It is based on someone else's translation of a Latin–German dictionary, which was first revised by its original German writer, then by an American scholar. Its genealogy is outlined in its full title (rarely used): *A Latin Dictionary: Founded on Andrews' Edition of Freund's Latin Dictionary: Revised, Enlarged, and in Great Part Rewritten by Charlton T. Lewis, Ph.D. and Charles Short, LL.D.* While Short, as befits his name, addressed only the letter A, Lewis had the rest of the alphabet to contend with. Such detail seems hardly worth bothering with; however, the cutting out of parts, even of dictionary titles, also deletes the multiple traces of this authoritative text. Similarly, traces of the ancient hearth have been variously outlined over the last two centuries, as we shall see.

According to Lewis and Short, *focus* has a number of subtly different meanings. It can signify the hearth or fireplace, but can also act as a metonym 'to signify one's dearest possessions', home and family. This was due to the placing of *Lares*, the gods of the household, in niches on the hearths, 'and for them a fire was kept up'. The term *arae et foci* (the altars and hearths) is common in Roman literature as a collective term for country, gods, home and family (for example, in the histories of Sallust and Livy). Virgil uses *focus* powerfully in his epic Roman poem, the *Aeneid*, to denote a funeral pile and the lyric poet Propertius signifies an altar by the same word. In addition, *focus* (or its diminutive *foculus*) could signify a moveable fire-pan or brazier, which might also be used for religious purposes – and was the same form as braziers used on public altars for fire and/or blood sacrifice.

Twenty years later, the American classical scholar Harry Thurston Peck edited an *Encyclopaedia of Classical Antiquities* (1898; see also Perseus 2012). This details the different types of Roman heating and cooking devices, their various uses and positions in the ancient house, and their association with domestic worship. Peck describes a gradual move from a single-roomed dwelling, where the *Lares* (household gods) were placed near a hearth used for cooking, heating and domestic worship, to a multi-roomed house which included kitchen, chapel, bedrooms and atrium (central court-yard). Many houses were centrally heated by hypocausts, underfloor water pipes heated with a furnace stoked by slaves. Although there is some doubt concerning the precise uses of different heating and cooking devices, the detailed descriptions, resting on source material from ancient writers, Pompeian houses and other archaeological remains, seem highly authorita-tive. Another, more modern authority on Roman architecture, Frank Sear, draws on the 1st-century Roman Seneca's Epistle 44, where he 'remarks that an atrium "crammed with smoke-blackened images" was a sign of the old nobility' (Sear 1992: 33). Like Lewis and Short, Sear states that the hearth for the *Lares* was in the atrium. While the Victorian dictionary takes the Roman authors as its authoritative source, Sear uses both literary references and the ruins at Pompeii and Herculaneum. In contrast, other writers claim that the altar of the household gods was associated with the cooking hearth in the kitchen (Camesasca 1971: 419; Perring 2002: 192).

Although this comparison of brief statements raises some uncertainty about the place and uses of the ancient hearth, the texts gloss over the many variants, dependent upon region, wealth, house form, social organisa-tion and cultural specifics. This might be due to lack of available evidence, necessities of space, an authorial focus that lies elsewhere, or a particular readership. It might be because the authors were working from other texts they assumed were authoritative and universally applicable, although this is conjecture. However, it is possible to look at other modern, expert schol-arly texts in which uncertainty regarding the authority of ancient texts, modern assumptions and the lack (or poor recording) of material evidence is openly acknowledged. It is precisely the space in-between these ambi-guities where these scholars work. A brief look at four authors' texts will demonstrate first, how acknowledging uncertainty and fragility produces meticulous archaeologies, and second, how hearths (absent and present, fixed and mobile) can be used in arguments questioning taken-for-granted assumptions about everyday life.

Doubt and ambiguity

The sacred concept of the ancient hearth/home/family/homeland that can be 'set in stone' is engraved into modern conceptions of home. Yet, some classicists, archaeologists and ancient historians now emphasise that they do not have a clear view of the past, but must look at it through the 'distorted lens' of ancient drama, poems and legal prosecutions, or interpret material fragments, often displaced, disfigured or poorly recorded (Tsakirgis 2007). Assumptions about links between national and domestic religious practices, the law, social relations, everyday activities and even what it was to 'be' Greek are all cast out of place through careful examination of (among other things) fixed and moveable hearths. This is the task of research: to disfigure and displace nostalgic images of cosy fires in homely nooks, throw into question what it is to 'record' the past, treading a dirty stranger's footprints across sacred ideas. As Douglas (2002) argued, dirt is only 'matter out of place', defined culturally, rather than naturally. And it now looks like modern madness to found an idea of 'home' on the past, since what these archaeologies make clear in their uncertainty is how much has been lost. Only ruins of what was set in stone remain, accompanied by a very few displaced, ambiguous and broken everyday artefacts, leaving so much still buried. Precisely how the idea of home is connected with the past, ' ... has very little to do with the past at all, and everything to do with the present' (Douglas 1986:69).

As more ancient sites have been excavated over the past century or so, and techniques for recording material remains have developed, modern editions and translations of ancient texts have also become more widely available. For example, Janett Morgan's work on Greek domestic religion (2005, 2007) argues that the fixed hearth is of material and symbolic importance in the home, in relations between public/private and human/divine spheres of governance. As an exemplar, she cites an ancient account of an adulterer getting divine protection by touching the hearth, thus avoiding the automatic death penalty (Lysias 1.27). Her argument, then, is that the Greek *hestia* (hearth) played an important 'ideological role' as well as being an architectural feature of the house (2005: 197).

This view is also taken by Barbara Tsakirgis (2007). Showing how domestic *hestia* and *oikos* (home) are synonymous in ancient writers' conceptions, she illustrates how this literary hearth must be taken as fixed for it to fulfil its many ritual functions. However, she proposes that there were both fixed hearths and moveable braziers in Greek houses, in a detailed review of archaeological evidence. Having established the sacred character of the domestic hearth, she argues that moveable braziers must have had the same functions and symbolic resonance: these were also *hestiai* for cooking, heating and ritual. Her specific argument is that the increasing use of braziers in Athens and decline in fixed hearths coincided with a change in house form and a new flexibility in uses of domestic space. The movement of braziers and functions of rooms were 'defined by the temporal activities of the inhabitants' (2007: 229). Notably, she also comments that the idea of a constantly burning domestic flame (implying an immoveable hearth), kept up for purposes of worship, is a misunderstanding caused by a long-term confusion between the domestic hearth and public religious hearths, due to long-accepted parallels between state and domestic rituals. What is clear in her description of ancient sites is that there was no fixed place for the hearth in the house, or, in many cases, a fixed hearth. She argues that central fixed hearths made sense only in simple archaic houses, where they could heat the whole space. In palaces and, later on, more complex ordinary houses, there could be numerous fixed and/or moveable hearths; wall hearths were particularly suited for cooking, often in a separate room.

Tsakirgis also acknowledges the contested notion that early hearth forms influenced the shapes of Greek temples – so often seen the other way round in the popular view of domestic fireplaces as shrines or altars – but points out that this is 'assumed' and without documentary support. Before presenting her own argument, she clarifies for the reader that the only evidence really is literary: ' . . . their sacred character is considered, this last matter seen largely through the lens, albeit somewhat and sometimes distorted, of literary testimonia' (2007: 225). In fact, only one buried ritual deposit has been found beside a fixed hearth, and there are (so far) no assembled remains of ritual material with braziers. Braziers are often humble-looking (and breakable) things, warranting little attention from earlier archaeologists, and ritual remains – such as bones – would no doubt be disposed of elsewhere.

While Tsakirgis focused on the co-emergence of flexible domestic space and everyday domestic practice in Athens with the moveable *hestia*, Eva Parisinou (2007) examines an earlier period to argue that studying the illumination of house interiors can inform new approaches to social interaction in domestic space. She emphasises the paucity of the material record and the danger of mistaking where an artefact is found for where it originally belonged in a structure. Combining material evidence with references to the *Odyssey* and a later book on household management (Xenophon, 4th century BC), she proposes, tentatively, that lighting was an increasingly important consideration in Greek housing, in the facilitation of social interaction and use of dark rooms. 'The absence of fixed hearths from a substantial number of surviving dwellings of the period may possibly suggest their replacement by artificial devices like portable braziers which provided warmth and light, thus becoming the focus of social activity particularly during the darker hours of the day' (2008: 220). With only a few fragile lighting devices excavated, and unable to designate wall openings as 'windows' in such early structures, or even distinguish houses from other types of building, Parisinou uses the absence of fixed hearths to build an argument about the illumination of 'living culture'. Her intent is to push the debate on 'ancient domestic' space beyond accepted spheres of chronology and gender relations (2007: 215).

Similarly, in her study of excavated houses in Crete, Ruth Westgate argues for the re-orienting of archaeological/ancient history away from an 'idealizing, Atheno-centric perspective of literary sources' towards a more regionalised, close-up reconstruction of ancient Greek life (2007: 424). Nevertheless, with the same proviso as Tsakirgis (2007) regarding literary evidence, she uses extant written sources to introduce her argument. Since ancient writers comment on the peculiarity of Cretan *communal* social institutions (in contrast to the private, family-oriented social organisation of Athens), she deduces that their domestic architecture and organisation must have differed too. Further, while 'the sources present Cretan social and political structures as uniform across the island (and through time)...it's clear from the epigraphic evidence that there was a fair amount of variation in reality. The variability of the houses adds another dimension to this impression of diversity' (Westgate 2012). Since older excavations were not adequately recorded and few extensive sites in Crete have been excavated, the material evidence is problematic. Referring to other recent writers, she comments on how '...the Pompeii premise – the assumption that the objects found in a room are a direct reflection of the activities that took place there – has been shown to be unreliable, even at Pompeii' (Westgate 2007: 426). And, as we shall see, chimneys and houses can be dismantled and moved out of place.

Examining the few sites currently excavated, Westgate notes how the 'curiously archaic-looking hearth rooms' have led scholars to date Cretan houses too early, contrasting the fixed central and wall hearths with the portable braziers in houses of a similar period elsewhere in Greece, as described by Tsakirgis. Whereas some scholars have invoked the climate as an explanation for fixed hearths in northern Greece, this cannot be the reason in Crete. Thus, having juxtaposed the 'othering' of Cretan social institutions in Greek texts with anachronistic Cretan hearths, Westgate then redefines the boundary, bringing Crete into the centre, and casting Athens out to the margin, to propose that 'the "norm" is not as normal as we might think' (2007: 454).

Thus, 19th-century certainty in classical/archaeological fields is tempered by complex debates drawing on texts, excavated objects and architectural remains. These three cultural materials are ways of knowing about social and architectural organisation in the absence of living voices. That might sound obvious, but it is surprising how much sociology is founded only upon what people say. Even without this dimension, these three artefacts – writing, things and buildings (that is, big things) – are combined to present arguments, contesting or supporting each other, transforming the solid edifice of Peck and his contemporaries into moot points. While recognising that this type of close-up, rigorous scholarly writing is not for leisurely reading at most breakfast tables or with half an eye on the television, I want to highlight the contrast between recent archaeology of the ancient house, linked to interpretations of social institutions, relations and interactions, with the daily fodder of popular design books, magazines and TV programmes. The next section focuses on accounts of the mediaeval movement of the hearth from the centre of the room to the wall.

Fireplace, walls, floors: the invention of necessity

This section first traces the movement of the domestic fire from the centre to the wall, and how this has been seen as making a place for display above the fire. Propelled by technology and necessity, this plot-line is inadequate, although poverty, locality, transport connections and technical concerns do play their part. Therefore, I then take a cultural turn, towards the interplay of architectural/domestic relations, for a different view of the narrative.

The central hearth

The central hearth's move to the wall, with its chimney becoming an essential load-bearing structure, before being supplanted by a central passage, with the Great Hall reduced to no more than a vestibule, makes a neat story of the 'civilizing process' (Elias 2000 [1939]; but see Johnson 1999: 71). The different perspectives presented here, unlike archaeological re-visions of the archaic/classical world, are not contested, in that each account is presented as a matter of fact, rather than an informed point of view. Yet jostled together, they do not make sense completely, as John Crowley's (2001) critique of 'the invention of comfort' points out.

Originally, houses in Britain were simply unwalled roofs for the fire (Prizeman 1975). The house form that persisted from the Romano-British period until well into Tudor times (and beyond in remote rural areas) was the single room with a central hearth, and a smoke-hole in the roof. Andrew Henderson, writing about the English family house, contrasts its Anglo-Saxon/Norse origins with the Roman atrium, 'so called because the rafters were black, *ater* [Latin for 'black'], with smoke from the central fire' (1964: 9). Nevertheless, smoke-blackened rafters are crucial evidence for modern architectural historians/archaeologists searching for traces of central British hearths in extant mediaeval halls (Hall 2005). In some regions, the two-roomed longhouse divided the animals from the people by a central passage. Examples of these can be seen in the Museum of Welsh Life, near Cardiff, where many old buildings have been moved, stone by stone. Numerous castles, manor houses and more humble dwellings in Britain survive from this period, although they nearly all lost their central hearth as upper floors were added, with rare exceptions such as Stokesay Castle, Shropshire, completed in 1291.

The wall fireplace

The movement of the main fireplace from central hearth to walls is well documented in architectural literature (for example, Wood 1965: 257–276; Drummond 1971: 99; Prizeman 1975: 106; Brunskill 1978: 99, 1981: 40–43;

Armstrong 1979: 51; Barley 1986: 245). This move to the wall fireplace, with a hood and chimney, is usually attributed to improved technology, health and safety concerns and the need to have more accommodation (but see Crowley 2001: 8ff.). However, this did not happen everywhere in Britain all at once; recent archaeological work brings regionalism and particularity to the fore (Tarlow and West 1999). Although some buildings in some regions of Britain had wall fireplaces in the 12th century, it was not until the mid-16th to 17th century that these were the British norm. Poverty, the use of local materials and poor transport links had their effects; other reasons recorded include an adherence to traditional beliefs (Aslet and Powers 1985: 39). Others note that 'the adoption of the fireplace in England was apparently attended with the same reluctance as its abandonment today' (Drummond 1971: 99; also Camesasca 1971).

The various explanations for the development of the wall fireplace and chimney that follow all make sense when read separately. Viewed here together as an assemblage, they are unsettling. Lyndon Cave argues that the construction of upper floors, and the use of stone and brick – increasingly prevalent materials – ended the centrality of the open hearth. A trained architect, deeply involved with the preservation/restoration of British buildings through various charities and societies, he writes that an upper floor, caused by 'the need for increased accommodation', was made over the two sides of the mediaeval hall. Covering of the central area might not happen until the 17th or 18th century, 'as the building of stone or brick chimney stacks and fireplaces removed the need for an open fire, originally a feature of the open hall' (Cave 1981: 48–49). We will now review this 'necessity' through two surviving historical remains: the Anglo-Saxon Chronicle and Rochester Castle.

The early 12th-century keep of Rochester Castle in Kent has one of the earliest examples of fireplaces on multiple floors (Fernie 2002; Hull 2006). Although this had stone 'chimney pieces', there were no chimneys; the smoke was supposed to dissipate through small holes in the wall near the fireplace. As one progresses from the storage basement, through the Great Hall, to two more storeys containing more private apartments (added later), the chimneyless chimneypieces become increasingly elaborate to suit a hierarchy of inhabitants. Until this time, most British houses were extended along the horizontal axis, but the Norman incomers, with their desire for defensive structures, built on the vertical. This type of defensive building would not allow for a smoke-hole in the battlement, or central fires on upper wooden floors. Thus the new Norman keeps, constructed for a new social order, pushed the fire to the wall. The construction of upper floors, Andrew Henderson (1964) argues, was as much in emulation of the new Norman order as the need for more space; nevertheless he asserts, like many others, that it was not until brick was widely used that chimneys became commonplace. However, there is some evidence of pre-Norman two-storey buildings in the so-called Dark Ages. The *Anglo-Saxon Chronicle* for the year 977 records that King Edward I held a council at Calne, Wiltshire, on an upper floor (Lapidge 2001: 125). This collapsed, leading to the death or injury of many councillors, leaving Archbishop Dunstan hovering above them, since his chair was placed above the floor beam. Timber and clay mediaeval chimneys have been found (Henderson 1964: 28; Hall 2005). John Kenyon dates the earliest chimneys and clay chimney pots in Britain after 1140 (2005: 168), even though these materials were easily available prior to this throughout Britain. This writer on mediaeval fortifications points out that few chimneys and pots have been found due partly to their vulnerability to the weather.

Linda Hall's thorough study of household furnishing shows a photograph of a 'very rare timber chimney' from as late as 1630, serving back-to-back fireplaces (2005: 177). The absence of smoke on roof beams is good evidence for this being an original site for the 17th-century fireplace. She also states that wall fireplaces were inserted into some open halls *prior* to the addition of upper storeys (2005: 170). Techniques for directing smoke, such as the reredos (moveable fireback) and wood/plaster hoods were used for both central *and* wall hearths, but a funnel, as such, would seem unworkable until hearths moved to the end of the hall, with screens dividing off the entrance and access to other rooms now situated beyond. Chimneys might be built against the exterior of the house on the side or end wall, so they did not impinge on the living space at all. In time, a large central chimney, serving the several fireplaces, would provide an essential support structure – and warmth – for the house. Some few hundred years later, the chimneys would move outwards, leaving a cold central passage-way, in the perfect symmetry of the Georgian house. The walls of this corridor were load-bearing, in place of the massive central chimney.

Therefore, teleological narratives, based on cause/effect relations between hearths, chimneys, upper floors, bricks, more space and walls, become circular. If 'necessity' is cast aside, other arguments can make sense. The massive, non-integral chimney could have worked well in the centre of a large single space, as in many contemporary houses. With this chimney retaining all heat within the house, the multi-functional, well-heated and relatively smoke-free hall would be technologically advanced. Open-plan living and working, and live/work spaces, are the height of modern Scandinavian-style chic. Great numbers of people can be fitted into a single room, negating the 'need' for more accommodation. Perhaps braziers (which were in common use) could have been used for all the cooking and heating.

Moreover, the brick has been around since the 9th century BC, reaching England by 300 BC, and is just as caught up in symbolic and social relations as the hearth (Higgins 2009). Its increasing popularity in the 15th century as a building material was not simply due to cheapness and ease of local production, but was also connected to the rise of powerful mediaeval craftsmen's guilds (Higgins 2009: 13–31). The Romans built in concrete and brick, and their multi-storey urban buildings were very often tenements for the poor, with the poorest at the top (Boardman *et al.* 1988). Concrete was not in widespread use in Britain again until the 18th century, apparently reintroduced to meet the Georgian desire for an affordable 'look' of fine stone with cheap stucco exteriors. At around the same time that upper floors were being added and fireplaces were shifting to the wall in many existing and new British houses, the Italian architect Alberti was advocating single-level houses, based on the drawings of the Roman Vitruvius. Further disrupting any notion of simple technological progress, Lewis Mumford views Alberti's designs as a 15th-century precursor of the 20th-century suburban ideal – the bungalow (1961: 552).

Thus, linking the need for more room, availability of building materials, heating technology and wealth with upper floors, chimneys, multiple rooms and wall fireplaces makes no sense by itself. The possible effect of the Norman keep, however conjectural, opens up the question of how changes in architecture might relate to shifts in social relations, which is addressed by numerous writers. A very brief review follows, which is intended only to suggest how things might have happened.

Modern patterns of social division and stratification have been traced as roughly contemporaneous with the shift from a feudal to a class-based society, in which power became increasingly centralised in the king and (later on) parliament. At the same time, a rising urban/mercantile middle class emerged, as mobile workers offered services for money, while paupers were now detached from feudal support (Mumford 1961; Henderson 1964; Johnson 1993). Having slept, eaten and lived in the main hall with the servants, often on truckle beds, wealthier families began to divide space between sleeping and entertaining, cooking and eating, upstairs and downstairs, front and back (Armstrong 1979: 512; Brunskill 1981: 43; Johnson 1993: 106–109). Eventually, a cross-passage divided servants cooking in the kitchen from the family and guests in the main hall. The 'master' might observe activities in the hall unseen from a spy-hole in the more private solar above. Extra heating was provided with moveable braziers (Wood 1965). Braziers are an ideal portable heating device, and negate the need for costly permanent chimneys in multi-room houses, as Tsakirgis (2007) argued in her explanation of the apparent rarity of chimney pots in ancient Greece, but permanent wall hearths eventually became the norm in Britain. Therefore, the persuasive teleological, technological narratives provided in different forms by numerous commentators are countered – both by each other, and by less certain accounts exploring the complex politics of home. The next section looks at the newly boundaried space: above the fireplace.

The space above the fire

With a fireplace against a wall, distinct from the kitchen cooking hearth, people could make a feature – a frame – of its surrounds. Extant mediaeval houses have beautifully decorated chimneypieces and fireplaces, with friezes, heraldic emblems, quatrefoil motifs and shields (Gotch 1909; Wood 1965). By the 17th century, divisions of social and domestic space were such that the kitchen was split off from the scullery, where dirty and wet work was done (by a scullery maid), and the corridor, 'this special organ for public circulation', further separated rooms and their inhabitants, who also now ate 'above' or 'below' stairs (Mumford 1961: 439). Not only was the wall fireplace part of the rearranging of the room and the house interior, it was also part of the exterior display of social stratification. It was associated with 'tall imposing facades' of two-storey houses, as opposed to the single storey, single 'public multiuse' hall that had been common to all social strata (Brunskill 1981: 43). Chimneys were status goods in themselves, bequeathed in wills as personal property and even, following demolition of the house, left standing to ensure a family kept its pew in the parish church (Cullingford 2003: 9). The chimney was not merely an analogy or metonym for the house; it *was* the house, but it was also the property of the person, and might even be removed when a householder moved house. Although the open space of the multi-functional mediaeval hall was symbolically divided according to one's 'place', new hierarchies, roles, gender divisions and even ideas of personhood were built into the walls, fireplaces, chimneys and storeys of the changing architecture (Johnson 1999).

The great aristocratic houses of the 16th century onwards, with their ornate wooden, stone or marble fireplaces, chimneypieces and over-mantels, decorated with family crests and carvings, are still standing in Britain. Although heavily influenced by continental Europe, their designs are more eclectic, due partly to the sea between, but also complex religious and state politics (see Fletcher 1989: 805–1066 for fuller details). As the customs of the court and grand houses filtered into an increasingly wealthy middle class, these were embedded into urban architecture and country houses. It would, however, still have been common for humbler houses to consist of one or two rooms, perhaps with an exterior chimney on a long wall, or for horizontal additions to extend gradually at the back of the house. Therefore, much of this available history necessarily marginalises what barely remains: houses built of mud; the houses and possessions of the non-literate; itinerant workers, to name a few of the excluded. The comments of William Harrison in Holinshed's Chronicles, first published in 1577, are also worth noting. In his 'Descriptions of Britain and England' he complains that the luxury of multiple chimneys (and therefore fireplaces) replacing open hearths with reredos has led to 'rheums, catarrhs and poses' and headaches. The loss of the open fire, smoking into the room, has weakened the constitution of British families in Harrison's opinion: 'For as the smoke in those days was supposed to be a sufficient hardening for the timbers of the house, so it was reported a far better medicine . . . ' (cited in Quennell and Quennell 1937: 51; see also Harrison 1577).

What might be seen as the dirty past can also be viewed as healthier – perhaps purer. Although new technologies rarely entirely replace existing technologies, this resistance to innovation in terms of heating is noted repeatedly by commentators on British social and design customs, as we shall see again in Chapter 2. In any case, these are not new technologies, but ones that are brought into cultural focus every now and again. Nevertheless, over the course of a few hundred years of known history, the fireplace and chimneypiece, with a decorative overmantel, had almost entirely replaced the central open hearth in the main room of the multi-room house. It is nearly time for the official entry of the mantelpiece.

Hearth, chimneypiece, mantel: the production of space

As a timely aside, we shall look first at the mirror, to think about how authorial viewpoint influences the timing of artefacts' appearances in written history.

Reflections on knowing: the mirror

Much has been written on the influence of designs by the 16th-century Italian Palladio, taken from 1st-century BC drawings of the Roman Vitruvius, on British architects and designers. Similarly, the continuing power of European (particularly Italian) design over architects such as Inigo Jones in the early 17th century and the Adam brothers over a century later is well documented (for example, Pevsner 1963). What is made significant, though, in Ian Gow's (2001) analysis of Scottish chimneypieces is how British fireplaces *differed* from European counterparts. In grander Scottish/British houses, the fireplace and chimneypiece continued to be architectonic, integral to the design of the whole house and therefore the responsibility of the architect or a skilled sculptor, in contrast to France, where masons were employed. Gow notes that, by the early 18th century, chimneypieces in wealthier French houses were already merely frames for mirrors up to 70 inches high, whereas Britain did not have the technology to produce mirrors of this size until the end of the century. The chimneypiece itself was the focus, rather than anything placed on what might be no more than a narrow horizontal strip above the fire.

On the other hand, in Sabine Melchior-Bonnet's beguiling (2002 [1994]) history of the mirror, she not only illuminates the role of mirror-making in the production of modern France but asserts that mirrors of any size remained luxury goods into the mid-19th century, receiving special mention in French property advertisements. In contrast to Gow's focus on the mirror's supremacy over early 18th-century French chimneypieces, Melchior-Bonnet comments that overmantel mirrors remained quite rare, and perhaps associated with a certain type of female vanity, even prostitution (2002: 84–86). She explores the reproduction of nature as spectacle, framed and reflected on the walls of fashionable rooms, and the peculiar reworking of self in the estranging, yet intimate gaze into the looking-glass. The mirror, like the brick, was not simply a technological matter. Gow chooses not to mention, for example, the 16th- and early 17th-century designs of Inigo Jones and Christopher Wren, who integrated mirrors into their royal chimneypieces (Hills 1985: 37–38). Contrary to his argument, then, mirrors were not necessarily precluded by architectonic design. The mirror was a luxury good in the 18th century, due to the high cost of mirrored glass (Saumarez Smith 2000), but the combination of mirror and candles shed precious light in an era of no artificial lighting. If this were their only purpose, however, we could ask why so many contemporary mantelpieces still present the onlooker with this same assemblage of things.

The line of division?

The mantelshelf, having been an indistinct part of the fireplace, is generally noted as a discrete feature at the start of the 18th century in 'fine rooms' when:

> The slight simplification from the massive chimney-pieces of Elizabethan and Jacobean times made the definite division of the mantel or fireplace and the overmantel covering the area of wall above the fireplace. The mantel-shelf became a more prominent feature.
>
> (Barfoot 1963: 62)

While there was now a separation of fireplace and display place, there was 'a continuing harmony of style for the two parts', notes another writer (Gotch 1909: 277). However, it is not completely the case that the mantelshelf appeared at a particular design moment, although this fits in with a narrative history. Nicholas Hills, for example, includes a photograph of a fireplace at Luddesdown Court in Kent dated c.1250 (1985: 25). Above the stone lintel is what he calls 'a moulded string course above'. His glossary describes a string course as a 'projecting horizontal band, usually moulded' (ibid.: 153). While this may be a quibble about terms (like my hair-splitting about 'chimneys'), the 13th-century 'string course' looks very much like a shelf above the fire. The key point is that no historiographical attention is given to this projection above the fire, and what people might have put on it.

The mantelshelf remained quite narrow, fitting with the plain style of interior design in the 18th century, but from the 1780s onwards furniture moved away from the walls and towards the fire, 'given the vagaries of the British weather' (Parissien 1995: 155). A design book of the time claims that the 'heightened prominence of the fireplace in principal rooms was a peculiarly British solution... [to the problem of the climate]... with the fireplace the "rallying point or conversational centre" of home' (cited in Parissien 1995: 157). It seems that the British weather (itself a cultural practice) explained the foregrounding of the fireplace as a site drawing the gaze, talk and bodies together.

Social historian Amanda Vickery writes that '... long into the 1700s, Londoners buried "witch bottles" under the threshold or behind the hearth', since both were 'apertures' into the house, with the chimney and hearth seen as 'weak points'. The hearth was conceived as 'breast, soul, heart or womb' and also as metonym for 'domesticity' (2008: 153). In this era of gentility, the house was still 'a body *for* the body' (Gell 1998: 252), an ancient and ubiquitous idea (feminised, in this case). Vickery continues with the story about the discovery, in 1963, of a bundle in a basket, containing [what had been] two live chickens, two strangled chickens, two shoes, a candlestick and a goblet. This was behind a hearth, walled up there in 1600 when the house – in Highgate, London – was built. I shall return to this in the concluding chapter; for now, we can contemplate the strangeness of this pre-modern practice in an early modern suburb.

In the 19th century the size of the mantelshelf grew, along with the enlargement of chimneypieces, even though this contradicted technological progress: Rumford's invention of an innovative grate in the 1780s should have resulted in smaller chimneypieces (Rumford 1796; Aslet and Powers 1985: 180; Parissien 1995: 156). Gow asserts that 'it was perhaps the French cult of the garniture, creating a new richness on the chimney-shelf, that led to the architect's supremacy over the design of chimneypieces being challenged in the mid-19th century by the upholsterer'. He goes on to attribute the reduction 'of the architectonic British chimneypiece to the status of a mere piece of furniture that could be seen as ephemeral' to the Aesthetic Movement's 'pursuit of the house beautiful' (2001: 64–65). However, this reading, based on a distinction between literally immoveable and moveable domestic structures, is not one taken up by other historians.

Mantelpiece displays: men, women and a tasteful morality

In this final section, we shall look first at the making of home as a place for women, and second as a site distinctly separate from work, dirt, the city and, in some senses, modernity. The shifting relations between work and home, men and women, middle and working classes were happening in parallel with a changing attitude towards home. As a site for consumption of mass-produced goods, the home was nevertheless a sanctuary from the dirty work of capitalist production. This tricky paradox could be maintained only by the conflation of good taste with a woman's moral duty to nurture her family. Professional style books and magazines proliferated, to guide the newly wealthy middle classes along the tightrope of being 'good' women.

Victorian altars

There are many paintings of families sitting around the fireplace, and photographs later on in the 19th century – although it is impossible to know to what extent the mantelpiece displays were staged for the artist's or photographer's frame (Weston 2002). Charles Saumarez Smith, former Director of the National Gallery in London, is careful to give his sources as he problematises the use of paintings, books and pamphlets of the time (2000: 234–240), just as other writers concerned raise the issue of curatorial authenticity when using sources such as 19th-century photographs (for example, Phillips 1997). Readers familiar with lifestyle magazines such as *House Beautiful*, weekly features in newspapers, and advice books will know that Victorian style books need bear little resemblance to everyday domestic practices (Gordon and McArthur 1986, Long 2002; Gregory 2003; also Daniels 2001). Therefore, the following discussion is based as much on the contemporaneous aestheticisation of the past.

From the mid-19th century, according to interior décor 'professionals' of the time, the clock, the candlestick pairs and/or vases and the overmantel mirror were reasonably constant parts of the display. By the late 19th century, writers of style books were commenting on the 'pretentious uselessness' of the symmetry and pairing of mantelpiece ornaments in 'lower middle-class drawing rooms' (for example, Mrs Orrinsmith's *Drawing Room*, 1878, cited in Forty 1986: 110) or the 'pity' of giving up the 'central opportunity of the room' to the clock, 'that is not worth looking at for itself, apart from its merely utilitarian purposes' (Cook 1995 [1881]: 119). Cook's explanation of the lack of interesting display on the parlour mantelpiece is that:

> [I]t is such a trouble to most people to think what to put on it, [and] they end blindly accepting the dictation of friends and tradesmen, and making to Mammon the customary sacrifice of the clock-and-candelabra suite.
>
> (1995: 119)

He urges his readers to take note that:

> [T]he mantel-piece ought to second the intention of the fire-place as the center of the family life – the spiritual and intellectual center, as the table is the material center... [and which ought, therefore to have on it]... things to lift us up.
>
> (1995: 121)

Cook was an American writer, who nevertheless used British exemplars in his advice book, perhaps because Britain has been viewed as the last bastion of the open fire (Muthesius 1979). It is noticeable that the British, unlike the Americans and continental Europeans, had not adopted other available forms of heating. Furnaces, central heating and stoves were all available (Cook 1995 [1881]: 111; Aslet and Powers 1985: 183; Long 1993: 98), but the British resisted these innovations (Camesasca 1971: 378), just as they had resisted the innovation of the wall fireplace in the 12th century (Drummond 1971: 99).

Another 19th-century American commentator argues for the continuing tradition of the open fire, as opposed to the stoves of America, seeing them as 'Lares and Penates of Old England', whereas the American stoves are 'fatal to patriotism... for who would fight for an airtight?' (Beecher Stowe's *Sunny memories of England*, 1854, cited in Long 1993: 98). This association of the fire grate, and hence its mantelpiece, with patriotism, echoes a rallying cry of time, written by 'an Ulster Cleric: "We have a great Home, and its hearth is a royal woman!" ' (Wilhide 1994: 75). As such, it accords with the increasingly gendered (and classed) division of space in industrial Britain, with the separation of the male dirty work of capitalism and the 'pure' home, tended by 'the angel of the hearth'(see Forty 1986: 94–119; Hepworth 1999; Tosh 1999; Davidoff and Hall 2002). At the same time, retro architecture and design flourished (Samuel 1994). The mediaeval, feudal past was celebrated in the quasi-religiosity of neo-Gothic style, while the Arts and Crafts movement recalled 'authentic' pre-industrial craftsmanship. These influences could be seen in grand houses and middle-class suburban villas, while workers choked in mines and mill-towns. The 'angel of the hearth' did not sweat in a factory.

Now, let us step back from the 19th-century fireplace and mantelpiece for a moment to reflect on what writers of the time were saying about it. Histories of the domestic interior have said that this was a time when the fireplace and chimneypiece expanded, following some restraint in the 18th century. This was despite the invention of Rumford's grate, and the fact that, as we have seen, fireplaces had previously existed without distinct mantelshelves. Mantelpiece displays came under attack for their conventionality and awful symmetry. Central heating had been available since 1800 (Aslet and Powers 1985: 183), and by law, gas companies had to supply homes on demand from 1855 onwards (Bowden and Offer 1996), but the British resisted introduction of new heating technologies. Writers of the time ascribe this to the association of home, family and country, with reference to *Lares* and *Penates* and the 'domestic altar'. The use of the display space on the mantelpiece without due thought to its position supporting (in a sense) the fire as spiritual and intellectual centre of family life is likened to a 'sacrifice' to Mammon, to consumerism (rather than to the gods of home and family) and to a lack of thought about the meaning of the mantelpiece, as a 'second' to the fire and its interrelation with the family table. Most of the literature available shows photographs and paintings of middle-class mantelpieces (for example, Hills 1985; Wilhide 1994), just as my interpretations are initially drawn from those who responded to the questionnaire, who were principally middle-class home-owners.

The Victorian overmantel could be perceived as the last flicker of the 'real' fire with the 'real' mantelpiece. In some ways, it was similar to the ornateness of the Elizabethan and Jacobean overmantel panelling (Parissien 1995). The noticeable departure is that, although the Victorian overmantel was also a materialisation of wealth and status, there were spaces in it for displaying moveable goods. While these might have been prescribed by stylebooks and convention (although this is not clear), the objects could be moved, unlike the 'pre-mantelshelf' time, when fireplace and display place were a single entity, in immoveable stone or wood and paint. There was no opportunity for 'matter out of place' (Douglas 2002 [1966]) or alienability when it could not be moved. This move to 'mobility' as the focus for style books – a new trend in the mid-19th century – parallels a growing, mobile urban middle class. They found a new need for interior décor experts' guidance in 'taste' when decorating their suburban villas.

Also interesting is the second shift, a little later in the century, in the gendering of domestic management. While, as Davidoff and Hall (2002) and Forty (1986) show, the construction of the middle-class home as private, feminised, aesthetic and moral sanctuary in early to mid-19th century Britain was a response to industrialisation and urbanisation, men were still principal managers of interior décor. 'The earliest home decoration manuals were written by married men for married men' (Cohen 2006: 90). Between the 1880s and 1930s, as marriage and property rights, then women's suffrage empowered (some) women financially and politically, they took on the mantle of domestic design, a trend that can be traced in the feminisation of these concerns in periodicals such as *Hearth and Home* and the *Lady's Pictorial* (Cohen 2006). Even Emmeline Pankhurst, future founder of the militant Women's Social and Political Union, owned a furnishing shop (ibid.). This move of domesticity into the female domain coincided with a literal shift in the 'place' of home. As home and work became increasingly distanced, the suburbs became a place for women, with men making a 'flight from domesticity', fearful also, claims John Tosh (2007), of the feminising influence on their sons. While Tosh is careful to point out that this 'flight' was not the 'loss' of a generation of men, his argument stands, that, in their very absence, save at evenings and weekends, men effectively made home a matter for women. However, the value of women's aesthetics and labour was low, with the loss of domestic servants and moves to the suburbs bringing middle-class women, as well as their former employees, into this private world of work (Sparke 1995; de Grazia with Furlough 1996; Attfield 1999, 2000).

Reluctant modernity

The open fire in the grate was, at that time, a seasonal as well as a daily event. In the summer, flowers, a fan or a *trompe l'oeil* of grate or flowers were put in the fireplace to replace 'the gaping hole left by the absence of a cheering blaze' (Parissien 1995: 162). This contrasts with most participants in my contemporary study, for whom the 'gaping hole' is a continuous daily event. Absences, as much as presences, are visible only to those who are looking for them. Despite its almost complete absence from houses in 21st-century Britain, the open fire was only reluctantly discarded by householders in the 20th century. Housewives surveyed by Mass Observation in 1941 did not want central heating, despite its efficiency, while the researchers themselves articulated the impossibility of a chimneyless urban skyscape (MO 1943).

The 19th century also marks a split between Britain and America and continental Europe, where other, more efficient forms of heating were adopted. The German writer Muthesius excuses this British attachment on grounds of temperate climate allowing survival of the 'domestic altar', but finds it unusual due to its 80% inefficiency (Muthesius 1979: 52). However, it did mean that the mantelpiece persisted atop these existing fireplaces, unlike the situation in America, where, despite furnace heating, people started to install fake fireplaces and mantelpieces towards the end of the 19th century, 'as if they couldn't bear to give up the memory of what had once been so pleasant' (Cook 1995: 111). This nostalgic re-attachment had other meanings in the US, as discussed in Chapter 8.

Central heating in Britain did not really take hold until the Clean Air Acts of 1956 and, more so, 1968, since the latter Act introduced smokeless fuel zones (Ravetz and Turkington 1995: 125). Urban space was controlled to such an extent that many people really had no choice but to turn to central heating, or at least replace the open coal/wood grate with a gas or electric fire, so that by 1979, fewer than ten per cent of mainland British houses were heated by an open fire (Utley *et al.* 2003). Alison Ravetz and Richard Turkington comment in their historical survey of British housing:

> The ghost of the candle lingers on in decorative, coloured and scented candles which form a stock-in-trade of gift shops and have little value for lighting...typically displayed on mantelpieces, when these are available.
>
> (Ravetz and Turkington 1995: 131)

They link this with a survey of bye-law houses when, despite the availability of cheap electricity, candles were still the 'second or third most important ornament', whereas in the semis and detached houses of the middle classes, these had transmogrified into electric simulacra, with 'imitation "drips"' (Ravetz and Turkington 1995: 131, citing Chapman 1955).

Shortly before the move to new technologies or, at least, attempts by modernist designers and suppliers of new electric and gas fires to move a recalcitrant British public into the future (Oliver *et al.* 1981; Attfield 1999; Stevenson 2003), the mantelpiece reached its apotheosis. The late Victorian overmantel reached from mantelshelf upwards, sometimes as far as the ceiling, often featuring a central mirror and surrounded by compartments for the display of many objects, now on several levels. Despite a trend towards simplified fire surrounds in new houses (Putnam 2002), the overmantel persisted in some homes even into the time of the 1937 Mass Observation *Report*. Moreover, not all late Victorians had the money to introduce the overmantel, or the new, costly pine surrounds. Similarly, many in the 1930s had the now-unfashionable marble fire surround, disguised with tasselled drapes (Long 1993).

This odd relationship between expert and novice, public and professional, teachers and learners, modernists and suburbians is seen clearly at a national level in the literature during and after the Second World War, when the rebuilding of Britain became a paramount concern (Brett 1947; Jarvis 1947). One architect argues for central heating in the mass-building programme, with good ventilation:

> But if we are to retain our open fires it would be as well if we were to improve on the designs of our fireplaces; the surrounds which have been used in many speculative houses, generally being ugly and over-elaborated with innumerable recesses and ledges which are neither an asset nor a necessity in the modern house... Manufacturers must give more care to this than they have done in the past and concentrate on designs of both simple and unobtrusive appearance.
>
> (Waring 1947: 53)

The battle for domestic space can be seen in the way in which architects, designers and town planners pushed one dominant reading of 'modernity' to the British public, through books such as the Penguin *Things We See* series and the design of houses. However, as we shall see in the next chapter, 20th-century Britons were not so easily moved into this version of the modern.

Conclusion

> In the intimate harmony of walls and furniture, it may be said that we become conscious of a house that is built by women, since men only know how to build a house from the outside...
>
> (Bachelard 1994: 68)

This historiography of the mantelpiece reveals it as a problematic material, bringing the paradoxical twinning of solidity and fragility into play.
It was not heating or building technology that refashioned central hearth
to mantelshelved wall fireplace, but symbolic spatial division; the ancient
hearth is elusive in archaeological digs. The mantelpiece has persisted into
the 21st century, entirely detached from the central, essential hearth in the
mediaeval hall, from the moveable heating braziers and the immoveable
ornamentation of the earlier wall fireplaces. They are hang-overs from the
past. Much of what people do with mantelpieces, and the fact that so many
people still want them, or at least permit them to remain, are accounted for
as effects of tradition and memory. As E. H. Carr pointed out, 'the facts speak
only when the historian calls on them' (1964 [1961]: 11). Many practices
are taken for granted, such as displaying a mirror above the mantelpiece.
These are traditional, and enacted without reflection or done with a different purpose from earlier meanings and uses, yet still evoking those absent
presences, just as the mantelpiece constantly invokes and makes present its
primary part, its absent past – the fire.

The majority of respondents to the questionnaire did not associate their
mantelpieces with terms related to such practices, such as 'shrine' or 'religious belief'. In a seeming contradiction, people in conversation about the
project immediately associated the mantelpiece with the concept of 'shrine',
echoing their Victorian ancestors. This paradox of differing perspectives, of
appropriation and detachment, can be seen throughout the partial genealogy provided here. The shift in attention from the (relatively) inalienable,
immoveable 'place' of the fire, to the moving display of things above, came
at a time when homes and identities, and the relations between them, were
undergoing great transformations. What, exactly, is being consecrated on the
mantelpiece today? What is set apart, raised up, foregrounded and distanced,
on this high shelf?

In Witold Rybczynski's unpacking of nostalgia as a method of dislocating from the present, he argued that domesticity is 'an idea in which
technology was a distinctly secondary consideration' (1986: vii). As an
architecturally-embedded 'past', the mantelpiece is, materially, a nostalgic
structure (Bourdieu 1977; Silverstein 2004). The chapter has highlighted
Bourdieu's observation of 'anti-genetic prejudice, leading to unconscious
or overt refusal to seek the genesis of objective structures and internalised
structures in individual or collective history'. Re-viewing the genesis of the
mantelpiece as 'patches...constantly undergoing unconscious and inten-
tional restructurings and reworkings tending to integrate them into the
system' (1977: 218) has caused the obviousness of the mantelpiece in
accounts of habit, tradition and commonsense teleology to become rather
less clear.

Bourdieu was writing about a non-literate culture, in which 'the absence
of the symbolic-product-conserving techniques associated with literacy'

leads to the house taking on the mantle of principal 'structuring structure' (1977: 38). However, this is not the practice only of non-literate groups: the house, and in particular, what lies within, are among the first things that children see. The ways in which people – scholars, Mass Observers, research participants – make the mantelpiece visible are inevitably bound up with what has been made 'look-able' to them, rather than the '... shadowed places in which nothing can be seen and no questions asked' (Douglas 1986: 69). Hearth, fireplace, mantelpiece, display: these four histories are connected, but not quite in the way that seems at first glance obvious, as commonplace, chronological relations. As Westgate argued, 'the "norm" is not as normal as we might think' (2007: 454).

Fraught with meaning, the mantelpiece is wrapped up not only in the making of family but in the politics of gender, class and culture: identity. Over the period covered in Britain, tax levies shifted from the hearth, to the chimney, to the windows and finally, to the person. The income tax, initially imposed as a temporary measure in 1799 to finance the Napoleonic wars, was seen by some as highly intrusive on the private person (Levi 1989: 138). This change from taxing externally visible domestic structures to the wage-earner also produced a new relation between individuals and the state. The domestic interior, and the economics of the home, were no longer behind closed doors. While this chapter looked at historiography – the writing of history – over several centuries, the next will look at smaller scales of history-making – in Mass Observation writing, and the small things on the mantelpiece. It will argue how critical scrutiny of these 'personal' materials might find similar processes of bringing certain meanings to the fore, and pushing others to the back, or transforming meaning altogether. As we shall see, the social spaces of home and family were to become more clearly enmeshed in the politics of the nation.

2
Mass Observation Mantelpieces

Soon after reading the New Statesman letter, Harrisson rode the train to London to meet Madge and Jennings. A witness to the meeting recalled 'Humphrey, with his elbow on one end of the mantelpiece, and Harrisson, with his elbow on the other end of the mantelpiece, both talking loudly and simultaneously to those present in general, without either of them paying the slightest attention to what the other was saying.' Madge was no doubt listening to and for both.

(Witnessed by Kathleen Raine, cited in Crain 2006)

Introduction: another way of knowing

Set up in 1937 by poet Charles Madge, anthropologist Tom Harrisson and painter/documentary film-maker Humphrey Jennings, following a chance juxtaposition of their articles in the *New Statesman*, Mass Observation (MO) was to be 'anthropology of ourselves' to counter government ignorance about the feelings and attitudes of the British 'masses' (see Mass Observation 2012). A principal aim was to collaborate in making 'museums of ... domestic objects' (Madge and Harrisson 1937: 35), and this perhaps prompted the *Mantelpiece Directive* as the first task for new volunteers, writing down 'in order from left to right' what was on their own mantelpieces and those of friends, relatives and acquaintances, stating, if possible, what was at the centre (MO 1937). The founders' first squabbles about what MO should be were never resolved, and they disbanded during the Second World War. Becoming a market research limited company in 1949, MO closed down in 1955. Soon after its renaissance in 1981 as the Mass Observation Panel, made up of volunteers responding to *Directives* about a wide variety of topics, the second *Mantelpiece Directive* was sent out (MO 1983); it offers fascinating similarities to and differences from the first, 1937 *Directive* in both form and content (Savage 2007). In this chapter I will focus on these responses to these two *Directives*, and look very briefly at responses to the 2006 *'Your Home' Directive* (MO 2006). The aims are threefold: to think further about how 'history' is made, as social/cultural material, both in MO and on the mantelpiece; to consider how the *Mantelpiece Reports* relate to home, household, family and identity; to relate these ideas to cultural practices today, in particular to memory work.

The inter-war period in Britain is particularly pertinent to a study of the home and (by extension) the mantelpiece for two reasons. First, it was a time of unprecedented mass speculative building programmes and the development of suburbia (Oliver *et al.* 1981; Stevenson 2003). Second, and entwined with this, there was a professional concern with bringing modernist architecture and design into the lives and houses of the 'public', who were seen as requiring education and enlightenment regarding their built environment and tastes (Putnam 2002). Advertisements of the time show this push to market modernism to the public, including domestic heating technologies such as replacing the coal grate with gas or electric fires (Oliver *et al.* 1981). However, modernist designers were to be disappointed, not only by the failure of British suburbia to be 'modern', with its mock-historical styles and attachment to traditional building techniques (Stevenson 2003: 37), but also by the 'public's' attachment to traditional technologies, as we saw in the last chapter. Design books, magazines and the modernist interiors that were 'geographies of transformation' (Darling 2009: 96) present images of the fashionable house interior. The desire to democratise the 'tasteful' home with high-quality mass-produced British goods might have been part of this modernism project (Darling 2009 in Sparke *et al.* 2009); however, Mass Observation offers different visions of domestic space. It was in this inter-war period, during which professionals sought to transform the taste, technology and material culture of the new suburbia, that Madge, Jennings and Harrisson, with other associates, got together. Following a year in Vanuatu in the Western Pacific, Harrisson's desire to carry out 'anthropology at home' combined ethnography with influences such as surrealism, psychoanalysis and Soviet documentary film-making in a democratising project to amass data collected through 'the observation of everyone by everyone, including themselves' (Madge and Harrisson 1937: 10).

There has been extensive writing on Mass Observation as social science, survey, history, surveillance, poetics, ethnography and representation of the everyday, by (among others) Liz Stanley (2001), Ben Highmore (2002), Nick Hubble (2006), James Hinton (2010, 2013), Mike Savage (2007, 2008), Murray Goot (2008), Mark Bhatti (2006); Louise Purbrick (2007), David Kynaston (2009) Simon Garfield (2009) and, its recent director, Dorothy Sheridan (1993; Sheridan *et al.* 2000). I discuss the methodological issues around using MO as sociological 'data' elsewhere (Hurdley 2013), since this chapter focuses principally on the content of the *Reports*. In brief:

although entirely statistically unrepresentative in terms of age, gender, class, education, occupation, ethnicity and locale, MO is uniquely able to give a glimpse (however partial) of mantelpieces in people's homes at two moments in the 20th century. As C. Wright Mills argued, 'the requirements of one's problem, rather than the limitations of any one rigid method, should be and have been the classic social analyst's paramount consideration', rather than objecting that historical materials are imprecise or not fully known (Mills 1959: 146). If we approach MO fully awake to its possibilities, not simply for comparative 'snapshots' of mantelpieces through time, but as a way of thinking about them, it will surely kindle our sociological imaginations.

Three questions about Mass Observation methods require attention in this chapter. First, the tension between the three founders' approaches was never resolved: was this social document, the simple collection of data, a surrealist technique to 'shock' new knowledge from the mass 'unconscious', through written collages in which a 'day in the life of' slum poverty, and leisurely wealth sat side by side (Jennings *et al.* 1937), or something quite different? Quite what MO was, and why it was, and who was involved, remain closely contested questions (Hubble 2006; Savage 2007, 2008, 2010; Hinton 2013). Second, how do the forms of the *Directives* frame particular ways of seeing the mantelpiece? Finally, how might the diverse array of reports make sense: narratives, lists, drawings, photographs, asides about other people and digressions on taste, tidiness and money? The chapter aims not to answer these questions, but to attend to how MO, with its inconsistencies, slipperiness and loose ends, opens up the way in which doing culture is a constant process of making choices, boundaries and things, even when it seems nothing is happening (Figure 2.1).

1937 *Mantelpiece Reports*: 'scientific value'?

In this section, I will discuss the *Directive* itself and how to interpret the mass of report writing. Following this is a collage 'mantelpiece', in the spirit of Mass Observation, made up of the many items and comments written by the 1937 volunteers. Next, we will focus closely on a single man's report, 'Male 240', and finally, think about narrative coherence and the permanence of 'ephemera'.

Directing the mass mantelpiece

Many of the 1937 *Reports* submitted about mantelpieces were from people who took part in the initial Day Surveys, in which they recorded the events of a day in their lives, the fourth and most famous of which was the Coronation Day of King George the Sixth on May 12th (Jennings *et al.* 1937). These named individuals were 52 men and 39 women. There were 22 other named volunteers, and 9 schoolboys who wrote short essays about their mantelpieces for homework. Another 12 (unnamed) schoolboys wrote lists of what was on their home mantelpieces, and there were 24 other *Reports* by unidentified volunteers. Therefore, there were 158 individual *Reports* about volunteers' own mantelpieces, and in most cases, mantelpieces in other people's houses. I read through these *Reports* twice during four visits to the Archive (housed in Sussex University library at that time), recording the form and contents of approximately half of them. A condition of access to the Archive is anonymity in print, so volunteers are referenced as they are in the Archive folders (for example, MO 1937: Men A-J); discrepancies are due to missing number slips on individual *Reports*.

X   12/2

D. Nicholson
_____

The Mantel-Piece

Starting at the left-hand end of the end of the Dining-room mantel-piece, its contents are as follows:

Firstly, a cut glass flower-vase, with a silver base which has been lacquered black to avoid having to continually polish it. This vase is a receptacle for two or three pencils, receipts from the Gas Coy., and hairpins. Between this and the clock in the centre is a copper oxidised ash-tray brought home from Weymouth by one of the family about four years ago. This is generally full of safety pins, collar stiffeners, pen-nibs, and matches.

The middle of the mantelpiece is occupied by a square green alarm clock (always about two hours fast) supported by an ornamental oak stand (Under this stand is kept the daily money for the milkman). Next to the clock is the inkbottle, and two or three dirty pens, on a glass block with places for writing materials. This block is always covered in ink-stains.

Beside this stand is a little china dog, two paws of which are missing. Lastly, there is the companion glass vase to the one at the other

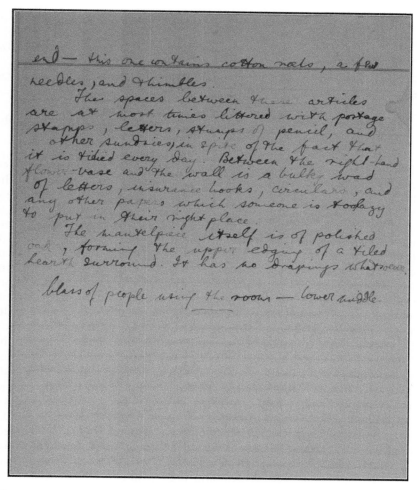

Figure 2.1 Mass Observation 1937: Schoolboys' *Reports*: included in the file of *Mantelpiece Reports* by volunteers who did not submit Day Surveys

The *Directive* asked them to:

> Write down in order from left to right, all the objects on your mantelpiece, mentioning what is in the middle. Then make further lists for mantelpieces in other people's houses, giving in each case a few details about the people concerned, whether they are old, middle aged or young, whether they are well-off or otherwise, what class (roughly)

they belong to. Send these lists in. If possible, also take photographs of mantelpieces.

(MO 1937)

Respondents were requested to 'report on yourself... sticking to the facts as far as possible'. Their anonymity was assured:

You therefore need not hesitate to write down your reports truthfully. Their scientific value depends upon your acuracy [sic].

Thus, while 'mantelpieces, the founders believed, displayed unexpected clues about religion, superstition, personal tastes and the entire life of the home' (Garfield 2009), the form of the *Directive* predicates the mantelpiece and its representation. This construction of the form of response (a series of lists) and the way in which the mantelpiece is viewed and reported (a line, with a centre point) is at odds with the decentring, surrealist notions of [some of] its founders, yet is appropriate, it seems, to the orderly collection of quantifiable data. Mass Observation's inherent contradiction, asking volunteers, conceived as 'subjective cameras', to write *Reports* 'with no distortion' (Mass Observation 1938: 66) of a place – the home – where concealment and presentation management are everyday practices, is encapsulated in the single mantelpiece photograph, sent in by a female volunteer. Written on the back of the small indistinct snapshot: 'Although a family secret, I think I should mention that the flowers [a very large bunch] are always arranged so as to hide a crack in the mirror.' These lists of 'observations' show only what is visible on the mantelpiece, what the writer wants to make visible, and, very often, what they can remember, since many of the accounts – especially of other people's mantelpieces – are written from memory. And a list is not simply a string of discrete objects; relations, resonances, indeed, what is *possible* to think, are set in motion through the ordering of things (Foucault 1989 [1966]: xvi–xviii).

In the lists, the objects named, and their symmetrically centred ordering look, at first reading, beguilingly uniform. However, not all volunteers confined themselves to the requested list format. While many write lists, usually with class categories (about which more later), others write long narratives about their current living conditions, or include parentheses about their family's behaviour, others' tastes and local traditions, or go off at tangents. Many provide sketches, with or without accompanying lists, or add details that – because they are partially obeying the 'rules' – require more explanation to make sense. The *Directive* does not take into account the possibility of an empty centre, or of objects on overmantels, layered mantelshelves, brackets, alcoves, walls above and hearthstones below. Neither the complex layering of objects, with the clock sitting over the rent book, the plate behind the vase, nor the decision of some volunteers to detail what is kept inside jars, vases and tins is taken into account. The collating of such material as 'data' through conventional content analysis is ridiculous (and I did try). To treat the mantelpiece as a fixed, universal structure or form is also impossible, extending as it does into various horizontal and vertical surfaces, layers and containers. Just as Mass Observation can be understood as the 'practice of understanding society as a totality of fragments' (Highmore 2002: 82), *Mantelpiece Reports* and displays can also be read as *both* wholes *and* parts (Strathern 2004), rather than materials that can be framed as *either* list *or* narrative, 'data' or digression, history or biography.

As a mass, the *Mantelpiece Reports* look almost – *almost* – homogenous; to leave it at that would be entirely acceptable as a broad sweep of social history. However, rather than making only that appraising overview one might give to a stranger's mantelpiece, I also looked at this 'mass' mantelpiece repeatedly, over a number of years – that everyday passing and sitting before, which makes *my* 'museum of domestic objects' distinct from yours. In doing this, the everydays of households, homes, families, lodgers, widows and schoolboys became separated and particular. However, a comprehensive comparative anatomy of the *Reports* would be unhelpful in this context. Stanley comments that 'twin but . . . contradictory impulses were consciously and deliberately part of Mass Observation from the outset' (2001: 95). Therefore, an approach which brings together a distant, impressionistic look at the vast collage of mantelpiece lists, tales, asides and sketches, with a close-up interpretation of just one of them, maintains the *both/and* tension that characterised the project from its beginnings.

Collage: tat, treasure, asides

Brass candlestick, once belonging to my grandmother (letters behind); photograph of sister, aged 3, in broken frame; orange Chinese vase containing pens, pencils and spills; bowl (originally a sugar basin) containing collar studs, coat button and clothes brush; pins, thread and needles; golf tee, cycle clip, gun cartridges and the usual oddments. Wooden elephant; ginger jar (behind it, postcard from friend on holiday in Germany – copy of Dürer self-portrait); perpetual calendar. In the centre: chrome electric clock (keeps good time) – rent book underneath it; ash tray from Austria (too pretty to use), matchbox (empty) and cigarette box (ornamental – present from friend); smelling salts and face powder (not supposed to be there); vase (the other's twin, slightly chipped) containing everlasting flowers, at present; Woodbine cigarettes, tobacco tin and ash tray (used); elephant (same as other one); toffee tin containing liver pills, darning mushroom, hat elastic (assortment of catechisms behind); one shilling (sub for my political party); framed photograph (friend's son killed aged 18 in the war); candlestick (matching other one); pipe cleaners, pipe lighters and pipe rack (never used). A cigarette lighter and coffee pot lid (newspaper cutting beneath, from Russia). Sometimes Dad's pipe at extreme right hand side. Two drawing pins and a ping pong ball (not mine).

This collage, made from numerous lists, drawings and other accounts, could be almost any mantelpiece in the 1937 *Reports*. Comparing it with the report written by the Schoolboy (Figures 2.1 and 2.2), we can see how similar they are, but also how the differences point to the daily processes which produce the politics of home and family. Many of the *Mantelpiece Reports* are variations upon a theme: symmetrical arrangements of candlesticks, vases and/or ornaments, with a clock at the centre and 'the usual oddments' in containers intended, even once used, for other purposes. Calendars are, if included, usually 'perpetual'. Letters, more often than not, are stored behind the artefact at the far left or right side, or sometimes behind the clock. Documents recording payments made or to be made such as rent, milk and insurance books, bills and receipts find their place on the mantelpiece, as do programmes for various political, arts, church and social groups. On display too might be photographs of framed formal groups or 'snapshots' (sometimes enlarged and framed), postcards and invitations to various events.

Ornaments, often in pairs flanking the central clock, of china, wood or brass represent human or animal figures, or baskets of flowers. Ships are also a popular ornament, as are old shell cases; propped behind the ornaments might be plates or paintings. It being autumn when these reports were written, a few vases display chrysanthemums and heather, but others contain dried flowers or 'everlasting flowers, at present' (MO 1937: Men A-J, 262). There are souvenirs, sometimes given by friends or relatives, of Europe, Asia and British seaside towns, as well as some inherited items and gifts. A few coronation mugs or other commemorative goods are listed in the *Reports* – of King George the Fifth's coronation in 1910, or the new monarch (rare, as there had been little time to produce them after his brother's abdication). Sporting goods, small household objects, grooming, sewing and writing implements form the bulk of 'odds and ends'; but almost universal on these mantelpieces are the paraphernalia of fire-lighting and smoking (even if the household members do not smoke).

Some objects are portrayed with pathetic fallacy – a poetics of things bound up with the politics of family. For example, one woman exhibits sympathy for objects on her brother-in-law and his daughter's mantelpiece:

> I don't like saying it, but to me the clock and everything on that shelf looks – lonely – still, it is *their* shelf.
>
> (MO 1937: Women H-Z, 153)

The criticism of her relatives is explicit, since the mantelshelf is so well-polished that she feels 'tired' to think of the 'energy which might so much more usefully be employed'. Comments on a family member's mantelpiece rumble with otherwise concealed conflicts and resentments. How could all this have been captured in a photograph? In another report, 'the clock sometimes arrives in the centre', while other objects very often find themselves 'stranded . . . with some other intruder' (MO 1937: Schoolboy). The objects that do stay somehow achieve tautologous permanent status: for example, at the very top of one overmantel 'stand those ornaments which no one has had the courage to throw away, because of their longstanding' (MO 1937: Schoolboy).

There is a noticeable presence of local traditional objects on some 1937 mantelpieces. For example, the 'large glazed earthenware dogs' on a Lancashire mantelpiece were not 'thought beautiful' and 'the younger generation dislikes them', but were used to comfort 'fractious children'. In addition to this display of place-specific culture are material signs of the times. One woman mentions a relative's reproduction Gandhi head: 'The Indian Leader of Revolt'. There is a bust of George Bernard Shaw on an Oxford undergraduate's mantelpiece, which, together with his Christian Union pamphlet, suggests an allegiance to Christian socialist values, although this is not made explicit. The fact that, on so many of the lists, there are programmes for Christian groups and churches, and signs of political engagement through societies' paperwork, newspaper cuttings and volunteers' comments, suggests that communal social movements based upon religious and political affiliation were common.

Signs of the times are not just materialised as display objects. Cleaning and tidying as a daily routine is evident in the *Reports*, either by the mother/wife or a char, due to coal dust. The aestheticised modern fireplace, free from the dirt of a 'real' fire, does not demand this daily practice. The centrality of the 1937 fire is also reflected in the constant battle for tidiness, which was similarly gendered in the *Reports*. This spatially gendered conflict is made particularly apparent in the Schoolboys' *Reports*, with, for example, 'father's end' and 'mother's side' by a boy who adds:

> Four of us at home are males; perhaps this explains why we are unable to keep the mantelpiece tidy, even after repeated pleadings from Mother, to, 'take that off there,' or, 'put it in its proper place' and so on.
>
> (MO 1937: Schoolboy)

There is constant movement on the mantelpiece – loose change, spectacles, playing cards, money for the milkman, insurance books, ashtrays full of collar studs and hairpins for grooming in front of the fire, and the storage of letters as a type of ongoing address book.

Furthermore, as one woman commented in 1937:

> Things vary on the mantelpiece according to the purse, fashion-urge, taste and whether they are in work (– insecurity here means mantelpieces among middle-aged are the last things to be changed). Then again as

opposed to well-to-do people workers often have useful things on the mantelshelves.

(MO 1937: Women A-G, no number)

This is a reminder of the time – modernist, maybe, in magazines and design books, but beneath the shadow of the Great Depression in homes around the country, where clocks were broken on heavy Victorian overmantels over coal fires. This can be viewed in connection with another comment, written by a schoolboy:

If all impressions were taken from the state of mantelpieces, I am afraid that untidiness would be the first and most prominent feature to strike people on entering our living room at home.

(MO 1937: Schoolboy)

These two seen together offer a synopsis of that curiously tangled role of the mantelpiece as metonym for home and perhaps its most visual artefact for visitors who were invited in. While an ideal, newly installed shelf might display only the 'permanent' artefacts of electric clock and well-polished ornaments in good condition, with perhaps some nicely framed photographs, economic necessity, the limits of domestic space and the contingencies of everyday life burst through these *Mantelpiece Reports*.

The literary report: Male 240

Taking the living room mantelpieces, here is revealed what artistic taste prevails in the house. Generally a neglected portion, with a clock that doesn't go, framed photographs, often opened letters stuck at the back. In season, sometimes a vase of flowers. Generally speaking, I find mantelpieces either too empty or too overcrowded. Full of oddments, and seldom lacking some snaps or framed photos. Seems to be the shelf for a piece or so of gaudy cheap china ware.

(MO 1937: Men A-J file: 240)

This *Report* was written by a 38-year-old 'writer of juvenile fiction', whose study mantelpiece in his mother's house is 'perhaps not as I would have it': candlesticks at either end and a clock in the centre, with his copy of *Gone with the Wind* at 'the extreme left hand, for reading in bed'. I have chosen his description of his own and other people's mantelpieces because he is a writer, and I therefore assume (perhaps wrongly) that he has paid close attention to what – and how – he is writing. It is typed, on thin foolscap paper, as, presumably, his professional fiction would be. An initial reading of the 1937 *Reports* confirms the judgement of 'Male 240' that this is a generalisable, much-used but ignored space. Almost every mantelpiece houses a clock at its centre, some of which run slow; good timekeeping is specifically mentioned too, as if this were noteworthy. Many of the twinned ornaments are listed repeatedly: birds on twigs, china posies, boy and girl figures, elephants and rearing horses. Ginger jars, jugs and vases – with or without flowers –, letters and photographs are features of almost every *Report*.

Yet Male 240's commentary on other people's mantelpieces is not as simple as it seems. Representing the mantelpiece as a neglected space, it nevertheless reveals 'artistic taste' (incidentally, he does not elaborate on who or what 'prevails' in this aesthetic: the exhibition of taste and the exposure of neglect. As a space that is either too full or too empty, the mantelpiece in this commentary is highly discomfiting: how can a display space remain in the background if it is never quite right in this viewer's eye? The writer sweeps over this shelf, filling it with a tawdry catalogue of other people's taste, an ill-fitting display 'seldom lacking' cheapness, brokenness, gaudiness and stale correspondence.

If we turn to the short list describing his own mantelpiece, however, it is a different story: he lists twin 'short, hand-carved candlestick[s]', in the centre a clock of ebony, 'neat, efficient looking' and, at the 'extreme left hand, my copy of GONE WITH THE WIND [sic], for reading in bed'. *His* mantelpiece, albeit, as he states, 'perhaps not as I would have it', is different from those he sees, or rather, recalls that he sees. From his account, we can infer that he has a study-bedroom in his mother's house, in which he has little say over the décor. He simultaneously defends the trilogy on the mantelpiece – these are *handmade* candlesticks, not cheap mass goods, and the clock 'looks' neat, presumably keeping good time – and tentatively distances himself from any judgement by the reader. The 'perhaps' allows him to side with both approbation and censure – the candlestick maker and the critic. We can see this man, his work life and his sleeping – we guess – confined to this room in the maternal home, reaching for his recently published American novel from the edge of the mantelpiece, his bed to one side, his desk, with the typewriter – the place that belongs to him – elsewhere in the room. The mantelpiece, save for its margin, does not belong to him; he only partially inhabits this space.

Whereas many other volunteers note down, 'from left to right' as instructed in the *Directive* from Mass Observation, the contents of their friends', neighbours' and families' mantelpieces, Male 240 does not; it is a blur of tat from which he stands apart. But looking for a moment in reverse, as one might look in a mirror to see the backs of the things on the mantelpiece, I suggest that the writer does not belong; he is excluded from the cultural mainstream, as a single man living at the parental home, without a room of his own which is free from the things and tastes of others. Like his bedtime book, he is at the edge of the space of the cultural majority. Using the art at which he is practised – writing – he dismisses the bad taste of the majority, and capitalises – literally – on his own identity of 'reader' in order to differentiate himself from the undiscriminated and undiscriminating mass. Dirt is only 'matter out of place' (Douglas 2002 [1966]);

by repudiating the taste of the cultural majority as, essentially, dirty, Male 240 can separate himself and his identity – as discerning writer, reader and aesthetic expert; as 'pure', rich in cultural capital (Bourdieu 1986). From the other side of this particular cultural boundary, however, he is the 'other'.

If another cultural line is drawn, however, similarities between him and 'them' start to emerge. There is the central clock, the symmetrical display – however partially he subscribes to this practice, he does not wholly reject it. While one mantelpiece list seems such a little thing, hundreds of them, all written within a few weeks of each other, accrete a massivity that, in its very repetitions, starts to beat out an impression of the 1937 mantelpiece, as history, as culture in the making. It is the very invisibility of these items to Male 240 that makes them culturally salient; the background of everyday life in autumn 1937. And Male 240's *Report* is not so different, in some ways, from the 'others', those whose taste he seems to despise. His brief mention of living in his mother's house is fraught with conditionality. With the interior 'perhaps not as I would have it', this is a trace of a life, of two lives and the stuff that binds them together (and keeps them apart). These are also written into many *Reports*: intimations of family and household relations, memories, identities and practices. And, just as his everyday habit of reading before bed is there at the edge of the mantelpiece, so are many routines – combing hair, fitting collar studs, handing out cigarettes, paying the landlord – on the 'mass' mantelpieces. His asides and comments are articulated, but it is impossible to know how many others have similar complex relations with a home that is not quite their own; not all volunteers would have had the writerly confidence or inclination to move away from the directed 'list' format.

Male 240 is not alone in having such a tiny space of his own. Many of the volunteers are living in 'digs' and describe the mantelpiece in the shared living room. This is filled mainly by the belongings of the landlady (usually a lone woman; sometimes a couple is mentioned, if the owners are described at all). Between these, a few of the lodgers' postcards, photos or smoking stuff might be dispersed (and also the bell, to call the landlady in). Often, these writers will also list the contents of their mantelpiece in the living room or bedroom 'at home', while several young women describe the mantel in their rented bed-sitting room, shared with another. The precision with which one describes the mantelshelf shared with a room-mate portrays lives carefully apportioned into small spaces (MO 1937: Women A-G: 21). Listing which possessions are hers and which are the Dutch teenager 'J.S.'s', she portrays the shelf divided into hers on the right and 'J.S.'s' on the right, a broken clock in between. The remembering and maintenance of social relations – the postcard, the photograph of the little brother – are crammed in beside the heat pad and the washing powder, things which would be in cupboards or other rooms in houses or family homes. These 'digs' seem to constitute unbelonging, in the broken clock, discomfort and a confusion of 'matter out of place' within which its inhabitants do what they can to control the space and draw boundaries. 'Female 21' lists, on her side, a 'cardboard box', but does not describe its contents. These at least can be kept hidden. She, like Male 240, is one of many 1937 volunteers who do not fit into the cosy image of 'home and family'. There are Oxford undergraduates, lodgers, their landladies, children and single young adults. Many adults live with their parents or alone; others, like the schoolboys, give a child's view of the mantelpiece where, unlike many of their 21st century 'peers', they are rarely appear. There might be a photograph of them as a baby or in a group, but the annual school photographs and the handmade ornaments which are so taken for granted now are not yet typical. A shockingly normal presence on the mantelpieces of 1937 – notably in lodging houses managed by single women – are framed photographs of soldiers killed in the First World War, pointing to a generation of women for whom 'home and family' were lost – indeed, never-owned – belongings and longings (Morley 2012).

Chance juxtapositions: not quite making sense

While not every list suggests the struggle for order, the careful negotiation of space and a sense of unbelonging, of small lives lived at the edge of the mainstream like 'Female 21' and 'Male 240', it is there in the broken clocks, the chipped ornaments, the endless old tea and toffee tins used for storing bits and pieces. Looking at mantelpieces 'from left to right' can present an image of a coherent narrative, an ordered metonym for home. Although this might be the ideal home story, the details tell different tales. Even the hairpins, hat elastic and collar studs, which now look charming in their simplicity, are reminders that most bedrooms were unheated, the fires lit only for the bedridden, and so much of what might now be considered 'private' took place before the mirror and the heat of the main fire. The descriptions of piles of letters, of 'intruders' managed by Mother and occasional comments about 'rules' such as 'Very little "junk" allowed to remain more than a few hours. Letters never appear there' (MO 1937: Men A-J: 262) open up homes where space was limited, legislated and fought over. The 'permanent' objects, like mantelpieces themselves, can be seen as the respite from these moveable (sometimes, however, unmoved) goods.

Rather than seeing the ad hoc containers, smelling salts and cigarette packets as the 'visitors', perhaps the 'permanent' symmetrical display of clock and twinned ornaments, vases and candlesticks could be viewed as inhabiting the spaces in between the cultural materials of everyday – really *every* day – social, gender, family and household relations, although there is something to be made, too, of these permanent inhabitants. Without them, the ephemera would have nothing to mess up, and unless the mantelpiece were considered a site for neatness and display, their presence would not be so problematic. Concealed in a kitchen drawer, the bills and buttons would be less of an irritant, but not so convenient to find or remember. It is precisely because the 1937 fireplace – with its cooking range or open fire – was central to domestic life that it was the 'carry-all' both for displaying treasures and keeping visible the little everyday necessities and reminders. Reading these accounts, it seems clear that the mantelpiece is the stage on which daily household activities and dramas took place in miniature, only because it framed the fire.

The very presence of the coal fire or range was not a technological necessity. A quick look at Mass Observation's 1943 survey of homes is a timely reminder that this was the case, and that economic explanations are insufficient for their continuing presence (MO 1943). This was a report on 1,100 interviews, mainly visiting every 11th house in 11 areas of England between August 1941 and April 1942. The aim was to contribute to 'the great task of rebuilding and rehabilitating Britain', according to the co-authors of the report, the Advertising Service Guild. The interviewers were female and carried out semi-structured doorstep questionnaires. Ninety per cent of the interviewees were female, and lived in areas that were identified by MO as working class. Interviewers noted differences in response according to age and sex. What is pertinent to the earlier collection of *Mantelpiece Reports* are three details of the findings. First, the report summary notes that the strongest desire for homeownership was in areas where it was possible to own one's home, and extremely low (seven per cent) where it was impossible, such as in council [public] flats and housing estates (MO 1943: xix). Desire for homeownership was strongest in the leafy Garden Cities, where the houses and districts were generally liked. The report also commented that 'Length of residence affects people's desire to own; the longer they live in a house, the more they desire to own it.' Second, the summary notes that most houses were still heated by coal fires in grates, 'and what is more, coal fires are still very definitely preferred to any other means of heating living rooms, even though it is realised that gas or electric fires and central heating have many utilitarian advantages, especially in bedrooms' (MO 1943: xiv). Third, the researchers themselves observe that an English townscape without chimneys is unthinkable.

Thus, according to Mass Observation's criteria, 'homeownership' was not a natural, a given. The effect of time on the desire to own one's own home was noted, as well as its feasibility and the aesthetics of house design and location. Moving on to domestic heating technology, we can see that respondents did not want newer, more efficient technologies. The people they interviewed still wanted a coal fire, despite its practical disadvantages. They were used to it, and time gave coal fires a legitimacy that superseded considerations of efficiency or common sense (Ravetz and Turkington 1995). Like, perhaps, the 'longstanding' ornaments on the Victorian overmantel, the coal fire and its seemingly inseparable relation, the mantelshelf, was there in the same entanglement of 'taste' and 'neglect' that Male 240 suggested. This culture of paradox, of 'both/and' can be seen on the mantelpieces of the 21st century. The clocks and paired ornaments remain, as do the ephemera of everyday life. Magazines and design professionals are still presenting smart fire surrounds, now with vases of fresh flowers, candles and careful arrangements of stones or antique artefacts on the mantels. However, there have been some changes in between. First, homeownership in Britain has become a given, an ideal state, with around 70 per cent of the population owning the homes they live in (often with a mortgage). While homeownership is becoming unattainable for young and vulnerable groups following the recent economic crisis, it remains the aspiration (Clapham *et al.* 2012). Second, the mantelpiece is there in many houses, but more often than not over a cold hearth or a 'living flame' gas fire or electric equivalent, in a centrally heated dwelling. Before moving on to the 21st century fieldwork in the next chapter, a discussion of MO *Reports* from 1983 will illuminate how these similarities and differences might matter (Figure 2.2).

1983 *Mantelpiece Reports*: a 'faithful account'?

Although the original Mass Observation ended in the early 1950s, the Mass Observation Project in its current form began in 1981, with three *Directives* a year sent out to volunteers, asking them to write about many aspects of everyday life, in any form they wished. Submitted for the 1983 Autumn *Directive*, this *Report* (Figure 2.2) was discovered years later in the file of a Mass Observation Panel member. The 1988 pass for the Glasgow soccer team Celtic's stadium clearly indicates that the person wrote it some years after the *Directive*, but not necessarily in 1988. As a man, this volunteer was in the minority for the 1983 *Directive*, for 261 women sent in *Reports*, and only 72 men (mostly aged 50 or over). The assemblage of items on his mantelpiece is also, at first glance, extraordinary, inviting the reader to imagine the man who wrote it. The list has a bare poetry about it, just as the barest mantelpiece makes poetics of things, a form that holds them. It is tempting to flesh it out, to the life (and death) of a man, a practice engrained into so many British schoolchildren through their compulsory literature studies. *About His Person* (Armitage 1992) is a particular pedagogic favourite:

> Five pounds fifty in change, exactly,
> a library card on its date of expiry.
> A postcard stamped,
> unwritten, but franked . . .

But perhaps we could leave the gaps. Charles Madge's working title for Mass Observation, 'popular poetry', is underwritten as much by these lists as the juxtaposed accounts of May 12th and other observations (Hubble 2006: 778). Modernist poetry, as commitment to 'the new' and ordinary experience, finds articulation in this mantelpiece prosody, curiously reminiscent of

C.1154

Mantelpiece.

Left to right.

1930's AA Badge

Avacado plant

Wooden cat from Mexico (ornament)

Kahlua bottle with candle therein

Wild Turkey bottle with candle therein

1950's matchbook with 'Merry Widow' cocktail printed thereon

Two Britains model cannon

One brass 'Carronade' from the Carron Iron Works factory shop

Photography pass for Parkhead dated 12/II/88

Grouse foot kilt pin

brass incensce holder

pheasant feather

Noritake cup

black ash tray with beach pebbles therein

Full packet of 'Mary Long' cigarettes from Holland

Pewter cocktail shaker made in Shanghai

Two 12 guage shotgun cartridges. Live. 0 spread.

Rubber plant.

Brass carriage clock

International Preess Card

1950's cigarette dispenser

Model of Panzer MkIV tank

World War One shell fuse

World War One shell case ash tray containing an acorn, twelve .22 rounds
of ammunätion, a .455 Eley round and a drawing pin.

Photo of Eric Liddell. (Chariots of Fire)

Souvenir of Algeria aan tray containing marbles and beach stones

Three 1930's plastic duck clothes brushes

Letter holder containg postcards and invitations. Holder in shape of a cow

1970's whizzwheels toy car

Wooden box of jewellers rottenstone. (Victorian)

inscense holder

World War one German fuse (used)

Jim Beam bottle with candle therein

Sol beer bottle with candle therein

Ends.

Figure 2.2   Mass Observation 1983: Male C1154

Walt Whitman's vernacular nationalism in *Leaves of Grass* (Whitman 2008 [1855]; I will write more on this).

The display of war paraphernalia, photography/press passes, references to (slightly exotic) smoking and drinking habits conjure up a certain lifestyle and identity. And yet, the 'skeleton' of the 1930s mantelpiece remains: the clock, the candles, the (often ornamental) ammunition, the letterholder, souvenirs, ashtrays and oddments such as matches and clothes brushes. The incense holders, potted plant and Mexican ornaments were not present in the 1930s *Reports*, but are notably common items on those from the 1980s. He lists the contents of a mantelpiece, but the display surfaces illustrated or described in 1983 are more varied than the 'pure' mantels of 1937: telephone tables, desks, shelving and so on. This section will focus on how the *Directive* and *Reports* have changed from those of 1937, in particular in showing the politics of home.

Curating the present

In 1983, the Mass Observation director of the time, David Pocock, sent out this *Directive*, prompted, he writes, by a visit from a museum curator who regretted the lack of Archive material about house interiors during the Second World War. He writes:

> If you have seen historical reconstructions of ordinary rooms in museums you will know how much they tell us about life in those times. I would like our written reconstructions to be as faithful an account for the 1980s as we can manage.
>
> In Section 4 the reference to mantel-shelves or mantelpieces will remind some of you how much the arrangement of our rooms has been affected by central heating... If you do not have a mantelpiece, you will be asked about its equivalent; the shelf, window sill or other surface where you might put ornaments, clocks, reminders, photographs, birthday cards and so on.
>
> (MO 1983)

They are also to describe every last cobweb and thrown-down coat in their living rooms, not tidying up in their 'mind's eye' in a search for veracity. Note the omission of the request to report on other people's mantelpieces and social class: the focus was on one's own home, rather than looking outwards to report (and judge). Volunteers were to detail their own living rooms and mantelpieces or equivalents, and their daily household tasks, giving a different context to their mantelpiece displays: not those belonging to other people, but the domestic space and (often gendered) roles around it. The multiplicity of spaces listed in the *Reports* is due partly to the absence in some houses of mantelpieces, but many Reporters list the mantelpiece display objects and various other surfaces in the home. The *Directive's* list of 'mantelpiece objects' could well have directed the gaze of the volunteers around their rooms to other sites for display and storage. This means that mantelpiece objects are often grouped with very large objects, numerous flat items and private papers. For example, fruit bowls (which would fit on very few mantelpieces) on sideboards; papers and postcards on pinboards, all visible to the eye (rather than piled up as they would be on a mantel); and the contents of desk drawers (many of them 'private' papers such as payslips and bank statements, and stationery goods such as pocket calculators) are itemised. It is December when some volunteers return their *Reports*, so Christmas cards and chocolates are listed by some; rare, but perhaps significant as little remembrances, are the Valentines or wedding anniversary cards from months or years before, Thus, while 'mantelpiece equivalents' may have proliferated in the home, and some of the lists seem to point to an increasing mass of 'stuff', the *Directive's* certainty as to what 'mantelpiece objects' are means that a multitude of places and things are drawn into the *Reports*.

Following the Clean Air Acts of 1956 and 1968, restricting the use of open fires in urban areas, the take-up of central heating in Britain increased, with complete removal of many fireplaces, perhaps to be replaced with modern units containing a gas or electric fire. Some original fireplaces remain, housing these new fires, sometimes with back boilers for the central heating system. Many homes described in the *Reports* have a mixed heating economy, with partial central heating, electric storage heaters, gas or electric fires and, in some cases, an open fire or stove, 'just in case' the new heating systems fail. New electric fires are not always used for heating a room, instead providing a coal-effect 'glow'. Other changes include the loss of the separate 'parlour' and dining room in older houses, with the removal of the dividing wall, and large open-plan rooms in newer houses and flats. A practical aspect of the mantelpiece remains, even if there is no coal fire beneath it, since it often supports a reading lamp. Its physical position in the room and its height makes the mantelshelf an ideal place for a lamp, a modern equivalent for the candles that were necessary in the 18th and 19th centuries. The candles remain on many modern mantelpieces as a past practice that is now transformed (like the clock, incidentally) in the light of modern technologies (Ravetz and Turkington 1995).

The early 1980s were a turning point for relations between past and present, home and other social worlds. Clearly, this knowledge is available from other sources, such as surveys, interviews, films, television programmes and documents of the time. The *Reports* are not proffered as further 'evidence'; they are too partial for this. Their special relevance lies in the fact that volunteers are – in the main – listing what they choose to record on their mantelpieces and equivalents, rather than narrating household relations and practices. Even without narratives, asides and comments, the 'mass' of the lists, especially when read together (and repeatedly) with those from 1937 does indeed produce surprising knowledge – as the founders of Mass Observation intended. Volunteers' *Reports* are cited according to their file numbers in the MO 1983 Autumn *Directive*.

Museums of domestic objects: 'the genuine article'

Altar, noticeboard, medicine chest, cemetery. A shrine laden with the relics of the recent past and a testimonial to the faith that one day the world will turn and the past come back into its own and there will be a restoration.

(Bennett 1980: end of Act I)

The way in which new technology had affected domestic space at first glance seems obvious: the multiplication of sites around the home for 'mantelpiece objects'. However, a second, parallel effect to this and similar losses was curation, in which the discarded spaces, materials and activities of ordinary life became central to a new heritage industry (Matthews 1999; Dicks 2000). This paradox was the topic of Alan Bennett's 1980 play, *Enjoy*, quoted above, in which the lives and belongings of the last couple in a Leeds back-to-back terrace are 'recorded' for posterity by an official. Considered a slum fit only for demolition to make room for smart new flats, the house is nevertheless moved, brick by brick, to a museum outside the city, with the Alzheimer-ridden 'Mam' still in residence, doing what she always did. Of interest to us here is how deeply unpopular the play was in 1980, only to be greeted with critical plaudits on its rerun in 2008–2009. In the 21st century, 'heritage' moves ever closer to the retro-chic present, 'period-style' pieces sitting beside sepia-tinted photos of today's museum visit, in a digital frame on the mantelpiece, between the flatscreen and the Xbox. However, in 1980, the brutal alchemy which turned yesterday's slum into today's museum piece was perhaps too current for ironic retrospective (see Bennett 2012, for the playwright's latest 'take' on the National Trust).

The 1983 Mass Observation *Reports* illustrate how the early 1980s marked a cultural turning point, from defining 'modernisation' as the replacement of 'dirty' open fires with new 'clean' heating technologies, to understanding 'modernisation' as an aesthetic project: the retro-fitting of houses with 'authentic' or 'period' features, accompanied by a new appreciation of houses which had retained their original features – perhaps with the addition of central heating (see Samuel 1994; also Baudrillard 1996 [1968]). For example, while the owner of a 200-year-old house has recently removed all five fireplaces to knock rooms together, another has replaced the 'ugly twenties style tiled fireplace' in his mid-19th century house (made by knocking together two cottages) so that 'now it is back to its original appearance' (MO

1983: Men 275). In a trio of 1935 houses, the writer of the *Report* compares his neighbours' removal of the fireplaces when they installed central heating (MO 1983: Men T527) with the preservation of the originals in his own house, while the young couple on the other side had just restored the fireplaces the former owner ripped out.

As 'original' mantelpieces and fires were disappearing, the collaborative 'museums...of domestic objects' to which the founders aspired were, by the 1980s, becoming part of the national 'heritage', a concept discussed further in Chapter 8. In the 1970s, 'living history' museums such as Black Country and Beamish had opened, focusing on the everyday lives of industrial workers and their families, with authentic reconstructions of their homes and workplaces, often in original buildings moved from towns and villages. In 1984, the Jorvik Viking Centre opened in York; there visitors could travel through a Viking village by train, not only seeing and hearing how they lived but also smelling the 'real' odours of their everyday life (the Vikings smell surprisingly like Lapsang Souchong tea). Membership of the National Trust, the principal charity for the protection and preservation of historic houses and gardens (as well as other national 'heritage goods') in Britain, increased from 226,000 to over 1 million between 1970 and 1981. In 1983, the National Heritage Act set up new forms of centrally funded heritage bodies, such as English Heritage, to protect, promote, research and advise on the built/natural heritage of England, followed by its counterparts, Cadw in Wales (1984) and Historic Scotland (1991). The 1983 *Directive*, then, can be seen as a parallel move in this trend: to curate not only the past for the present, but also the present for the future, and to do it as authentically as possible. Few volunteers comment on this directly, but one exemplar points to how many of the *Report* writers display at once a 'mass' similarity and a singular conviction of difference: 'I don't suppose it is at all typical and therefore would not be much use to a museum curator' writes one woman (MO 1983: A-C108), before mentioning that her mantelshelf 'should have' a clock, two candlesticks and a hand-bell, but there are many 'extras', which she lists, together with all that is 'hidden' in a pot. In effect, she removes herself from this project of curation, but her list of objects, and the authentically 'confessional' tone, place her *Report* firmly in the mass.

A young married father (MO 1983: 169) has replaced the 'nasty modern fireplace' in the 1917 house he bought two years previously with a 'rather fine old' one dating from 1890–1910, from an antiques shop. All their display items on the mantelpiece 'have a period flavour'. A woman (MO 1983: C041), having no television and an open fire writes that 'ours is a "genuine" mantelpiece', although her display items are no different from those on electric fire tops, televisions and window sills. A man (MO 1983: S-Z 541), following the developer bricking up the original fireplace, writes that 'we have further disgraced the fireplace by putting in a gas fire', nor can they afford to open up the original. Another writes that 'perhaps the authenticity was spoiled when we redecorated but ... I have tried to be as realistic as possible in all aspects' (Men A-C 005). Authenticity, the 'genuine article' and ideas of keeping or refurbishing 'period features' had started to enter the vocabulary of home. Thus, different eyes were turning on the fireplace and its surround, as central original features in the living room in older houses. These were often the first to be ripped out when central heating was replacing open fires (if money allowed), leaving only those in less public rooms such as bedrooms. Their comparative rarity, then, made them highly desirable.

The politics of home

The notion of authenticity being mutually constitutive of home and identity is perceptible in the above accounts, but is particularly salient in the few *Reports* by those who had bought houses they had recently inhabited as tenants of the state. These reflect the social revolution that changed the housing landscape in Britain: tenants' right to buy their council houses (public housing) with discounts of 33–50 per cent. Margaret Thatcher's new Conservative government had passed the Housing Bill in December 1979, fulfilling a central promise of its electoral manifesto. Its aim was to appeal to traditional council tenants – 'respectable' working class families in work – with the aspirational lure of homeownership. While tenants could make some changes, they had to apply for written permission for 'approved alterations'. In moves to establish themselves as owners rather than tenants, householders replaced gates, doors, windows, curtains and kitchens, the 'original features' marking out state-owned housing (Dolan 1999; McVeigh 2009). In August 1980, Thatcher made a well-publicised visit to Harold Hill housing estate in Essex, to hand over the keys to the 12,000th family to buy their house. In 1983, another Harold Hill tenant who had exercised his right to buy (MO 1983: W636) described how they had 'demolished the old GLC [Greater London Council] fireplace, and I built a natural stone fireplace' with a mantelpiece moulded and cast *in situ*. Another former council tenant described how he was 'redoing' the whole fireplace, facing the tiles with stone and building shelves on either side (MO 1983: S473). The mantelpiece might seem to belong only to the politics of family and home, but these two examples show how the politics of home and homeownership had been placed at the very centre of social policy, brought home in turn by these two appropriations of the domestic fireplace in an imperishable material: stone.

In time, the right to buy was to lead to the residualisation of council housing, as less popular housing stock in depressed areas, particularly flats, increasingly housed tenants who were in receipt of state benefits and themselves marginalised (Cole and Furbey 1994; House of Commons Library 1999). The distinction between the new homeowners and council flat tenants can be perceived in the report of a young man (MO 1983: 220) who drew diagrams of his own mantelpiece and others in the block of council flats where he lived. He puts only letters to post, keys and the occasional postcard on the narrow electric fire top, measuring 18″ by 2″. A long-term unemployed male neighbour has 'nothing' on his mantelpiece, like the young woman in the flat below him; another (working) man has 'an improvised ashtray, alarm clock and empty metal locket'. While the narrowness of the available space might have been a factor in this, studies such as that by Miller suggest that a failure to appropriate 'the state', even through simple strategies such as creating a 'facade' (1988: 15) of biographical display objects is indicative of alienation. In contrast, for example, Rosalind, a participant in my fieldwork, determinedly searched for and bought two small figurines to put on the narrow modern mantel in her privately rented house on an exclusive cul-de-sac. Thatcher's drive to make Britain a 'property-owning democracy', enthused by 'popular capitalism' which gave choice and responsibility to the individual and the family, 'rolling back the frontiers of the state', redrew the boundaries between public and private – which has continued, with 'making home' as an 'obvious materiality' in this Do-It-Yourself (DIY) world (Macdonald 2007). The new nation of consumer/homeowners did not, however, include this type of council tenant: on low wages or unemployed, often single or not within a conventional family unit.

While the mantelpieces of 1937 had included signs of communal endeavour based around religion, arts practices and political allegiance, different relations between the home and what lay beyond its walls can be traced in 1983. While home (as property) and family (as the social space for a new social contract) were being placed at the centre of the national political stage, home as a site which had formerly faced outward to political and social engagement looks, from the 1983 *Reports*, like a place where politics (in that sense) was turning inward (Featherstone 1987; Clarke 2009). One of the few noteworthy artefacts portraying political engagement is a postcard displayed on one mantelpiece: a photograph of Thatcher waving, entitled *Crime Wave* (MO 1983: Male A883). Many items relating to new forms of consumption and entertainment are listed: discount vouchers for theme parks, travel, washing powder and food; restaurant take-away menus and wine lists; shopping lists of goods such as herbs and spices and newspaper bingo cards. Different financial arrangements are visible in the replacement – for the most part – of shilling subs, rent and insurance books. The money for the milkman and window cleaner is still there, but supplemented by cheque books, bank and credit card statements; National Savings Certificate leaflets (a state-run bank), state welfare provision cards and pamphlets. The National Health Service, founded in 1948, is there too, in the Blood Donor session and medical/dental appointment cards. Signs of local communal activities are rare (though still present), although membership of national charities and organisations such as the National Trust, motoring associations and children's charities is apparent in badges and cards. Among the many new display spaces cited as 'mantelpiece equivalents' are the television and the telephone table, signalling new relations with 'the outside' which perhaps parallel this domestic semi-detachment from daily, localised political and communal practices. Membership of national organisations extracts the local and the specific, just as the television and the telephone distance forms of communication and entertainment.

In tandem with this abstraction and distancing is a turning inward to the children and their activities, cleaning and cooking, eating in front of the television (traceable in the 'cruet sets' – salt and pepper shakers – and take-away menus on many of the living room mantels). The place of children in the family has changed on the mantelpiece. In 1937 children were visible in posed family photographs, the odd informal snapshot or in 'baby' photographs of long-grown adult family members. In 1983 the annual school photograph is prominent, as are materials connected with children's activities. College graduation photographs (of daughters as well as sons) can be seen in 1983 – another type of commemoration. The School Parent–Teacher Association programme, badges for sporting achievements, home-made cards and craft items are listed, together with a variety of toys. The mention of children's home-made items, kept sometimes for years on display, are perhaps related to other changes in objects (or at least, vocabularies for objects) which have not been bought. Whereas in 1937 some artefacts are described as old, perhaps with the date/period of their production mentioned, or 'was my grandmother's', and items such as vases or clocks might be 'broken', by 1983 the language of the gift and inheritance is prevalent. Also notable is the use of the '-style' suffix, such as 'twenties-style clock'. This 'styling' of the past – its modernising – and emphasis on gift/inheritance moves in tandem with changes in what to 'make' of the past and social relations inside/outside the home. The next section focuses on one dimension of this: the gendering of homemaking practices.

Daily dust; occasional DIY

Whereas DIY jobs are listed as undertaken by men in 1983, it is women who manage (or justify their 'failure' to manage) the ongoing construction and maintenance of the home as a clean, well-provisioned, tidy space. I have noted the 'confessional' tone of many of the *Reports*, perhaps responding to the *Directive*'s request for 'veracity'. While mention of 'intruders' on the mantelpiece, contrasted with 'permanent' members (often anthropomorphised in the *Report*) was common in 1937, the only gendering of the management of this ongoing transience was by the schoolboys. Although no children write in 1983, the 'confessing' of dust and untidiness is prevalent in both men and women's *Reports*. Similar to the 1937 Schoolboys' *Reports*, but different in one crucial respect, is the following report by one woman (MO 1983: M340) about the kitchen dresser: ' . . . the watershed of the varying states of order that reign in our household'. On the day of her *Report*, the assemblage on it, which runs to several dozen items, is a mess, but of the sort that can be 'put right during the day'. She then departs from the list to write:

> not the type that makes you absolutely despair every time you look at it and think, 'I must clear that dresser, but I don't know what to do with half of it, and it's not my bloody mess anyway so why the bloody hell should I have to clear it up'.

Nevertheless, she adds that when 'visitors (neighbours)' come for a meal, it is 'polished with *Pledge* and nothing [on it] but a jug of fresh flowers'. This *Report* echoes many of the women's writings. Very few of the men write the detailed housework timetables submitted by the women. One man excuses the dust on the grounds that his wife is in hospital, while women make comments such as 'I don't like dusting' and write of 'muffled cries of rage' when moving papers off the mantelpiece daily to the letter-rack, followed finally by a 'purge'. In contrast to this awareness of dirt and comments by women about their role as cleaners and tidiers, 'dust' is rarely mentioned in 1937, when open fires would have created soot daily during colder seasons, and cooking ranges at all times. As we have seen, the schoolboy group commented on their families' 'laziness', the 'look' of the visitor and 'mother's' constant pleas for tidiness, but the only women who comment are those who refer to 'the char'.

In contrast, a 64-year-old married man, like many of the male volunteers in 1983, focuses on DIY jobs, rather than describing the mantelpiece as if it were 'only' a display space. He keeps things in compartments of a flap-top desk, and it is a 'job I take on once a month' to go through it. It is curious that he names the desk as his mantelpiece 'equivalent', even though what is in it is compartmentalised and concealed, since it is the first place to look for 'anything', as mantelpieces were in 1937. Yet he also has a mantelpiece which looks purely decorative – except the clock – although he himself does not count it a useful object. In his view, then, the mantelpiece of his childhood, transposed now to the desk, was a space for storage of necessities and the temporary refuge for things to be 'gone through'.

Like the schoolboy of 1937 who saw the mantelpiece as the 'state' of his home and family in plain view to the visitor, one woman writes in 1983 that the mantelpiece is 'not as it should be', just as the house is not as it should be, following her recent divorce. As a result, DIY jobs have stopped, and her single parenthood can be seen in the daily, untidy comings and goings of her daughter's school- and playthings from the mantelpiece – rather than the 'father's side' of 1937. As expected, no such narratives of family breakdown are provided in the earlier *Reports*; the commonality lies in the equation: between the state of the mantelpiece and that of the household.

I have represented the 1983 *Reports* in ways designed to suggest a few juxta-positions, not only between 1937 and 1983, but also between ways in which some had appropriated the 'state' of their mantelpieces and those whose connections with the space were more fragile, even apparently absent. It is not my intention to draw conclusions from these; this review of Mass Observation is part of a process of understanding how the mantelpiece relates to doing culture. A brief glimpse of the 2006 *'Your Home' Directive* will connect the oblique perspective of MO with the 21st-century mantelpieces 'observed' in the fieldwork (MO 2006).

Your Home, 2006: memory, identity, home

To me it's the personal things that make a home. All the bits and pieces you collect which you can look at and have an instant memory of a place, a person or an event.

(MO 2006: Female H2418)

My friend's wife was a bit sarcastic about it once [a big mix of furniture styles] as she has all Edwardian furniture in her living room and said she would not mix any other period with it. I said I would pop over and view her Edwardian TV.

(MO 2006: Male H1806)

The incongruity of new technologies and an adherence to 'period' features, together with an ever closer connection between home, memory and iden-tity, marks the domestic sensibility of 2006, a glimpse of which can be seen in extracts from this *Directive*, commissioned for a project led by Alison Clarke (2009). As the 1943 Mass Observation had found, the British adher-ence to the open fire was noteworthy even then, but with the Clean Air Acts and the advent of near-universal central heating, the return to the fire was remarkable. While this could be reconciled as part of a general trend towards neo-historical styles (Samuel 1994), the open fireplace had never quite left the domestic stage. Despite the 1943 MO researchers' surprise concerning the 'reluctance of residents to offer any subjective opinion regarding their homes and interiors' (Clarke 2009: 262) the persistence of the open fire and fireplace in Britain, against all technological sense, had been remarked upon since the previous century (Beecher Stowe's *Sunny memories of England*, 1854, cited in Long 1993: 98; Muthesius 1979). Even if it were unvoiced to doorstep surveyors, this attachment to the fire was not practical even then, and by 2006 it was astonishing to 'strangers' to British culture, used to the enclosed stove. For example, Clarke discusses respondent T3775, who has moved into a new-build home with efficient insulation, but also a vast inglenook fireplace. Invoking his Swedish ancestry for failing 'to understand the "sooo conservative" British obsession with the open fire', he writes that this was 'a "monster in brick that totally dominated the room and completely ruined a wall that could have been perfect for a very large bookcase" ' (Clarke 2009: 265–266). In contrast, a divorced woman in her seventies (MO 2006: H2447) has undertaken DIY with her daughter to open up and line her fireplace, before commissioning a beech mantelpiece from a local cabinet-maker. This is another turn in the process of recovering the fireplace and mantelpiece from the destruction of the 1980s, towards a high, yet homely aesthetic. Perhaps an unintended consequence of the Clean Air Acts and new heating technologies was a growing interest in the fireplace as a space of authenticity, as its 'realistic' use faded ever deeper into the past. Although some surfaces might be changing in the home, the display of ornaments, family photographs and clocks can continue, if not on the new flatscreen television, as one respondent comments (MO 2006: Male H1543), then certainly on new and restored mantelpieces.

Conclusion:... 'everlasting flowers, at present'

A final extract from a Mass Observation *Report* brings the two periods together. Writing in 1983, the volunteer looks back to a time when – despite mantelpieces being the 'norm' – an acquaintance, in order to maintain domestic perfection, had rid herself entirely of the 'trouble' that mantelpieces brought:

> Apropos of mantelpieces – may I quote the most austerely tidy woman I ever knew? One day – some forty years ago – I heard her remark that she could not possibly live in a room that had a mantelpiece. 'Whyever not?' I asked. 'People would put things on it,' she replied.
>
> (MO 1983, Women K308)

Tidiness is a kind of death without decay, denying movement, disorder, complexity, dust: a wasteland. The little shelf over which Tom Harrisson and Humphrey Jennings squabbled in the 1930s, employed as a 'test piece' for their new Mass Observation volunteers, could be construed as a site for contesting different ways of knowing, and a place for the practice of observing 'home'. Without it, the family squabbles, rivalries and negotiations over what home was for, and who 'did' it, would no doubt carry on elsewhere. However, as a central site in the main living room of the dwelling, it was a limited, visible space where the business of 'doing' home was intensely distilled. Further, the 1983 *Reports* illustrate how popular capitalism located the individual, family and dwelling as the social spaces for exercising choice, rights and responsibility. The politics of home and family were at the centre of government policy.

The mantelpiece has survived the 20th century, unlike its outdated peers, such as majority rental occupancy, ink pens and, indeed, coal fires. Although its centrality to household practices had seemed attached to the importance of the fire, this triptych of Mass Observations opens up other ways of thinking about it. While practices might have changed, the linking of mantelpiece displays with doing family relations, memory and other cultures of home and identity is always there. Like the clock at its centre, its meanings may have shifted, but the mantelpiece, for now, remains. In the following chapter, we turn to the fieldwork for a different method of observing this peculiarly resilient little monument: personal memory.

3
Materialising Memory

Was it fate? I remember the marvelous Shelburne Museum in Vermont where, in thirty-five houses of a reconstructed village, all the signs, tools, and products of 19th century everyday life teem...The display includes innumerable familiar objects, polished, deformed, or made more beautiful by long use; everywhere there are as well the marks of the active hands and laboring or patient bodies for which these things composed the daily circuits, the fascinating presence of absences whose traces were everywhere.

(de Certeau 1984: 21)

Introduction

I have sat and nodded encouragingly through many 'mantelpiece memory' stories. There were the participants' interviews, set apart by dint of research aims, our roles, ethical guidelines and a recording device. Then there were the myriad others, told in conference or seminar rooms, across kitchen, cafe and rail carriage tables. This is the collective tracing and retracing of absent presences; it is not a practice distinctive to my interviewees. Moreover, this type of everyday aesthetic labour flies over analytic vigilance, creeps under the fences of critical thinking; the professor's granny's china dogs are recalled with the same warm glow as the waiter's mother's trinkets. The mantelpiece, and its attachment, the fireplace, are material 'structures of feeling' (Williams 1977: 128–135), embedding and embedded too as 'nostalgic structures' (Bourdieu 1977). The work of this chapter is to tease apart the doubling of the mantelpiece as fabric and fabricator in this collective labour of memory.

Following a brief review of literature, the chapter draws on interview and questionnaire accounts from the fieldwork. In the first part, we will focus closely on Shyam's narrative around the brass and glitter of her grandmother's 1940s mantelpiece. Following this is a brief overview of other participants' memories of childhood homes, ranging from the 1930s to the

1990s. The second part organises participants' accounts loosely around four themes, as a way of thinking towards how people actively construct identity through 'memory work'. 'Memory' cannot be cut into distinct categories, but writing forces such division (Strathern 2004 [1991]). First, I examine how the passing of time is constructed. While some distinguish their lives today from the messy, dirty, laborious or static, old-fashioned past, others regret the changing pattern of life in the home. One participant, Andrew, makes an extreme distinction of the 'Victorian' era of grief, pain and economic constraint, which those born even in the last years of the 19th century carried into the next – a period which he sees ending with the Second World War, when he was a child. Second, I look at how space is dissected. Within homes earlier in the 20th century, for example, the categorisation of mantelpieces depended upon the distinction of rooms for different purposes. While this would not be the case in all houses, many participants in this study lived in then-typical urban working class terraces: narrow, four rooms deep with the 'kitchenette' (as it is called in Cardiff) – the scullery – for dirty or wet work at the back. Third, then, comes the division of things, between, for example, useful and precious. Further, the evolving distinction is made by some – but not all – between the fireplace/mantel and the objects on display there, as the years of 20th century progress and fireplaces are removed. Finally, I explore how mantelpiece memories unfold how persons and identities are defined through separate roles and tastes, among other distinctions. A prominent theme is the gendered division of labour: so many memories from the 1930s and 1940s circle around the dominance of women's activities around the 'working' fire – washing, preparing food and baths for children and men in heavy industrial jobs. Even later memories frequently refer to 'mother's' or 'grandmother's' mantelpieces and possessions on display. But division of persons is not only along gender lines; Wendy, for example, born in the 1970s, classifies herself as not a 'mantelpiece person', in contrast to her parents.

Although mantelpieces are undeniably solid, often too solid masses protruding from the centre of living room walls, their potency as disappeared objects, as subjects of memory accounts which delineate empty space, leads to the question: what are they *doing, here*? This chapter will examine how mantelpiece memories – as accounts or as material traces – accomplish particular sorts of work. They circumscribe the often tacit boundaries between particular times, spaces, things and persons, by effecting divisions, expulsions, enclosures and compressions. The emphasis here is on the processual character of pulling apart and pushing together: these boundaries are not brick walls. However, just as the oscillation of presences and absences tends to manifest contradictions, the both/and character of such movements produces ambiguities, as we shall see. Circumscription has another definition: the limiting of power. One focus, then, is how power is organised into and out of these spaces of memory.

The materials of memory

If we look at artefacts as parts of a society's 'characteristic ways of history-making' (Mills 1959: 7), then we can see a link between the small objects on display at home and public monuments and museums as 'memory work' (Douglas 1993). Rowlands (2002) examines small objects and monuments in their role as props in processes of belonging, remembering and – notably – forgetting, thus linking in effectively with work concerning public monuments (for example, Loukaki 1997; Low and Lawrence-Zuniga 2003; Schwarz and Schuman 2005). Loukaki suggests that interference in state monuments (in this case, the Acropolis in Athens) disturbs national identity work, and that it is important to acknowledge the 'poetics' of space, things and monumentality. Noting that artefacts have scale, Saunders' (2002) interpretation of war objects emphasises both the 'promiscuity' of material culture and also how the living and dead 'find proximity' via small objects from the battlefield. The transformation to 'memory objects' (ibid.: 177) and 'collectables' by changing their context to domestic space effectively alters the symbolic relations of the artefact. The examination of such object biographies and transitions brings into sharp relief relationships between different constructions of time (Adam 1995; see also Kwint *et al.* 1999).

Attempts to change traditional elements of domestic design can therefore be conceived as attempts to displace identity, such as Khrushchev's modernist efforts to remove the nucleus of the petit-bourgeois hearth by removing the stove (Buchli 1999; see also Hanson 1998; Attfield 1999). Studies such as Drazin's (2001) study of Romanians' relationship with wooden furniture have shown how seemingly private constructions of identity around traditional domestic artefacts also resonate with cultural, social and political categorisations and the struggle for meaning. The importance of objects doing memory work is conveyed in a wide-ranging survey, in which 37 meaning categories were constructed (Csikszentmihalyi and Rochberg-Halton 1981: 57). These included general memories or memories of a particular place, and the finding that one object was usually categorised in many places highlighted the nuanced complexities of biographical relations between people and things. Notably, the stamping of identity by processes over time added 'value' to an object, such as an informant's mother painting, and her husband then sanding, a wooden chest (ibid.: 62).

Douglas makes an explicit connection between museums and houses as 'memory machines' (1993: 268), the former for public memories and the latter for private, by means of storing goods. de Certeau, on the other hand, calls 'memory a sort of anti-museum: it is not localisable'. He terms places as 'fragmentary and inward-turning histories', where memory is both held and unfolded as personal, spatial practice (1984: 108). Maleuvre (1999) makes the connection between collecting and displaying objects in the home, and its transition from a building to a place that is constitutive of identity (see also Belk 1995). Historical surveys of domestic art and culture emphasise the constructed character of practices of collection and display, and their historical, cultural specificity (for example, Camesasca 1971; Halle 1993; Saumarez Smith 2000). This emphasis on the importance of close, local empirical work is iterated in Miller's essay 'Accommodating' (2002), to uncover object relations and meanings that accumulate and change over time, again contesting the ability of grand narratives to engage with the complex mediations of cultural consumption within individual experience (see also Miller 1988). The power of houses, rooms and objects to evoke memory is not always read as a benign effect (Bahloul 1999; Taylor 1999) and has been criticised as a masculine discourse of home (Morley 2000). The relationship individuals have with their material goods is not necessarily comforting, and their materiality can be problematic (Miller 2001b).

Edited collections by Cieraad (1999a) and Miller (2001a) likewise show how memory is an ongoing accomplishment by means of the material culture of home, in displayed goods and other practices such as cooking (Marcoux 2001; Petridou 2001). One study is especially significant (Chevalier 1999), in that it shows how audience assumptions about a plate picturing the pope are confounded by the personal memory motivating display of the picture. It is not seeing the pope that was the memory on which the picture 'turned', but a visit by the informant's daughter. This suggests that local, contextualised fieldwork inhibits easy, universal concepts about consumption and display of ornamental goods.

Part one: where there's brass, there's muck: cleaning up history

The oppositions, ambiguities and conflations apparent in the varied concepts discussed above, relating memory with the materials of home, can be seen in the accounts that follow. We will see that the deployment of memory as a way of accounting for oneself is an important strategy in the construction of identity. First, Shyam remembers her grandmother's mantelpiece.

Shyam's 'lovely memory'

> Can I talk about my grandmother's mantelpiece? My grandmother had just a straight slate mantelpiece. I can see it now and it was a very old-fashioned coal fire with an oven. Have you seen them? So you'd always have a kettle on the hob but you could cook in the oven and I mean people cooked, actually cooked in the oven. She had the most amazing brass collection. And every damn thing seemed to be on this mantelpiece which on a Saturday, ugh, we had to go there every Saturday and it was our – my sister and I had to clean the brass and everything was brass. The candlesticks, the clock. She used to have a button box with the most

intricate pattern on it. It wasn't very big, but you had a little brush to scrub the, you know, clean the Brasso [cleaner] in between, but every- thing used to sparkle. You'd see the reflection of the blackness against the brass because she had, I don't even know what they call it, they're kept in the fireplace with a shovel and a long-handled brush, all on a brass stand. And I've actually seen them in the Argos book the other week and I thought, "Oh god, you know if she'd kept those things". But her brass was never discarded. When she died, none of us wanted it. My cousin came over from America and grabbed it willingly: "Oh my friends will go mad when they visit me and see all this lovely brass". When you can have things, you don't appreciate – ... Yeah, lovely memory apart from the hard work.

(Shyam, 74, 'Welsh/Arab, middle-class')

The sensory vividness, the old-fashioned details of the Brasso and the button box, the familiar vision of the candlesticks and the clock produce the mem- ory as an immediate, intimate presence. Narrative, biography, memory and identity can be so closely bound up that it seems only this way of telling is the story of a life, where memory and identity knit together in the making of the person. And when 'home' and 'family' are woven into the fabric, it is tempting to sit back in a nest of nostalgia, into the comfort of things and 'pastness'. Is it simply the case that 'People turn to the past because they are looking for something they do not find in the present – comfort and well-being' (Rybczynski 1986: 215)?

There were plenty of memories such as Shyam's, rich and detailed, that made me yearn for times I had never known. These were made vivid in the telling, but I was aware, too, that a confusion of my own memo- ries lay over them: of films, 'living history' museums, novels, postcards, my stepfather clearing the ashes on winter evenings. Mixed in were Mass Observation *Reports*: 'my' memory and 'hers' comingled with something col- lective, cultural. In seemingly recasting the 1937 lists of Mass Observation as biographical narrative – for Shyam speaks of a similar period – the extract seems more alive, more real, drawing the audience in to sympathise with the girl who, 'ugh', had to work the Brasso into the pattern, yet rejoice with her in the 'sparkle', wonder at the 'reflection of blackness'.

The narrative leaps between different temporalities, places and modes of telling, in a way that has parallels with the construction of memory through things on the mantelpiece. Although seemingly sequential, it moves from the eternal kettle on the hob to the weekly routine of going 'every Saturday', visual to tactile engagement, first person to second person viewer, from the 1930s to 'the other week' and back again to her grandmother's death. Shyam's sister is her silent Cinderella companion for part of the story, disrupted by the dramatic entrance of the cousin, rapturously imagining her friends' reaction in America, regretful aside about the old fireside companion set, and reflection about not appreciating what you have. Quoting the American cousin coming over to grab the brass, and seeing a fireside set (like the one her grandmother discarded) in the Argos (a popular, mid-range homeware store) catalogue are features of the story that would appeal to many British readers' sensibilities. *Our* castoffs are *their* heirlooms. What was once rubbish is now valuable, ripe also for *Cash in the Attic*-style programmes, where the alchemy of television turns junk into auctionable goods.

A closer look at Shyam's enchanting tale therefore suggests that, while telling, listening to or reading such accounts are taken-for-granted forms of interaction, the work involved is intricate, reflexive and laborious. It is a commonplace to state that interview accounts are processual, co-constructed and contingent (Hurdley 2006a). Biographic narratives constructed around things are the focus of Chapter 4, about objects that are *here, now*. In such cases, it makes sense that accounts of absent times, places, identities and people are made around these material presences in the home. However, while accounts such as Shyam's make present absent places, times and people, they also include the things themselves: the mantelpiece, the brass, the button box. The account conjures a lost world. Recent work by Kate Pahl and Andy Pollard (2010; also Pahl 2012) focused on how lost things, 'disappearing objects', were constructed through various and varying accounts during interviews with family members. Making a museum exhibition of replacements for these 'lost' intergenerational belongings, they argue: 'Objects, too, tell different stories in different times. By focusing on lost objects and the many meanings of objects, this complexity comes to the fore and creates a more open interpretative landscape that is constructed across homes, communities and museums' (Pahl and Pollard 2010: 17). I will return to these relations between different groups, museums and home in chapters 7 and 8, but the point here is to consider how 'museums...of domestic objects' (Madge and Harrisson 1937: 35) work as memories of the lost, rather than what is still here. An immediate impression from Shyam's account is of things, people, times and places being made vividly present. However, if we accept that interview accounts are processual, co-constructed and contingent, a more considered response might be to eye the fragility of the button box, the mantelpiece, the brass.

In a further reflection, then, the solidity of stuff that is *here, now* becomes precarious; if potent accounts of family, home and identity can coalesce around non-existent things, what are domestic display objects for? For now, what this approach suggests is that accounts and things are both artefacts, being made and unmade in processes of *oscillation*, and that presence and absence are not necessarily either/or choices (Strathern 2004 [1991]; Law 2002; Mol and Law 2002). While Shyam's story appears to make these absences present as subjects, it simultaneously makes visible their absence.

In this sense, it is not about bringing things, people and events back into here and now, but circumscribing, literally writing around, the space they do not inhabit. Are these *vacant* presences? When the thing around which memories are constructed is present – the wedding gift, holiday souvenir or family photograph – that vacancy is filled up by the 'thingness' of the object. But if we accept that the thing itself can be nothing more than a sparkle, a reflection in the blackness, we are left to contemplate what that circumscribing is doing.

Narrative accounts can be interpreted as description – writing (or talking) *about* something or other. Of course Shyam's tale is about her and her sister cleaning the brass every Saturday, and her cousin taking it to America. But it is also circumscription: making a boundary, drawing lines, separating out times, spaces, things and people. For example, the past, hard work and keeping things clean, is opposed to the present; her and her sister's relation to the brass was not primarily visual and aesthetic, based on desire – in contrast to her cousin. Back then, Shyam did not know that the future would transform everyday useful things into valuable antiques, costly even as mass reproductions: 'alienable' and 'inalienable' become oscillating, ambiguous properties. The memory itself is partitioned into 'lovely' and 'hard work'. Moreover, Shyam writes in her questionnaire response, 'You could hardly see the mantel for the amount of brass.' The surface which made the brass display possible, and which was the foundation of her account, was itself a 'disappearing object'. This contrasts with her own mantelpiece, which, shortly before our interview, had been emptied of all but a small clock on the advice of her daughter, who, having restored her own 'beautiful' period house (as Shyam calls it), advises her that her display of photos and ornaments is 'old-fashioned'.

Shyam was a young child at the time that the Mass Observation *Mantelpiece Reports* were being written. Many of the older participants in the study were growing up in the first half of the 20th century, when mantelpieces and 'real fires' were common. Others recall the electric fires and simple wooden surrounds of the 1980s, as children or adults engaged in 'modernising', just as many Mass Observers were in 1983. Even the younger adult participants grew up with fireplaces in their grandparents' or family's homes, and attitudes towards the presence or absence of a mantelpiece vary widely, even within generations. While 'real' fires were almost universal when the oldest participants such as Shyam were children, they were also mentioned in the memories even of people in their twenties. The great difference in uses of the fireplace was the change from it being an important source of heating, and, in the kitchen, a cooking device, to a place for sitting beside, hanging stockings at Christmas, family gatherings, collections of ornaments, cards and photographs, or feeling 'cosy' and 'homey', especially in winter. Memories of each generation point to changing activity over the decades of the 20th century. Shyam, together with many of her peers, recalled hard repetitive labour: not only cleaning brass, but also black-leading the grate and the daily task of emptying the ash, then going down every morning to stoke the fire. Combs and brushes on the mantel were used daily, with girls and women leaning dangerously towards the fire to look in the mirror above. Letters were put there until they were answered, bills and vouchers kept in a container, and things left for 'father' to see and pick up. The shelf itself could be removed and used as a bed warmer for children; stories were told round it; anything you wanted to find was up there on the mantel; as Shyam adds, 'it was the focal point of your whole being'.

Other memories: a brief chronology

What follows is a fleeting timeline of other participants' accounts of childhood memories, from the 1930s to the 1990s. In the 1930s, there was a pot or kettle on the fire, and mother or grandmother cooked daily on it, as Charlotte (John's wife) remembers: 'it was a different world then, and I haven't entirely left it behind'. Bernie, growing up in a terraced house recalls 'everything that was, like, valued or like family heirlooms value' and family photographs was on the well-polished front room mantelpiece, compared to the living room mantel, on which sat his mother's box for coupons and vouchers, brushes and combs. On Monday, which was always washday, clothes would be hung round it on a cord or rail. Andrew, Liz's father, comments that 'they were much more of a utility purpose than a decorative purpose', although photographs of the dead – his unmarried aunts' fiancés, killed in the First World War – were a constant presence. In contrast, he says that the 21st-century mantelpiece is 'only a picture'.

Belinda, growing up in the 1950s, calls 'the good old days' 'garbage', remembering only the dirt and work of the fire, without Shyam's memories of the stories, the cooking and the warmth. David recalls the 'sacrosanct' character of his parents' mantelpiece in the suburban semi-detached house where he grew up in the 1950s and early 1960s: 'a clock in the middle, two candlesticks, two brass ornaments...lovingly polished' which stayed there for 30 years. Rosalind remembers her mother's 1950s 'forbidden' mantelpiece, where her best china was displayed, but not to be touched – and where cleaning was 'hazardous'. Cleaning is a practice set apart from everyday, careless handling, since it remakes these fragile artefacts as tangible (and dirty). Annette, born a decade or so later, recalls her grandparents' coal fire – 'such a mess' – which her parents did not have. Adrian, growing up at the same time with 'real fires' means he associates the mantelpiece with home. Yet Dan, also a child in the 1960s and 1970s, talks of the 'grotty surround' of his parents' two-bar electric fire, as 'fireplaces were going out of fashion then'.

Many children of the 1980s and 1990s have nostalgic memories of the mantel. In Bronwen's home, the display changed only at Christmas, when a bit of tinsel was put up and they would sit round the fire, rather than the television. Similarly, Karen recalls the 'proper fire' in winter, her mother's display of inherited antiques unchanging on the mantelpiece. In Victoria's parents' home, the mantelpiece has always been somewhere for an ever-changing array of cards, and important family photographs. The furniture is arranged around it, 'people get up and they'll go and look at the photos', while she, on visits home, goes straight up to look at the latest cards. Wendy is 'not a mantelpiece person', because her parents had 'dark wood' and 'bits of brass' on their mantel: 'to me they're not modern colours and styles; they suit my mum and dad'. But any movement of photographs and well-loved objects would have prompted her to ask, 'Why has she done that?' Now that her parents have moved into a modern, smaller house, 'I haven't got a set idea in my head of where they are anymore.' Her parents' move has prompted her to realise that 'It must be more about the things, the actual ornaments and the memories, rather than the actual mantelpiece.'

Part two: organising memory

Following the detailed analysis of Shyam's memory narrative, and a brief introduction to how other participants 'told' memory in the first part of the chapter, is a thematic look at memory work. During interviews in partic-ipants' homes, these were densely worked narrative accounts, or loops of question and answer, loose strands and half-told yarns. How these are tidied up into themes leaves threads hanging, and entanglements.

Time, cold and dirt

Although I was asking people about the mantelpiece, many participants produced memories of the fireplace. This took on a particular salience when those who did not have fireplaces in their current homes articulated this absence through memory accounts, in terms of cutting time (and space) – into then/now (and here/there). Four examples convey the force with which participants separated out past and present in their memory accounts, which were often related to their current choices or desires in having/not having a fireplace. John and Charlotte currently have an electric fire that can be moved into the stone fire surround they recently commissioned from a local stonemason. The fireplace/mantelpiece is a very special place, then. Charlotte says the mantelpiece is made different from the multitude of display surfaces in the living room – shelves, windowsills and cabinets – because it is above the fireplace. She longs for a coal fire again. Her rea-son for this is threefold: she sees gas and electric fires as 'meaning very little'; the work involved 'gives you something to do' as a retired person; the house 'feels cold without anything there' and unless there were a fire, it would be 'something cold and drab'. Thus, past and present are divided into warm/cold, vivid/drab, meaning/emptiness, action/inaction. Saying, 'it was a different world then, and I haven't entirely left it behind', she demonstrates the misalignment between *her* world, of sensory, bodily, intellectual fulfilment, and the present world. Bringing a coal fire into her home does not change *her* world, it changes *the* world (Strathern 2004 [1991]; Munro 2005).

In contrast, both Annette and Belinda have chosen not to have fireplaces in their recently built houses. Belinda, also in her mid-sixties, thinks the 'good old days' are 'garbage', appreciating the marvel of pressing a button for the central heating and walking around in shorts. The coal fires of her childhood gave out an uncomfortable, laboriously made, one-sided heat, and, with the mirror and combs on the mantel above, were 'dangerous' for girls in their nightdresses combing their hair. A generation younger, Annette dislikes fireplaces – 'get rid of it' – which she connects with old houses – 'damp, dusty and depressing'. She remembers her grandparents' coal fire – 'such a mess' – recalling that her parents did not have one. She thinks that might have 'rubbed off on me', 'but as well it's by choice'. Having spent most of her adulthood in Royal Air Force (RAF) houses, she covered up and ignored the fireplaces, with their electric fires – 'you wouldn't want to decorate it'. Rather than a fireplace in this, the first home she has owned, she has a long, low mobile shelf unit as she likes to be 'slightly different', but laughs when I point out she has a clock in the centre, exclaiming, 'It's a very classic mantelpiece!' Although she says, 'I don't know how that happened,' she explains that it is 'handy' and 'probably very similar to mantelpieces I've seen or what you see in magazines'. For both Belinda and Annette, the past/present division is a nuanced reverse of Charlotte's. The past is worse than just garbage and mess; its affective, sensory dimension offers discomfort, depression and dampness. However, Annette has not entirely turned away from the conventional fireplace, invoking utility, the sight of other people's mantelpieces and magazine pictures. Note how she shifts from 'I' to 'you', as if looking at magazine images were a universal activity, distinct from her personal viewing of actual mantelpieces. Similarly, she mobilises distinction/difference and ignorance/inheritance to explain both her dislike of the traditional fireplace and imitation of the 'classic mantelpiece' on her mobile shelf.

The power relations at work in the organisation of memory can also be seen in a conversation I had with Andrew, Liz's father, born in 1934. He makes a clear break at the end of the Second World War, from his parents' and aunts' generation, who 'felt that when they died that was the end of the suffering'. His mother, 'the last of the Victorians', the only sister to have married and had a child, burnt all the family photographs on the mantel, including those of her four sisters' fiancés killed in the First World War. He says, 'my parents didn't want me to remember the stress, the worry and the fear', 'that bad memory should not be passed onto the next generation'. He finds the 'present generation's' 'vigour and enthusiasm' for commemorating Armistice Day 'gross over-romanticisation', that they 'can't feel the misery it caused', in contrast to the 'generation in it [who] wanted to forget'. The mantelpiece no longer has 'utility purpose', being 'a piece of art that you look at', so he concludes, 'throw it out'.

The violent deletion of the past (memory, photograph and mantelpiece) through burning, forgetting and throwing out, has itself been violated, para-doxically through romance, art and vigour (in contrast to fear, utility and misery). The multiple divisions in Andrew's account are organised along a fault line he perceives between the 'present generation' and his, born into the world of 'the last of the Victorians'. What he construes as the present generation's improper processes of memory, artifice and preservation can be understood as another exercise in erasing the past – or rather, *a* past. In re-membering this past differently, the present organises the materials and practices of memory in ways that Andrew feels excluded from. His world, and that of his parents, has disappeared. However, in producing accounts such as this one to make that world visible, he paradoxically re-members precisely the pain, fear and worry he was told to forget. Both remember-ing and forgetting, deleting and producing, are simultaneously present in our conversation, which, incidentally, he takes over from his son-in-law, the 'official' participant in the study. The rest of the family drift away as Andrew argues against the novel aesthetics of memory as romance, made material in the mantelpiece.

Space: sight, function, effect

Bernie, growing up in a terraced house in the 1940s, lives in a house built in 1985 on the land where these very terraces had been condemned and demolished. Brain-damaged and physically disabled, he spends a lot of time at home. He distinguishes between the fireplaces in the front room (kept smart for visitors), the back living room, and the narrow bedroom mantels, underneath which a fire was rarely lit, recalling, 'I can see it in my own mind, the difference between the living room and the front room and the old kitchen.' Bernie is going to remake his mother's front room mantel, 'a display one', with her three vases and family photos, by purchasing one from B&Q (a stockist of house and garden goods). He says, 'I don't need a fire at all, just a fireplace effect,' since 'I think it looks bare without it,' citing a visit to a friend of his who had a modern, minimalist home interior as an example. The differentiation of space in his childhood home, between display and utility, family and guest, fire and cold, upstairs and downstairs, valuable and everyday will be transformed and compressed in his version. Like Charlotte, he dislikes the 'bare' modern interior, but is happy to have the 'effect' of a fire, for display and looking at, rather than warmth and physical activity. The division between different domestic spaces according to function is impossible in his small, modern house, where our interview in the sitting room is accompanied by the roar of the washing machine in the kitchen. Nevertheless, despite this (audible) invasion of space, Bernie plans to make his own spatial distinction with the new mantelpiece for an abridged version of his mother's collection.

Bernie's acts of distinction are expressed visually: the memory of the rooms he 'can see', the 'look' of the bare interior, the 'display'; even the 'effect' is for the sight, rather than to warm the body. For the moment, it is worth bearing three questions in mind. First, is Bernie's intention to install a new mantelpiece and fireplace 'effect' into his centrally heated modern house no more than an aesthetic choice of the late modern individual? Does the 'effect' re-present the fireplace as a non-fire, a 'non-place', detached from memory (Augé 1995)? Finally, if a fireplace no longer necessarily provides heat, what is it doing here?

This last question is pertinent to the division of space that some participants performed on a larger scale than the rooms of a house. One example will be helpful here. While Adrian recalls the 'real fires' of his childhood home in the 1960s, he did not have one in the modern apartment he later inhabited in Singapore, where a mantelpiece would have 'looked rather bizarre' and a fireplace 'out of place'. In his current home, where he lives with his wife and three young children, he thinks that 'in the context of this kind of house, it is appropriate to see a fireplace and a mantelpiece there'. The house is as modern as the apartment, and centrally heated, but climate and house design have their effect on what he expects to see. His connection of the fireplace with 'home' is not emotive, but because it is the 'central point', the 'focal point' which he grew up with. The effect of repeated looking, over years, upon the fireplace and display above has produced such an expectation, that Adrian would have fitted a fireplace into his own house had that 'focal point' been missing. The boundaries of house design and climate are what he uses to categorise the fireplace and mantelpiece as in or out of place (Douglas 2002). However, this circumscription is an active process, in that he would have installed these materials, to cast out 'empty space'. Emptiness is as material as things, as visible as 'focal points', if it is outlined as something *else* lost or missing. This is not an absent presence, as such, rather a *vacant* presence. While participants themselves might articulate this 'other' which has left a gap, the difficulty is in delineating emptiness that is *not* circumscribed.

In this case, Adrian's memory of the 'real fire' which 'explains' his current liking of a fireplace does not 'count' in Singapore, where 'context' takes its place. However, climate and form of dwelling are manipulable things, brought into and out of participants' mantelpiece accounts, as is memory. Adrian divides countries and houses into 'hot' and 'cold', appropriate and inappropriate places for a fire/mantel, but does not make the same distinction for his dwellings. Memory, climate and architecture are worked together to produce explanations of what is fitting. It is noticeable how Adrian also employs 'look' to explain his circumscription of the right place for a fire/mantelpiece, even though temperature is felt by the whole body. It is as if the eye is metonym for the body, a part standing for the whole, just as the 'effect' stands for the fireplace in Bernie's vision of the future.

Things: house, fireplace, mantelpiece, clock

Once parts start standing in for wholes (Strathern 2004 [1991]) and emptiness becomes absent presence, it is possible to see other effects at work. Christine, a similar age to Bernie and living in the same modern development as Adrian, sees her fireplace as 'just a decoration', which she likes 'as a feature'. As an adult, she has always lived in modern houses, since she remembers the old houses of her childhood: 'there are always nooks and crannies and horrible dusty areas. So I reckoned I wanted something clean and modern.' Since she does not 'like the idea of not having a fireplace', she does not link the dust, the labour of blackleading the grate and the danger of her mother leaning over the fire to do her hair with this feature in her current home. Unlike Annette or Charlotte, she does not construct the fireplace as 'the past', with its divisions of clean/dirty and so on. Instead, she has separated the fireplace from the house. Just as Shyam partitioned her memory as 'lovely, apart from the hard work', Christine separates her memory of the dust/danger/labour associated with the house and *that* fireplace, from the fireplace as 'feature' of a clean, modern house. The fireplace could be conceived as a double negative, rather than a positive decision: 'I did not like the idea of not having a fireplace.' By detaching it from all the practices it once had, it can become an idea, the 'not not' fireplace, where there is no danger, no hard work, no dust.

Clutter is the enemy of the modern, or so it seems from questionnaire and interview accounts. Memories of childhood mantelpieces frequently name 'clutter': so many family photographs that individual faces cannot be seen, crowded china ornaments, acres of brass, dust. No separating work is done in these abridged memories; it is assumed that the highly condensed meanings are universally understood. Another way in which memory gathers up the past mantelpiece and fireplace (often viewed as one and the same) is in words such as Christmas, grandmother, mother, homey, homely, cosy, warm. These too assume shared meanings which seem universal and eternal, with no need to unravel the links between them. It is as if 'the past' is either crammed up in a dusty muddle, or all cuddled up in a cosy nest, although both constructions effect the same refusal of close examination. What this chapter has shown so far is how dense even the simplest memory account is, and how much work goes into making boundaries of 'what counts' – even when and how memory itself counts as a strategy for explaining the present. As we saw, Annette found herself with a 'classic mantelpiece' display on her mobile shelf unit, explained by the accident of what has 'rubbed off', 'choice' after seeing others' mantelpieces and what 'you' see in magazines. This is a double process of bricolage: first of putting together selected modes of memory – childhood homes, mass media, visiting others – and then choosing how to construct the present. Taste is both 'naked' and elective (Bourdieu 1986).

The house, the fireplace, the mantelpiece and the things upon it were taken as a whole, albeit with parts and effects – until Christine's account separated the fireplace from the rest of her memory, as a 'feature' of the modern house. Dismantling the fireplace/home/memory construct presses forward different understandings of accounts, and the relations between home, fireplace, things on the mantel, practices and affective, sensory dimensions. For example, Harriet lives in a traditional terraced house, which was modernised before she and her young family moved in. Her husband put up a small pine shelf above the sofa, which is against the (former) chimney breast. She has decorated the humble ledge with a fine cloth and silver ornaments. Although anyone entering the room can see it, it is invisible once one sits down. She would like to install a fireplace one day although, as she says, 'it's not exactly a burning issue'. In fact, a fire in what would have been the fireplace is currently impossible, due to the positioning of the furniture, yet Harriet calls the shelf her 'mantelpiece'. It is neither a focal point nor above a fireplace, but presents a 'traditional' display of silver-framed photographs and ornaments, to which Harriet attaches memories of family. The most important thing for her is the picture hanging above, painted by her great-great-great-grandfather, which she has hung in every place she has ever lived. In a similar move, Nick and his partner Liz have put a cupboard in the living room of the modern house where they live with their four young children. It is diagonally opposite the television, and although the things on it are like the things displayed on mantelpieces in his earlier homes (as a child and an adult), it now has no attachment with a fireplace. As he says, 'we've fabricated a sort of artificial focal point that the fireplace might have been once'. What Shyam called 'the focal point of your whole being', because of the practices around it, which depended upon the fire itself being 'in place' has now been wholly supplanted by an 'artificial' focal point, for centring the gaze (if not directed at the television), rather than one's 'whole being'.

While Annette's shelf was moveable, Harriet's mantelpiece is 'makeable' and Nick's cupboard is a fabrication. Whereas the mantelpiece and its display were once 'givens', dependent on the fire in its fireplace for their centrality, and intimately bound up with home and being, they are now represented as active, mobile constructions. A 'traditional' or 'classic' display does not need an actual mantelpiece, a 'mantelpiece' does not need a fire, and the fireplace itself can be replaced by a cupboard. These three examples, however, are partially constructed through memories of childhood homes. These are invoked as continuing attachments to some form of traditional or classic display, focal point or mantelpiece. In the next example, childhood memory has no part to play.

In Alison's last house, a Victorian property in north Wales shared with her (former) husband, she had a 'very conscious wish to have that room looking very traditional and the mantelpiece and candlesticks came from that. I mean it's always something I associate with Christmas.' This had no connection with her childhood homes in the 1960s and 70s, in which there were no traditional fireplaces, but, 'they were images that I admired ... from *Woman and Home* [a monthly magazine] or whatever'. The house itself was a 'period' property, which Alison invokes as another influence on the mantelpiece display she created, but the same sort of 'candlestick' display, with the same slate clock she bought specifically to fit in with her former home [in an area near a slate mine] is now on the mantelpiece in her modern house.

Alison's memory is entirely constituted from magazines and 'whatever', a 'conscious wish' built from 'admired images'. How does this mode of memory differ from the childhood memories of others? However they construct their present 'mantelpiece', none of it is built from dirt, dust, bareness, danger or toil, but from their own particularised forms of purity, in which memory is another method of circumscribing, drawing around and controlling what is visible. However, viewing these accounts together also makes visible the ambiguities, oscillations and partiality of these connections. One person's 'warm' past is another's damp mess; Adrian's memory is an important constituent of what 'home' is – depending on context; fires and mantels are in all sorts of different places and pieces. Memories can be articulated in fabulously sensuous detail, such as Shyam's, or a single word: 'Christmas' or 'mother', 'dust' or 'clutter', heavy with unuttered echoes of collective memory.

People: identity, culture and power

What are people doing when they put together mantelpiece displays and/or talk about them? This is culture in the making, the casting out, pulling apart, encircling of meaning, in which time, space and things, even memories, are divided, abridged and transformed. But what about persons? Women, especially mothers and grandmothers, are in some accounts metonyms for memory, or home, or family. This will be discussed more fully in Chapter 5, but there is a little more to be said here. Norah, who grew up in the 1920s and 1930s, simply leans back in her chair at one point in her reminiscences to utter 'Mother, mother!' As early as the 1930s, Norah says her mother had got rid of the mantelpiece above the kitchen range, infuriated by her husband's persistent use of her neat 'two by two by two' display of brass candlesticks to store papers behind: 'so she didn't have one, and she had him then'. This account conveys the power at work in replacing contested space with emptiness, which is perhaps hard to see except at such moments of disposal. Anyone looking at that space after the disposal would have no knowledge of this: his practice, and the act of replacing his world with another, had disappeared. By ridding herself of her property, Norah's mother took possession of a man's world.

A final example will sharpen the point that absence, as much as presence, is crucial in the management not just of not just space, but also time, identity and worlds. The 'danger' trope, which is part of Belinda's memory, is also used by Nick's partner, Liz, to justify the absence of a fireplace, and its replacement with a cupboard:

> *Liz*: Yes well, it was because in my old house, Henry my little boy, we had things over the fireplace, and it had a mantelpiece and it had a – I had a photo on it. But he was playing with a ball in the sitting room on his own; he knocked the photo down and it set alight – there was a pilot lit and it lit.
>
> *RH*: Oh my God!
>
> *Liz*: And he was in the house, him on his own, and it put me off. You know, when you –
>
> *RH*: Yes, yes.
>
> *Liz*: It was sort of potentially there, I thought. And when we came home – he was only three so you know, he was only little. Now you know, it's different because of course he's so much older.
>
> *RH*: Yes.
>
> *Liz*: But that put me off that.
>
> *RH*: Yes, so you had an actual experience of sort of –
>
> *Liz*: Yes. You know, the kiddies and the fireplace; and my father used to light the fire every day and the cats used to get really close to the fire. And then a coal would spark and they – it would come out and land on the cats.
>
> *RH*: Oh my God!
>
> *Liz*: And they'd start sizzling away.
>
> *RH*: Oh!
>
> *Liz*: And they didn't notice.
>
> *RH*: And the fur would singe.
>
> *Liz*: Oh yeah. All you'd smell was burning fur!
>
> *RH*: That's a terrible thing to happen!
>
> *Liz*: And the cats would be fast asleep.

The family pet, a playing child and a family photo – such 'homely' ideas – are turned into the possibility of stinking, fatal inferno. She juxtaposes her experience as the 'careful' (albeit absent) mother of a 'kiddy' with her experience as a 'kiddy' with a 'careless' father. That carelessness, and the stench of sizzling fur (and maybe flesh?), become attached to the mantelpiece, in a powerful mingling of smell and moral dirt (Drobnick 2006). *Not* having a mantelpiece is perhaps so abnormal that its absence must be justified by making other 'normal' concepts dangerous. By replacing the mantelpiece with a cupboard top, Liz has deleted this precarious future, and, further, presented herself as a good mother.

Dirty and clean, warm and cold, abundant and bare, homely and depressing, real and fake, safe and dangerous, forgettable and memorable, rubbish and treasure, smell and sanctity: memories have so much to say about the present, and the future, in these accounts, especially in what lies silent. However, there is something more pressing than the perpetual tussle between whether past or present is the 'good', although this is important. This is a battle for meaning. Since culture is the making of meaning, these accounts can be understood as the politics of culture at work. Whoever wins the battle makes culture. The practices of division apparent in these memories enable their makers to draw the 'other' – be it the present, another place, the friend or the cold – as the boundary-markers for a space they can fill with meaning. In doing so, they organise meaning into and out of the spaces of memory. The power of these meanings depends upon appealing to more than just intellectual sense-making; the senses and the emotions are folded into complex modes of constructing memory. Artefacts – accounts, houses, mantelpieces and display objects – are all brought into play by participants in this complex work. This depends upon an assumption of implicit moral consensus; and who would dare contest the culture that is contained in these memory spaces: cleanliness, homeliness, goodness, realness, plenty, safety, comfort, beauty, utility?

Conclusion

The house is a primary 'structuring structure' in Bourdieu's theorisation of *habitus* and is thus the principal site for the interiorisation of practices of distinction, which are so implicit that their origins are forgotten. He also highlighted the 'mythico-poetic' symbolism of domestic space and structures (1977: 118), an aspect of the meaning of home that Bachelard (1958) in particular brought to the sociological imagination. 'Home', heavy with memory, is laden with concepts such as 'ontological security', in that its routines, habits and familiarity are crucial for the maintenance and construction of identity (Giddens 1991). Moreover, there is a common conflation of woman and home (Forty 1986; Davidoff and Hall 2002), home and memory (Douglas 1993; Maleuvre 1999). This can be related to women's management of the hearth and hearth goods for centuries (Filbee 1980; Pennell 1999). As mother/partner, women were pivotal both in memory and in present orderings of the domestic spatial economy.

The cuts, between inside/outside, public/private, space and place, places and non-places (Augé 1995), invite a romantic intertwining of memory, home and meaning. In terms of appropriation and ownership of meaning, 'place' can be wrought out of 'space' by the ongoing construction of everyday practices and lived experience (Lefebvre [1973] 1991; de Certeau 1984). Marc Augé makes a distinction between 'place' and 'non-place', in that place is 'relational, historical and concerned with identity' (1995: 77), and in his criticism of 'non-places' proliferating and intruding into most practices of daily life represents the pessimistic viewpoint that de Certeau resists. Kim Dovey's extensive critique of architectural practice argues that, for example, the fireplace is now an 'arbitrary fragment of discourse', conflating ideas such as heat, hearth and home and commodifying this deep-seated distinction between inside and outside to sell houses (Dovey 1999: 148). Such an argument relates the meaning of home to differing conceptualisations of public/private, local/global and space/place. However, in jumping over to the other side of the fence, Dovey maintains this firm boundary. Mantelpiece as memory, memory as mantelpiece and the 'mantelpiece memory story' are slippy, fond, sly things, working like smoke into the cracks of our own memories of houses from childhood, films, imaginings. While boundaries are useful for tracing concepts, and to understand how practices are shaped by what is already there, their rigidity has to flex and soften to mould around practices.

The artistry that goes into the production of such a narrative as Shyam's is easily missed when listening; this is as aesthetically expert a construction as Walter Benjamin's (2006 [1932–1934]) writing on his childhood, its intricate temporality more complex than any clock mechanism. And yet this is everyday work, made routine by repetition, and taken for granted in its seeming appeal to nostalgia, that mix of comfort and regret. However, as the previous two chapters have shown, history does not have to be made like this – for this is history, as much as any scholarly article, expert history or archive. This is the kind of memory that is the stuff of 'ordinary' history, the 'fish and brass day' recalled in Birmingham slums (Upton 2005). All three modes turn around the idea that things – a house, a ruin, a fireplace, or a brass candlestick – are reliable foundations for constructing the past. Even though the interpretations of that past may vary, the things themselves, like cultural memories and collective assumptions, are taken as unchanging, solid presences. Things, however fragmentary or partial, cannot disappear, can they?

The embodied character of 'ordinary' memory, conjured by de Certeau at the start of this chapter, produces memory as labouring, patient bodies, making things tangible and dirty, working them clean. Memory becomes synaesthetic, as sight, touch, smell entangle. Sight is no longer the privileged sense in this domestic museum (Hetherington 2003), this 'ordinary', affective memorialising (Carsten 2007a). However, is this 'better' than the public museum, where bodies and senses are ordered into legitimate modes of being (Bennett 1995; Hetherington 2003)? While the optic might be construed as 'touching' (MacDougall 2006) and multisensory worlds of participants portrayed as more authentic (Pink 2009), I suggest that all the senses are as deeply trained, or constrained, as sight (Packard 1957; Classen 2005a, 2005b; Howes 2005a; Drobnick 2006; Hurdley and Dicks 2011). The skilful artifice of multi-sensory stories delights us precisely because we 'know' how to feel.

Pierre Nora, referring to his work, *Les Lieux de Mémoire* (1984–1992) sets memory and history against one another:

> History has become our replaceable imagination – hence the last stand of faltering fiction in the renaissance of the historical novel, the vogue for personalised documents, the literary revitalisation of historical drama, the success of the oral historical tale. Our interest in these *lieux de mémoire* that anchor, condense, and express the exhausted capital of our collective memory derives from this new sensibility.
>
> (Nora 1989: 24)

In being 'validated' these everyday fictions become legitimated, even enhanced as appealing to senses and sensibilities attuned now to museums where smell, touch, even taste are celebrated as modes of organising the past. In Britain and the US at least, we are accustomed to multi-sensory performances and performing of 'Retrochic' in *Theatres of Memory* such as our own homes (Samuel 1994; see also Baudrillard 1996 [1968]: 73–106). Further, if individuals now 'are left to look to oneself as the biographer, the story-teller, detached from any solid institution such as family, "society"' (Czarniawska 1999: 53), is this 'collective' memory, or rather, is 'memory' a mode of ordering, that disciplines us into a circuit of value, that is quite different from a 'collective'? Barely visible is the careful working in of taste (Bourdieu 1986; Bennett 2005), of cultural, social and educational distinction into the patterns of these sensuously wrought tales, that invite only nostalgia and complicity.

Part II

Presents: Ordering Identities, Things and Home

4
Telling Identities

> At one extreme, one finds that the performer can be fully taken in
> by his own act; he can be sincerely convinced that the impression
> of reality which he stages is the real reality. When his audience is
> also convinced in this way about the show he puts on – and this
> seems to be the typical case – then for the moment at least, only the
> sociologist or the socially disgruntled will have any doubts about
> the 'realness' of what is presented.
>
> (Goffman 1959: 28)

Introduction: once upon a time

A house-martin flew in through the front door, over the kitchen table and
out of the window at the very moment I began this chapter. It shocked me
out of the normal run of things, took my breath away. When it flew in, my
first sensible thought was, 'How do I get it out again?'; the second, 'Will
the dog go crazy?' When it flew away across the field, I felt relief – and
regret: I really have to start writing now.

Had I not written this little story down, I would no doubt have forgotten
it, but because it is recorded, here, I will always remember the time and
the place the chapter was made. And now it is shared, but a strange way
of sharing: you cannot imagine the place, the time, but you have the story.
Rather, you have this story, rather than any other I could have told – about
the dog slumping in the hallway, the crows' indignant croaks, the sheep
calling their lambs, the fly crawling on the table. As time passes, I will forget
the other untold stories. Only having this artefact, the book, materialising
'The House-martin' story, keeps *that* memory – at least, the account of that
memory – present in the 'here', 'now' of each re-reading. Not only is this
story a strange way of sharing the *what, where, who* of 'now', 'here', it is also
a particular tale of the extra-ordinary moment, rather than the mundane
rumble of what passes for normal round here.

In contrast, many mantelpiece stories – the ones that are told – are tales
of the expected. Some objects commemorate momentous events in a life,

101

such as the death of older relatives, a wedding, a birth. Taken together, they produce the rhythm of a culture that marks such events through the prominent display of certain objects, such as photographs, wedding presents, invitations, cards and heirlooms. Others mark out the smaller rhythms of lives: daily medication, easy-to-find spectacles, or walks on the beach. Things remembering events, people and other places – holiday destinations or former homes, even souvenirs of others' travels – are put on the mantelpiece. Collections, prompted by a single object picked up on holiday or given for a birthday, gain a tautological momentum: people give them because you have them (Belk 1995). They are a different kind of story from the trivially existential 'house-martin tale', to which the listener's response might be, 'Oh, that's interesting', before moving on to discuss the weather. It is expected that objects on display can be accounted for through family history, autobiography or aesthetic sensibility. In producing such accounts, people account for themselves, as culturally proficient members of a 'knowing' society. Further, seemingly dissonant counterpoints and gaps enrich these productions. Listening for these syncopations and silences enhances our understanding of how culture works through small stories 'about' things.

In this chapter, I present short extracts from four interview transcripts; little scripts intended to highlight how participants perform identity (as do I) in these two-handers. One aim of the chapter, then, is to undo the fixing of objects as autobiographic: to consider the 'how', rather than the 'what'. Certainly, a person can sit and relate her autobiography through the objects around the house, and in turn, tell the biographies of things through family or personal histories. The storying of objects, the idea of artefactual biographies, is now common parlance in material culture studies. As Kopytoff (1986) emphasises, things have a 'cultural biography' and are embedded in frameworks of time and memory (Tilley 2001; see also Appadurai 1986a, 1986b; Attfield 2000). Their role as consumer goods is only momentary. Biographies of things are important in the construction of individual and family autobiographies (Csikszentmihalyi and Rochberg-Halton 1981; Woodward 2001; see also Mason 2004). By appropriating mass-produced objects to create 'meaningful décor' (Chevalier 1999: 94) people can move from being supposedly alienated or passive consumers to active producers of meaning (see also Miller D. 1988, 1995, 2001a; Jackson and Moores 1995; Cieraad 1999a; Clarke 2001; Drazin 2001; Marcoux 2001). Further than this, however, objects have been construed as becoming meaningful *only* through autobiographic narration. For example:

> It is not a particularly visible owl. It stands among the other ornaments on the mantelpiece, along with brass candlesticks and bowls – very much the sort of ornaments and souvenirs one expects to see these days on mantelpieces, although this one doesn't happen to have the typical invitation cards, vase of flowers and clock that are found on most.

The owl only stands out from the rest through the filtering effects of Dominic's own narrative [...] but even then the owl does not really fly out of its own accord.

(Miller 2008: 194)

But what if people do not make their belongings 'fly out' from 'the rest'? There were many instances during the interviews with participants in their homes when they had very little to say about certain objects: 'I just liked it,' or 'I don't know why that's there.' Often, the 'meaning' of things was not 'consciously' thought about until I asked them. For many people, it is the assemblage on the mantelpiece – the 'look' – that matters, rather than individual pieces. Some objects are not mentioned, some members of a household are silent or speak little, and some people simply do not take part in this kind of research. As I commented about Mass Observation *Reports* (see Chapter 2), to base an interpretation only on objects with particularly 'tellable' narratives would be to distort both their part in the practice of everyday life in the home, and the ways in which people account for them. Some objects are not considered important as 'autobiographic' artefacts, nor is everyone engaged in telling those kinds of stories (see Plummer 2001; Pahl and Rowsell 2010).

There is a danger in ignoring the fact that not everyone participates in the popularised social scientific practice of the narrative/biographic interview. The social character of these 'life stories' must be recognised, since in the 'interview society' interview narratives are not transparent reflections of lived experience or the self, but are interactive performances (Holstein and Gubrium 1995; Kvale 1996; Gubrium and Holstein 2002; Czarniawska 2004). As Paul Atkinson and David Silverman point out, the emphasis on narrative in interview interactions results not from any essential superiority of this interview type, but from a 'preferred subjectivity' (1997: 19) that is currently popular not only in the social sciences but more widely in society. This is particularly noticeable in populist reality shows, where a juicy backstory is vital (Skeggs and Wood 2009). Stories are culturally ubiquitous, seemingly 'natural' phenomena (Flyvberg 2011; also Chase 2011). Indeed, Coolen *et al.* (2002) express concern about empirical studies of the meaning of home in particular, which have tended to use small-scale, qualitative interview samples for data collection to the exclusion of other approaches. In Chapter 7, discussion of Becky and Pete's interview will centre on 'telling' inarticulacy.

Clutter, laziness, dust, hesitation, failure, frailty, anxiety, squabbling and things-yet-to-be-done shadowed stories of grandmother's vase, the school photograph, father's clock. Often forgotten in the home/memory/family elision are the 'other' stories: divorce, bitter dislike, arguments, ongoing grief, loneliness, deprivation. These, as much as the well told tales of mantelpiece tableaux, are cultural productions, and accounts of the making of culture.

It is too easy to settle a study of mantelpieces into that comfortable rut of home, family and memory, chuckle knowingly at tales of matronly irritation or nod and sigh at that shared reluctance to dust. In that rut, the 'other' stories can be seen as caesurae (Carsten 2007a), breaks in the neat pattern. But this *is* the pattern: to exclude dissonance is pretend that home and family are cosy compositions. Nevertheless, the fact that so many of 'us' (whoever 'we' are) want to chuckle and nod along with the tune, ignoring the background hum (and the silences) requires scrutiny.

Beginning in boxes of fragile documents, piles of library books, swathes of photographs, questionnaires, emails, phone calls and scrappy dialogue, the book now has the appearance of a static artefact. The following interview extracts recall, however partially, the processes that can so easily be cast aside and forgotten in the quest for completeness (Law 2007). Further, these bits and pieces of dialogue move beyond narrative, with a teller, and a listener 'sitting comfortably'; they are performances. As such, they awaken the dramaturgy of display, belying the seeming slumber of things at rest on the mantelpiece. Bourdieu wrote of 'genesis amnesia' (1977; see also Douglas 1986 on 'structural amnesia'; Halbwachs 1992), referring to the tendency of sociologists and societies to forget the beginnings of practices, and take them for granted – be that the origins of neat academic arguments or ways of dividing up space and time. Of course, each is one version of many possible versions of the same stories, but they all enact that 'genesis moment' when an object, through 'accident' or deliberation, was put on the mantelpiece. The ongoing process of maintaining stasis is also performed; the effort of thinking and doing display. Further, the permanence of some things – such as Eric's pills – is mobilised as daily routine. They also show something of the first moments of scholarly knowledge productions. Therefore, I suggest that you read them as *very* short plays, rather than interview extracts, with one glaring inversion of Goffman's (1959) settings: the 'props', and the 'backdrop' are centre stage.

None of the four interview extracts is a 'telling case' (Savage 2010); the extracts are not selected for their salience in illustrating a common way of doing things in the home, but to introduce the idea that, while people may have very particular ways of doing things, there are commonly accepted enterprises in the home and ways of talking about them. What individuals' stories can do is show how these seemingly (to the visitor) static tableaux are processes, bound up in the ongoing politics of identity, memory, home and family. They illuminate the 'shadowed places' that the institutions of collective memory practices can obscure (Douglas 1986: 69). The extended sequences here illustrate how object biographies (Kopytoff 1986) are enmeshed in dialogue; while a few might be told from beginning to middle to end, these were rare. Although these can be plucked cleanly from the body of the text, such anatomisation dismisses the 'rest' as waste, when, as we shall see from Chapter 6 onwards, the 'rest' matters. Indeed, keeping things (and people) in their rightful places is a great concern for some participants.

Of the four participants, only one (Julia) lives in what can be seen as an 'ordinary' family: a married British-born white heterosexual couple with two school-aged children. In Julia's modern house, the mantelpiece surrounds an enclosed gas fire. Eric, a twice-divorced grandfather, shares his house with a long-term male lodger, who has a bedroom and the 'best' room in the house – the knocked-through living room. Eric's sitting room is the narrow back room, leading through to the kitchen. Having ripped out all the fireplaces in the mid-1970s, he uses the top of his piano as a mantelpiece. Annette is divorced and has no children, living now with her female partner. Her deep dislike of traditional fireplaces was fostered, she says, through years of married life in unpleasant Royal Air Force [RAF] houses, while working as an RAF dentist. Bronwen, recently split from a long-term boyfriend, has moved out of their flat to a house rented from a family member, shared with her sister and a friend. The television is placed below their original mantelpiece, also in the narrow back sitting room (as the front room is a bedroom), due to limited space. Their biographies and photographs can be viewed online (Hurdley 2012).

Performing identities

The too-big pebble: Julia

RH: And would you say you're kind of – I suppose, the way you think a fireplace and mantelpiece should be; do you think that comes from childhood memories or from somewhere else?

Julia: I think it's whatever you see around. I mean obviously they're quite personal to me but I think a lot of people would think, well, I suppose, 'She's got a VW van stuck on there', do you know what I mean? And the pebble, I mean I started collecting pebbles when my brother died four years ago, so I think that's why I pick up – it's just that one won't fit in my pot, do you know what I mean?

RH: Yes.

Julia: So I think it's quite personal probably to me. I don't know, I'm sure other people have got very – things like out of a magazine, you know. I mean, to put on ... but that wouldn't be me, you know.

RH: No, so you're not influenced by –

Julia: I put it there because I think the colours look nice but I've also put things that are personal to me, rather than just because I think that would look good because I'd seen it in a magazine, you know.

RH: No, so do you get those sort of magazines like, oh, was it *House and Home* [a glossy home interiors monthly magazine] and –

Julia: – yes, well, I work in – I am a district nurse so all the old dears give me all their magazines.

RH: Oh.

Julia: So I do get quite a few, but yes. So I do look through them but I don't you know, often – I wouldn't go and buy them then.

RH: No.

Julia: Yes.

RH: And so do you –

Julia: Does that make sense?

RH: Yes – no, I know exactly what you mean. When I was in hospital, it's like, I'll read them in hospital –

Julia: – yes –

RH: – but I won't –

Julia: – yes, or if you're going on a train somewhere, you think, 'Oh, I'll pick these up', but you wouldn't normally – you wouldn't get them regularly.

RH: No, no. And so you don't get that – because sometimes I look at them and think, 'Oh, my god! My house is nothing like that!' You get that sort of –

Julia: – yes, yes. And I mean, you could go on forever doing your house but you know, your house is here long after, isn't it? And you know, you've got to get on with living and I think –

RH: – yes –

Julia: – that's how I think, anyway.

RH: So you're not kind of – like *Changing Rooms* [a popular home makeover television programme]. You're not sort of –

Julia: – no. I like it to look fairly tidy and nice, but it's not always the case! If you'd seen the dust on it earlier – because with working, you can't do it, so something has to go and that's what it is for me really, you know.

Although Julia's husband, Dan, filled in the postal questionnaire, I ask if I might also interview her separately. Both the pebble and the VW van model flank the hearth, being too big for the mantelpiece, and the pebble is too big for Julia's pebble pot, yet neither has been sidelined to less prominent positions in the house. The couple's accounts refer to both, but with slight nuances of meaning. Whereas Julia mentions her brother's death in relation to her habit of pebble-collecting, Dan says only that they got the pebble on the beach because it was 'smooth and round'. On the other hand, he mentions that Julia's brother used to drive a VW van 'almost identical' to the model she gave him. Not only is this a kind of remembrance, it is a 'nice' 'funny' thing to have, whereas Julia comments only that it was for Dan's 40th birthday. Neither is what could be called an heirloom, but both are enmeshed in processes of grieving and remembering, within the practice of family life, birthday celebration and selection of things to display in the home.

Dan invokes Julia – her taste, colour sensibility, DIY, purchase of fresh flowers, birthday card from her mother – throughout his account of the mantelpiece display. In turn, she uses the first person singular and the term 'personal to me' during our dialogue. This wholly circumscribed system of doing the display is set against those who turn outwards to magazines for their 'look', and who might criticise her idiomatic 'look'. An aesthetic without this idiom is implicitly criticised – it is for those who do not work. They regularly buy and consume what for her is rare leisure reading or accidental gifts, accepted to please her patients (Goffman 1959: 51). In a way, by reading the magazines while she is travelling, she is excused by being taken out of herself; her identity is in transit. Nevertheless, it is important for her to demonstrate that she is familiar with these fashions. Further, by asserting that 'living' is, by default, *not* striving to make the house perfect, she implies that those who do are *not* 'getting on with living'. The comment that houses outlive people is juxtaposed with her brother's death, marked by the happenstance pebble, in contrast to the fashion mob who attempt domestic perfection – a delusion since magazine fashion, like life, moves ever onward. And the melancholy counterpoint to the story is the strange partnership of housebound 'old dears' and glossy exhortations to perfect the house. They cannot get on with living, nor can they do more than view – and pass on – the shiny paper dreams of the House Beautiful.

This short morality play addresses mortality, and seemingly mundane ways of dealing with it: picking up pebbles and doing less around the house. It is also about sacrifice; house labour has had 'to go' for the sake of work outside the home. However, Julia lets me know that she has done house labour prior to my visit, despite her busy work schedule outside the home – pressing me to imagine her vivid recollection of the dust. The agonistic strategy that she uses, contrasting her way of thinking and doing things with that 'other', is tempered by her occasional magazine reading, her dusting for me, and her non-confrontational 'for me', makes it impossible for me to disagree. By questioning me with 'Does that make sense?', deploying other rhetorical questions and her scenario of 'you' on the train journey, Julia calls for the same complicity. Through these devices to engage me as an audience/spectator – for her mantelpiece display and her account of it – her idiom becomes universal sense.

The proud candlestick: Bronwen

> *RH*: And could you just talk me through one or two things? I know you labelled them in the questionnaire, but maybe, talk about where they come from and if they've got any particular meaning to you?
>
> *Bronwen*: Yes, okay. The two, like, candles at either end, those are, those are additions because we've just been sort of buying things in Ikea and they weren't deliberately put there. We've just had a barbecue outside

and when we've come in it's just been put, so they're a sort of accidental decision.

The plant on that end my mother bought for me years ago, which I never really took to, but it's growing. So, it's stayed there. The post-card's from my mum from when she went away.

This blue candlestick with the flower in, my oldest sister got for me years ago when I first went to university. So that's come with me from house to house to house. But part of the reason that's there is, my ex-boyfriend hated it and made me keep it in a cupboard. So that now I've come down here and I've got a new place and everything, I said, 'It's got to have pride of place', and put it right in the front there.

RH: Restored.

Bronwen: Yes, so I'm quite happy with that.

RH: Do you particularly like it or is it just ...?

Bronwen: Yes, I do but as well, it's more, when people give you things, you do get given objects that you feel obliged to put them around the house, but the stuff here is stuff that I like, otherwise it wouldn't, you know, I'd have to look at it all the time basically. If I don't like it, I find somewhere better for it. But no, I do like that, we do. It reminds me of my sister and it reminds me of that time in my life, really.

RH: And is it bound up with kind of joy at leaving a relationship?

Bronwen: I think it's the situation because I wasn't, I wasn't happy and all that stuff. My guess is, as time goes by and you get more confident in yourself again, it's nice to think, 'Well, this is mine now. I have owner-ship and I'm happy'. Not that I think it consciously when I look at it though.

RH: Is there at all, that kind of memory, when you look at it, or is it just in sort of telling me that you remember?

Bronwen: It's more in telling you. I mean, when I put it there, I thought, 'Oh yes, this was from my sister'. But it's not, I don't think you con-sciously think of it. I think you put them there because someone's given them to you. You think, 'I'll put that there and then it's on display'. But I don't look, not every time I think, 'Oh, my sister', or anything. I wouldn't sit and look at my mantelpiece, but you're kind of aware of it being there aren't you?

Throughout our interview, Bronwen emphasises the care she has taken to avoid making the mantelpiece display 'personal' to her, as it is a shared house (note the 'we' in this extract). The fact that she, unlike the other two, has previously had a living room of her own, means that she has lots of living room 'objects' which can go on a mantelpiece; also she would lack the room in her bedroom for these now. She has left the wall space above the mantel bare, however, because it is so 'focal', and wants 'the girls' to choose something with her. Although they do not feel dominated by her display work, she feels wary, and wants them to take part. The more obvious negotiations and conflicts about possession space in a shared rented house also illuminate the often hidden or unspoken processes that go on in other 'shared' houses – of couples (like Bronwen's former partnership) and families.

Bronwen and her housemates moved into the house two months previously, and like so many recent movers, have been to Ikea (a popular homeware store). This seems so ordinary it is barely worth attending to. However, three points need emphasising. First, not everyone goes to Ikea. It is not the cheapest place for domestic furnishing and equipment. Second, not everyone who has decided to buy certain goods there also does that picking up of extra minor purchases such as candles and tealights – the little bits and pieces that fill up a house. Last, a trip to Ikea is an alternative to other sources of cheap – and cheaper – furniture. Second-hand furniture shops were once the only place for cheap furniture. A long-time owner of two of these shops (where I once worked) has seen prices and sales drop since the rise of Ikea in Britain – even of once-prised 19th-century dressers and chests of drawers. A sample of one is not 'data'; however, while participants gave accounts of goods from 'Ikea', antiques, gifts, things passed on by 'family', or 'finds', they did not talk of 'second-hand' items. The candles, at either end of the mantel, look like the fixtures of traditional display, but this 'look' belies their contemporariness. Placed there without thought, by someone coming in from a barbecue in the back garden, they are part of a more recent tradition of summer socialising at home. In contrast, the plant has earned its place on the mantel, through survival, rather than any fondness for it. Not Bronwen's choice, like the candlestick from her sister, it is a gift that she feels 'obliged' to display. However, gifts she really doesn't like would be put somewhere 'better'.

This obligation to the giver has some limits. The fact that her ex-boyfriend made her put the candlestick in a cupboard highlights the difficult negotiations couples can go through to display objects one does not like (Chapman 1999b), and where one cannot balance this dislike with an attachment to the giver, or the memory of the time of giving. Her memory of her sister, and the time in her life when she was given it, now has another layer of meaning: restoration and possession of both domestic space and a happier state of mind. Highlighted in her account is the moment of putting the candlestick on the mantelpiece, rather than an ongoing reiteration of meanings with every glance at the mantel. After all, this would be exhausting. Like the postcard, placed there after reading, it is as if that first emplacement brings with it a laying down of the meanings, brought out (and transformed) only when voiced to another. Noticeable also is how 'looking at it all the time' is set up in opposition to 'wouldn't sit and look' and simply being 'aware'.

The dating agency: Eric

RH: Then your medication?

Eric: Oh, my pills, sorry about that.

RH: Is that to remind you to take them?

Eric: Yes, I think a lot of people do that. I mean they're out of the reach of children and yes, they're there to remind me. I'll always forget them. They make me feel unwell for a while, a bit nauseous, and my hand shakes like that [holds hand out]. Sometimes I've got to use two hands. It's only for about an hour. First thing in the day, never mind.

RH: And a mug.

Eric: I bought that in Barcelona, the year I married my first wife. We bought it in, do you know Barcelona?

RH: I was there this year, yes.

Eric: You've been there, lovely. Well, did you go to the Spanish Village?

RH: No.

Eric: Well, there's a place called 'The Spanish Village', which is a sort of park, it's like a theme park. It's not a theme park, it's rather like that. But the themes are Spanish culture. So they have a glass-blowing works, they make pots like that out of corkwood. You know, sort of crafts. And it's very interesting. That's in Barcelona, or in the outskirts.

RH: Then you've got a, is that a jewel box?

Eric: That's my hearing aid.

RH: Ah, hearing aid jewel box.

Eric: Terrible, isn't it?

RH: And a magnifying glass, is that?

Eric: That's, I don't really need that. I use it for some things; if I examine my hearing aid, I really need that to blow it up. It just magnifies well.

RH: And then some letters, are they letters?

Eric: No. My worst complaint is loneliness. A few years ago I joined one of these dating agencies and I lapsed and rejoined in April this year. I've been out with two nice women in the last month. One of them is a County Councillor, no less, and she's very nice though. I'm very fond of her, honestly. But she's so busy I just don't see her. So I don't want to go out with one or two at the same time. But I spoke to one who is on the list and I met her last week. But I won't let it go on for long and I hope it resolves itself soon. So there we are. I'm a bit old-fashioned like that.

So many married couples had wedding gifts on display, and things bought that were memories of places visited 'together', that it was a surprise to hear an account of an object that was a souvenir from the first year of a failed marriage. What this story did was question the conventional way in which objects are understood as connective tissue in joint memory-making, and celebrating union (Purbrick 2007). Eric is neither celebrating his former marriage, nor 'hiding' the memory by hiding the pot away or getting rid of it. This illuminates the work that goes into *making* memory and meaning, and using these to construct particular identities, particularly as a joint enterprise. Eric apologises to me for the sight of his ageing body's requirements. Yet to hide them away would cause problems for him. Good display practice and management of the body conflict. As if to repair this, he emphasises he doesn't 'need' the magnifying glass – his sight is not failing, and it is a 'good' magnifier. My sight, however, fails, in that I view the hearing aid container as a jewel box, imagining adornment where none is intended.

Although apologetic about his physical frailty, he is very firm about his moral standing; the descriptions of women from the dating agency are not a sign of a Lothario, but a temporary situation while he waits for resolution. Like many of the objects he has on display, the things we talk about in this extract are for the day, the moment, and useful, with a few 'permanent' goods such as the cork pot as decoration. One of only three participants who spoke of loneliness (Rosalind, who moved frequently for her husband's job, and Sheila, who moved from her neighbourhood following divorce), he opened up that seemingly unbreakable bond between 'home' and 'family'. Eric accounted for himself as lonely, ageing, but hopeful. Further, the late modern assumption that identity is fluid, and its construction an endlessly positive project came into question. Is 'loneliness' the counter to 'individualisation', and can it, too, be reshaped through treating the self as a mouldable unit?

Not the green bunny: Annette

RH: But not – do you – is that display for you as opposed to – ?

Annette: Oh yes.

RH: Yes.

Annette: It's definitely for me yes, and in fact I have such specific ideas about it because Carol dusts round and things but I move things a millimetre back to where they were.

RH: Yes.

Annette: I mean that's how much – I know, I know if there's something out of place there. In fact probably the picture [the photograph I have taken], you might see even angles and things, but I do, I have – yes, very specific – maybe not on the shelves, but you know, everything has got its own exact little place that I know, and if it's turned slightly I'll have to turn it back.

RH: Does that drive her mad?

Annette: Yes, yes, and it drives me mad as well because she comes and moves it and, you know, and I'll move it back.

RH: And what happens? [Annette laughs] But she – do you both dust it?

Annette: Yes, yes.

RH: But what would happen if she were to say, 'Oh, I've got this, and I really like it, and I want to put it there'?

Annette: We'd negotiate on that.

RH: You'd negotiate, yes.

Annette: But with the sheep, the four little sheep, they've been negotiated in.

RH: Right –

Annette: – yes. I sometimes think they're a little bit much, but you know, it's not that bad, but more – so there's not much more we can put in there I don't think, without then moving stuff apart. Yes, so it's – but I mean we're pretty much in agreement with our style anyway so there's none of the great –

RH: No, and so would you say the display – are you the person who is kind of in charge, would you say, of what goes out?

Annette: Yes, yes, I would say, although there's been little imprints I've allowed in, like this little bunny and things that probably look a bit childish I suppose, but then, so you know, it's not high art or anything, you know, it's just something to put on there.

RH: Yes.

Annette: If it had been a green bunny I would not have accepted, you know, it's got to at least blend in a little bit I think, if that makes sense.

In this case, I interview only one partner. Whereas Julia takes complete possession of the mantelpiece in her home, Annette says that objects her partner, Carol wants to add can be 'negotiated', although it is clear that she 'allows' these in. This implicitly calls into question their 'shared' taste, particularly as she separates Carol's choices from the rest of the display as looking 'a bit childish'. The mundane conflicts over minute fractions and infractions of space, and the fact that additions will eventually result in subtractions of other things might seem trivial. Are tiny movements of objects to and from their proper place meaningful? Matter 'out of place' was the very foundation of Mary Douglas's (2002) cultural analysis. Further, the way in which Annette imagines the unacceptable 'other', the green bunny that would not fit her pattern of display, brings another dimension into play: how is presence made through absence, through the imagining of what is not to be made present? The limitation of surfaces available for display in the home requires boundary-making, not only materially, but also in the imagination. Although this is seen as a creative, personal attribute, what people invoked was something else in its commonality – a social imagination, in appeals to me, sympathetic spectator of the stage-set and complicit audience for its narrator. While the conventional image of 'home' puts women inside, managing comfort and display, Annette's account counters this. Between the two women, spatial subtractions and additions are marked out in careful double-entry book-keeping (Munro 1999) where taste also counts. How might this relate to social memory? The care, artifice and expertise of the builders of memory in Chapter 3 suggest much of the attachment to social memory is made in the telling, and knowing how to listen. Auditory culture, as much as visual and material, is bound up in these networks of belonging (Bull and Back 2003).

A host of other identities, people and worlds crowd these little dramas. Not so easily split into past, present and future, these oscillate in and out of focus, as 'what if' Carol turned up with a green bunny and 'if only' the County Councillor would make up her mind. Things accrete meaning as time passes – the sister's gift is now a statement of ownership – but not in archaeological layers – the new meaning both depends upon and transforms the last. Meaning is both palpable and manipulable around these objects, and conventional terminology such as 'wedding present', 'heirloom', 'souvenir' become doubtful. Ideas of ownership, control and negotiation are also tentative and conditional, as is the very question of what 'making home' means. Annette says this is not 'high art', yet the effort of maintaining her aesthetic space requires an finely honed sensibility for colour and spatial relations. What are the 'rules' for this folk art?

Conclusion: imagining others

These are not stories in the conventional sense, with a beginning, a middle and an end, since they all have an active listener, prompting, agreeing, asking questions. During interviews, there were narratives such as these, some of which will be discussed in the chapters to come. But 'off-the-cuff' stories within a conversation tend to have this interactive character, as the question or encouraging 'yes' from the listener leads to expansion or focus, a new direction, or clarification (Holstein and Gubrium 1995). However, they story objects in a particular way, which also present their tellers as moral beings, as everyday heroes. As such, they are conventional narratives (Plummer 2001), political in that they produce and reproduce what is considered 'good' action. Although these stories may seem deeply ordinary, this is their potency as cultural materials. The absent 'other' is always there: the bad man; the follower of fashion; the domineering ex, the old dear, the disruptive partner, the dead. This other is not always another person; it is a possible, imagined alternative identity for the teller. In Bronwen's case, her past identity as an unhappy part of a couple is 'in the cupboard' now that the candlestick is out on her mantelpiece.

They are also stories of the negotiation and control of domestic space, awareness of the gaze of others, the multiple ways that an object ends up on the mantelpiece. This dramaturgy, re-enacting the moment that something went on display, is rarely told but is what gives these displays their implicit momentum, which – as Bronwen says – is no longer 'consciously' there if she happens to glance at the mantelpiece. But that 'beginning', so to speak, is what stories of objects relate. Julia's pebble is there through happenstance, as so many objects are, since it would not fit in her pot of pebbles. But that decision to place it on the mantelpiece makes present all those other pebbles, and the reason Julia collects them. At the same time, it is 'just' a pebble, she imagines, to the visitor. Yet the fact that she includes this imagined visitor in her account is as significant as the meaning of the pebble 'personal to me'. Even in this private process of remembering and grieving, she is not alone. Each of the extracts show how people circle round meanings, sometimes seeming to contradict themselves, confront or align themselves with imagined 'others', produce object biographies which seem intensely 'meaning-full', that are then cast aside.

I was shown round many houses – the photos in the toilet and on the kitchen wall, the shelf unit in the bedroom, beyond which a husband slept. I was offered cups of tea, fed salmon cooked in the dishwasher; dogs, cats and babies inspected me, children stared; a father-in-law took over one interview, while the rest of the family wandered off; one interview happened in a pub, and one couple talked so much the recorder ran out of space, although they said very little about the mantelpiece. As such, although a stranger, I was also a guest invited in to the home and into the workings of family life. As such, too, I was the visitor participants so often talked about – the judging, interpreting 'other', a role they also filled when visiting others.

While it would be highly unusual for someone to walk into a house in the normal run of things and urge its inhabitants to talk about what was on the mantelpiece, the fact that I did means that I have an anthology of stories about these displays. Of course, these interviews could not pass for normal conversation; these were extraordinary events. Asking people to tell me about what was on their mantelpiece produced a lot of stories, with very little talk from me, which again is a bizarre form of dialogue. What I was told were narratives of how an object came to be on the mantelpiece, rather than what 'really' happened, as if that were ever knowable. The stories I heard were chosen from a range of possible accounts a person might tell a stranger in their house, asking odd questions. And most people commented that they hadn't thought about many of the objects overmuch until I asked them, nor did they 'consciously' think of the stories when they looked at an object. Frequently, people explained the reason for displaying a particular thing as 'just because I liked it', or 'I don't know, I never really thought about it.' Couples told different stories about the same object, or picked out different things to talk about; children had very little to say. One artefact might have several narratives wound around it, and people might contradict themselves as the interviews progressed. As I suggested in Chapter 2, the mantel is not an 'either/or' space, but 'both/and', a site where ways of looking and knowing oscillate. A temple to permanence, the mantelpiece mobilises uncertainty, doubt, anxiety at the same moment that home and family, moral identities and deep social relations are embedded. While at times neither the stuff on there nor its accidental arrival seem to matter, at other times its precise position is crucial, or its visibility as a reminder for action, or even protagonist.

The mantelpiece, with its height, central position above the fireplace and limited, linear platform, raises whatever is placed on it above the ordinary run of things in the home – whether the inhabitants like it or not. The act of putting things – anything – on a mantelpiece makes meaning. The display on the mantelpiece may look static, but the possibility of a new photo, birthday card, coins pulled from a pocket, a good dusting, leaves it forever unfinished. The thought of a bare mantelpiece is 'strange' to many; none in this study had an empty mantelpiece (though this would be a striking design). Filled with ornaments, or a choice few, perhaps crammed with toys, invitations, bowls of screws, or a mix of china and oddments, the mantelpiece is looked at, commented on, judged, haggled over or ignored in favour of the television. Similarly, the absence of a mantelpiece is justified, disliked, substituted or unthought of. In having or not having a mantelpiece, in using it for a tidy display, tinsel at Christmas, or the remote control, and in looking at and commenting on the mantelpieces of others, people make homes and participate in the making of meaning. Part of this activity might be about a 'look', a 'period feel' or some notion of 'homeliness', and this aestheticisation of the fireplace is a cultural process. Bound up in this are other processes: the production, maintenance, negotiation, presentation and performance of identities through practices of display. While the connection between home, family and memory is taken for granted, the precise ways in which this works out as everyday process, together with aesthetic and identity work, is a complex, happenstance, uncomfortable negotiation.

Although individuals might shrink from any notion of 'conscious' meaning-making practices, this is what every one of the study's participants was doing – even if they did nothing at all. Culture is making materials meaningful through selection, management and order – what can and cannot be put on display and where; what arrangements of things are appropriate, and what stories are good to tell, if some strange guest should happen to enquire. It is also about where to look, and how to look. The child who did not look at the mantelpiece, because he watched the television against the opposite wall, was as much part of making culture as his father, who had nailed the shelf up, his mother who had put things on it, and his long-dead great-grandmother, whose vase, unknown to her, was on this makeshift mantel (see Chapter 3). Bronwen's term 'accidental decision' expresses the politics of paradox – of 'knowing what not to know' (Taussig 1999) – that characterises some participants' accounts. To permit 'accident' is a decision in itself.

As this chapter ends, a low-flying RAF fighter jet roars above the cottage, the sound threatening to crash through the ancient walls. The house martin, a presence in these hills for centuries, seems like the fragile creature of a moment compared with this modern beast. Raising my eyes, I look above the kitchen range – oil-fired now – to see only flat wall, the mantel long gone. A fly still sits on the table; the dog still slumbers, although days have passed. The fighter jet is the violent uproar of movement through vast space, of time as global, technological progress. But what of small, uncounted moments and movements that seem like nothing at all? Careful scrutiny of the dramaturgy expressed in and through interview dialogues suggests understandings are never prescriptive nor complete, but ongoing and nuanced. The 'genesis moment' of an object's distinction as a 'mantelpiece object', the territory wars over mere millimetres, the daily decision to live, rather than dust, are fleetingly touched upon, yet are as significant as the big stories of life changes.

In her study about sex workers and 'memory', Day challenges the dominant discourse of 'what biographies should be', in the timing and social recognition of transitions, such as marriage, births, school and wedding photographs, '...metaphors of continuity and integration that are so prominent in biographical idioms and yet so clearly untrue to life' (2007: 173). The measuring out of lives in mantelpiece millimetres seems such common practice, and so comforting, that the effort that goes into making these lives 'countable' gets lost. As Douglas commented: 'The high triumph of institutional thinking is to make the institutions completely invisible' (1986: 98). The interview interaction, the mantelpiece, and biographical narratives, are 'telling' of how this world shapes, and is shaped by consent: 'Our social interaction consists very much in telling each other what right thinking is, and passing blame on wrong thinking. This is indeed how we build institutions, squeezing each other's ideas into a common shape, so we can prove righteousness by sheer numbers of independent assent' (Douglas 1986: 91).

As I talk over this chapter with David Morgan, his reading of it has prompted his memory of a story related in Bede's 8th-century history. A human life is likened to that of a sparrow flying momentarily into a warm hall, before flying out once again into the winter darkness (Book 2, Chapter 3). Even a little, serendipitous story becomes refracted with meaning, intelligible in different ways once it is heard, retold and effectively, remade. This chapter looked at how things are made 'telling', and in turn, how people make themselves 'tellable' and 'intelligible' (Bourdieu 1986; Butler 2004a; Skeggs and Wood 2009). It might have seemed that choice, and its twin, chance, were in the hands of those tellers. The trick of the concept of the individualised 'self' (for example, Giddens 1991; Beck 1992;

Rose 1998; Bauman 2001a; Beck and Beck-Gernsheim 2002) is to make it seem as if that were the case. But there is one particular shape of thing that is persistently entangled in relational practices, in the telling and retelling – remaking – of things and persons. The next chapter pursues the genesis of this distinct and meaning-full thing: the gift.

5
Relating the Gift

> To ask about the gender of the gift, then, is to ask about the situation of gift exchange in relation to the form that domination takes in these societies. It is also to ask about the 'gender' of analytical concepts, the worlds that particular assumptions sustain.
>
> (Strathern 1988: xii)

Introduction: negotiating ambiguity

The last chapter focused on how relations between things and people are remade in social interactions, including talk, writing, dusting, commemorating the dead and the other work of home. It emphasised how seemingly static displays of objects can be understood as ongoing processes of identity, as both relation and performance, intimately connected with the politics of family, home and beyond. This chapter focuses on a particular sort of thing/process, the gift, since this allows close scrutiny of the frictions between the different demands of identity work. In late modernity, the aestheticisation of everyday life by individual consumers (Featherstone 1991) is a sociological concept embedded in, and also confirming the notion of the late modern individual. However, the ambiguous status of the gift-for-display is a dimension of domesticity that questions this. Working through the idea of the gift as a 'structuring structure' (Bourdieu 1977, 1979, 1986) also disturbs other 'givens', such as the mantelpiece and, in turn, the home as present practice.

The gift-for-display is especially salient for examining relations between identity of the person, his or her home and family, since all of them, effectively, are recipients of the gift. Over time, identities might change, but things stay the same. If identity is so wrapped up in the selection and orderly display of things in the home, how can people incorporate the disruptive potential of gifts? And how do they negotiate the equally delicate act of giving, or passing on, such things, knowing that these might not 'fit in' with the aesthetic of the house or the person? If the gift 'relation' unavoidably attaches things to people, and gift-giving constitutes social belonging, how can unwanted gifts be disposed of? Four threads of the 'problem' of the gift were particularly noticeable during the interviews: such gifts are commonly given to women; the female partner/mother commonly had more to say about gifts' provenance than men (in heterosexual couple/family households); the materiality of gifts was problematic; and people called some things 'gifts' even when they had chosen and/or bought them themselves.

Women's interview accounts form the greater basis for this chapter. This was not my selection practice; it was principally women who received gifts for themselves that were also gifts for the home. Further, it was more often women who said they bought themselves domestic display objects if they received money as a present. This is similar, if not analogous, to the conflation of woman and the domestic interior in traditional Berber houses (Bourdieu 1977). Bourdieu provided a critique of gift society as 'collective deception' and the advancement of market capitalism as a disenchantment, a refusal to continue with the cost of this colluding delusion (1977, 1979). The unequal relations of gift-giving have been related to the maintenance of gendered emotional and domestic work and consequently to social and economic anxieties concerning inequality, divorce and the commodification of emotion (Cheal 1987; Hochschild 1989; Belk 1996). For example, the commodification of social relations invested in gifts, and the 'symbolic violence' of gift hierarchies, has been a concern for sociologists (Bourdieu 1977; Cheal 1988; Godbout 1998 [1992]). In particular, Christmas has been a focus for the view of the gift as commodity (Belk 1993) and the domestication of previously socially explicit hierarchies of exchange (Nissenbaum 1997), with specific attention on the parent/child relation (Werbner 1996), as well as gendered tensions highlighted by the event. Christmas, therefore, is a central ritual in the temporality of the gift (Miller 1993), as are weddings (Purbrick 2007). The 'calendar' of gift-giving is produced on the mantelpiece as event cards, for Christmas, birthdays, anniversaries, Mothering Sunday and Fathers' Day, which stay up for varying periods of time. However, the gift-for-display is ever-present in domestic performances of belonging. The mantelpiece is a key site – a monument, if you like – in the landscape of this gift relation.

Gift exchange within modern commodity exchange societies is now seen as complex and research has centred on unpacking the rules, meanings and functions of the gift relation (see Agnew 2003). For example, the anonymity of money (Simmel 1978) has been contested by work on the gift relation (Zelizer 1994; Miller 2001c). Zelizer argues that impersonal, alienated/ing goods and meanings of the market are constantly appropriated by consumer practices. This accords with Appadurai (1986b) and Kopytoff (1986) arguing that the form of the good as 'commodity' is only a moment in its biography. The embedding of gift exchange in the market has led to a review of commodification in general. For example, Miller (1998) has argued that everyday shopping practices have replaced gift exchange, rather than the now commodified world of gift-giving. In a conflation of market and reciprocal circuits of exchange, the notion of 'gifts-to-self' questions both the validity of separating the two spheres, and the value of consumption theories that ignore the continuing hold of 'the gift' over the social imagination (see Mick 1996). Cash is not put on display in the home (Leal 1995: 316), but reconciling taste and the varying sentiments of household members with the gift relation is difficult (Chapman 1999b). However, cash is often given as a gift between close family members (Douglas and Isherwood 1979).

This blurring of rigid boundaries between market and gift economy is most interesting in the gift-to-self. It was noticeable how many of the informants said that most of their display objects were gifts, even though they had bought many of them (for) themselves. Thus, 'the gift' – even this paradoxical 'gift-to-self' – is made more visible than 'the commodity' in interview talks. Bourdieu (1977) argues that a period of time must elapse between receiving and reciprocating a gift, the 'visible manifestation' of one's social relations. The gift-to-self apparently deletes this passing of social time – as well as passing a thing between persons. Is this disappearance of difference and periodicity in gift exchange the same as the removal of gift exchange as a *'préstation totale'*, a total social fact (Mauss 1990 [1950])? How do people negotiate the gift, gift-to-self, gift-for-display as materials of/for belonging and identity, self and others? The first interview account with Ruth unwraps the complexities of contemporary gift practice, detailed in the later sections. The participants are named at the head of each section, so their photographs and biographies can be viewed online (Hurdley 2012).

To thine own self be true? The problem of the gift

Reciprocity and the reverse heirloom: Ruth

I asked Ruth what she would save in the event of a house fire. She has many display areas in her living room, filled with heirlooms, presents, things she has bought and photographs of her family. Yet amidst all of this stuff, she would take one object besides the photographs of her children and grandchildren: a small china dog. Some 20 years previously, Ruth gave her daughter £4 to take on a school day trip to Tenby. Rather than spend it on sweets or things for herself, the child returned having spent all her mother's money on a gift – for her mother. This perfect gift exchange, in which money given was immediately translated and reciprocated in the form of a material object, is perhaps the most intense example of the process by which people embed or crystallise social relations in inalienable goods. It does contend with Bourdieu's (1977) argument that a period of time should elapse between reciprocal gift exchange, and raises interesting questions regarding hierarchies of exchange and symbolic violence (Bourdieu 1977; Werbner 1996):

> Alison came round with the teapots because she sent for them, and said, 'Oh, I don't like this one, you can have this one'. The Peter Pan one, she bought as a present to come home from Disneyland [...]. It's not that I don't like the teapots, but if you're thinking of just grabbing and running, I think it would have to be [the china dog] – it means quite a lot, because, as I say, she didn't have all that much money, and to give her four pounds, and she ends up coming home, and 'What did you buy – spend all your money?' I knew that she must have spent most of her money on that, and she was about eleven, I suppose, twelve, so I would try and grab that, and all the pictures, obviously, because you don't like the thought of pictures going up in flames.

Ruth does not mention all the heirlooms she has gathered about her, from her parents, grandmother and husband's family. Although most families no longer inherit large objects, many continue to receive small heirlooms such as ornaments. A well-known elaboration of 'curatorial consumption', for example, highlights one woman's role in memorialising her family and thus granting herself 'belonging' by filling her house with inherited goods (McCracken 1991: 44). However, this once taken-for-granted passage of goods through time has become incommensurable (in some respects) with expressions of taste in dressing oneself and dressing the home (Miller D. 1995; Banim and Guy 2001). This is a theme in many informants' accounts, highlighting the difficult interaction between traditional inheritance rituals and the conflation of taste and self-identity.

Ruth does, however, mention the huge collection of teapots that covers a broad display shelf in the living room and has spread to other areas of the house. This collection was not her choice; her daughter joined a teapot collectors' club, but gave her mother any she did not like. She then started to buy her mother teapots from holiday places, and then other family members began to give Ruth teapots too. They take up a lot of space, but are imbued with little meaning by their owner. Nor does she use them for their designed function. Other informants had 'suffered' aspects of this fate: the designated collector, the recipient of souvenirs or the repository of unwanted objects still labelled as 'gifts' – reverse heirlooms, in a way.

The giving of money, particularly to one's children for the self-purchase of presents, has also become prevalent (according to people I interviewed), thus transferring the responsibility and the power of selection from giver to recipient (see also Douglas and Isherwood 1979; Corrigan 1995). In this account, Ruth's daughter turns this transferral on its head, just as she reverses the heirloom process by giving her mother unwanted objects as gifts. Many informants told me stories about choosing their own presents, of contributing to the cost of their own gifts, and one even bought her own heirloom. Many also spoke about the problems of storage and disposal of objects; in particular, things they had received as gifts. The 'throwaway society' is not so quick to destroy things which are still so powerfully invested with memory, emotion and relations with others. Yet at a time when 'stuff' has never been so cheap, and the private space of home has been opened up to scrutiny as a place of and for consumption, ritualised gift exchange can no longer be taken for granted. Various aspects of the gift in transition will be explored, which Ruth's tale of teapots and china dogs has opened up for us.

Sorting out junk and treasure: Shyam

There has clearly been a transition from the accounts of display practices in Mass Observation *Mantelpiece Reports* from 1937 (see Chapter 2). Then, volunteers reportedly displayed objects whether they liked them or not, and kept things on display even when they were broken. Souvenirs from relatives, from the Far East, the continent and British seaside resorts were put on the mantelpiece. Older people in the contemporary study also recalled similar assemblages, and some had retained this custom of display on their current mantelpieces. However, there was a sense of a change in attitudes towards this customary form of home décor, as Shyam, aged 74, related:

> Until last week the cabinet was full of china that was about sixty/seventy years old. Foreign china there was because my dad kept a boarding house and the men used to bring mementoes home. They brought these two tea sets and a coffee set and when you held it up to the light there's a woman's face at the bottom of the cup and I actually seen a piece in the Echo [local paper] last night about it: 'For Sale', a china cup, it was a joke really, 'For Sale', a cup with a lady's face in the bottom. Well that was the two sets that I had and I thought well I know my girls; if anything happened to me they're just going to bundle everything up. That may sound morbid but you do, you don't always want all the old rubbish your family has collected but they both said they wanted the tea set. So I said well there's only a tea set and coffee set, you can choose between yourselves. As long as one of you takes the cabinet so now I am waiting for the cabinet to go. Linda [daughter] has on her mantelpiece, as you say probably from me, a candle, candlestick and a clock and a vase, I think.

Shyam's story is interesting, since I visited her just after her daughter Linda had prompted her to clear her living room mantelpiece and, as she relates here, clear the old china cabinet that her husband has always thought a waste of space. Although Shyam has retained and displayed all her family's goods, she knows that her daughters, both aged around 40, do not have the same attitudes towards heirlooms (see McCracken 1991). Their houses are carefully renovated period properties with, as she thinks, beautifully ornamented interiors. That old assumption, that one's inalienable family goods can be entrusted to the next generation, is no longer valid (contrast Weiner 1985; Chevalier 1999), and Shyam is dealing with this transition with a pre-mortem clear out to save her daughters the bother of getting rid of unwanted, antiquated (as opposed to antique) objects.

Paradoxically, her daughter continues to decorate her period mantelpiece in the same way as her mother has done; she has, however, selected the items for display herself. Shyam's mantelpiece display includes a bird ornament that belonged to her dead sister, a perpetual calendar (so popular in the 1930s) from her aunt and an ornament that her daughter gave her. Like Ruth's daughter, she was disposing of unwanted goods by giving them to her mother. Whereas Ruth had to keep the teapots because they were quite costly (and therefore could not be thrown away), Shyam's daughter was given the ornament as a leaving present from work; the morals of gift exchange preclude throwing it away. By giving it to her mother as a 'gift', she avoids destroying the network of relations imbued in the object. Shyam, therefore, has a dual responsibility: to dispose of unwanted heirlooms, and to store unwanted gifts. She finds the current absorption with certain antiques – such as the china cups – amusing, thus highlighting the curious distinctions that are made between desirable antiques and junk shop bric-a-brac.

Buy-it-yourself heirlooms: Harriet

Harriet tells me this story about a pair of silver candlesticks on her mantelpiece, which is covered with a lacy cloth and an entirely silver display. It was interesting that her mantelpiece was a pine shelf her husband had put up on the wall behind the sofa, since the original fireplace had been removed. This demonstrates how people construct their material environments; it was Harriet's house, Harriet's mantelpiece and Harriet's heirloom. It was comforting, at a time when lifestyle magazines and supplements are promoting certain orders of taste and design, to discover idiomatic constructions of home interiors (Gregory 2003):

> The candlesticks my mother gave me, she had a burglary about two years ago and they cleaned the house out basically and she had lots of lovely antique stuff and like, with the insurance money, she said that I – my brother, sister and I – were to choose something, so that's what I chose with the money she gave me.

What was most noticeable, however, was the way in which Harriet had translated a cheque from an insurance company into a gift from her mother (see Keane 2001 for money's 'vulnerability to slippage' – used by Harriet to advantage). In fact, this was more than a gift, it was a replacement for an object that had been in her mother's possession, but also contained its potential role as heirloom. Such a transformation was conditional on her mother's death. This implied condition had been destroyed, however, when her mother's goods were stolen. In effect, that thing had 'died'; the relations invested and made material in it had been transferred to the candlesticks. Whatever object had been assigned to Harriet would now be an object for purchase, for new meanings – a new biography – in a shop or stall.

Since the intended transformation had been prevented, a new transformation took place. The original objects were converted to insured, stolen goods, which could then be turned into money. However, rather than Harriet's mother going out and buying herself new display items, she bypassed this stage in the conversion process of money: to her object, thence daughter's heirloom. Instead, she allowed her children to buy things with the insurance money and ascribe to these objects the role of pre-mortem heirloom. Whereas Shyam had undertaken a pre-death clearout of objects, effectively ending their biographies as heirlooms, Harriet's mother had dealt with the problem of inheritance by giving her children the power of selection and ascription. This also offers a solution for the problematic gift relation when different family members contest ownership of a symbolically significant heirloom (see Finch 1997). She had 'insured' the heirlooms.

Counting clocks: Adrian

Adrian spoke to me in his university office, using a sketch he had made of his mantelpiece display on the back of a letter from Sky TV. It was an ordered mantelpiece, however, and easy to understand in terms of conventionalised display. There was a mirror above it, and a clock in the middle:

> The clock was a wedding present and I think we had about three carriage clocks! And one of them just ended up there. I have to say I never – well, infrequently use it to tell the time because there's clocks on the video [in 2012, a DVD player] and all kinds of things around the room that I use in preference.

The clock is not used to tell the time; it is, as Adrian says later, the 'automatic' clock at the centre of the mantelpiece. It is, similarly, the automatic wedding gift. As markers of important ritual events, clocks also take a central role; changes in their function as gifts and time displays therefore suggest other transitions in social practices and relations. Older informants, such as Eric, spoke of the clock on the mantelpiece as a special object, only to be wound by father, an expensive object that might be given as a retirement present, and used to tell the time (even if it was wrong).

Adrian and his wife received three wedding clocks; two are stored away, and it is unlikely they will be displayed. It is also unlikely that something so ritually bound up and so costly will be thrown away at this point in their lives (mid-thirties). Both the stored clocks and the displayed clock are taking up space in the home. All of them were given automatically; Adrian cannot recall who gave them the clock on the mantelpiece, so that particular, personal relation is not present. It is associated with a happy event, but also connects with the unwanted clocks; all three are displayed in a way, as a reminder of the problem of materialising ritual events in objects: what is to be done with them? The 'wedding list' is increasingly used to deal with this problem, and cash is now the British couple's 'most wanted' gift (Purbrick 2007). This is seen as distasteful by some people, but makes sense at a time when many couples live together and assemble many necessities of home life before marriage. Also, without the guidance of a list, guests are stuck with the problem of choice, and resort to the conventional – resulting in a multitude of the same objects, none of which can be redefined as 'alienable goods' and cast out (Gregson and Crewe 2003; Gregson 2007).

'No ... no more ballerinas': Annette

Storage of wedding gifts is not the only problem. There is a certain equivalence between the 'automated' ritual of wedding presents, and the way in which some people have collections imposed on them accidentally, but to the great convenience of gift-givers. As one can see in every city centre, there are shops that exist with the sole purpose of providing this particular species of gift that has no function or role besides those of solving the problem of ritual gift-giving at a time when many people have everything they need, of being 'the wedding gift' or 'collectible'. Such a shop sells a particular type of china ornament that I encountered only in this exploration of mantelpiece displays: figurines from Lladró pottery in Spain. There are many websites devoted to selling, buying and telling stories about these figures (for example, Lladró 2012). Each one has an official story and is usually part of a collection or 'family' of figurines. Some are made with specific events in mind, such as the birth of a child, Mothering Sunday, Valentine's Day and, of course, weddings. They could be viewed as representations of the absolute commodification of social ritual and gift relations, and were displayed on many mantelpieces, irrespective of any socio-economic categorisations. However, their recipients did not view them as commodified relations; many of them were much-loved objects and were connected closely with accounts of memorable occasions and family relations.

However, such 'collectibles' – unlike books or chocolates or kitchen utensils – could become problematic, should the recipient rebel or the occasion they commemorate change from a happy memory to a different life. The following account, concerning a collection of Lladró ornaments and Scottish crystalware, shows the problem that an individual contends with following a complete change in lifestyle and identity. The second, in which a woman tells of her burgeoning collection of hedgehog ornaments, contrasts with the first, in that the narrator is less troubled by the assignation of 'collector' identity (see Dittmar 1992: 98).

Annette has changed her lifestyle and, to some extent, her identity. Previously married and living in RAF houses, she is now divorced and lives with her female partner in a modern house that she owns. On her move to Wales, she started to collect sheep, which I shall discuss later. She also has a collection of Lladró china figures. These are expensive gifts from her parents:

> I think luckily my parents are in Scotland so they don't visit very often because their taste and my taste in somewhat removed, hence – though I do still keep the Lladró pieces through there because they tend to buy me them. They've stopped now I did say, 'No, no more Lladró, no more ballerinas and stuff because that's not just me', so I have said no to that.

She has put the Lladró figures in a cabinet in her dining room, separate from the main display unit that is the focal point of her living room, and which contains a careful selection of ornaments that commemorate aspects of her biography she wants to recall. As well as the china, wedding gifts of china and Scottish crystal are kept in the cabinet:

> That's from my previous marriage so it's more – I look on that [in the dining room] as definitely as a storage area... but this [in the living room] is more reflecting my personality. That's a different mood, but I do think it's a shame not to show the pieces off because some of it's quite expensive. [...] They are a different part of my life so they don't perhaps fit in with my lifestyle now as they did, but I still think the crystal stuff is beautiful, sort of Edinburgh crystal which of course because I'm Scottish I've got a sentimental attachment to that.[...] But it's functional as well because I have to store it somewhere. I suppose I could wrap it all up and put it in the garage but I do like it on display but I very – no, I use them very rarely. I have other crystal I prefer to use which is much less ornate than that stuff. [...] It's very much the old me I suppose but it still was a part of my life so I don't suppose I want to erase it altogether. [...] But it's not like a constant reminder of the past. [...] I just think it's quite nice stuff that doesn't deserve to be put away. [...] Not quite yet anyway.

In response to my question whether it is partly the expense of the items that stops her putting them away, Annette says that this is the case (although she had not thought of it in this way before):

> It does seem a shame to put it all away when obviously there's a lot of money spent acquiring it all for me so perhaps there is an element of that...

This story does emphasise the complications that have arisen from the habit of equating social relations and rituals with material goods. Divorce was not a commonplace until the 1970s, and the disposal of old wedding presents following divorce is a new concern. In addition, people married younger, before setting up home together, meaning that wedding presents performed a different purpose from today's routinised exchange (Purbrick 2007).

Annette also has an extensive collection of sheep, begun when she moved to Wales, due to their common association. This decision foregrounds the way in which tourism has spectacularised culture (Urry 1990; Stanley 1998; Haldrup and Larsen 2004); this has progressed from the small 'Souvenirs of Whitby' on 1937 mantelpieces and highly prized mementoes of the Orient brought back by sailors for Shyam's family. These tourist objects have become an area of production and consumption in themselves, and further-more, have become a field for constructions of meaning entirely detached from the everyday practice of – in this case – sheep-farming, wool produc-tion or eating delicious spring lamb. Indeed, the association of sheep with Wales is often a focus for lewd jokes and anti-Welsh sentiment (and in a strange turn, anti-English insults in a popular rugby song). However, these multiple meanings and practices do not destroy the particularity of Annette's decision to collect sheep, and this could be viewed as an aspect of an interest in connecting material culture to place, and hence connecting herself (as can be seen in her account of the Scottish crystal).

The original motive of her decision to collect sheep has nevertheless been appropriated by other people and undergone a transformation. She now receives many sheep from various friends and relatives, but displays only her favourites. As new ones arrive, older ones are sidelined, and eventually are stored upstairs in a spare bedroom. She has not yet thrown any away, as she has plenty of space in the house. It has four bedrooms and she has no children; the sheep, therefore, are not currently 'stealing' space from people. Logically, however, the collection will have either to be stopped, or older or unwanted sheep figures disposed of at some future point.

The accidental collector: Gina

What began as Annette's decision to make a link with her 'new country' has been transformed into an easy gift-making decision by her friends and family. This transformation of an individual decision to select specific goods to a collective decision, in a way, *not* to have to select gifts, resonated in many people's accounts. For example, the next account is given by a woman who has had to confront this problem, since she lives in a three-bedroom house with her husband and three sons. Gina likes hedgehogs, although she became a collector by 'accident'. They now take up a lot of space at home, and even in her office. She therefore has occasional 'culls', but good-humouredly continues to accept hedgehogs:

> I started collecting them when my oldest son was a baby, and it was com-pletely by accident. I saw a glass blower, and I've always been intrigued by

little hedgehogs, and he made two glass hedgehogs, and my mother-in-law bought them for me, and it stemmed from there, because once people know that you collect something, the floodgates open! So, some are more special than others; we have several hundred [laughs]! A lot of the soft toy ones, I cull and give them to the school when they have fairs or whatever. [...] I let them carry on, because they know that it's something that gives me pleasure, the fact that I have them all around my workstation at work as well [smiles], because I have so many, and they're going up the stairs [laughs]. But I like them, people know that I like them, it gives them pleasure to give them to me, so I haven't got the heart to say, 'Look, I think I have enough'.

As is clear from Gina's account, she does not mind this ascription of 'hedgehog collector' identity, nor does she have a problem with disposal – although note that the creatures join that circus of school fairs, charity shops and jumble sale, the 'deserving' arenas of second-hand culture (Gregson and Crewe 2003). It is a different world of goods and gifts from the sphere of objects bought in 'objects' shops. Gina lets people give her hedgehogs to give *them* pleasure; they, conversely, think they are giving her pleasure. Therefore, although the hedgehogs are taking up too much space in the house, and she has nowhere to store them, unlike Annette, they do perform a role in the process of building and maintaining social relations. This does, however, break down when an individual no longer wants that ascribed collector identity, when there has been a significant change in lifestyle and self-identification, such as Annette attempting to remove herself from the label 'Lladró collector' by putting the ballerinas in another, less prominent place (but could not hide them away).

Collections can also fulfil other connections of memory and friendship, perhaps because these particular sorts of objects, including tourist goods, have become curiously immaterial. Not everyone appreciates tourist objects for aesthetic form, such as Jesus figurines from Brazil, but these sorts of display gifts can become a form of communication between partners and friends. For example, Kate and David have a habit of picking up iconic tourist trash for each other, such as Eiffel towers, and also specific cultural goods such as Venetian masks on their many travels. These are displayed on their mantelpiece, together and without fuss, as material memories of travels and this ongoing private joke. This fusion of aesthetically pleasing objects and memorabilia of various types that did not 'fit' with the order of things was a common feature of many mantelpiece displays and other decorative assemblages around the home. Some people were troubled by this disorder, or 'matter out of place' (Douglas 2002), but could not reconcile an aesthetic design with maintaining a display of gifts that might be beloved objects, or have associations with loved ones. One couple solved the problem by telling their adult children what they wanted as souvenirs from their far-flung travels, thus maintaining their control of their home décor. However, other individuals could not wholly reconcile contesting demands on their space, as can be seen in Sian's story.

Attachment, detachment – the magic of the gift: Sian and Hannah

Sian lives in an Edwardian villa with her husband and three children. There are period fireplaces in both reception rooms, which she has decorated with collections of Wedgwood and Moorcroft pottery. She likes these features, as they look 'authentic'. There was a tiny carriage clock on one side of the mantelpiece, and this decentring seemed deliberately to contravene the 'rules and regulations' that govern mantelpiece displays, such as symmetry and a central clock (to which many still adhere). Her explanation shows how she negotiates a path between her aesthetic designs and displaying a problematic gift (see Madigan and Munro 1999:70):

> I know I think it's because it's too tiny to be central. My mum bought me that; I think it was for my 18th or something. I saw it in a shop in town and I just love it as well, but I just think to have that in the middle would be rather – well it would look a bit odd so I tend never to put it in the middle.

She does recall that it was an 18th birthday present, an event that is viewed as the ritual passage from childhood to adulthood in Britain, and for which, appropriately, she bought a clock. As with many other informants, the fact that she chose the clock does not interfere with her perception of the clock as a present from her mother. She loves the clock and her mother and these considerations override her desire to have a quite traditional display on the mantelpiece. This decision can be seen in reverse in a short story by Hannah, who displays three tiny mice on her mantelpiece, despite the fact that she detested her grandmother, from whom she received them:

> The mice are from my father's mother. That's the one thing of hers I have because I wouldn't have anything else of hers in the house. I hated her. She was frightfully snobby and was very sexist [...] She was a witch. From the age of 12 onwards I refused to see her after that. I didn't see her until she died. I allowed mice house space on the, I think it was William Morris, 'nothing that isn't useful or you believe to be beautiful.' I believe them to be beautiful. They have no sentimental value whatsoever other than they've been in all the flats George and I have lived in and I like them.

In this case, Hannah has divested the mice of their socially related meaning and located them in a culturally specific frame of reference that allows her to see them as aesthetic objects. It emerges that they also perform a function as a music box to silence screaming children; the mice therefore fulfil

Morris's joint remit. This divestment contrasts with the way in which she, along with other informants, can also invest objects with social relations and memories of absent times, places and people. It is important to note this ability to invoke narratives about objects from an array of accounts, dependent on their effectiveness as materials in the construction of objects as 'fitting', as aesthetic, memory and/or identity goods. This 'calling to account' finds an analogy with the way in which individuals are taking the responsibility for the selection of their own things with money gifts. It also connects with the removal of 'automatic' rights to house space for inherited goods (McCracken 1991), as the home becomes a contested space for strategies of social belonging, which are neither cohesive nor, at times, coherent.

Conclusion: keeping women

The current political emphasis on choice, rights and responsibilities seems to have moved into the system of gift exchange, in moving choice from the giver to the receiver. However, this 'democratisation' of the gift is not all it seems to be. We have seen in all the accounts so far the specifically feminised gift relation, not only in the giving and receiving of gifts, but also as repositories of the provenance of objects – as a kind of 'memory machine', perhaps, as Douglas termed the house (Douglas 1993; see also de Certeau 1984; Maleuvre 1999). This connects with the idea, discussed in Chapter 3, of mothers/female partners as not just the keepers of memory, but the makers of memory. Further, as we will see in Chapter 6, the mantelpiece can be made an adult space, removed from the milieu of tangible, childish things in the low-level plains of home. I therefore suggest that there is also a process of the 'mothering' of place: separating and distinguishing this from the rest of domestic space, 'othering' into memory and the imagination.

The problem of the gift is complex. For many individuals, gifts continue to play an important part in the building and maintenance of social relations, life histories and memory. They can recall absent times, places and people by merely glancing at an ornament on a shelf. This is possible even when they have chosen the gift for themselves, as they translate the money and the accompanying human connection into the object. A particularly nice object can, conversely, be divested of the connection and appropriated as an aesthetic object. Both these processes are important at a time when home and self are so closely bound up, and symbolic/cultural capital of artefacts invested in identity (Bourdieu 1986). Who wants to display a horrible old vase from a little-known relative? It could, therefore, be said that there is no simple nexus of material culture and social relations, allowing individuals to select gifts in complex performances of taste and social attachment.

Does this equate with a commodification of social relations? Is it ethically correct to dispose of unwanted objects, to turn the inalienable into alienable and therefore destructible goods? This is clearly not what is happening, since people continue to store unwanted gifts, or transpose them into another circuit of gift exchange in charity fairs and shops (Gregson and Crewe 2003; Gregson 2007). People also continue to follow the imperatives of giving gifts at ritual events, despite the fact that so many of these items are from a peculiar market of 'gift goods' that are highly commercialised (Caplow 1984; Werbner 1996). There is also the ongoing gendering of gifts, which was very clear in my fieldwork (Cheal 1988; Corrigan 1995; Godbout 1998). Women received ornaments for the home, and were often the 'managers' of the home interior (Hunt 1995). This analogy of woman and home means that they seemed to feel a responsibility to be repositories of all the stories of every object on display in the home, just as their homes could become repositories for unwanted things. Adrian thought his wife might remember the provenance of the one on the mantelpiece, just as many other men could not recall the provenance of many things on display, but knew their wives would remember. All the accounts suggested that women – like houses – are 'disposed' as the repositories of memory, of unwanted objects: both safe-keepers and dustbins. If women/mothers, houses and mantelpieces – like gifts – are at once containers of treasure and holders of rubbish – that cannot be discarded – how can this paradox be related to gendered conceptions of home and identity?

This duty to retain memories, and to invest objects with meaning, means that, despite assumptions regarding 'throwaway society', many women (and men) continue to harbour unwanted goods in their homes (Evans 2012). This begs the question: what is home for? It could be argued that, while there is certainly a spirit of entrepreneurship in gift exchange, just as there is in the home, there is also a steadfast adherence to moralities of gift exchange and the role of home as repository of memory. However, if the culture of giving either money for transmutation to object – or of objects themselves – continues, the only possible conclusion is that the mass of stuff bursts homes apart: they are, after all, only walls and a roof. The material and symbolic heaviness of both 'gift' and 'home' in maintaining relations of attachment and belonging clearly emerges from this focus on the gift. Nothing is lost in the disposal of the gift (see Munro 2001).

Cheal argues that gifts are redundant; this is their value as 'used to construct certain kinds of voluntary social relationships' (Cheal 1988: 14). However, I argue that they have become almost more 'employed' in the constitution of identity, and used as a counterweight to the incursion of the market, a re-appropriation of the moral economy that the gift affords (Miller 1998). This can be seen in the continuing transubstantiation of money-gift to artefact-gift, rather than the display of cash in the home (Leal 1995). Similarly, the trope of 'gift-to-self' is enmeshed with this: is there a boundary at which purchased goods can be separated into two distinct categories of commodity and gift? These accounts show how the tradition and traditional accounting of 'gift exchange' remains necessary, and that this relation is not 'voluntary', but enmeshed in the powerful tropes of 'home', 'memory' and 'family'.

The 'gift' is therefore a potent thing and process for 'showing' and 'telling' identities. The 'gift relation' is so closely bound up with the relations between accounting-for-objects/accounting-for-self that this way of 'knowing' seems almost indistinguishable from modes of 'being'. To understand and participate in the gift relation is, simply, to be. However, opening up the multi-dimensionality of viewing points, positioning accounts and ordering practices also exposes misalignments, conflict, paradox and difference. The frictions and tensions necessary to maintain the home, family and memory as sites of security indicate who and what has to be excluded from this nest of shared understanding. Participants such as Gina and Shyam 'othered' themselves to allow the fiction of an easy gift relation to continue, disturbing the connection between 'self' and home to keep up the performance of good mother, good friend. While Shyam emptied out her house, Gina filled hers up to enable others' conception of inherited and gift objects as inalienable to remain coherent. Adrian keeps a clock on his mantelpiece from an unknown 'other'; the visible attribute of the gift is its connection to social ritual, rather than the person. This means that two more clocks can stay in the attic (but not move elsewhere), since that particular attachment has been accomplished in the traditional form of the clock on the mantelpiece. The givers and these other clocks no longer matter, provided this one clock stands in for them as 'the wedding clock', even a material metaphor for 'marriage' as a cultural time-marker.

Activating constructions of the gift relation, the gift-for-display and the gift-to-self might not make for coherent narratives *altogether*. However, such articulations display the craft of identity and home, relying on the materials at hand, as sophisticated, yet pragmatic folk art. In the next chapter, I turn to consider how these powerful notions of 'home', 'family' and 'memory' relate to the 'focal point' of the mantelpiece, and hence how these 'givens', these traditional cultural tropes – seen so often as a singularity – can be viewed as an archetypal 'gift'.

6
Focal Points

It is not the work of a moment for a society to generate (produce) an appropriated social space in which it can achieve a form by means of self-presentation and self-representation – a social space to which that society is not identical, and which indeed is its tomb as well as its cradle.

(Lefebvre 1991 [1974]: 34)

Introduction: the blindingly obvious?

In this chapter, I focus on how the mantelpiece – as space and matter – works and is worked in organising people, place and time. Arranging these modes of organising into headings and sub-headings was difficult, as they are so entangled in home life. Further, if mantelpieces are practices of auto-archaeology, perhaps these traces were the hardest to distinguish, buried in the very ground beneath my feet. Snobbery, squabbling, childish indignation, resentment, pride and intolerance are easy to practise, and easier to deny. The mobilisations and impositions of space and matter are deeply implicated in the politics of 'home', micro-practices of power as regulation and division, expectation and attrition. Through practice, the body, the senses and the person are organised into where and how to look, touch, judge and order. Who decides what is clean or dirty, sacred or profane? How do I know not to read the back of the postcard? When does the holly go up? And who dumped those keys here? Not everybody defines the mantelpiece as a special display space, but some of their visitors will (and everybody knows *that*, don't they?). The struggle for space and matter in the home is the struggle for meaning: this is culture at its most petty, trivial and ferocious. Global geopolitics can be left at the front door; the door keys cannot.

We have looked upon the mantelpiece as a thing so far; now is the time to refocus on it as both matter with deep (albeit shifting) foundations, and lived space – as embodied, embodying spatial practice (de Certeau 1984; Lefebvre 1991). Mantelpiece 'talk' is dominated by 'tradition', 'symmetry', 'clutter', by 'conscious', 'deliberate' and 'accidental' wishes and decisions. The ways in which these are assembled into discourses of family and home, of self and other, power and resistance, transform this focal point into an horizon of practice:

> The central location makes it the focal point of the room. I mean it's the place that everyone has to look at wherever they sit in the room and when you come in the door.
>
> (Adrian)

The gap between viewer and viewed, and the limitations of visibility *up here* for mantelpiece objects, as opposed to 'the rest' *over there* might be articulated as no more than serendipity by Adrian, but these divisions of space and things produce meaning, and are produced as meaningful (Douglas 2002). Many participants thought I was either mad or stupid for asking what they thought made the mantelpiece different from other display areas, and what it was for. Harriet asks, rhetorically, it's 'just a traditional thing and pictures and things that go over the mantelpiece isn't it?' Yet that word, 'just', and the frequency of rhetorical questions – 'isn't it?' and, 'you know?' – oblige reciprocal assent. Similarly, the 'focal point' demands focus, to avoid a contradiction in terms. These commonplaces resonate with Mike Savage's (2003) 'universal particular', the quiet violence that the powerful do, in mild assertions, non-committal nods, dismissals of others, and the omnipotence of the blindingly obvious. Is this our contemporary gift as 'total social fact': the etiquette of returning sight and voice always as expected? But the mantelpiece (so far) has belied confident assertions. Dissembling, paradoxical, contrary: it is a study of awkwardness.

The questions I should have asked (ah, hindsight!) would have invited participants to go beyond dismissing the mantel and the things on it as mere accidents of domestic geography or topography. These are the questions I address in this chapter: 'How do *you* make the mantelpiece different from other spaces? What work is the mantelpiece doing here, now, in your house?' However, I am not sure what responses such direct questions would have invited. Obliquity, disjointedness, layering and distancing all articulate identity. As we shall see, the mantelpiece might be a focal point, but unless one approaches it, there is a 'critical distance' between it and the person at the doorway, sitting on the sofa or watching the television. Is it possible to 'watch' the mantelpiece, or contemplatively rest one's elbow on the television? The mantelpiece is a boundaried space, placing limits on what goes 'up there', just as the television limits what goes 'on' there. The way in which the two objects elicit different registers of standing, sitting, looking, doing, suggests how thickly enmeshed human bodies are with the materials and spaces of home. To paraphrase Joey's question in an episode of US sitcom *Friends*, 'Without the TV, where do we point the furniture?' The chapter is divided into five sections, loosely arranged around themes of couples and children; time and space; and the television.

Negotiating couples

'My little space': Sian

In the interview extract below, Sian is talking about the mantelpiece in the bedroom she shares with her husband. No ordinary visitors will sit and look at this focal point; here is the field where their relations as a couple are made, through disputing of space and time:

> He dumps his handkerchief and his change on the mantelpiece and it drives me mad, that does. I think he leaves receipts on the mantelpiece. I can't – I'm not sort of obsessively tidy – but I can't stand clutter on the mantelpiece [...] It's my little sort of space and he just dumps some money on it [laughs]. 'Well', I think, 'I'm not going to touch them now and see how long he lets' – I think he would be happy for it to be a mountain.
>
> (Sian)

Sian's 'little space' is intruded upon daily with her husband's rubbish. The gaps that make her display meaningful are filled up, laying waste to the distinction she has made between her things. For him, it is a convenient shelf for the contents of his pockets, but in transforming her space, he changes its meaning, from aesthetic display to dumping ground. In her eyes, this is occupation of her space, which she can repossess only by removing the rubbish, reclaiming the meaning. The gap between her seeing the intruders and touching them is crucial; the transition from visible to tangible matter is carefully timed to test whether he will move into her world, where the mantel is her pure space, and his stuff is dirt. But every time, he starts to build his mountain, meaning that she must make the move to pull the mantel back into her sphere of meaning (Douglas 2002 [1966], Strathern 2004 [1991]; Munro 2005). This everyday practice of time and space is, therefore, more than it seems. It is not merely an outcome of relations, but makes them, in the never-settled struggle for meaning. It might seem at first that Sian is in control of the space; most of the time, the mantelpiece display looks as she wants it to. But it is those times in between that constantly destabilise her world through ongoing anxiety, that mix of fear and anger which Sian dismisses with a laugh. The wars over space and matter extend into more public areas of the house. In the 'quiet' living room, Sian has placed her collection of Moorcroft pottery, because she likes to look at the figures as aesthetic objects. Her husband (an accountant) does not favour this, since he views them as investment goods that should be kept safely stored away. By putting them in the quiet room, Sian has protected them, she says, from children kicking footballs, but she will not put them away.

Her husband would rather put out his 'horrible grey sports trophies', which are kept in storage. The mantelpiece is therefore a contested space in terms of what is revealed, and what is concealed in boxes in the loft (Hockey 1999). One might chuckle over these squabbles, but this is not trivial: children, who might be moved around bedrooms and have constricted space, do have rooms of their own, while couples do not (Dovey 1999). Where is the room each can call their own? 'Co-habiting' sounds so cosy, but modernity demands we are all individuals now, according to dominant sociological theories of the person (see Introduction). However, in his book on the 'little quarrels of couples', Jean-Claude Kaufmann (2009) demonstrates that the resolution of minor rows requires the utter transformation of the person. With the assumption of an autonomous individual, negotiating coupledom and individual identity is central to the problem of life in late modernity.

Space invaders: Phillip and Jo

Not all are overt players in the politics of the mantel: 'What to put on the mantelpiece beats me,' says Phillip, who would like to replace the traditional-style mantelpiece with an ultra-modern 'hole in the wall' fire. His wife, Jo, on the other hand, expresses annoyance about a male friend of theirs who always leaves his car keys on there when he visits, a detail unknown to Phillip until our interview. Preferring to have a flat wall there, Phillip is absent from the ongoing ordering of the mantelshelf. He justifies their friend's intrusion on grounds that he is merely replicating what he (being tall) does in his own home, to keep the keys away from his small children. Ignorant or not of the disturbance his casual move causes, the friend, this tall male body, silently reconstitutes that space (Lefebvre 1991 [1973]: 170; Puwar 2004). In contrast, other male participants said they either 'wouldn't dare' to leave pocket contents on the mantel, or leave things temporarily, timing the removal of things carefully to avoid annoying their wives. While they would use the mantel as an 'in-tray', their wives' organisation of it as a display space is dominant. Some submit to this completely, whereas others syncopate the regular rhythm, slipping guitar plectrums, wallets and coins in a mantelpiece 'sieve-order' (de Certeau 1984).

The music of memory: Victoria and Luke

A gendered distinction can be seen clearly in Victoria and Luke's flat. They are in their early twenties and this is their first home together, as opposed to childhood homes and shared student houses. It is a flat rented from Luke's father and does not have a mantelpiece. The focal point is a television/stereo unit, but there is a shelf unit in one corner that Victoria nominated as her mantelpiece. She wants a mantelpiece eventually, and has a well-formed plan of what will be on it. Her display on the shelves is a combination of heirlooms, gifts and memorabilia of self, family and home (objects and photographs). Many of the items have been transferred from her bedside table at the family home and in shared houses. Like several younger participants, Victoria sees the progress of these things – their biographies – as intimately linked with her own life course and housing career. Their transition from bedside table to living room, and finally to mantelpiece, is analogous with her movement from child in the family house, to young adult tenant, to home-owning 'settled' part of a couple/family, whose mantelpiece will similarly fall into the same kind of 'place' as her parents'.

Although the array of things on the shelf unit is not what will be on her future mantelpiece, Victoria has designated this space for display of decorative objects. The bottom shelf on the unit is Luke's place. This is a storage site for practical things like a screwdriver, penknife, glue and personal stereo. Victoria likes him to keep it tidy, although he points out that she has put her sewing kit there. They agree, however, that this is Luke's space; well below eye level and for the storage (and temporary dumping) of tools and practical items. Nothing on the display shelves is Luke's. This might suggest that Luke is absent as a producer of the room. However, he is very much present, since the focal point of the room is the 'entertainment unit'. For people sitting on the sofa, the most visible items – apart from the television, DVD player and stereo – are the DVDs and CDs, which are mainly Luke's. This collection is significant for the recollection of his autobiography, just as Victoria's display is. When he plays a film or piece of music, Luke recalls who gave it to him and when. Social relations are made and remade at the playing of a song or film, rather than looking at ornaments.

It is easy to assume that the production of 'home' is women's work, because men are not always active in what counts as 'décor' which 'reflects my personality', to use a commonplace. Victoria made the eye-level, decorative display; Luke used an unseen area for tools and so on, in a hierarchy of goods, space and, by extension, genders in the home. He also owns the entertainment media – typical *man*! Yet this reading ignores the meanings that both partners had constructed around the two sites. It also omits the memories that Victoria and Luke have of their childhood homes: whereas Victoria's parents' home has a mantelpiece and pictures on the walls, Luke's parents do not have many areas of display in their home. She therefore has an inherited notion of the aesthetic function of home. Luke, on the other hand, is not accustomed to these practices; he has made his own biography through other media – songs and films – a collection of images and sounds (Bull and Back 2003). Therefore, to give primacy to dominant assumptions about the gendering of domestic space is to detach objects from these biographic accounts. And who is to say that televisions do not count in the making of home?

Perfect asymmetry: Christine and Harry

In contrast, Harry equates the symmetry of their clock/candlesticks display with 'the way our minds work'. He goes on, 'it's at eyesight level, you can't get away from it', compared with other spaces in the house such as a large display cabinet 'just in the corner of the eye' filled with things collected while living abroad, 'half the world'. His wife, Christine, considers the mantelpiece an ideal modus vivendi which she strives to achieve: 'That's how I'd like to be. That's what I want my life to be. Uncluttered, neat, tidy and clean.' This perfection, inescapable to the gaze, from the doorway, chairs and sofas, is possible because 'the rest' has been amassed in the corner of the room, analogous to the corner of vision. Its symmetry, as Gombrich (1995) argues, might pacify the gaze, but also produces discontent. Set apart from the mass to please the eye, this seemingly static display mobilises unrest. While Harry equates the display with their ordered mentality, his wife sees only disjuncture with her life. In dividing up domestic space between 'clean' and 'half the world', they have divided up their life between their past elsewhere and this ideal, present perhaps in the mind, but forever deferred as 'life'. However, this seemingly simple division of spatial practice blurs when viewing their year-long photo-calendar (Hurdley 2012). Christine was loath to participate in the auto-photography project, since she thought her mantelpiece display never changed. Yet the gaps in the 'ideal' permanent display are periodically filled with event-markers such as birthday, wedding anniversary and Christmas cards, photographs of a daughter's wedding and a new grandchild. The stockings are put up at Christmas for the grandchildren. Certain types of 'mess', at certain types of times, are permissible for the performance of family relations and temporality, yet so taken-for-granted that they are forgotten the moment that 'time' passes, when the clutter once again disappears from view.

Children: home schooling

The place of the mantelpiece as a focal point means it is also one of the first things that children see; a place that becomes more visible when they are being carried about by adults, and then as they grow up. Therefore, from babyhood, it is a grown-up place, where exciting objects like the remote controls, mobile phones, DVDs, sweets and shiny things are put out of reach. This was such a commonplace, I had barely thought about it, until an interview with a retired child psychiatrist:

> I was interested that people were taking notice of the rooms that children live in, you know, and the things that children have to look at.
>
> (John)

Listening again to the interview and reading transcript, I realised the double meaning of 'have to look at', suddenly resonating with Adrian's 'place...everyone has to look at'. The gaze possesses the thing it beholds, but the things themselves demand the sight, especially when the world one inhabits is very small. That looking and relooking, over days, months, years: how does that shape a person? I name the participants in each section, so their relevant photographs and biographies can be viewed (Hurdley 2012).

Intangible/visible objects: Hannah, Harriet, Rosalind

We can develop a perspective on the 'focal point' as a place where an object is on view, not only for aesthetic pleasure but as a site for educating children in civilised social interaction, the meaning of things and spaces, and the disciplining of the senses and the body. The mantelpiece is a place of punishment for Hannah's children. It was only during our interview that she realised how 'child-focused' her mantelpiece was. She feels extremely proud of her three children, since she was adopted, and so they are her only known blood relatives. This is a very strong connection for her, made visible on the mantelpiece by the photographs of the children. However, it is also a stage for teaching her sons how to behave. If the two boys have fought over a toy, it goes up on the mantelpiece for 24 hours. They can see it, but they cannot touch it. The boys are now tall enough to reach it, but have been trained not to touch anything up there. Similarly, Harriet's sons had broken an ornament on the mantel – the silver windmill – by playing with it. Whereas the windmill had once doubled as ornament and a toy, the children's part-ownership of it had been replaced by their mother's singular view of it as 'ornament'. They had overstepped the limit of its 'toyhood', and this transgression into the adult territory of 'ornament' had banished their boyhood practice. The toy is removed from the arena of play, childhood and tangibility, to a different order of object – for consumption by sight alone, as the boys are trained into adulthood. A development of this notion can be drawn from Rosalind's memory of her mother's mantelpiece as a 'hazardous place' filled with her best china. Despite her dislike of her mother and the unpleasant memory, she nevertheless imitated the display as an adult:

> When the children were tiny, I did start off putting really lovely things [on it], but when they were broken, I was so gutted. So I had to be practical and take them away until I got past that stage and they were taught never, ever to touch the things that mattered to mummy on the mantelpiece, and they never did.

Thus, Rosalind learnt from her mother this particular treatment of the mantelpiece, as a place where children were dangerous intruders, and where the frangibility of objects obviated their tangibility: sight, rather than touch, was the civilised sense, keeping objects distant and precious. The effect of viewing children as objects' risky relations is to displace the display, temporarily. Objects on the mantelpiece have sanctuary from the low-lying, childish territories of home, either as ornament or as a part of pedagogic practice. In both cases, they are hazardous relations for children who dare to touch them or treat them as toys.

Justice, safety and sanctuary: Hannah, Nick, Dan, Victoria

The inverse of this is the practice of keeping children safe by putting risky objects on the mantelpiece. It is common to put screws, nails, broken tools, scissors and other sharp objects in bowls on the mantelpiece, as well as medicines and hot drinks. The mantelpiece is also the 'home' for things temporarily out of place. For example, Hannah was fascinated to see her young son imitating what his parents did: picking up a puzzle piece from the floor and putting it on the mantel.

The presence of children in Nick's household has entailed the absence of a mantelpiece: it brings with it the danger of an open gas fire (see Chapter 4). In contradiction to this logical explanation, Dan – living in the same development – chose to have an enclosed gas fire under the mantelpiece, for child-safety reasons. Accounts do a lot more work than simple explanation. What is the effect of invoking children's safety for the absence of mantels, the presence of dangerous objects on the mantel, and, in turn, children as dangerous creatures, to be kept away from things that 'matter', limiting the empire of domestic senses to sight alone: the adult, civilised sense?

While adults might justify certain spatial practices by talking about children's safety and the safety of things, these accounts also produce children as disordered bodies, senses and persons that need shaping (Classen 2005a, 2005b; Howes 2005a, 2005b). As much as children constitute space, space – above all, domestic space – constitutes children (Lefebvre 1991: 170). An adult visitor usually knows how the relation between space and bodies works. As Victoria says of her parents' home: 'People get up and they'll go and look at the photos. And I will when I go home, I'll straightaway go and look at the cards and the important things like that.' These polite registers of closeness and belonging, of seeing and touching, however, can be overthrown by a visitor who is accustomed to being up high and using up a lot of space, such as a tall, male visitor, throwing his keys on the mantel (Puwar 2004).

Keeping time: the quick and the dead

Family photos, seasons and rituals: Sian, Dan, Geoff

Many parents and grandparents had photographs of their family elsewhere in the house, such as 'collage-style' on a board in the kitchen, or a photo wall, but the mantelpiece was unusual in that many of the photos were frequently of children in the family, but much younger than their current age. Others were 'ideal' photographs. Sian had selected the photographs for her mantelpiece because the children were 'altogether' and looked unusually 'tidy' in their school photograph, and all looked very 'sweet' in the bath. Similarly, Julia and Dan's 12-year-old daughter was pictured aged five on the mantelpiece, which she found 'embarrassing', she said, to the surprise of her mother during the interview. On the other hand, photographs of Geoff's toddler daughter were very frequently updated, even over the course of a year. The older children became, it seemed, the fewer the photographs on the mantelpiece, until they graduated, married or had their own children. Increasing age reduced mantel presence. While digital photo frames might have augmented these 'permanent' displays, they have not displaced them: some photographs 'keep' time in ways that others do not. The way in which some people kept photographs of their children 'close', in the sense that they were displayed on coffee tables near favourite armchairs, in the kitchen, on bedside units or even on the walls of the downstairs lavatory, sharpened the distinction the mantelpiece conferred on these particular photographs. The mantelpiece might be highly visible, but is particularly so to visitors, who do not inhabit these other spaces in the house. This attribute of the mantelpiece, its impact on the eye at the moment of entering the living room, gives its display a special salience.

These childhood photographs present children out of time, framed in ideal moments and ages, just as wedding invitations mark out those invited as participants in an idealised version of social time. As well as this social aesthetic of time, a further dimension is apparent in the way in which mantelpiece 'time' has changed since Mass Observation *Reports* from 1937. It no longer plays the role of calendar of the everyday, but as a calendar of foregrounded social rituals – focal points of social life. Mundane prompts for appointments, shopping lists and bill payments are kept in a diary or mobile phone; only aesthetically pleasing 'reminders' are put on the mantel. The extra-ordinariness of time-keeping on the mantelpiece is highlighted in the prominence of its relation with Christmas, which came across in most accounts, highlighting the transition from the mantelpiece as daily 'calendar' to marker of special social events. Although it might be easy to call events such as Christmas 'seasonal', that would be a misnomer, in that the mantelpiece 'year' has little to do with the weather and seasonal changes. A look at the auto-photographic snapshots of 'Christmas' suggests it is constituted of conventional bought items, such as cards, holly, candles and tinsel. Its normal display is displaced, replaced or augmented by transient yet important shared cultural markers that it upholds for everyone to see. Participation and non-participation in these social events – for putting up Christmas cards is as much an event as the day itself – signals cultural belonging or non-belonging. While participation matters, the materials themselves are important for fine-grained distinctions (further discussion in chapters 7 and 8).

Anachronistic aesthetics: Alison

Alison leaves aesthetically pleasing birthday cards on show on her mantelpiece, concealing less artistic ones behind, or moving them to another place. She also displaces her 'normal' display for events such as Halloween and Christmas, which are marked by special decorations. Her unusual – for Britain – focus on Halloween, with orange candles and autumn foliage – is not simply to demonstrate a liking for seasonal change in home décor, but also to represent her experience of working in the US, where Halloween traditionally entails decorating the home and garden, as we shall see in Chapter 8. The festival is therefore used as resource to perform her identity as a well-travelled professional person, familiar with a non-indigenous aesthetic tradition. However, like so many participants, Alison is not quite up to speed with changing her domestic display 'calendar'; her demanding job in another city means that decorations stay up for weeks beyond their time, only changed when visitors are coming. Yet this anachronism enables her to maintain home as a place that inhabits a different temporality from that of her work. Home, as well as being a place to display aesthetic competence, is a place where asynchronicity is another performance of control. Like Julia's dust, related in Chapter 4, Alison's orange candles are a form of decay that shows her command over her home and domestic time.

However, unlike Julia, Alison employs cleaners due to her job's demands on her time and space, since she must live elsewhere during her working week. Although they keep the house clean, these domestic workers constantly profane Alison's space, by disturbing her careful organisation. While the cards and other backstage objects need not be symmetrical, the front display on the mantel must be; how her cleaners 'can leave it asymmetrical is completely beyond me because I just can't live with it'. In paying to have the dust removed, Alison loses her 'liveable' space. The dirt might be gone, but as matter out of place, her precious display is polluted. Also, unlike any other visitor, the cleaners see and touch everything; they see the unattractive cards shoved to the back, the out-of-date decorations and the dust. Through their movement of objects, they confront Alison with the mechanics of her performance, as she is forced to rearrange her 'setting' (Goffman 1959: 32). However, having been a 'socially disgruntled' domestic cleaner before I became a sociologist, I suggest that they cannot pause to contemplate that mantel, to measure the millimetres, since their time is paid hourly, measured out in the routines of removing other people's dirt (Goffman 1959: 28).

Moving bodies: Hannah

Time on the mantelpiece is visual, palpable and manipulable, for those who have expertise in deploying temporality – in the shape of 'period' displays, seasonality, ideal photographs and enviable wedding invitations – to perform attachment and belonging. Paradoxically, however, the ability to move within these 'sticky' social norms demands mobility and detachment; in particular, the ability to imagine oneself as 'other', and to shift within and beyond multiple temporalities (Adam 1995):

> I put it there after he died, partly because it doesn't seem likely for him to be dead. Every now and then, I sort of look at it; I can still chat to him there but I can also look at it and go, 'Han, move on. Dad's not coming back. He isn't on a business trip'.
>
> (Hannah)

In the last chapter, we saw how the passing on and display of family heirlooms was not a simple process. Reverse inheritance, purchasing one's own heirlooms and getting rid of potential inheritance objects were some of the ways in which this process of 'passing on' becomes a more complex social choreography, to maintain both social relations and identity performance. Yet such processes were hidden, since these 'moments' were unspoken, leaving the material objects as silent remnants, either on display or boxed up for disposal elsewhere. Similarly, the moment at which Hannah marked the death of her father, by moving his photograph from the living room wall to the mantelpiece, has passed: who would know now that this tiny journey was her act of remembrance? And that, further, her daily domestic life is now punctuated by moments where she both 'chats' to him, and also uses the image to remind herself he is gone? Rarely spoken of in the day-to-day, the skill to mobilise these multiple articulations of time (places and people) was a common thread in many interviews. The mantelpiece in Hannah's living room was 'family' space, filled with an assortment of display items and children's toys, bowls of screws and so on. By moving the photograph of her father there, into the 'day-to-day' space, she put it in the place which showed what was 'happening' with her family. His death, in effect, had been incorporated into the day-to-day flow of family life, yet could be set apart for those moments of contemplation, another mode of 'immortal ordinary' (Garfinkel 1988), when she chose. Although commemorating a past event, the photograph also pointed to a future when Hannah no longer needed to remind herself that her father really was dead, rather than simply not here.

Hannah's repeated act of looking mobilises persons in plural spaces and times: moving her father both into the here/now and into the past/elsewhere, while moving herself beyond here/now, in which her father remains as an absent presence, to a future acceptance of his death. The mantelpiece is a shifting horizon, moved by her gaze. This ongoing process of mourning through the active production of new meanings around the photograph demonstrates how routine markers of life events, such as photographs and cards, disrupt the notion of a routinised domestic 'passage of time'. Although the process Hannah related was personal, the commemoration of the dead through photograph displays, on the mantel or elsewhere, is considered normal practice in Britain; at least certain types of photographs of certain types of people. Whatever the private processes of mourning and commemoration might be, these memorials are, after all, only photos standing among candlesticks, clocks and pictures of nice-looking children.

The hidden expectations surrounding this practice of marking a life passing, however, were revealed by the drawing made by one participant in the postal questionnaire. Her living room mantelpiece was different from other display areas in the house because it carried 'mementoes of my still-born daughter, Eve'. These were fresh flowers in memory of her, and a framed religious poem, rather than a photograph (Bleyen 2010). Would anyone put a photograph of a stillborn baby on the mantelpiece? The silence of photographs makes them ambiguous in the eyes of unknowing others. It is so 'normal' to display photographs of people to mark their passing that it is unquestioned, unshocking, until this wood- and silver-framed culture of grieving is broken. The participant has three living sons, but nothing of them is displayed on the mantel. The drawing and comments illuminated the profound connections between death and 'lookable', material remembrance (Forty and Kuchler 2001; Hallam and Hockey 2001; Hockey *et al.* 2010a, 2010b). While I was doing this study, Sarah, the wife of the then Chancellor, Gordon Brown, gave birth to a daughter who died soon afterwards; I wrote to her to express my sympathy. I have never written to any other strangers about such matters, and this unusual move led to an equally unusual response. A card arrived from Sarah Brown thanking me (among others) for my sympathy. On the front of the card was a photograph of Jennifer Brown, a tiny, translucent human. I quietly put it in the 'personal' section of my filing cabinet. To display the dead *as* dead – or to displace 'ideal' photographs of children and newborn babies with this doubly disturbing person out of place – was unthinkable. Not a keepsake in a drawer, nor grief rising in the hollow hours of the night; a photo of a dead baby lays sorrow bare.

You got the look: making space, making people

In this section, we will look at how participants ordered, and in turn, were ordered, by ways of looking, and organising spaces and things. In particular, the place of 'the other' is crucial in the complex imaginaries that institute the 'gaze'. This is simultaneously unfixed and fixing, of self and other, home and elsewhere. We will see how 'the other' – and the 'gaze' – is used in strategies of belonging and distinction, but also how they constrain.

The ideal s(h)elf: Bronwen

First, Bronwen, a psychology postgraduate, articulates the transposing of her body, from being at home as a host, to being a visitor hosted elsewhere; the changing gaze that this demands, and which she herself expects from others:

You go to other people's houses and you kind of get an impression, that's just what goes on a mantelpiece... you wouldn't put a saucepan or something up there, would you? [...] [It] must be clean because if you've devised it as a focal point, you don't particularly want people looking at it and thinking, 'Oh God'... it is for other people, but I wouldn't expect them to focus on it. You don't want things that don't look nice on there and you don't want it to be messy, whereas that shelf [a shelf unit next to the mantelpiece] seems a bit stuck back in the alcove a bit and that's more functional. That's got an old radio on it that works, but I don't want people looking at it *per se*. And the phone's up there and the teddy that the dog keeps chewing to pieces. So that's more functional.

(Bronwen)

For Bronwen, the mantelpiece is a focal point, whereas the shelf hidden in the shadow of the alcove is not, and therefore has a function of storing things that are used. However, she also calls the mantelpiece 'half storage, half display', but what is stored on the mantelpiece must also have aesthetic value. This is, in a way, an imperative, an order *by* space, which obliges her to keep this place clean and tidy and aesthetically pleasing. However, there are other 'orders' at work here: although the gaze might, through domestic topography, be directed towards the mantel, Bronwen combines that spatial directive with expectations about where and how people will look. To look at the shelf askance would be to decentre the proper 'subject' of the gaze: the mantelpiece. Viewers must ensure they avert their eyes from the 'functional' clutter to maintain Bronwen's performance as culturally competent. However, actually to focus on this focal point would also break the rules. Not only the precise measure of the consuming 'look', but also what Bronwen devises as an appropriate vision is regulated. Her provision of a 'nice', not 'messy' display depends both upon what she has herself seen as the visitor in others' houses, and also, she says later, on what her mother puts on the mantel. Knowing what belongs here is to perform belonging. A combination of intergenerational channelling of correct view and viewing and an endlessly returned look, at others, by others and as 'other' produces this continually refracted practice of looking at and doing display as matter *in* place, rather than dirt, clutter and saucepans.

Other ways of seeing: mass visions

The performance of belonging and proper looking need not be drawn from the lived experience of domestic space, but from idea of home, as mediated through the perfecting lens of 'ideal home' magazines (Gregory 2003). Further, cultural capital is not necessarily through the intergenerational transmission of taste for particular things, but in knowing how to present the 'look' one wants. For example, Alison (see Chapter 3) disliked her parents' display, seeing it as formal, but in a different way from hers, and 'modern' (as was common in the 1960s and 1970s). Although the 'very select range of special ornaments', were not to her taste, those attributes of 'special' and 'select' can nevertheless be seen in her careful divisions of space and things in her home. She says it was the image of an old-fashioned looking Christmas mantelpiece in her mother's copy of the periodical *Woman and Home* that produced her 'conscious wish' to recreate that image in her adult home. The traditional, symmetrical display on her Adam-style mantel is a central assemblage in her recently built house. The magazine and the distinction practice of her parents are used as resources to make the home of her imagination. By making that unfitting 'modernised past' of the 1960s only partially visible, to focus on the desired 'unmodern' past for the 'look' of her contemporary house, Alison regulates not only space and matter, but also time in a precise production of home.

Popular media therefore provide other ways of looking – at other homes, perfected homes – rather than the houses of friends and relatives. Julia, who, as we saw in Chapter 4, denies the influence of such images, nevertheless associates the mantelpiece with 'family things because it is like in magazines, with the TV [programmes] and things like that, so it's family and home, especially after we lived in that [rented] house for a while with no mantelpiece. The room seemed terribly strange.' The connection of *no* mantelpiece with being in transit, looking for the home they wanted to buy, further fixes the relation between 'family' and the 'mantelpiece'. While popular media might not influence her own practice, they provide frequent reiterations of the traditional 'look' that binds together ideal homes and families. Yet Julia combines mediated images of mantelpiece as family/home with lived experience of domestic space differently from Alison. She selects the idea of the mantelpiece as unavoidably conflated with family and home from this ubiquitous image to explain the special position of the mantelpiece in the home. Its absence alters domestic space, making the familiar strange. Therefore, although popular media do not inform her practice of mantelpiece display, the constant reiteration of the family/home/mantelpiece relation is invoked in her performance of familiarity rather than strangeness – of belonging – while detaching from the mass of TV-watching, magazine-reading consumers. 'We're not "Clock on the Mantelpiece" people' says her husband, Dan, similarly displaying both knowledge of the traditional look, and detachment from it. Passive reproduction of tradition is set against the discriminating practitioner of space. Symmetry, the archetype of tradition and formality, mobilises resistance, cited, for example, by Karen as the dominant order. She has 'consciously gone away from putting something in the middle. If I found something that would look good, I would put it there, but I didn't want to sort of you know, middle, two things left, two things right', and 'I deliberately put them [two candlesticks] on the side.'

Distinguishing between the 'sacrosanct space' of his parents' 'neat, clean and orderly' inalienable display and his own mantel, with the 'stuff that just grew there', David sets himself apart from them and their way of living (see Chapter 3). While many of the individual things on the mantel, and their combination, might be entirely unique, the bricolage 'look' is nevertheless common. Although there is no clock, candlestick or mirror here, the look is strangely familiar. In resisting the sanctity of the mantelpiece, bricolage as a form, rather than the content itself is a tactic in practising this space as ongoing, momentary, apparently non-discriminating and organic. Not to interpose things with gaps; in effect, choosing 'clutter' – the enemy of choice – is *choosing not to choose*, a practice to which I shall return later in the chapter.

In a different mode of choosing, Gina cares nothing at all for her mantelpiece, an 'ugly' makeshift structure of three planks above a gas fire in the front room, which is used only for eating at the table and for her sons to use the computer. Much more time is spent in the back room (where the television is), where her sons' sports trophies are displayed on top of the gas fire. This is where 'family' and 'home' are practised. She has put family photographs on the kitchen wall. As a site for the routine preparation of the evening meal, she had also produced this as a dense space and time for reconnecting with her family. When family and home are accounted for elsewhere, the mantelpiece is no longer the focal point; in fact, to gaze at it would be strange. Gina has *stopped* the mantelpiece 'look' entirely by moving on to other sites for doing home and family, yet the traces of that other, passed-over space are outlined still, by the unfinished 'look' of those bare planks.

Looking at others, looking at me: Hannah and Sian

Hannah displays pretty wedding invitations partly for the attention of her National Childbirth Trust group; patently a 'reminder' of a future, the display also performs important work in the present, as do other, more formal displays:

> ... [like] going round to other mum's houses and thinking, oh, you collect paintings as well. It was almost an automatic, "Oh, you're a middle-class de-de-de-de-de-de", you know. It sounds terrible... [I'm] very hesitant to split into classes, but other than, you know, you do get to a certain point at which you can't do any social categorisation without it, which is a very middle-class thing to come up with.
>
> (Hannah)

Hannah said this was 'just what you do', as if this display of events in the family calendar, unlike the decision to move her father's photograph, were done without 'conscious' thinking. In 'choosing not to choose', like David talking of his 'stuff', she removes herself from the position of active constructor of meaning. Yet this very ability, to move oneself in and out of the role of decision-maker, making certain moves meaningful and others not – when they are *the same action* – is a practice of misrecognition, in which some participants were particularly skilled (Bourdieu 1986; Butler 1993, 2004a). The relations between landlords and lodgers, parents and children, visitors and hosts, cleaners and employers, partners are political, in the micro-struggles over space, matter and meaning. Some are powerless, or absent themselves from the field (Bourdieu 1986), although this can itself shift the frontier – from dirty/clean objects on the mantel to the mantel/television, or to my fireplace/other fireplace.

Sian asks rhetorically, 'You can't help it, somebody's house, can you, you look and you know it just reflects my taste…?. The fireplace would be the first thing I would look at.' However, she then hands over agency completely to the fireplace, for it 'would catch my eye…draw your eye, nothing nosy or anything'. The simple morphology of the living room presented by Geoff at the start of the chapter can be changed in a moment to perform distinction. Metamorphosis of this domestic structure, through the inflecting of its parts and its past to seize meaning, unbalance domestic relations and engage in asymmetries of power produces spatial practice and discourse that extend beyond the home.

The telling television: 'not one of those people'

While my focus on the mantelpiece or its equivalent probably sharpened participants' perceptions of the relations between the two, the spatial arrangement of many living rooms made it undeniable, with the television beside the central fireplace, its top, at about the same level as the mantel, used as a display space (unless it was a flatscreen). In Bronwen's house, the television sat in the fireplace due to lack of space. More recently, flatscreens are hung above the mantel, a shelf, or 'hole in the wall' fireplace, containing no more than a heaped pile of logs, with tall candles around. The display of 'mantelpiece objects' is to be found on a window sill nearby; they have been literally sidelined. In some homes, it is impossible to see the display space when seated without twisting the head round, since the furniture points at the television. This makes Belinda's comment about 'two focal points' salient, since it is easy to miss the problem of 'double vision' when the two are juxtaposed:

> We now sit around the television…. I wouldn't like two focal points, […] it would just clutter. [Pointing at the shelf opposite back entrance to room, selected as her mantelpiece] I mean, I'm not going to sit around that, am I? But if I had a mantelpiece, I might try to arrange the furniture

around that, and I would also be trying to arrange it around the television. And as I am quite a tidy person ...

(Belinda)

For a 'tidy person', spatial practice encompassing two centres is impossible. When looking at one, the other intrudes; as Karen says, it 'competes'. Looking at one makes the other invisible: how can this be settled, except as a constant oscillation? Memory and biography, identity performance and social relations; we have seen how these are mantelpiece practices. The television is as much a focal point; often, it is more dominant than any other object in the room, even when it is switched off, so it cannot be ignored in favour of the ideal, traditional focal point, can it?

'Before television, people used to sit round the hearth,' says Annette, as if television had entirely replaced the mantelpiece as the focal point. The following collage of comments suggests that television has partially supplanted the hearth. However, the two things are not equivalent, nor are the practices of looking that are associated with them. While Belinda was never going to 'sit round' the shelf unit, she still thought the television, her husband's choice, was too 'big and black', wishing they could have something smaller that could be brought out for specific programmes. The mantelpiece or its equivalent was seen as fulfilling 'different meanings' from the television for Nick, whose cupboard top was 'for photographs and memorabilia, stuff like that', whereas the television, diagonally opposite, was 'for information ... it's part of the family'. For Bronwen, the mantel and its display gave 'colour and shape and form', which the television could not. Phillip was certain that mantelpieces 'will just die' with the move to wall-mounted flatscreen televisions.

I had to ask a few people to switch off the television when I was trying to record our interview; it was part of the background of their lives, whereas others, such as Eric, 'tried' only to watch the television after 7 pm, 'unless the cricket's on'. In families and couples, the mantelpiece was noticeably favoured as the 'focal point' for women, who saw the television as their spouse's 'obtrusive' choice, the focal point for 'them' (husbands and children), although many enjoyed watching it to relax (Morley 1995, 2000). Mike, Shyam's husband was worried when she rearranged the front room, updating the mantelpiece display and moving the furniture, asking, 'Well, where's the TV going?' For Karen, the mantelpiece is a 'nice feature' that 'competes with the television', unless guests are present, when 'we'd just chat'; at other times, the television is the focal point. However, she goes on to say that 'I've got all my TVs second-hand and I'm not one of those people who wants a really big TV.' Eyes are 'dragged towards the TV, which is bad enough' as Julia said. For her and Dan, the mantelpiece helped in a 'balancing act' which gave symmetry to layout of their sofa and chairs, whereas 'in a lot of places they have them pointed directly at it'. When Harriet's son pointed out the television as his focal point, she sighed, 'Terrible, isn't it?', and Sian emphasised that, although her children watched television, they were educational programmes such as those on the History Channel.

Conclusion: choosing not to choose

In Chapter 4, we saw in Annette's account of the squabble over putting ornaments in and out of place – a matter of millimetres – a demonstration of territory wars that were not gendered. Other participants who lived in shared, single-sex houses and flats articulated fraught, often silent contests over space – the mantelpiece, the kitchen worktop – that were as much about the desire for one's own 'little space' in apparently communal sites as Sian's complaint about her husband. In other communal spaces in rented houses, nothing is displayed, as no one feels able to occupy communal space with 'personal' things. The delicacy of maintaining the balance of 'shared' space' was made clear in Bronwen's house, where, despite her management of the mantelpiece, the space above was blank, since she did not want to risk offending her housemates by choosing a picture herself. This would be a step too far in her organising; choosing not to choose facilitated good relations, through spatial communality. In contrast, while Karen's lodger could display his birthday cards in the living room 'if he wanted', she did not think he would. Had he chosen not to choose? She owned the space, without intent, or words being spoken. His 'memory' and 'identity' was absent from the 'front' regions of the house; nor did he mark out his 'time' in birthday cards or bunches of keys. Awaiting the transition from renting a room to owning or renting a 'whole', he is a partial domestic presence, who occupies space only when his body walks in the door. These different modes of doing home serve to highlight the delicacy of household micro-practices. In the 'ordinary' family or heterosexual home, these assemble along gendered and generational boundaries. However, these alignments are not fixed; other hierarchies come into play when these conventional divisions are not present. For now, however, I would like to look at three aspects of these practices: memory, gender and class.

As an extension of the domestic relations produced through the mantelpiece, the television/mantel opposition was used between family members in the balance of power (see Crewe *et al.* 2009 for television 'presence'). Mike sidelines his wife's reordering of domestic space by focusing entirely on the television. When Harriet's son points at the television as his focal point, he decentres his mother's spatial practice by centring the room around his viewing practice. By looking at me and saying 'Terrible, isn't it?', Harriet detaches from her child's still-unformed gaze, reorienting this discourse around the matter of class. Emphasising that her children watch only educational programmes, Sian transforms the potentially 'bad' television into an instrument of pedagogy, just as she and others mobilised the mantelpiece. Although Julia dislikes the television being the focal point for the rest of the family, at least they are not like other people dispensing with the symmetry the fireplace offers, who point their furniture 'directly' at the television, 'don't they?' Using the mantelpiece as 'balance', she performs the asymmetry of power between her family and uncultured others. For some, the television as both constant focal point and background to everyday life (like the mantel) was unproblematic, and it was left on most of the time, or watched for information and relaxation. The mantel was for mementoes and so on, with no competition between the two spaces. Expanding on Skeggs' and Wood's work which presents the television as part of working class 'domestic architecture', but a 'bad, powerfully corrupting object' for the middle-classes (2009: 242; also Fiske 1992), I suggest that the unstable relation between the television and the mantelpiece offered a hinge – to some – for identity 'turns'. As Skeggs cites, 'nothing classifies somebody more than the way he or she classifies' (Bourdieu 1986: 19; also Lawler 2005).

The mantelpiece was particularly the field for the practice of female, especially middle-class identities. Their 'hold' on the home depends upon maintaining the purity of the space (remembering that clutter or dust might constitute purity). However, the key word here is 'maintaining': process is all, enabling the constant renewal of identity as relational, with partners, children, cleaners, mess, the television or kitchen wall and 'them' (whoever they are) as the 'other'. Yet alternative household formations demonstrate how home is spatial, temporal, embodied practice that needs no gender. Still, the dominant perception is of the 'pure' relation between woman and home, family and home, woman and the gift, mantelpiece and memory, tradition and aesthetics constantly under threat from a decentring modernity, masculinity and mess. And what is this mess? More often than not, it is the stuff of everyday life, separated out as functional, to be cleared up or stored away. Somehow, these parts of home have to be swept under the carpet. One of the participants in the Cardiff study, Hannah, is particularly prominent in this chapter. She was notable in that she most explicitly talked about class, as a child of the north Oxford cultural elite. Sian was less open about it, but what is clear is how, in talking about others, she, like many participants, was classing herself. The 'mess' of separating oneself out from 'the rest' is an implicit, 'dirty' practice. Who would say now 'I'm posh and rich' unless they want to be mocked, in making explicit their own extreme practice of distinction?

The idea of the mantelpiece as a domestic museum seems comforting, but the way in which children's bodies, senses and comprehension of space, matter and time were disciplined through mantelpiece practice unsettles this notion (see Foucault 1977 [1975]; Bennett 1995; Reay 1998; Hetherington 2003, 2011). From birth, then, 'what children have to look at' constantly delimits the horizon of what can be made visible and how (Berger 1972), what can be practised, as 'home'. Some of them will learn how to use home – and their senses and bodies – as strategies in performing middle-class identity, because they just 'can't help it'; others will not, for the same reason. The domestic learning of 'naked taste' distinguishes legitimate 'knowing' from other forms of education, such as school or 'semi-legitimate legitimising agencies such as women's weeklies or "ideal home" magazines' (Bourdieu 1986: 77). This disciplining of childhood memory, beyond the affective dimensions it does itself constrain – of warmth, Christmas, mother – is where myth lies sleeping. As a cenotaph, the mantelpiece stands as monument not just to those who are already dead, but as memento mori for the living. As curators of family heirlooms, or keepers of photographs, the participants prefigure their own deaths, perhaps not as explicitly as Shyam with her pre-mortem clear-out (in Chapter 5), but as surely. This curious mix of celebratory maternal cosiness, and the cold (untouchable?) tomb: is this 'home'?

Myth lies heavy over other unseen, forgotten practices. Why is it that memory and remembrance are so closely attached to displayable, 'useless' domestic objects that 'matter to mummy'? Why is memory so completely oriented to the past, or to a future where death lies waiting? Is usefulness profane? Where does the middle-class, feminine, past-oriented, pure, dead home leave 'the rest'? And is modernity masculine dirty work? In the third part of the book, we shall step outside this domestic space to ponder these questions.

Part III

Cultures of 'Home': Other Ways of Looking

7
Defamiliarising Home

A further caveat. There are lots of good grounds for doubting the kind of analysis about to be presented. I would do so myself if it weren't my own... Nevertheless, some of the things in this world seem to urge the analysis I am here attempting, and the compulsion is strong to try to outline the framework that will perform this job, even if it means other tasks get handled badly.

(Goffman 1974: 13)

Introduction: migrating home

In this chapter, mantelpieces in Britain that do not sit comfortably in the 'ordinary' domestic sphere will be examined. As the Introduction mentioned, this book is narrative, in the sense that it progresses from the centre, the focal point, of mantelpiece culture, as elicited in the first phase of fieldwork. Those who volunteered to answer the postal questionnaire, and, further, to be interviewed in their homes, were principally female, and defined themselves as white, British and middle class. Memory, identity, family and home, produced through displays of objects on mantelpieces and other 'set apart' spaces (and narratives around those) therefore cohered at some points. Some of these, such as the ways in which stories about display practices articulated 'moral' identities as performances, discussed in Chapter 4, are quite visible. However, others are not so clearly on view. It is easy enough for a sociologist to point out from scholarly high ground the 'taken-for-granted practices' of others, but fail entirely to sense the rock of embedded practices holding her up there. It is impossible to dig this out entirely, but this chapter will shift the ground, and the frame, a little.

In the first part of the chapter I turn to participants who, for one reason or another, offered an 'outside' perspective on what is going on in the construction of domesticity and belonging in Britain. Most of these were deliberately selected as a second group some time after the principal fieldwork, since it takes time to notice absence. I have placed them 'outside' the frame of the ordinary mantelpiece for two reasons. First, as discussed in the Introduction, no one person's mantelpiece practice fits neatly into 'ordinary'. This would presume a structural normality lies somewhere beyond the micro-processes of everyday life (de Certeau 1984). Second, the preceding chapters suggest that, 'on the whole', these complex materio-spatial practices on the mantelpiece produce little tableaux of juxtaposed things which look ordinary. The mantelpiece, background and focal point, in contestation with the television but also 'balancing' it, where gaps are spaces to be both filled up and emptied out, permits such contradiction. I have called this a drama of quiet violence, but have so far kept this agonistic harmony within the confines of 'home' and 'family'. Setting apart a small group of participants makes it possible to see more clearly how the interplay of familiar surfaces and ongoing micro-politics produces big pictures.

In the second part of the chapter mantel displays in museums and 'heritage sites' change the field of practice to that of professional curatorship. These are the 'museums of...domestic objects' that the founders of Mass Observation anticipated (see Chapter 2). Formal presentations of the 'home' as heritage and comfort, they are consumable cultures for the tourist gaze. The colonising, classed, raced or ethnicised 'gaze' of these spectators has been well documented (Bennett 1995; Harvey 1996; Hetherington 2011). The value of looking at these spatial practices is that they are produced as generalities, surfaces that, 'on the whole', depict historically-accurate house interiors or desirable homeliness. This opens up how domestic, heritage and market practices work in the production – and reflection – of 'universal particular' value (Savage 2003).

Part One: Outsiders?

The conversations discussed in this section open out these surfaces in different ways. Becky and Pete are social housing tenants living with very low income, long term disability and other indices of deprivation. Nina defines herself as second generation British Muslim, with a different take on the 'British mantelpiece' in her accounts of childhood memory and current practice. Finally, Matthew and Laura are White South Africans, recently arrived to work in Wales. None of these interview extracts is intended to produce a comprehensive interpretation of their complex, multiple 'home' practices. They simply unsettle 'ordinary' ways of doing home, memory and identity.

Becky and Pete I: life, strength, warmth

Becky and Pete could be perceived as living on the margin of mainstream society, with little in the way of cultural, educational, economic or symbolic capital (see Rogaly and Taylor 2009). Their small Victorian terrace smells of baking. When I walk in, it feels like home.

The mantelpiece, around a 'living flame' gas fire, is Victorian in style, made of wood with floral tile inserts and, they were told by the seller, original ironwork. When they moved in eight years earlier, there was 'just a blank wall', 'but we always fancied a nice fireplace, we'd seen them':

> *Pete*: We decided to buy that to give us a focal point plus some extra heating... [Although the radiator is efficient, it] just doesn't do it [laughs]... I like to see the naked flame... and of course, all that adorns it, really: the tiles, the flowers, the plants, the photographs.

More recently, they have replaced their television with a flatscreen, since the old one 'took up so much room'. I also ask them what informed their decision to buy a fireplace, which they installed with the permission of the Housing Association (HA), using an approved builder. The HA would have had to maintain it if they had installed it, so unlike the rest of the fabric of the house, it is the couple's responsibility. After 13 years in their previous HA property, neither of them could settle down. Becky 'kept wanting to go home', and when Pete came downstairs in the morning, 'it felt like somebody else's house'. Pete says the room was 'bare' and 'cold', and it did not 'flow' when that wall was a 'cold block'; 'it never felt warm, you couldn't sit down and relax'. The fireplace helped to turn it into a home, and now, 'It's the first thing that hits you when you come in the door; it says, "Welcome".'

> *Pete:* [At Christmas it is] nice to have, because I like that Dickensian look. Christmas *is* the Victorians, they had Christmas down to an art form. These days, it's far too commercial.

Pete comments that the house 'needed' a fire, since it was built with one. Even though the large one they chose is an 'appropriate style', it is not quite what the house would have had originally. However, he emphasises that they chose what they liked, rather than seeking authenticity with the house design. He wanted a wooden surround as wood is 'tactile'; it 'still has a bit of life to it', unlike paint. They chose the fireplace together, and Becky thinks 'it brings the room alive'. Central heating is 'dry' and the walls are always 'cold'; there is 'no charm', 'no life' to it. In the time of 'real fires', they were kept burning all winter and spread warmth along the wall. Although their fireplace contains a living flame gas fire, which is 'clean' and 'quick', they nevertheless 'wanted to come back to the fireplace', because they both grew up with them. Becky recounts how the fire downstairs would heat up the middle wall, making the lid rattle on the boiler upstairs and keeping the bedroom she shared with her sister 'lovely and warm'. Her father would not use the central heating when it was fitted. Pete's memory is a little different, of the boarding school he attended as a young boy, when his father was in the army. The school was partly accommodated in two 'big ornate buildings', the 'ex-mayor's house' with 'astonishing fireplaces' and the 'Bishop of Derbyshire's residence', with 'really big fireplaces' which were 'magnificent'. If the boys wanted to watch television, they 'all sprawled out on the floor' in the housemaster's living room, where the 'big fireplace was always on'. 'So,' he explains, 'my love of fireplaces was really deep-rooted when I was a kid.' His parents divorced when he was young, and he spent the rest of his childhood in south Wales.

Their mantelpiece display comprises two dark brown vases (though it emerges that one is a candle), two photographs in brown frames, a wooden tealight holder and a clock; nothing is in the centre. When I first ask them about what is on their mantelpiece, Becky says, 'I don't know what to say – Pete, talk about your pictures,' then:

> *RH*: 'Is there a story to the two vases?'
> *Becky*: No, not really.
> *Pete*: Just what we've picked up. We found the vase and then Becky found the candle, which was a similar shape to the vase, so she thought, "I'll have that" [laughs].
> ...
> *Becky*: [The tealight holders] were a pound in Primark [a popular high street budget store]! [laughs] I loves Primark... I've had some nice things in Primark. I like it in there.

One photo is of Pete with their twin daughters holding a box of gifts, awarded to them as the 'millionth free children' to visit the Museum of Welsh Life (St Fagans 2012), where original houses and buildings are moved to and rebuilt. The other is of Becky's mother (deceased) with the twins as babies. Level with the mantelpiece is the top of a bookshelf, where there are two vases containing imitation roses, two cat ornaments (all from British Home Stores, a high street department store), because, Becky says, 'I likes two', the other tealight holder and batteries for the television remote control. There are two more photographs: Becky's father (deceased), who 'sometimes' moves to the mantelpiece, and Pete holding up a 13½ pound carp he caught. 'He don't care where I puts it, as long as you can see it!' exclaims Becky. Scented oil diffuser sticks are in a vase on a side table, but Pete says Becky moves them 'if she wants more strength in the room'. Other ornaments, gifts from their daughters and friends, are on lower shelves, as is their daughter's school award for geography. Becky does not know why it is not more prominently displayed. On the lowest shelf are albums of old photographs, no longer added to as digital photographs are now loaded onto the computer upstairs, including Pete's fishing pictures, which are also displayed on his angling club's website. His passion is fishing, which 'gets me out into the countryside, clears my head. I'd have a *lot* of fishing stuff up there, but I'm not allowed.'

Becky is 'in charge' of the display:

> *Becky*: I moves things around, Rach. I change it, don't I, Pete?
> *Pete*: I'll come down, I'll have had my shower, and I'll think, 'Huh? What? That's gone there, that's gone there', type of thing. Rebecca's very fond of moving things around.
> *Becky*: I moves things around. Don't you do that? [to me].

Two things, they say, never move. The clock is 'always' on the mantelpiece, and a photograph of Pete's father (deceased) is always by the phone. Pete emphasises, 'that's *his* private place there. When I'm sat here [in the armchair he always sits in], I can see him.' He adds that photos of relatives are 'to remind us of them and get the feeling they're still with us in one shape or another'. Photos of other older family members are upstairs, but 'when their time comes, no doubt they will end up in the gallery'. Becky says, 'I like candles and I like my pictures.' The principle of the display is colour, which is currently a dark brown, seen in the frames, vases and so on, and the cushions. As Pete explains, 'They weren't bought together, but sort of married together as we've found them.' Becky comments that 'I'll probably get fed up with all this next year and I'll just change it all then,' including the unifying colour and the ornaments. She also repaints the walls quite frequently. The old cushions and ornaments are usually thrown into the bin or given to a charity shop, but Becky now plans to pass such things on to her oldest daughter.

Becky and Pete II: longing for the future

I ask them where they get the ideas for these frequent changes. They visit show homes on new housing developments, as they are 'somewhere to go on a Sunday', explains Pete. They can see what the designers are doing with 'cheap and cheerful' things, since the stuff on show is not expensive (Chapman 1999a). Trends such as 'accent walls' with 'dramatic impact' are 'nice ideas' that make him think, 'I can do that or adapt that.' This is better than 'looking at a piece of paper in shops'. They both feel that the ornaments on display in show homes are too 'modern' for their older house, but they can follow the trend to 'keep it minimal... not too cluttered, leave space between and things like that'. He has seen how style 'has evolved' from graduated displays of photographs on the mantelpiece which could be seen from all over the room. Becky focuses on the things she sees, 'things I can't have', unless they 'won the lottery', but, 'There's no harm in *looking*, is there?'

Pete wants a high shelf to display tankards, just as his father, who was in the army, displayed tankards from all over the world around his house. Becky is vehement that this will not happen, saying, 'I'm in charge!' He feels the house is too small, as he would love to have a second room downstairs, a 'blokey room' for all his 'bits' that are currently stored in the attic. He would 'have to acquire' the other things, things 'I've wanted all my life' for this room, which would have a log-burning fire. Here, he would keep his fishing tackle, tie the flies on in there, keep the computer. It would not be private, but would be, 'dare I say it, a masculine room' with which Becky agrees she would not interfere in terms of décor. He has a clear vision of the house they would have, in the Vale of Glamorgan [a desirable rural area] like 'my old colonel [the colonel of his father's regiment]':

> *Pete*: ... stone-built, farmhouse-style –
> *Becky*: – but it's been done absolutely stunning –
> *Pete*: – stunning, but I'd want fireplace features –
> *Becky*: – character –
> *Pete*: – in the style and character of the building, so similar to the age of the building, so that it would look as it should do.
>   ...
>
> *RH*: So do you think if you lived in a house like that, you would still be tempted to get out the paintbrush, Becky?
> *Becky*: Yeah –
> *RH*: – yeah –
> *Becky*: I just don't sit down do I really? I'm always looking for something.
> *Pete*: But in some of those buildings, there wouldn't be as much paintwork to do, because there'd be more stonework around and what have you –
> *Becky*: I've always been like that, Rach, but there again, he's going to buy me the horse that I want, so I'd probably be out chasing that! [laughs]

This future is deeply imagined in wood, stone, paint, informed by detailed knowledge of fashion trends and rooted in the memory. It will never happen, and is intangible in that sense, but what is 'touching' is how they make this image-space as a couple (Casey 2008). Their idiomatic hybrid taste, learnt from show homes and museums, would not be legitimate in Bourdieu's terms. According to him, their décor, produced through 'necessity', exhibits ' ... the taste for trinkets and knick-knacks which adorn mantelpiece and hallways [that] is inspired by an intention ... of obtaining maximum "effect" ... at minimum cost' (1986: 329). Yet the effect which Bourdieu imagines has no bearing on what Becky and Rob 'effect', which bears comparison with Bernie's fire 'effect' (Chapter 3), for warmth that is beyond mere heat. Bourdieu's theory of taste bears some comparison with Veblen's (1953) much earlier reading of classed values, in which poorer/working social strata seek to emulate the conspicuous consumption of the 'leisure class'. While Becky and Pete might be 'at leisure' were worklessness, part-time menial work and visits to museums and show homes to be some perverse analogy for leisure, there is also something else going on. Becky and Pete's accounts open a door into another way of doing 'home' and 'identity', where concepts of culture based on capitals and legitimated consumption tread too heavily to feel this tender ground. Is there another 'culture' here?

Unlike those of the middle-class women we have seen so far, Becky and Pete's home is not for the gaze of others; it is a place of comfort that is made and remade cheaply enough (Garvey 2001). Many of the artefacts are there, not for memory's sake, but to 'colour' the room. It bears the traces of Becky's labouring body, and Pete's patient body too, worked into the walls and the talk criss-crossing years in that room (de Certeau 1984: 21). These conversations also trace out this imaginary space of the future, invested in the fireplace and pictured in fishing photographs. This is not the 'human sensorium' (Howes 2005a), or the cultured 'touch' and affect that rely on dominant cultural narratives (Classen 2005a), but bears something of the 'textual tone' of home that touch can bring (Edwards 2005; see also Pink 2004).

However, the point of this analysis is not to sit back and eat cake, enjoying the comfort – itself a fairly recent fashion (Crowley 2001). Becky and Pete are still very poor, unable to access most of what is taken for granted by the middle class, although they do their best in taking their children to free museums (and show homes). 'Every material inheritance is, strictly speaking, also a cultural inheritance [accomplished] by moving in a universe of familiar, intimate objects' (Bourdieu 1986: 76–77). This universe of objects, the empire of things (Myers 2001), is colonised by values that Becky and Pete cannot access, let alone share, 'lacking' even the right stories to tell (Lawler 2005). However, looking back at the 'mainstream' participants to reflect on what Becky and Pete's story can 'tell' of them, we can see an intensification of home as multi-sensory, time spent together dreaming – 'dwelling' in affect, perhaps, and 'just-talk' (Bachelard 1994; Benjamin 2006 [1932–1934]; Latimer and Munro 2009; Pink 2009; Skeggs 2011). In longing for a future embedded in the past, they illuminate more brightly how physically intangible, yet embodied sensory/imaginary memories of 'home' 'keep' the future, as much as the present (Chapter 3). The past holds the house fast. While, in Chapters 3–6, we saw how accounts are strategies for keeping one's place in 'circuits of value', Becky and Pete make visible links between this circuit of middle-class/classing home owners or future owner-occupiers, and the margin. The 'universal particular' (Savage 2003) of 'telling' accounts has an horizon, beyond which other modes of organising time, space, materials and persons is possible, perhaps, in a new democracy of things.

Nina I: making Englishness

When Nina was born, the family lived in a 'working class Pakistani area' of Rochdale, a mill town in the north of England, in a house with no mantelpiece. Their move to 'a mainly white' village was, for her mother, 'a real step up', connected with 'displaying they'd got the economic status'. Since the house needed renovating, she made it

> ...exactly as she thought a house in [the village] should be and she got that idea from visiting posh friends...and when they were viewing houses in that area before she moved in, she got an idea of what a house in [the village] *should* look like. It should have this fireplace, this mantelpiece, it should be a special place. And it was her idea of what a house in [the village], an English house should be like.

However, over the last 20 years, Nina has noticed the display on the mantelpiece changing. Her mother displayed china at first, since 'it was a very English thing to have on display', but all the china has gone now, except for an egg, a gift from an old woman they used to know:

> Initially [in 1989], they were always Muslim, but they weren't what is known as practising Muslims, in that they didn't pray regularly – they were very Pakistani, but not obviously Muslim. So on that display, there were little china ornaments of people – like a basket with a lady holding it. In Islam, it's *haraam* – forbidden – to have images or a living thing, an animal...if you have images, you're almost kind of worshipping – you're not supposed to worship anything except Allah. But they had little china rabbits...and they had images of animals...But as they became more Islamic, now their mantelpiece, they won't have images of any living thing, an animal or a human being around their house. So they've removed all that kind of thing from the mantelpiece. And now they display, maybe, verses from the Qur'an, which are normally quite intricate, because of Arabic scripture. You can buy them. They got theirs when they went on Hajj, for their pilgrimage to Mecca as well...The idea of the mantelpiece being a special place in the home is still very English, but it has changed, it's a more obviously Muslim house now. I think the idea of the mantelpiece was as well, rather than having an ethnic look to the room and the house, it was, 'Let's have a more English look instead'.

These days, she sees fewer houses that have 'chintzy sofas and china ornaments', except among recent migrants. In her generation, there is a lot more diversity, but, if they were born here, people are not keen to display what they perceive as Britishness:

They're not sure what the British identity is – part of the problem is whether a British identity can incorporate a Muslim identity of equal, if not more importance...

The *behtak* – main formal sitting room – where male visitors are received, is traditional in the Indian sub-continent, near the front door and with its own bathroom. Her father-in-law misses this layout. In Britain, the front room might be designated as that formal sitting room and remains a place that has 'all they want to show of family life to people from the outside'. It might contain Islamic images and texts, but no personal items. There are no souvenirs of beach holidays, for example, in the *behtak*, as these are very personal things not to be shared, not 'the done thing'. Besides, 'Pakistani people don't do that [send postcards] – it's an English or British thing...':

> That sitting room is quite bare, that place they put on display...[it's] normally quite anonymous.

I ask Nina whether souvenirs from trips abroad are a common feature of mantelpiece displays in Muslim families. She replies that they might have

> ...something to remind them of back home, the place they originated from. People who are born in Britain are less likely [to do this]. The one place they will have images and things on their mantelpiece is if they have visited Mecca and Saudi Arabia. They might have pictures of the Ka'bah, which is the one shrine for Muslim people and it's the point of the Hajj pilgrimage...'We've been there or someone we know has been there', and they're very proud of that as well.

A trip 'back home' to Pakistan might also mean a framed cloth from Dubai is on display, bought en route, as this is a Muslim country.

Nina II: doing hybridity

The giving of Christmas cards and presents is a practice Nina considers dependent on how 'practising' families are as Muslims. As children, she and her siblings took part in school nativity plays as 'part of being British' and displayed Christmas cards on the mantelpiece. Now, 'we do celebrate Christmas a little bit' for her children, so they do not 'miss out' at nursery and school. This will 'phase out' as the children grow old enough to understand that it is a Christian and not a Muslim practice. However, she would not want a Christmas tree, saying that different families 'pick and choose' Christmas practices, although she considers Christmas a 'high point' for the mantelpiece, which is more 'cultural' than Christian.

Nina also considers the display of family photographs as indicative of how 'practising' a family is, although her account illuminates the complexity of this concept. She displays photographs only in the bedroom, not the main room, because she feels her father (when he visits) would not like it, while her husband also finds photographs of them and their children too 'personal' for public display. However, her sister-in-law, who was brought up in Pakistan, initially displayed lots of very formal photographs. She has, however, 'toned down' this display, not because she has become more 'practising' but because she has come to realise that it is not acceptable among practising Muslims in Britain. Nina explains this as a transition from identifying principally with 'culture' to identifying with 'religion', as her generation in Britain see themselves as Muslim first, rather than Pakistani or British. This can result in 'minimalist' interiors in public rooms, with no 'cultural reference' to Pakistan. 'If they have anything, it will be an Islamic reference, or nothing at all.' The absence of religious references is a custom she has seen in upper-class or professional Muslim families, regardless of how 'practising' they are. However, she nuances this point, with another exemplar of a 'very practising' family with pictures of their family members in Malaysia on show:

> The father said, 'I know it's not right within Islam, but how are my children going to know, 'This is my uncle, this is my grandfather?'

Nina makes it clear that, while 'you've got the two paths' of culture and religion, 'it's not quite as clean-cut' and 'needs unpacking'.

Unpacking cultures

Trevor Jones (1996) and Tariq Modood *et al.* (1997) presented comprehensive empirical studies of the diversity and changing lived experiences of diverse ethnic minority groups in Britain. Tensions in living as a Muslim/Asian illuminate the 'fragility of the local' (Appadurai 1996), while their experience could also be termed 'glocal' (Eade 1997). The things of 'home' in Asian families in Britain have been characterised as hybrid, travelling, encompassing 'roots' and 'routes' (Gilroy 1993; Clifford 1997; see Tolia-Kelly 2004; Pahl and Pollard 2010; Pahl 2012). The migrations of people from Pakistan and other parts of South Asia to Northern industrial towns in England have been well documented (Werbner 1990; 2004; Blunt and Dowling 2006; Phillips 2006). Pnina Werbner (2004) writes of insular new families, whose children stress their Islamic identity but do not, for example, speak Urdu, emphasising that Muslim identity is a choice, not universal (see also Basit 1997; Ali *et al.* 2006). The complexity of British/British Muslim identity is discussed in detail by Sophie Gilliat-Ray (2010), while her work with Jonathan Scourfield *et al.* (2012) perceives an increase in religiosity – the expressing of religiosity – from first-generation to third-generation British Muslims.

Ghassan Hage notes also the 'turn to Islam' as a reaction to 'assimilation' fatigue among young British Muslims, 'as opposed to the desire for "recognition" by first-generation immigrants' (2008: 509).

Simon Schama argues that British national identity is tied to landscapes, which '... are culture before they are nature ... constructs of wood and water and rock' (1996: 15). Since I have seen things of wood and rock on 'British' mantels, I ask Nina whether pebbles and pine cones, say, might go up on the mantel. Laughing, she replies, 'walking is not a pastime, it's something you have to do' in rural Pakistan, and many people are economic migrants from rural Pakistan: 'Pakistani people don't do woodland walks.' She walks, but 'that's our middle-class upbringing'. She never did it as a child, but does it with her children 'as it's an important part of their education', as is visiting museums and castles, for example. Nina performs a contemporary, inflected version of 'middle-class Englishness', moving on from her mother's practice. She performs it through country walks and museum visits, in a similar way to Becky and Rob, for her children.

If we look back at earlier chapters, taken-for-granted ways of belonging, like walks on the beach to pick up pebbles, family Christmases, framing family in photographs and materialising taste in ornaments, Nina's account accentuates how such simple practices produce particular topographies, temporalities and materialisations of belonging. Strathern (1992) 'turns' class into 'Englishness'; this fine work elicits the ambiguous connection between the two concepts. Nina's adoption of walking shows her cultural expertise in belonging to the class which does '... walking and tourism, movements without any other aim than physical exercise, and the symbolic appropriation of a world reduced to the status of a landscape' (Bourdieu 1986: 55). Country walks, castle and museum visits: these exemplify the 'National Trust' culture in Britain. It is seemingly universal, but always exclusionary, as the deeply unlikeable National Trust agent in Alan Bennett's latest 'heritage' drama encapsulates (see also Chapter 2):

People are ineluctable, Lady Dorothy. They are endemic. They are unavoidable.

While of course as a growth organization we are concerned to maximize our percentage footfall, do please bear in mind these are not just people. Our membership is made up of self-selecting individuals who appreciate the art and craftsmanship of the past.

(Bennett 2012: 33; also Macdonald 2002)

Thus, just as Becky and Pete's account tempered the shaping of home, identity and culture through class in Parts I and II, Nina's etches out the entwined patterning of class and national identity (Savage *et al.* 2010). The 'past [is] a scarce resource' (Appadurai 1981), limited by the comforting, constraining binds of belonging.

Nina also clarifies how absence – of photographs in this case – is as much a process of identity (Wetherell 2009) as presence. However, it is only through her circumscription of this emptiness (or, in her sister-in-law's performance, a material reduction) that the process becomes visible. Juxtaposed with Becky and Pete's non-stories of present 'stuff' (in contrast to their vividly presented future imaginary), this circumscription also outlines how power works quietly. The hesitations, pauses, stops in talk during conversational interviews, the miniature 'heritage dramas' where people's and things' biographies are neatly tied up, are obvious gaps. Silence is silence only if the audience is aware that there is nothing there, in a closed circuit of tautology. Is this a circuit of value where only 'noisy' silence is heard, gaps made meaningful by the things interposing them? What about the absences which have nothing to lean against and give them substance?

Matthew and Laura I: looking outside in

I visit Matthew, Laura, and Lydia (Laura's mother, visiting from South Africa), in the manse, a modern house on an estate in East Wales. The four of us talk about mantelpieces, Welsh dressers and African culture. Quite quickly, the conversation moves on to violence, corruption, poverty, disease: portrayed by them as the legacies of empire and apartheid, mixed with fragile hopes for the future, through the work of 'African journalists' and the 'new new generation of children'. Asked how he understands British identity, Matthew recounts a memory of the mid-1980s (compare Chapter 2 for 1980s national 'belonging' work). At the time, he was working in a South African mine with British graduates:

> One day, we were sitting in my room or somebody else's room, and there was a picture of Africa, a political map of Africa. And they were, he was talking with other British guys, four or five of them sitting there having a natter. And they sat back and they folded their arms and shook their heads, and said, 'Do you remember when it was pink, from Cape to Cairo? Oh, those were the days'. Such a sense of pride of that history, and I thought, I was quite, like, 'Hold on, how can you think like that? Colonialism's bad!' And yet, a lot of their identity – my understanding of their identity – was based on this: having gained so much, and lost it all.

While his story of 'British identity' is of men sitting together gazing at a paradise lost, Matthew goes on to say how moving to Wales has 'blown a hole' in this long-held impression, especially on learning that 'the Welsh were part of the oppressed'. Seeing British identity now as complex, fragmented and politicised, he and his family can no longer fix it down. Lydia grew up in what was then Rhodesia, 'accepting that I was a British subject, [so I] couldn't understand why, when I first came here, why I was treated as a foreigner, and that I found quite hurtful. But since then, I've realised the different boundaries.'

Recently moved into a new home in Wales, Laura and Matthew's mantelpiece is 'in transition', as they came with very little luggage, having disposed of most of their possessions in South Africa. Laura's family has been accustomed to moving countries and continents, rather than just houses, for several generations. Her brother is currently digitally scanning 'everything', such as letters from his daughter and old celebration cards, before he moves to Europe, since it costs 'a living fortune to transport'. A family friend is scanning all her photographs prior to a move to a smaller apartment in a retirement complex, before destroying the originals. These forms of travelling produce different practices of disposal, enabled through technology. Quite the opposite of the souvenirs that people fit into their suitcase from travels abroad, these moves to new homes prompt gift-giving as a means of casting off, different materialities of memory inside a screen, and careful selection of things to display.

Matthew and Laura II: looking inside out

A box is shortly to arrive with some of Matthew and Laura's 'sentimental things', although none of these is specifically 'African', nor are there any heirlooms in there. For Matthew, home is where his wife is, and he has no 'outer museums of life', although he appreciates her work in making a 'physical sense' of home. Laura comments:

> In the future, I can see a need to have memories of South Africa there [on the mantel], for the sake of explaining that we came from somewhere else too, and especially if we do have children. A place to connect, that there's more than just Wales in our home. I can almost *feel* that there's going to be a need to connect. I can imagine I would choose *modern* African art, that it would be aesthetically pleasing; actually, that's what motivates it, not about life back in South Africa. Because life back in South Africa is very similar to here.

Connecting with this heritage of 'elsewhere' will be affective and aesthetic practice, rather than displaying reminders of a different way of life, in the sense that home in the white suburbs was 'really extremely similar' to Britain. She is looking forward to unpacking the candlestick holders because 'I just love them'; all their display goods are what they both 'find beautiful', rather than attached to history or memory. However, as we carry on talking, the similarities become overwhelmed by the differences. Laura recalls the jolt when a friend asked her to view her new house in Johannesburg on Google Earth: 'The first thing you see is bars in every window and door ... [it was] a shock again to see it.' Home has become strange, in a double sense: neither South Africa nor Britain is quite what it once seemed. 'Home is a sanctuary within the prison, but you have to be barred in,' unlike Wales, where houses 'are so open'.

In turn, the couple's strangeness is emphasised by the bulky travel guide to Britain on the mantelpiece. This is neither souvenir of another place, remembrance of a distant home, nor an artefact to signal a kind of belonging, such as (in Chapter 5) the sheep that Annette, a Scot, chooses to put on her display shelf at home in Wales (for what could be more Welsh than a sheep, in the eyes of an outsider?) In terms of ownership, a guide 'to tell us where to go and what to do' is the reverse of a map of Africa, coloured pink. Although it denotes separateness, it also signifies a desire to transform oneself, rather than mark out territory, through going to and doing what is outlined in the book. Also on the mantel is a very recent purchase, a print of Tintern Abbey, which the three of them visited. That shared memory is important, since Lydia is soon to return to Africa, but Matthew draws a parallel between the ruins of the Abbey and the contemporary church in Britain, which is 'broken and old and a museum' where no people go except 'to gawk as they would at any other museum piece'.

Is British heritage a sacred practice of keeping 'ruins' and 'detritus' (Hetherington 2008)? Heritage is not simply museums and ancient buildings, but ways of doing culture, memory, identity and belonging. Has the colonialising gaze that yearned for a map coloured pink undergone a sea-change? Have class and ethnicity intersected in such a manner that the topology of the English (or British) landscape is transformed? The practices instituting 'home' that we saw in Parts I and II produce margins, force out certain practices and make exclusions. The mantelpiece is a 'telling' materialisation of these, lending its weight to certain meaning-making practices. As Matthew and Laura show, memory and home can be 'light', almost weightless. Conversely, they also offer a different concept of 'nostalgia'. Rather than Odysseus and the other original *nostoi* making long journeys home from the Trojan war, sick with longing, Laura views a digital image of 'home' only to be shocked into a sense of its pathology. Prisons, like the 19th-century sanctuaries where angels of the hearth kept home (Chapter 2), are pure places, keeping out unwanted strangers and dirt, just as they keep in those who might want to break out. A practice of home so deeply entrenched in the material, and where past, present and future are constantly refracted in what seems like a closed room of mirrors, is heavy, enclosed.

As we saw in Chapter 5, the closely kept relations between people and things made home a site of security, maintained through fictions, where tensions and frictions were carefully negotiated. Proposing alternative ways of doing 'home', Divya Tolia-Kelly writes of 'new cultural nationalisms [that] rely on souvenirs and sacred objects, contributing to a new moral aesthetics of home and thus creating an inclusive culture of Englishness' (2006: 341). Visits behind the scenes at two museums of home and design will explore more deeply how belonging as purificatory homely practice extends into cultures of national memory and identity (Macdonald 2002; 2007).

Part Two: curating memory, cleaning up the past

The Georgian country house became a 'culture industry' for a 'newly emergent consumer class' (Arnold 1998: 18) and the staging of houses for tourists was already a feature of 18th- and 19th-century social life, particularly since wars in Europe demanded that the Grand Tour have a domestic substitute (Thomas 2007). Therefore, these houses became the focus for the type of touristic experience fictionalised by Jane Austen in Elisabeth Bennett's visit to Pemberley, home of Mr Darcy in *Pride and Prejudice* (2008 [1813]: Ch. 43). This practice of visiting old country houses continues, and was popularised in Britain as a pastime by the National Trust's purchase of grand houses made unaffordable to their owners through taxes and repair bills. While what is seen on the mantels of these houses might not precisely mirror those seen by Georgian ancestors, the National Trust ideal of the British country house is powerful in the conception of 'Heritage Britain' (Hewison 1987). Sites such as Tintern Abbey, currently under the care of Cadw (the Welsh equivalent of the National Trust) are precisely the places that construct 'heritage Britain' as a museum piece to 'gawk at'. The aim of this second part is to examine the construction of such sites of memory, and how they might guide viewers 'where to go and what to do'. Becky and Pete's Sunday drives to show homes are a strange tangent from the commonplace British middle-class visits to country houses, museums and their attached shops. To tease out the practices of 'curating' home, I visited a preserved slum, and interviewed two museum professionals, walking and talking around the spaces and materials they curated.

The Victoria and Albert Museum archives

I met museum curator and design historian Charles Newton in 2004, in the cellar archives of the Victoria and Albert Museum in London, where exhibits are stored with varying degrees of protection. This visit highlighted the 'crisis of representation' (Atkinson 1990), since 'exhibiting authenticity' has been a longstanding problematic in museum curatorship (Phillips 1997). Charles had curated the 1990 'Household Choices' exhibition, part of a project that also produced a book (Newton and Putnam 1990). A variety of methods were used in the production of both book and exhibition, including photo-elicitation, auto-photography by children and adults of their own and others' homes, and what is conventionally understood as 'expert' photography of domestic interiors. The card boards hosting the photographs are stored together in wide wooden drawers in the cellars, but can be removed and viewed. In contrast, a small sliver of William Morris wallpaper was kept, untouchable, behind glass in its own frame. In the depths of this museum,

I wondered at the changing regimes of value since those domestic interiors of 1937 (See Chapter 2), with their few photos of family on the mantel.

Indeed, as Charles commented, it was almost impossible to have any idea how most people decorated their homes prior to the advent of mass-produced, cheap cameras after the Second World War, since any photographs earlier than this are staged and normally middle-class (see also Weston 2002). As an expert curator, he views television costume dramas as inaccurate portrayals, since they draw on a very few sources from a brief period in the late 1880s and early 1890s and a small section of the upper middle class. As a result, they tend to be full of overstuffed, over-classed houses that do not reflect how most people 'did' home in the 19th century. The television, close neighbour of that other 'period drama' in the living room, the mantelpiece, thus presents another mirage of heritage for viewers to gaze at.

Extant old houses, photographic images, curated museum houses, staged displays of country houses and castles, or Victorian style books, paintings and literature therefore offer limited sources for interpreting 'past' hearth and home (see Wood 1965; Phillips 1997; Arnold 1998; Long 2002; Scholz 2002; Stange 2002; Weston 2002; see also Chapter 1). Curators have access to inventories, but these are not the 'everyday' stuff (Meldrum 1999). Consequently, the 'authentic' study and display of historical homes is problematic for museum curators (Phillips 1997), and for design historians (Saumarez Smith 2000). To explore this further, I visited the last three back-to-back 'slum' houses in Britain, meticulously restored by the Birmingham Conservation Trust and National Trust at Court 15, Hurst Street Birmingham at a cost of several million pounds (Upton 2005). There are a few photographs extant of these back-to-backs between 1939 and 1941 (Bournville Village Trust 1941; Upton 2005). The mantelpiece over the range in the back-to-back was recalled by some previous inhabitants. One account resonates with the 1937 Mass Observation accounts discussed in Chapter 2:

> There are many ornaments on the high mantle [sic] shelves – flowery vases which are often used as repositories for letters, money or sweets.... The art consists of family portraits, often hazy from enlargement, framed certificates and prints from Victorian times – Highland stags, the Infant Samuel and so on.
>
> (Anon., cited in Upton 2005: 68–69)

Another recalls Friday was 'fish and brass day' when the ornaments were polished. Yet what a visit to the expensively-restored Court 15 highlights is that this is heritage, a history cleansed, literally, of soot, rats, filthy water and poverty. As tourists of the past, we were free to turn over the cigarette cards on the mantelpiece, inspect the 'hazy family portraits' and nose into the vases. But we could not sit there after dark with the candles lit, coughing into the smoke, or, as a child, stay out on the street until bedtime, due to lack of space in these cramped rooms.

The Geffrye Museum of the Home

Having noticed how the prevalent the practice of 'curatorial consumption' (McCracken 1991) is in the management of mantelpiece displays, I was interested in how expert curatorial productions are made. I therefore interviewed Eleanor John, head keeper at this London museum, in 2009. The principal display is 11 period rooms 1600–1998, arranged chronologically along a corridor, which visitors walk down to view each roped-off room (Geffrye Museum 2012; Dewing 2008). These contain mostly original furniture and décor from the date in question, focusing specifically on the homes of the 'middling sort' in London. A fireplace features in all but the two most modern rooms. Interpretations for each room are provided in antechambers, together with examples of the materials used for visitors to touch. During our interview we focus on the changing fashions in curatorship, especially in the move from a 'design' framework to putting objects in context. Eleanor explains how they are in the process of curating the rooms according to this principle, pointing out that, 'If you're looking at any period room, you can tell not only the date people were trying to represent, but the date that it was done' (see Douglas 1986: 69).

In the rooms from the earlier period, this changing practice involved the exhaustive analysis of probate inventories, together with paintings, diaries, Old Bailey records (post-1674) and some fictional sources. The main resource, the probate inventories, underwent, 'broadly speaking', content analysis to see what objects came up repeatedly for a picture of what a particular 'strand' of the middle classes in London owned at that time. Although these are 'a key body of evidence for that period', there are a number of problems with them, such as the fact that each listed what only one person owned in a household, 'things are removed, things are left out', and 'getting to the detail, the happenchance stuff, what happens to be left on a chair is more difficult'. Further, understanding how rooms were used, 'who's getting invited to the dining table and under what circumstances' is challenging (Meldrum 1999). Having decided what furniture to put in the rooms, Eleanor and her colleagues tried to find the objects, but 'those very middling sorts of furniture that the middling sort would have had just weren't really in museum collections'. As a consequence of this absence of 'ordinary' goods in museums, they 'had to go out and buy them from auction houses'. In practice, the museum had to buy the things that people no longer wanted to consume 'curatorially' in their homes:

> I think, how does this stuff come onto the market? I think it's associated with that point of death, isn't it, clearing objects? I don't know how people decide when, what they want to get rid of. There has been a huge

fashion movement away from 18th century stuff and that's been quite useful for us, because it meant we got a lot of things quite cheap, but it also meant they weren't coming onto the market so readily.

For the 19th- and 20th-century rooms, photographs add to the 'body of evidence', but with the same caveat that 'things are put in place for photographs, just in the way that you have to think about paintings and the reason paintings were created'.

The latest move in curation is 'revisiting', 'layering' the displays by observing people's responses to them, and 'placing a value on memory', together with feedback from the museum's website to produce a participative framework. Eleanor comments:

A memory is a part of the collection in the same way as an object is. And objects on their own, they can't speak. That fundamentally is the problem. And they take up an awful lot of space and you spend an awful lot of time looking after them and actually it's the information surrounding them that makes them really interesting.

However, she adds later that 'I struggle with memory, because I absolutely realise it's a reconstruction.' Connecting the curatorial fashion with both the growth in technology that allows for constant, pluralistic feedback and the popular interest in history, she says:

... it's about hearing people's voices, isn't it. And then you've got the problems with that, that people have in terms of – is everybody's voice *as* valuable, and that you actually, there might have to be some sort of weeding out process and that is, presumably, where curation comes into this whole thing, that there is a weeding out of what is valuable and that's an ongoing process [...] you can't escape your time. What is kept by curators is the curator's view. Not everything can be kept or captured. You have to be aware that what you're doing *is* a version, it's always a version of what's going on. You can't merely reflect what's going on ... Everything is down to the framework you're looking for.

What if the past does not want to be curated (Hetherington 2008)? How do we assemble different pasts, in different ways, pasts of intangibles, hybrids that have no narrative, that do modernity differently? And how might housing futures veer away from the aspirational spectacles of show homes (those modern descendants of Georgian country 'show' houses), beyond anxious aestheticisation of ruined slums, made precious by rarity – because so little survives of poverty (see Bennett 1980)? The cultural practices and values of the powerful keep their potency precisely because they seem so 'natural' (Bourdieu 1986). 'The practices of institutions of collection and exhibition

[are]... key sites for making up, acting on and transforming social worlds through the distinctive kinds of assemblages of persons and things that they effect (Bennett 2005: 102). Hetherington calls 'museumification' a space of death' (2008: 290). 'Museumification' looks strung out, a clumsy assemblage of too many syllables – usually a sign that *doing* has been ordered into a grand circuit of meaning and value (only think of 'interdisciplinarity' to understand my line here). I am thinking about something else: a way of doing exhibiting that some anthropologists and curators are bringing forth (for example, Pahl and Pollard 2010). Is narrative, stories of things, a way of telling that everyone can articulate? 'Narrative seems to exist in all human societies, modern and ancient, and that it is perhaps the most fundamental form for making sense of experience... but if something is everything, maybe it is nothing, and we are back to square one' (Flyvberg 2011: 311). The practice of 'making home' involves an 'obvious materiality' (MacDonald 2007) which imbricates nation, gender, class in ways that are so very everyday, they are elusive (Scott 2009: 2).

Conclusion: 'museums of the future'?

Avtar Brah writes that 'home' is a 'mythic' place of 'no return' in the diasporic imagination, but also the 'lived experience of a locality... a cold winter night might be differently experienced sitting by a crackling fireside in a mansion as compared with standing huddled around a makeshift fire on the streets of 19th-century England'. She questions the implications of 'eras[ing]', that is, forgetting this history of inclusion and exclusion, of the multiple affiliations and conflicts, both between those with different origins 'on the street', and between them and the mansion dwellers (Brah 1996:192). There is no one way of doing 'museum', but 'museumification' kills these multiple roots, routes, attachments and detachments. In telling the history of the fire, the mantel and its assemblages, it is too easy to freeze out those 'huddled' outside, to see their makeshift hearth as a lack, rather than as the making of a network. 'The large and powerful are able to delete the work of others in part because they are able, for a time, to freeze the networks of the social' (Law 1999: 95). The *Nation's Mantelpiece* (Conlin 2006) is a lovely coffee-table book about the [English] National Gallery. The mantelpiece, the coffee table, the National Gallery: this indeed is belonging in circuits of value. As Savage argues, 'the power of class lies precisely in the difficulty of articulating it clearly' (2008: 478). Those who cannot articulate the narrative, yet assemble things in their own domestic museums, live not with futures, but with precarity (Skeggs 1997), on the edge of the network that *matters*. 'How do people inhabit personhood when they are positioned as the constitutive limit to it?' (Skeggs 2011: 503).

In making nation, belonging, home, conditional on 'obvious' 'natural' 'everyday' ways of remembering, memory, museum-making, we keep it to ourselves (see Skey 2012). If only the 'ruins' and 'detritus' could be replaced by the messy multiple pasts of the unordinary masses. Further, in 'keeping', we are kept within a space of home that requires constant maintenance, and where frictions and tensions must be smoothed over, the folds in the social fabric smoothed out. This ongoing process is what Bruno Latour called the paradox of modernity (1993), where constant attempts at purification produce more and more hybrids. Perhaps, then, the oppositions which troubled the end of Chapter 6, in which home as feminine and pure countered masculinity, mess, and modernity, can indeed be clothed together in the warp and weft of the modern. But what modernity is this, which both imprisons those who belong and pushes out so many? In the next chapter, we shall explore China and the US, to examine more deeply the homely geographies of modernity.

8
Genealogies of Difference

Let's face it, we're undone by each other. And if we're not, we're missing something.

(Butler 2004a: 20)

Introduction

Chapter 1 narrated how Roman design, in the form of Italian neoclassicism, together with other Continental trends, translated into a British idiom, attached always to the open flame and more recently, to the 'garniture' on the mantelshelf. In this chapter, two different genealogies of the mantelpiece, in China and the US, offer reflections upon the different ways of 'history-making' in Part I (to view images and websites relating to the Chapter, see Hurdley 2012). It explores how the absence of mantelpiece culture in China, and the careful preservation of New England fireplace practices, dig deeper at the foundations of home and identity – in the sense of homeland, or nation. I chose China as a country which until recently had very little cultural exchange with Britain, and New England precisely because it was an early colonial territory. I was also taken by the serendipitous discovery that a complete and exactingly researched traditional Chinese house now has its home in this US state. By looking at other countries, at how the 'white middle-class Anglophone identities' (Savage *et al.* 2010) have fared in colonialising domestic architecture, we can understand how the 'universal particular' makes its world everywhere (Savage 2003).

The first part of the chapter draws on interviews with two Chinese academics, Lok and Jun. The aim was to hear their views on how Chinese domestic display practices have changed over time, and how they compare with Anglo/American practices. Three points were of particular interest: first, the cosmology of architecture and interior décor; second, the contemporary irrelevance of the hearth and the historic absence of the mantelpiece; finally, the rapid changes in domestic practice over the past

sixty years, in connection with national, political and economic transformations. Their common focus on these prompted me to explore histories of the
Chinese home. As a caveat, Lok, like Jun, emphasises that he can talk 'about
the mainstream, but not all people', 'because the Chinese have many kinds
of families'. Both use online photographs of preserved traditional Chinese
houses and new apartments, together with hand-drawn sketches, as starting
points for our conversations. Each refers in passing to his own home, but
this is not the focus of the dialogue. The aim is to reflect on how another
cultural vernacular can make the familiar strange.

In the second part of the chapter I focus on New England and the
Eastern Seaboard in the US. As this is the first area of America settled by
the English, I was interested in tracing how the English fireplace fared
as colonial 'material'. I trace how the New England fireplace threads into
networks of remembering and belonging that stretch beyond the narrow
boundaries of home and family. While the development of US architecture and domestic interior décor is pluralist and complex, the work of this
condensed interpretation is to build an argument about changes and movements of meaning in American houses. Such an overview elicits three aspects
of design history: first, the change in meaning of 'Colonial' architecture;
second, the transfer of meaning from domestic architecture to the architecture of domestic things; third, the transition from nation-building to
'homely' national belonging. Following this is a detailed analysis of an interview with an expatriate Scottish family who have lived in New England for
ten years. While, as 'outsiders' to US culture, they note the clutter and uni-
formity of mantelpiece displays, they nevertheless attribute New England
fireplaces to necessity – the climate. As a further interrogation of commonsense explanations for everyday familiar practice, I therefore conclude with
an exchange I had with a sociologist from sunny California. Why do all of
this, now? Because from here, in Wales, this looks very far away. As we shall
see, it is all very, very near.

Part One: China: history, cosmology, culture

In this exploration of house, home and family in China, I divide the
genealogical sketch into two necessarily brief chronologies, drawn from
common themes Jun and Lok expressed. 'China' and 'Chineseness' are
'capacious umbrellas to wrap any generalisation' (Knapp 2005: 4; see also
Yeh 2009), so local and ethnic differences in domestic architecture and practice can be extreme. However, there were few apparent changes in the design
and decoration of Chinese houses until very recently, in contrast to the clear
historical periods of European houses (Lo 2005). The historical overview is
based on three principal sources (Berliner 2003; Knapp and Lo 2005; Pow
and Kong 2007) to reflect on how a national genealogy of domesticity can
produce different home cultures.

Chinese homes and families pre-1949

The house is the oldest Chinese building form and 'in traditional Chinese society, house, home and family and all that they touch are seamlessly interwoven' (Steinhardt 2005: 13). Cultural practices around 'home and family' – *jia* – rather than religious belief were central to Confucian concepts of hierarchy, patriarchy, balance, harmony, security and control (Taylor 1982; Bray 1997; Lo 2005). Protecting *jia* with doorway deities, ancestor worship and other practices was equated with protecting the country itself (Lo 2005). The practice of siting the house, its furniture and ornamentation auspiciously, according to the geomantic principles of *feng shui* (rooted in Confucian and Daoist worldviews), was part of this ordering, based upon symmetry, pairing and centrality. The colours, materials, house size, construction type and decoration were governed by sumptuary laws, although these may have become ineffective by the 16th century (Pomeranz 2002).

Things did not embody an aesthetic of 'beauty', but cultural symbolic practice based on 'the word as a duplication of cosmic patterns, numerology, ornamentation, ordering of spatial elements...' (Liu 2005: 157). Concepts of affiliation and duality were embedded in the language, and since homophonic connections made things homologous with articulations of harmony, the auspicious pairing of ornaments was vital (Berliner 2005; Lo 2005). Therefore, the 'visual vocabulary' of home was in part analogous with the spoken word. It was not 'ornamental' but designed to 'express and embody a family's aspirations for good outcomes... good fortune generally, as well as longevity, (male) progeny, prosperity and peace' (Jervis 2005: 230). This can be seen in the positioning and decoration of the altar table, in the formal reception hall of larger houses. Ancestor worship, 'fortified by the Confucian canon', was embedded in Chinese ethical and intellectual structures, including domestic practice through honouring, nourishing and protecting the home and family (Lo 2005: 175), and thus the nation. Living and dead family members, including the broader lineage, were linked through rituals in a prescribed calendrical sequence, particularly at New Year.

The 'form and extent' of the family's housing was 'inextricably linked to its own form and extent' (Cohen 2005: 235), with clusters of 'houses' developing in a residential compound around a 'collective stove' (Faure 2005: 284). Families descending from a common (male) ancestor were therefore divided, but commensal, pooling resources and sharing meals. The stove was central both physically and symbolically, with the stove god in his niche playing a central role in the calendar of domestic ritual (Flath 2005). In smaller rural houses in, for example, Heilongjiang province in northeast China, it was common to have a central open room with two or four stoves which vented via side rooms under built-in beds (*kang*), thus heating them. Family members' bed 'place' was dependent upon their position in the family order, since 'discipline and hierarchy took precedence over intimacy and emotionality' (Yan 2005: 376). Young married couples would be separated by no more than a cloth from other members of the family, and were subject to 'surveillance', with no autonomy in their management of home (ibid.: 389). With no formal reception/living room, the beds were platforms during the day for daily chores, children's games and sitting with visitors.

Since villagers shared a common lineage, there were ancestral halls in each village, as centres for affirming common ancestry and performing family rituals (Ho 2005). For a funeral, the altar table might hold an arrangement of two candlesticks, two vases and a central incense burner (for example, Berliner 2003: 62). In larger family houses, there was also a formal reception hall which functioned partly as an ancestral hall, partly as a place to receive visitors and for daily household activities. An example of this is the Yin Yu Tang House, built in 1800 in Huishou province, southern China. Directly opposite the entrance, the altar table was central in embodying order. Similar in position and design to a long, broad mantelshelf or console, the altar table was quite high and placed 'facing conceptual south in the centre of the [house] structure...the most auspiciously located and esteemed place' (Berliner 2003: 148). In Huishou province, *dong ping xi jing* [east vase, west mirror] was a common arrangement on the table (ibid.: 149). Since the homophones for *ping* and *jing* are 'peace' and 'calm', the auspicious placing of the vase and mirror were articulation of and aspiration for the key Confucian concept of harmony. Above the altar table might be calligraphy hangings expressing good fortune, while at New Year, ancestral portraits and tablets would be hung up. Furniture was 'symmetrical and standardized' (ibid.). However, furniture position was not fixed; its Chinese name, *jiasheng*, means 'active objects'. Understood as 'portable architecture', it was moved around according to occasion, making this formal space flexible, which was crucial in more modest households (Lo 2005; Knapp 2005a). Thus, constitutive of this cosmological orthodoxy was mundane pragmatism. Despite freezing temperatures and snow during the Huishou winter, there was no fixed domestic heating. People wore multiple cotton padded layers, and used mobile charcoal braziers (compare Greek/Cretan houses in Chapter 1).

Into now: 1949–present

With the formal establishment of the People's Republic of China in 1949, and particularly during the Cultural Revolution, there was official repression and destruction of the principles and materials of traditional cultural practices. Defined as one of the 'Four Olds', *feng shui* along with anything else defined by the Communist Party as 'old' was banned or demolished during the Cultural Revolution from 1966 (Spence 1999). Ancestral halls and tablets were destroyed, and it became common to hang a portrait of Mao above the altar table in the reception hall at New Year, as the Mao cult replaced ancestor worship (Berliner 2003).

From 1978, the official introduction of the 'Four Modernizations' brought China into an era of economic reforms and different global relations, particularly since the 1990s (Evans 1995; Hsü 2000). The 'Three Represents', formally adopted by the Communist Party of China (CPC) from 2000 onwards, supporting economic, cultural and political advances, also implies that, in order to maintain dominance, the CPC takes a constantly changing approach to modernisation (Hepeng 2004). These reforms produced changing house/family forms, a new conception of conjugal and domestic privacy, less restriction of traditional practices and changing relations between home and identity. In traditional reception halls, the altar table became a hybrid space, where rituals such as weddings and New Year were celebrated with calligraphic hangings, pictures and cloths, interwoven with the materials of modernity, a music centre and a clock being common features (Berliner 2003: 20–21; 148). The new mass production of printed paper 'gods', such as the stove god has made them cheap and widely available, and subject to freer interpretations than the old orthodoxy (Flath 2005). Reworked into 21st-century Chinese family life, the god of wealth, for example, has become newly popularised since the economic reforms, and celebrations of New Year show both respect to tradition and aspirations for the future. The formal hall has been transformed into 'a family's multi-purpose room often without ancestral tablets, but often with photographs of deceased parents and others, but also cluttered with a television, refrigerator, dining table ... ' (Knapp and Spence 2006: 76).

In the 1980s and 1990s, there was also rapid, extensive demolition of traditional houses as young men wanted comfort, new modern lifestyles and an attractive home for a wife – crucial for the production of a male heir (Berliner 2005; Yan 2005). A sofa – a new modern piece of Western furniture – will not sit easily against a round column. In Heilongjiang province and elsewhere, the influence of urban house forms brought back by young people working in the city led to the introduction of an intermediary 'living room' and private bedrooms in smaller village houses (Yan 1997; 2005). This introduction of *yinsi* – the Chinese translation of Western 'privacy' – remade spatial and family relations, and a new division of home into the 'public face' and intimate space. This new division into 'front' and 'backstage' (Goffman 1959) means that economic status can be concealed, with the distinction of some visitors as 'intimates' who still come into the main bedroom, and a different spatialisation of activities and family members.

In a rapidly urbanising society, the new home/family unit is a couple with a child living in an apartment, where an entertainment centre replaces the altar table. Lifestyle experts and publications proliferate, and young people prefer to swap a valueless antique chair for a comfortable sofa (Lo 2005). As well as the mass construction of high-rise apartment blocks, a particularly interesting phenomenon is the construction of gated developments of Western-style houses, analysed in a recent study (Pow and Kong 2007). In wealthy suburbs of large cities such as Shanghai and Beijing, the 'house is a hotly sought after consumer good... and a prime venue for the articulation of taste and status' following the 1998 housing policy reforms to introduce mortgage loans and privatize all state housing (ibid.: 135). These market 'the exotic' of Western-style modernity, such as 'Tudor cottages' and 'English manor houses' in 'Hopson town' (with areas named England, Northern Ireland, Scotland and Wales) together with the Chinese elite aesthetic 'nature' tradition (ibid.: 146–148). While these conflate modernity with Western-style housing and lifestyles as symbolic and cultural capital for a new urban middle class (Bourdieu 1986; Bennett *et al.* 2009), this is not simply a result of recent globalisation, but 'historically inflected' by nostalgia for the 'glory days of old Shang Hai' (Wu 2004; Pow and Kong 2007: 150, 156). The construction of English, New England, French and 'compradoric' hybrid-style houses in the late 19th century is embedded in elite urban Chinese heritage. In contemporary Western-style villa developments, the use of *feng shui*, internal Chinese variations, such as putting the kitchen in the garage and, since 2005, a move to sinicise development names further demonstrate the complexity of relations between westernisation, modernity and constructions of Chinese identity, home and nation (Dong and Tian 2009).

In tandem with this programme of modernisation has been a new focus on heritage preservation (see also Chapters 2 and 7). Traditional towns and villages in China started to gain United Nations Educational, Scientific and Cultural Organisation (UNESCO) listing from 1997 onwards (UNESCO 2012), with other towns and villages named in China's own listing of historic towns and villages from 2003 (Doar 2005). The mass dismantling and selling off of parts of pre-1911 houses led to new regulations for trading in cultural relics in the later 1990s (Berliner 2005). Architects 'attuned to international practices', 'aspiring home owners' attentive to 'real estate values', 'eco-tourists' and 'awareness of the problems posed by industrial pollution' have contributed to the turn to conservation in China (Doar 2005). However, poverty is paradoxically 'the most potent conservationist' and 'unfettered economic development' is conservation's 'greatest peril'. Thus in turn, heritage tourism is contradictory, causing both harm and protection (ibid.), as seen in recent debates around plans to build a £3bn Tibetan culture theme park outside Lhasa (Global Voices 2012). Cultural heritage plans also include a £67m theme park around the abandoned childhood home of Mo Yan, winner of the 2012 Nobel prize for literature. The government will pay farmers to start growing red sorghum once again (an uneconomic crop), to create an authentic 'Mo Yan Culture Experience' for readers of *Red Sorghum* (2003 [1988]). Open air museums and historical 'living villages' similar to those in Europe and the US are recent phenomena, but the selection of specific sites is perhaps not representative in a country with a vast, diverse range of different, yet locally systematised practices, rendering of heritage as leisure. The historic Yin Yu Tang House mentioned earlier, curated by Nancy Berliner, has now been reconstructed in New England as part of a cultural exchange programme, a large-scale version of the transposing of old buildings at St Fagans and other 'living' museums in Britain (see Chapter 7; Berliner 2003; Peabody Essex Museum 2012; St Fagans 2012).

Meanwhile, 'China style' has entered the Western mainstream as a means of 'blending' East/West styles (for example, Leece and Freeman 2006; Lim and Corrie 2006; Taschen and Guntli 2006). In this aesthetic discourse, Taoism, Confucianism and *feng shui* are seen as decorative (marketable) resources: 'As the pace of modern life gains tempo, more and more city dwellers – both in China and around the world – are finding that such classical serenity fits neatly into contemporary living.' *Feng shui* is 'simple common sense' for living in an uncluttered home which meets a 'basic desire to live in conjunction with the natural world' (Lim and Corrie 2006: 9; contrast Jun and Blundell Jones 2000; Hwangbo 2002; Knapp 2005b).

Interviewing Lok: displaying education, Chineseness and modernity

We first look at a traditional rural house, with a formal reception room/hall, on a Chinese website. Lok explains how the altar table in the main living room, which he calls a 'desk', would be the equivalent of a mantelpiece. This has a vase on one side and a clock on the other. The homophones of these two objects [*ping jung*], are 'a whole life' and silence', so the two together express and embody a peaceful life. Symmetry is important: 'two means good thing, one means single, so not good'. He and his wife live alone in their apartment, in Beijing, with families still living in rural areas. In such apartments, the 'combined style' of 'ancient' and 'Western' or 'modern' is popular for 'upper class' Chinese people with a 'high education'.

The question is 'how to do tradition' when televisions and other entertainment units have changed both lifestyle and room organisation. These have taken the place of the altar table, and 'no one wants a picture of grandfather anymore'. They 'put their memory in some kind of book or computer, because it's changed'. The use of colour is important in creating this 'combined style', using brown or grey:

> Times are quite different. Within fifty years, great change has happened, so no one knows what's [the] next step, so they just want to have a quiet philosophy and a quiet life is enough, they just want to put it [décor] simply, like this.

To be able to combine ancient and modern gracefully is admired among

...people who have a very good education, [who] want to express their ideas in their families. [But] a merchant with a poor education, but they have money, lots of money, they put the decoration as rich as you want, it's quite different...Education is a very important factor to dividing the style.

I ask him about the types of villa developments examined by Pow and Kong (2007), with Western-style fireplaces. These are not for heating, merely for decoration. His response echoes that of a university lecturer interviewed by Pow and Kong, who mocks the 'uncouth' 'new rich' for wanting 'vulgar Western styles' (2007: 153):

Nowadays, we think it's not good, but it's just a period of time. They just want to attract customers: American British, French styles... Because the customers have money, but they have no ideas – [he mimics the customers] 'Oh, what is the feeling if I live in Britain, if I live in America?' – 'So, you can try this villa!'...But many have changed their style to ancient or Chinese style, to combine together. They want to show, 'I have knowledge, I have education'...

Thus the symbolic and cultural capital, combined with affectivity, which developers are promising house buyers, through investing in Chinese tradition/heritage and Western exoticism/modernity is subverted by Lok's hierarchy of capital, where displaying education is paramount. He turns affective/symbolic/cultural capital into no more than fleeting fashion, pure economic capital and a simplistic 'cut and paste' attitude to Western lifestyle/architecture (Kuson and King 2000).

When I ask Lok whether he displays family photographs in the living room, he replies that, whereas his father and grandfather gathered family photographs in a corner of the wall to show them all together, he does not. He says that 'memory is not necessary to do in the families, they want to put their families more modern, especially in the 1990s'. So calligraphy and paintings are taking the place of photographs. His explanation is that, with urbanisation and the breakdown of traditional (rural) household and social formations, more people used their homes to entertain people they did not know very well, with wider social and career circles. The new 'Western' concept of privacy captured by Yan's (2005) ethnography of village homes, imported from urban house forms, has returned to the cities, inflected by Chinese rural family-oriented culture:

[mimicking a visitor] 'Oh, this is your younger sister' – it's not good to tell them, it's private. Some people do not want them to know this, so collected them together in the drawer.... they want to protect themselves, their families.

While family members might no longer live as a corporate unit, the Western practice of constructing families as 'absent presences' through the public display of photographs is supplanted by keeping families safe in a drawer, book or computer. No longer guarded by doorway deities and strictly followed rituals, they are nevertheless protected (Lo 2005). It could be argued that the display of calligraphy and paintings is as much a display of 'family', in that it shows a high level of educational capital.

Lok's apartment is on the 26th floor, where he cannot see trees, like many people living in cities. He explains:

> More and more young people want to put the vase in their living room. In my room, I have three vases, I put the flowers in, fresh flowers. It can make the air fresh and make me feel comfortable.

This too is linked to a 'good education, and their feelings towards nature. In modern families, they have to see green, fresh trees and flowers...they want to make the room more ecological'. Thus, although apartment dwellers might not have the private gardens offered to the very rich, this miniature, domestic interior performance of the traditional Chinese 'nature' aesthetic is important in the construction of the family as 'modern'.

I explain to him that British décor is often about family and history, looking back through inherited objects, family photographs and certain stylistic features, including the mantelpiece. He responds that there is no difference, because Chinese people 'also want to remember'. However, the key division is 'the principle' of *feng shui*, which he considers to be 'more and more important for modern families'. He explains that it was 'forbidden' because, in 'the new Chinese society' the past, and the old, had to be 'demolished'. Now, the state does not promote *feng shui*, but permits it, in order to maintain their 'own Chinese culture'. 'If we demolish, we will have to use the culture of the West.' Although he did not have the time to use *feng shui* for the interior decoration of his apartment, he has ensured that there are two goldfish in a water bowl, auspiciously positioned, and also used *feng shui* principles to choose the apartment location. It seems that our understandings of 'memory' diverge, with his constructed around working ancient formalised cultural practices into modern houses, and mine centred around displaying images and belongings of family members.

I ask him how he perceives the British construction of the home:

> I think in British [homes], their principle would be family circle together, and it's family life. But in China, it's the order, it's for parent, grandparents and sons and grandsons – it's the hierarchy – positioning in the room – grandfather in the middle, father on left hand, grandchildren in the last

one, grandfather chooses the TV channel. So the location of the facili-
ties of the living room will [depend on] listen[ing] to their grandfather,
grandparents' ideas.

This is in extended family households, where the grandfather/parents might
have a bedroom still decorated in the 'traditional' style. The portrait above
the altar table might have been replaced by control of the TV remote and
best position on the sofa for the venerated patriarch, but this demonstration
of 'order' shows how ancient principle is performed in everyday life. The
'person' does not matter, rather his or her position in a vertical, gendered
generational order. Similarly, his or her ability to practise modernity as
the skilful, graceful hybridisation of new and ancient practice, rather than
the personal attachment to things as performative of family/social networks,
is dominant in this account.

As we conclude the interview, I remember something I read somewhere,
and ask casually whether Lok is familiar with shrines to Buddha in the
corners of reception rooms. He closes down the conversation immediately: 'I don't talk about that; it is too powerful.' Confused, I ask him what he
means. 'No, I don't talk about that,' he repeats, and fearing I have somehow
trodden clumsily over a boundary I could not see, I thank him and end the
interview. Later, I realise how this connects with the way in which power is
a process which delineates only certain empty spaces, gaps which are mutually constitutive of artefacts; at least artefacts which *matter*. The skill with
which participants produced accounts of things, and of themselves, in earlier
chapters, shows how they know what to see and what to do. But they can
exercise their craft only with what is available, a pragmatic approach to a
world *which is given*.

Interviewing Jun: pragmatism, tradition and Westernness

If Jun had a mantelpiece in his Cardiff flat, he would display Chinese art
and photographs of his family, using the fireplace to show where he is from.
He currently displays these in his flat, together with British and African souvenirs from his travels, as these too are 'a memory of my life'. He likes the
open fire in Britain 'because people sit there, drink, read a book, enjoy it'.
However, he has only been in one home inhabited by a British family, and
is uncertain whence this idea of enjoyment originates, thinking perhaps it is
from films. When Jun visited his colleague, he did not look at the display on
the mantelpiece, noticing only that the fire was lit. He suggests that this is
because he does not have 'the habit of looking'. It is not in his 'background'
so he is not 'attracted' to them, in contrast to 'if you always live in such an
area and realise fireplaces can show memories and mental ideas' when visiting other people's homes. British, African and Chinese objects are displayed
in his office, where we hold the interview. As I ask him where each object is
from, he explains that one small silk decoration, similar to a doll's dress, but

without armholes, was originally given to his British colleague when they were on a work trip abroad. The colleague then gave it to him, and at the end of the interview he gives it to me. I am troubled by this souvenir of somewhere I have never been, a thrice-given, seemingly always unwanted gift which I do not know what to do with, nor have I any attachment to the series of givers. It is a 'memory of my life' as an interviewer of strangers and acquaintances, which after some months in the back of the car, gathering dust and guilt, is disposed of as rubbish.

In China, Jun considers the living room is not for 'private memories', but for 'their belief, their wishes', with photographs kept in bedrooms or photo albums, excepting perhaps a newly married couple's wedding photograph. He emphasises the future-oriented character of display in public rooms, for good fortune in terms of money, family and career. Modern rooms are organised around a sofa and the television. Remembering that when he was a boy, the slogan was 'to demolish all old things', he explains that 'old' was equated with 'weak' following occupation by the Japanese and Germans, and in the face of Western military/industrial modernisation. Ideas and technology were imported from the West to 'become the New China' but he emphasises the complex character of the relation between 'Western' and 'modern':

> ...for layout of the sitting rooms or decorations, the change to modern –I cannot say modern – it's kind of Western-style, but it's not exactly Western-style, because we do not have a fireplace, something like that, but it's kind of, modern styles has been a long history.

He makes a strong distinction between 'local people, ordinary people' living in rural areas, who still maintain 'layout tradition', and the 'great change' in urban areas. In 2004/2005, he comments that there was a change in governmental approach to Confucian ideas, which had been officially forbidden during the Cultural Revolution. Interpreting this as political pragmatism, because they realised these ideas were 'in the hearts of the people' and could not be changed, he says that the government now encourages tradition. However, this is not a cynical top-down new ideology, but the character of Chinese people, who 'are very pragmatic'. For example, the lack of religion in China is because Chinese people pray for wealth, luck, more sons, rather than worshipping a deity. In contrast to Lok, he views this state move as rooted in ancient Taoist belief, in establishing a 'harmonious society', with harmony between nature and people. It is not, therefore, in opposition to Western ideas, but because traditional ideas are 'useful' for government.

Returning now to the Yin Yu Tang House, owned and inhabited by the Huang family from 1800 to the 1980s, the following comment by a family member illustrates a future-oriented attitude to the heritage of home and family:

[This] arrangement is the best solution for preserving the house. It's actually a big favor for us descendants. We can preserve the house forever and it will help us to remember that our ancestors had glorious achievements, and that we must keep forging ahead ourselves and make progress in our own careers.

(Huang Binggen, quoted in Peabody Essex Museum 2012)

As Jun explains, heritage is a new concept, constructed because living standards have improved. People are richer and therefore have more time to think about it, rather than merely surviving. I introduce Rybczynski's (1986) argument that nostalgia is caused by 'discomfort' with the present, but he counters this, asking whether the British were interested in heritage a century ago. There was no legislation for the protection of old houses in Britain until 1945, while the open fire was resurgent in the US in the late, industrialising 19th century. Was this discomfort, or was it comfort that enabled people to look around them and value what was being lost in the rush to be modern and enjoy greater domestic comfort?

In the second part of the chapter, we move to New England, to explore how the hybridisation of 'heritage' with modernity and orienting to the future is a strategy for nation-building and belonging.

Part Two: America: gentility, climate and homeyness

As 'history' and contemporary practice, the mantelpiece in the United States can be viewed as partially connected with the British mantel; it is the points of apparent disconnection that suggest different ways of understanding home and identity. In particular, the linking of 'private' domesticity with a strong 'public' national identity resonated with the culture of home and family in China. I chose principally to question how British expatriates viewed the American mantelpiece, since this illuminated the sharp edges of what was considered 'American' and therefore 'other'. Focusing on New England and the Eastern Seaboard, rather than studying a vast, diverse mix of cultures and localised practices, meant that the 'other' was itself shaped by a historical legacy of northern European – dominated by British – colonialism. Nevertheless, I was also interested in how mantelpieces were viewed by a Californian, Marie, since 'climate' – a popular justification for fireplaces as 'necessities' – could not count in her city. Before discussing these conversations, a brief history of the 'American' fireplace follows.

The birth of an American mantelpiece

The typical household in 18th-century New England used firewood in quantities that were 'unimaginable in timber-starved England (Brewer 2000: 1). The great wood stacks in front of each house held both the promise of comfort and the effort required to achieve it: the American dream. 'It is important to note the lengthy dominance of Georgian architecture in the Colonies involved much more than an architectural style: it represented the material aspect of an evolving, stratifying culture', which 'filtered down the social levels, reaching those who, unaware of its origins, knew only that it was somehow desirable' (Foster 2004: 34). The Georgian aesthetic was to be found 'especially in parlors [where] fireplace walls were enhanced by moldings, mantel shelves, raised paneling, and even painted landscapes' (Brewer 2000: 17). This spread beyond New England through the use of pattern books imported from England, and newly arrived colonists, including artisans, who spread westwards. As the 18th century progressed, 'the dominant English culture, exemplified by its Georgian symmetry' (Foster 2004.: 39) took precedence over Dutch and German house designs in their former colonies, even supplanting French/Creole styles on the lower Mississippi by the early 19th century. Eastern Anglo-American architecture spread into California during the 1848–1859 Gold Rush, although here, as in many settlements, it combined with the availability of local materials and existing building tradition to produce hybrid vernacular styles.

Nevertheless, the new republic also sought the weight of neoclassical allegory to create nationalistic motifs. The fireplace was an ideal symbolic and physical focal point to add these to existing homes. Following the concept of Adam's 'edifying' chimneypiece designs (see Chapter 1), the entrepreneur Robert Wellford set up his 'American manufactory' in Philadelphia producing composite ornamentation – synthetic paste forced into intricately carved moulds (Reinberger 2003). From the late 18th century these cheap, mass-produced and, crucially, American-made decorative motifs adorned mantelpieces in middling homes along the East Coast. These transposed the British–European neoclassical tradition into domestically-produced material allegories of the early republic, also including 'story' pictures such as the *Battle of Lake Erie*, portraying an American victory against the British. Wellford also set up a 'Fancy Ornaments Store' selling marble and bronze decorations for the mantelshelf, thus integrating the two elements of an 'American' display (ibid.: 29).

Despite its European roots, from France and Italy as well as Britain, the 1820s Greek Revival has been called the first 'American' architecture, producing the ideals of republican democracy in built form, particularly in the work of Benjamin Latrobe (Fazion and Snadon 2006). Pattern books for craftsmen, builders and the new professional architects spread ideas quickly; detailings around the doors and windows could be seen even in Midwest villages, detached from this political significance (Foster 2004). Following the Civil War, however, nationally available catalogues of designs and building parts created 'mail order architecture' that reduced regional differences (ibid.: 274). The withdrawal of architects and craftsmen from mainstream housebuilding during the mass growth of urban and suburban populations led to a decline in 'pattern books'. A new genre of books and periodicals about the domestic ideal, many of them British imports, entered the popular market (e.g. Beecher and Beecher Stowe 1869; Caddy 1874; Eastlake 1969 [1868]; Cook 1995 [1881]). It is impossible to know how closely these design experts were followed in home decoration practices, but the growth in this market points to popular demand, at least for reading about homemaking and taste (see Chapter 1).

As in Britain, the increasing division between the male domain of work and the female place of 'home and family', from the mid-19th century to the 1930s, was paralleled by an increasing emphasis on women as homemakers, and as writers about home décor, rather than the earlier emphasis on the house as reflective of a man's character (for example, Downing 1969 [1850]). A further explanation is that, following the Civil War, and displayed at events such as Philadelphia's 1876 Centennial Exposition, a 'cornucopia' of household furnishing flooded into the US (Gordon and McArthur 1986: 15). Many of the newly rich urban/suburban population originated from small towns and rural areas where the practice of 'taste' was rare and Puritanism continued, albeit implicitly, to taint personal display as 'sinful' (ibid.; also Bercovitch 1975). It was therefore crucial to make connection between domestic display and morality, for the consumption and display of interior furnishings. Works such as 'the gospel' of the British artist Charles Eastlake, as the New England writer Harriet Spofford called his Arts and Crafts-influenced *Hints on Household Taste*, were vital. His book encouraged a new fashion of DIY handicrafts, dispensed with the need for inherited goods and dismissed the luxurious French rococo style as passé (Gordon and McArthur 1986: 106). In making a virtue of handicraft, 'new' money, an simplicity, and an 'evil' of 'ugliness' Eastlake not only developed the idea of home décor as a moral practice, but also denied the ability of the 'ordinary' person to discriminate between 'good' and 'bad' design without expert guidance (Eastlake 1969: 15). Her particular duty was to nurture Christian values in her children through home décor; also to 'reflect her own accomplished individuality' (Cook 1995: 351). The mantelpiece, associated with the 'family shrine' was a particular focus for this activity (Cook 1995; see also Brown 1988: 127).

While more efficient devices, such as the airtight stove in living rooms, and the cooking stove in the kitchen, had become common during the early 19th century, mantelpieces remained a feature. In, for example, New England homes with stoves and, later on in the century, central heating, mantelpieces were still fixed to parlour walls, with 'bracketed shelves, reminiscent of the mantelshelf' in bedrooms (Garvin 2002: 166). Fireplaces 'returned to favor in the late 19th century and have remained an affordable luxury ever since' (Garvin 2002: 158). This has been interpreted as a 'backlash' against stoves (Reinberger 2003: 141) and nostalgia for the symbolic connection of the open fire with 'hearth and family' at a time of urban industrialisation, albeit one that women, for whom the stove saved labour, did not share (Brewer 2000: 93).

From the late 19th century, better technology and mail-order, pre-fabricated houses enabled eclectic hybrids of modern technology and historic styles in the new ideal: the detached suburban family home (Gowans 1986). Styles such as the Craftsman bungalow with its 'strong expression in the mantelpiece' (Garvin 2002: 166) and building methods such as the balloon frame demonstrate how experimentation and divergence from Anglo-American tradition gradually produced a distinctive US 'high' domestic architecture (Peterson 2000). Even though, like other architectural trends, these had some influence on vernacular residential styles, they were not popular designs. Despite many different modernist-influenced designs in urban apartment buildings and high-end housing, the suburbs still display – in diluted and often vague form – the 'Colonial Revival' that was, paradoxically, instigated by the Centennial celebrations of independence in 1876. These often contained Federal or Adamesque-style fireplaces (Garvin 2002: 166). The architecture of domination has thus become the material of heritage, seen in 'three-car-garage "Colonials" ' (Foster 2004: 286). The 'somehow desirable', yet much-altered fragments of Georgian gentility proliferate in these neo-Colonial designs, with fireplaces still common in New England suburban houses and beyond. Mantelpieces are also constitutive of the visual nostalgia canon, in, for example, the wistful black-and-white photo-essay of pre- and post-Depression era rural America, *Mantelpieces of the Old South* (Baldwin and Turk 2005).

USA today

In order to reflect on how the first British incomers brought their house-building traditions to America, I questioned how contemporary British immigrants to the Eastern Seaboard of the US viewed the now strange homes of their neighbours. It was striking how, when so little could be imported from Britain, these migrants used the mantel, or an equivalent shelf, to make a microcosm of their displays at home. Further, their accounts resonated with how 'outsiders' such as Nina's mother, Matthew, Laura, Jun and Lok perceived British display practices. Heritage, as a 'national' practice, and 'memory', as a supposedly individual practice, are parts of ongoing processes of making identity. The salience of examining a genealogy of the New England fireplace and mantelpiece is how 'individual' colonisers, as a collective, built a nation.

Therefore, rather than interview Americans about American mantelpiece displays, I asked British expatriate participants to contrast their mantelpiece displays with those of their American friends and neighbours. The questionnaire participants were all members of the British military or civil service (and their family members) on secondment to Washington D.C. Few of them could comment about actual American homes, since none had American acquaintances, partly because many lived in an 'enclave' of rented houses for British civil servants: a little Britain. Their own mantelpiece displays were often direct transpositions of their displays 'at home' although some had deliberately brought objects to remind them of 'home': for example, a slate clock and lovespoon on a Welsh woman's mantelpiece. Several commented on the decoration of American gardens, with 'patriotic displays' and seasonal ornaments: 'I would guess they also dress the inside of their homes similarly.' Others recalled US mantelpieces that displayed 'lots of things, lots of anything', 'faux fruit' and 'family photos'.

In order to focus closely on how 'Americanness' was made as everyday home and family practice, I interviewed a family who lived as both strangers and insiders to the American home. The questionnaire accounts of the little-known interior were supported by this Scottish family (Ailsa and her daughters), who had relocated to New England a decade previously, and who were well-integrated into a wealthy middle-class American neighbourhood. For Sasha, who has been at boarding school in Scotland for two years, the fireplace is a 'comforting image' – the objects move to each house, it reminds her of 'mother', 'home'; 'I can smell it almost.' Clarifying that they cannot generalise about American mantelpiece displays, they discuss the mantelpieces of people they know, who are white middle-class New Englanders. It is 'very New England' to have woodstocks outside the house, and living room fires are used because 'it's sooo cold' so 'come and drink hot chocolate by the fire'. However, expectation that there would be no fireplaces in the warmer climate of the South is confounded by my description of the mantelpiece photo-essay of the 'Old South' (Baldwin and Turk 2005).

The type of mantelpiece and its contents vary 'not just [according to] a question of taste, but how affluent you are', and it is common for wealthy householders to employ interior designers to 'theme' rooms and houses, choosing all the colours. They agree that domestic display practices are more 'traditional', since 'they don't have a sense of old...their sense of old doesn't go back many generations', explains Ailsa. Noting that it is very rare to have the elegant 'bare' symmetry of a typical Georgian-style mantel display, she comments that 'they like to put a lot on the mantelpiece...little frames that say things like, "I love you, Daddy", and it's all piled up there', albeit symmetrically. The mode of décor is 'excess', which automatically denotes wealth, even though a different minimalist aesthetic might characterise dwellings such as converted lofts. An extension to the mantelpiece is the huge American fridge, filled with postcards, photographs of holidays and magnets, explained by Sasha as imperative: 'you have to decorate that vast expanse of white'.

The conversation starts with a discussion of photographs of Ailsa's friends' mantelpiece displays, as well as her own. She does not consider her few very close friends as 'American', since they display things from their travels, rather than their 'cultural background'. People like them are 'keen' to show that they are 'travel-y', through showing souvenirs of elsewhere, says Sasha, demonstrating, as Ailsa puts it, 'I am not American.' Displaying European taste is particularly important, although she disagrees with her daughter's claim that 'they're trying to be European'. Ailsa notes that they do not put 'tactile objects or nice beautiful things up there [...] I like the feel of objects too. As you move the giraffe to dust them, they feel really lovely. You pick it up – not that I dust that regularly.' The principal focus of our conversation is the mantelpieces of other families, including those of Sasha and her sisters' schoolfriends.

A typical mantelpiece in these homes is a graduated, symmetrical display, with either a wedding picture or photograph of the whole family in the centre. Extending from this is a chronological sequence of the children at different ages, culminating in the graduation picture. For the older generation, pictures of grandchildren would be included in this sequence. These are expensive studio portraits, which 'everyone' does, says Sasha. They are taken against a studio backdrop which might be on a 'beach' or against a 'picket fence', rather than 'documenting a good day or a memory or a party or something, it's so fake'. The principal purpose of the mantel is, rather, 'a display of their family, but proud it's an American family', since 'displaying their love of America is very important', especially since 9/11 (although Halle 1993, comments on this). This incorporates the Stars and Stripes as the background to a studio portrait, or into the photograph frames themselves:

Sasha: If you're an outsider to a tradition like that, it just seems so empty. I suppose all traditions are like that. There are probably things we do that they think are weird.

Ailsa: Americans have this formula for decorating.

Sasha: It's expected. You *have* to have your child's graduation photo up there, otherwise [she mimics 'the American'], 'Are you not proud of your kid? Are you not happy they graduated from High School?' It's a look: 'Our family functions the way it's supposed to, we're happy, we have great kids, we had a gorgeous wedding, our children are accomplished'.

Ailsa: You know how grandparents are very proud and put up photos of children and grandchildren? Americans seem to do that from Day One and they don't wait until they're that generation to start displaying. I've very rarely gone to a house where somewhere you don't see photos of themselves at different ages.

Sasha explains the 'formula' as 'you have to do it to show you know how it's done'. This is structured by seasons and annual events, with autumn being marked by chrysanthemums, Christmas by lights and figurines of snowmen and 'horrible German-type Father Christmases' on the mantelpiece, Hallowe'en by 'a pumpkin between Child One and Child Two'. Thanksgiving, Easter, Valentine's Day, Mothering Sunday and Father's Day are other points on this social aesthetic calendar. I ask them about poorer families, to which Sasha comments that she thinks they follow similar patterns of display, but they live in a 'very white middle-class town'. 'We're not avoiding them, we just don't see them,' she adds, underlining the closed circuitry of distinction. While many of the participants comment on the taste of others, they are, in the main, commenting on the taste of others who are very similar to them in terms of class and ethnicity. Yet this is not a simple reproduction of social stratification, but an ongoing and complex process of friendship, intimacy and belonging. While much of the calendrical display rituals might be external shows for any passer-by, Christmas among friends is a competitive event, centring on the production and display of cards. It is convention for Christmas cards to be studio portraits of the family, so plans for when to visit the studio, and which one has been selected are the first subject of conversation. When cards have been sent, visitors check the mantelpiece to see whether or not certain cards have been received, and conversations then centre on the portraits themselves, judging the 'look' of the families.

Therefore, displaying 'family' (Halle 1993) depends upon both presenting one's own family together with the 'right' others on one's own mantel, and displaying one's own family correctly on others' mantelpieces. Knowing how to 'do' Christmas includes not only the purchase of the correct Father Christmas figurine, but also purchasing the correct 'look' from the right studio, for the gaze of others in numerous domestic galleries (Belk 1993). However, if a picture is missing from one's own gallery, that too constructs the family as lacking. Nevertheless, participation constitutes belonging, since even a poor picture or absences perceived (by the looker) in the display (however full up the mantel might be of snowmen and Santa figures) is an intimate practice of belonging. Hospitality in the home is less common than in Britain, comment Ailsa and Sasha, with people meeting up in restaurants unless they are close friends and family. To take part in this contest is to take part in small circulations of bodies sitting in studios, framed in pictures, displayed on mantels, visiting houses, looked at and talked about and belonging.

The enclosure and safekeeping of family portraits in Chinese homes, in bedrooms, albums and digital files, rather than in these constant processes of extensions between persons not only produce different identities, but produce identities differently. The process, as well as the 'product', matters in the making of meaning. These different treatments of family – as storage and display goods – produce different versions of 'family'. Since they are also accounted for here as national practices, the relations between family and nation also produce 'nation' differently. 'Who sees what' is not simply a matter of whether a birthday card is opened up and read by an inappropriate visitor. It is an action that constitutes families as 'doing' America, as belonging to a nation and a social group. It is an action made possible by a Chinese man not being 'good', and failing to pursue the 'Western' notion of *yinsi*, but putting a photograph of his little sister on the wall (if he has siblings).

American 'style' houses in China are products of quite different processes from these New England houses. Similarly, the surfaces where families are constituted and circulated in Britain and America might be the same Georgian-reproduction mantels, but have quite different genealogies and parts to play in the making of identities. While Sasha comments that 'I've never met an American; they're always half this, a quarter that' in terms of their heritage, conceived as genetic components, 'it's compartmentalised so there's no friction. On the one hand I'm American, and on the other...' This account of the frictionless separation of parts, between 'their make-up' and being 'American now' is a process of making history, persons and nation that throws being 'British' into sharp relief, especially when compared with Nina's account (Chapter 7):

> *RH*: What you makes you different from Americans?
> *Sasha*: I have a British passport, but apart from that, I don't consider myself British. I know I am, but –
> *Ailsa*: – our family doesn't have a British identity –
> *Sasha*: – Tea!

This is a conception of the American mantelpiece as centripetal, in a sense moving towards a cohesive, coherent picture of nation through the display of family, with no memory-objects of other places, and binding social groups together. The 'New England' firewood and fireplace culture is also important, and explained by the climate. To interrogate this entirely reasonable explanation, I interview Marie and visit her home and family in San Lorenzo, on the east coast of San Francisco Bay. We also correspond by email. She considers that fireplaces are 'sought after' for two reasons: as adding to the market value of the property and embodying the 'ultimate sense of home'. As 'homey' goods, their dual values are connected, since 'People move so quickly here, they want to turn a house into a home quickly'. In later email correspondence, I ask Marie to confirm that the climate has no significance in this construction of 'homeyness' (McCracken 2005). She replies:

> It gets a little blustery [in San Lorenzo], but nothing compared to many parts of the state. Californians often talk about their 'micro climates'. We do not need a fireplace and have not lit it in several months. The last time we had a fire it was Spring and only because it made the house feel homey. In fact, we don't even use real wood. We use 'Duraflame Logs'.... You can even buy logs that crackle, to make noise like it is real wood. Anyway, in California we have 'spare the air days'. On those days, one is not

suppose to use the fireplace. Many people have converted their fireplaces into gas. All new houses are equipped with these because it all together helps the environment. I think they are better at putting out heat. But, all in all, they are more for looks... We hang our stockings up at Christmas and our wreath is pretty low, knowing that we don't have much to worry about in the way of a hazard.

Conclusion: moving worlds, keeping modernity

Georgian gentility thus enters a different sphere of meaning, of morality and taste and family, from early nation-*building* and *supporting*, to nation-*keeping* (Latimer and Munro 2009). Yet still its attachment to the old country is manifest in the keeping also of 'Colonial' architecture, no longer the material of domination, but of 'heritage'. If we look at the overall 'move' of the American mantel, we can see three things happening. First, its part in the translation of 'Englishness' as the dominant architecture of 'gentility' to the new White Anglo-Saxon Protestant nation, and its pioneering spread to the South and West. Second, a change in the architectural scale of meaning in the making of 'America': from the house to the fireplace. Even a Californian bungalow has a fireplace – perhaps 'only' for the 'look', but looking makes worlds. Third, and attached to this, a transition from 'Englishness' to a material of nationhood and personhood – of making and being 'American', of 'homeyness' and 'family' (see Rybczynski 1986, on Ralph Lauren stylings of the American 'home'). Yet nothing is entirely lost in the 'disposal of meaning' (Munro 1999; Strathern 1999). A hybrid of Englishness, class and gentility carried over in the continuation of the mantel, built into the Georgian frame for the fire that first found its place on the Eastern Seaboard, carried over in ships and pattern books, and keeping its place in the patterning of 'home' – as nation, as family, but still framed in the notion of the 'Old Country' (Munro 2001). Through this rescaling of the architecture of meaning, the 'right' Christmas family photo-card on the 'right' mantelpieces in town, and the access for looking at these, remakes 'circuits of value', networks of belonging and property, as the 'genteel', cluttered domesticity of Anglo-American middle-classness – and classing (Skeggs and Wood 2009, following Bourdieu 1986).

Having 'taken' the mantelpiece, the British were then very successful at translating that into American landscapes, in its powerful connections with 'gentility', perhaps from its 'original' Georgian ancestor. Its *affect* here is nostalgic, family-oriented, with 'homeyness' and the plenty of New England woodstocks close by. To 'do' the mantelpiece is to *be* American. Such is the flexibility of the British (neo-Georgian style) fireplace, that it flips over in China, as an attachment of modernity and/or Westernness. The fact that it manifests nouveau riche lack (of education) in some of its forms only enlarges its reach in the 'disposal of meaning' As Savage *et al.* (2010) note, these multiple transposings do not indicate 'simple cosmopolitanisation', but rather 'the cultural imaginary of the (post) colonial white British, a 'weakening of a Eurocentric white identity and its replacement with a more Atlanticist, Anglophone version'. Cultural referents from Asia, Africa, South America and Eastern Europe are invisible in the cultural tastes of their representative group of white Britons. Following Savage's and Skeggs' (among others) ongoing pursuit of class and *habitus*, I suggest that Englishness, middle-classness (see also Strathern 1992) and a historicism that stops at (neo-)Georgian gentility are enshrined in the small world of the mantelpiece and its assemblages. Although the poor might always be with us, 'we just don't see them', as Sasha says.

Now, we could reverse this line of thinking by arguing that, in China, political pragmatism has incorporated Westernness/modernity with Chinese past/future as another hybrid entity, to strengthen a Sino-centric world that will 'go beyond the West' (Anagnost 1997: 85). In her argument, Anagnost shows how the concept of *wenming* embodies not only civilisation as 'an advanced stage of historical development', but also 'civil behaviour', bound up with a concern to transform the 'masses' into 'persons of quality' [*renmin de sushi*] (ibid.: 75–79). She notes a discourse of 'lack' in this current articulation of power through the inflecting from 'quantity' to 'quality'. Nevertheless, these complex tensions between past, present and future, Asia and 'the West', modernity and tradition are bodied forth as state practice, modelled, Anagnost argues, on the 'illiberal capitalisms of Japan and Singapore'. In taking this stance, she contests the traditional genealogy of *wenming* from the ancient Chinese classics, in a similar move to that Westgate (2007) made (see Chapter 1). However, these traditional genealogies are effects of a particular world-making, just as Anagnost's is a 'turn' to make a critique of them:

> A genealogical critique refuses to search for the origins of gender [...] rather, genealogy investigates the political stakes in designating as an *origin* and *cause* those identity categories that are in fact the *effects* of institutions, practices, discourses with multiple and diffuse points of origin.
>
> (Butler 1999: xxix)

What this elicits is a tautologous temporality of past and present, if the past is made always as an effect of the present (see also Douglas 1986). Modernity may indeed be reflexive, but in a mode that always folds itself in, enclosing the past. Thus, as Mao displaced ancestors with images of himself, tradition and the 'four olds' were to be seen as weak in the face of Western enemies, to legitimate the Cultural Revolution. When China turned towards the markets of the West, a pragmatic recovery of tradition produced hybrid 'Chinese' modernity. The 2012 election of a new CPC Central Committee will produce further changes. With the (relative, partial) wealth and leisure of industrialisation comes a recent remaking of the material past as heritage, since little denotes global modernity better than a UNESCO world heritage site. 'America' persists still as the 'other', a dream place of escape, an imaginary that we can see also in the architectures of villas and lifestyles in Shang Hai. The American dream, however, looks similar – if not the same – from the 'common ground' of both nations: wealth, the ability to consume and produce 'America' in the same civilised move, safely housed within circuits of value. Note how English 'Colonial' was revived as American architecture in the 19th century, just as the technology of the photograph was incorporated into tradition, framing nation, home and family on the mantelpiece, a century later. In Chapter 2, we saw how Margaret Thatcher placed home and family firmly at the centre of state policy at a point when the 'National Trust' was expanding its principally middle-class membership, who paid up to wander through the once-private houses of the old elite. Home and family: these twin institutions effect and are effects of a particular dominant narrative. 'Traditions', 'heritage' and 'dreams' sound so much pleasanter than circuits of value, quality, exclusion.

Wells (2012), drawing on Dwyer (2000), argues that, after the great era of nation-building, and monument-raising in the 19th century, there was still a focus on 'events of national significance' and 'great men'. However, ' ... the myth of a unified national identity unravels as the contested claims of vernacular histories struggle to make themselves visible in a public landscape of memorialisation' (Wells 2012: 153). Yet the dominant narrative is retold and remade, in the small spaces, materials, visibilities and shadows of that most 'vernacular' of spaces, the home. In her writing on 'cutting the network' (1996) Strathern contests Latour's notion of the:

> ... proliferation of hybrids as the *outcome* of the purificatory process ... But heterogenous networks [i.e. those not contingent on people's interactions] also have their limits. I shall argue that if we take certain kinds of networks as socially expanded hybrids then we can take hybrids as condensed networks. That condensation works as a summation or stop. The Euro-American hybrid, as an image of dissolved boundaries, indeed displaces the image of boundary when it takes boundary's place.
>
> (Strathern 1996: 523)

The trouble with Latour's notion of modernity, once he has clarified that 'we have never been modern (1993), is that there is no 'stop', in the great mass of stuff waiting 'out there' somewhere for us to stitch into the network. Just as the mantelpiece in America is a hybrid entity, working the genealogy of nation, home and family, it is also a condensed network of modernity, tradition and class. Where is the 'stop'? Strathern proposes:

...an indigenous, Euro-American mechanism for cutting [the network]: ownership. Ownership is powerful because of its double effect, as simultaneously a matter of belonging and of property. Euro-Americans will not have to look far to determine network length; they have always known that belonging divides and property disowns.

(Strathern 1996: 531)

The dominant network is made of people who tell stories about things, and make things with stories: connecting their biography, tastes, memories, losses, aspirations and everyday lives with the assemblages on the mantelpiece. This network makes a seeming heterotopia in which each person is the fabricator – the inventor – of relations between time, space, things and persons. Like a spider's web, each thread vibrates with the move of another, as they are connected through alignments of practice: stories, clocks, photographs, cleaning, keeping. Some of the efforts at keeping things apart – or keeping them in line – such as the television and the mantelpiece, or the ugly card and the line of vision, are spoken of. Others are completely invisible. Savage *et al.* (2010) contest Said's (1978/2003) notion of orientalism as 'eroticized visibility of "the other" ', with their extensive and detailed data concerning the cultural tastes and practices of the white British, which 'indicate mundane invisibility'. I would take this further, to bring gender back in – or back out.

We can remember, now, that the migration of South Asians into industrial Northern England (Chapter 7) brought another hybrid into the network. An effect of industrialisation – in early 19th-century Britain, later on in the US and Asia, with a mid-20th century revival in England, was nostalgia, the hybrid of tradition and modernity. Leisure, an after-effect of industrialisation, makes time – really, *makes* time – for heritage, and museums, and a concern for belonging to what is now a global matter of concern – producing the past for consumption (see also Chapter 2). Seeing the past as consumable makes it a modern material, and the mantel nurtures the discerning gaze. Nostalgia has been viewed as a masculine discourse, since the '...feminisation of modernity...is largely synonymous with its demonization...the idea of the modern becomes aligned with a pessimistic...glittering phantasmagoria of an emerging consumer culture' (Felski: 1995: 62). To continue the 'turn' at the end of Chapter 7, are mantelpieces modern, masculine, nostalgic, feminine, kept-but-consumed messes (hybrids)?

Goffman (1983:17), observing 'the social arrangements enjoyed by those with institutional authority...who are in a position to give official imprint to versions of reality', is cited by David Macdougall (2006) in his critique of dominant visual practices. The mantelpiece constructs a reality of 'distal' knowledge for the 'masses', a domestic museum where 'proximal knowledge' (see Hetherington 2003) is given only to those who clean and tidy, or who are in the recognised group of those who can walk up and read the insides or backs of cards. The 'god trick' (Haraway 1991) of a finished, distant tableau is maintained for many visitors to the living room. The busy work of ongoing maintenance and repair – of 'care' or 'curation' – is done when visitors are absent. Dust is incorporated into the acceptable finished product by apologies which maintain the caring, aestheticising worker as an absent presence. Sight, therefore, remains the dominant sense. Industrialisation in Britain and the placing of women as angels of the hearth were synchronous, as was the birth of the modern museum (Bennett 1995; Hetherington 2003). No longer keepers of it in the practical sense, when it was the site of their power and property in terms of 'hearth goods' (Filbee 1980; Pennell 1999), women now manage the mantelpiece in an entirely different mode, in the practice of maintaining that domestic museum. The twin of this practice is that of the 'show home'. As we have seen, practices of showing and telling, hiding and silence are never 'natural'. Just as contemporary museums rely on a certain construction of authenticity (through memory accounts) to make their historical 'worlds', developers depend on other versions of reality to sell their brand of 'home'. Their aspirational worlds are built on spatial illusion, where some furniture is reduced in size, bulky pieces are excluded, and mess is absent. Thus are time and space organised into the 'furnished frame' (Goffman 1986 [1974]).

This third part of the book has exaggerated the boundary between those contained within its margins, and those who built cultures of domestic space and time in Parts I and II. My intention was to show how, as Strathern argued, the boundaries between those in the centre and what they apparently place beyond are modern hybrids: purificatory practice is illusory, in one sense, within this network. As an analogy, think back to Adrian's wedding clocks in Chapter 5. One of many was in the centre of the mantel, keeping time, standing in for that vital part of the social calendar – the marriage. The others were in the attic, not thrown out as rubbish, because they were gifts; what has been given cannot be cast out, unless one breaks free from the person/thing/narrative relation, the nexus of culture. Clocks, mantels, attics, houses, persons, weddings, social time, social space – they are at once parts of, and the whole of a cosmology of modernity. This modernity is made of dense matter, myth and mess. Such comfortable clutter requires the greatest skill to navigate. And the horizon of this world looks like a 'stop' where 'belonging divides and property disowns' (Strathern 1996: 531).

I will never know what Lok would not say about a practice or material which was 'too powerful'; analogously, those of us moving within these circuits cannot know what gaps in culture – in meaning – are really vacant presences, worlds of persons and things that have been deleted. The only way to elicit these is to ask rude questions, posit queries that sound stupid even to the enquirer, overstep the mark to try to see, speak and touch what is invisible, unspeakable, intangible. This third part of the book has unsettled the twin artefacts of past and present in Parts I and II. It is matter out of place, juxtaposed with the others in this literary mantelpiece. As we have seen, people make biographies, linear narratives of stuff on the mantelpiece, fleshing in the gaps with the connective tissue of their lives. However, the Mass Observation lists (Chapter 2) laid this bare, to show how any joining up, like any analysis pulling it apart, is cultural practice. We have also seen how contriving the past as matter – moving a house across continents, restoring a ruin, growing red sorghum, framing a photograph or giving it away – is contested, political and powerful. Who decides what matters – who chooses – makes meaning; culture is power at work.

This is not a conspiracy theory of power; power is an effect of what is already in place. Parallel cosmologies show how the slips, slides and frictions of 'different' cultures work always to keep some in the centre of contemporary networks of belonging, while 'the rest' fall off the edges. In the final chapter, I will sum up, as is the tradition, but also push open the door that Becky, Pete, Nina, Matthew, Laura, and our American and Chinese guests have left ajar.

Conclusion: Culture, Clutter, Contemplation

> I should never be able to fulfil what is, I understand, the first duty
> of a lecturer – to hand you after an hour's discourse a nugget of pure
> truth to wrap up between the pages of your notebooks and keep on
> the mantelpiece forever.
>
> (Woolf 1929: 5)

Introduction

One spring morning, a couple of months ago, I was back in the cottage where
the house martin had flown in through the window, as told in Chapter 4.
While I was editing the final draft, I looked again at the ancient fireplace. The
plaster above the hearth had been stripped back to reveal a worn wooden
beam, twisted with age, set into the wall. No ornament could ever have
rested on that; it seemed to be holding half the house up. I kept the window
closed, to prop my iPhone against the frame, hoping for a glimmer of 3G
to beam through the pine forests and mountains. An email arrived, asking
me to contact a BBC researcher, to talk about Mass Observation *Mantelpiece
Reports* (Chapter 2). I called her, my face and phone pressed to the window in
a confusion of half-heard broken shouts. A fighter jet roared overhead. Later
that week, I made the long journey to the MO Archive at Sussex University,
to talk to a reporter from a popular current affairs programme.

Strangely, it was a reporter known for his work in war-torn countries who
interviewed me. I spent nearly an hour telling him how complex a space
the mantel could be. In particular, I pressed home my point that it was
only after repeated looking at the 1937 *Reports*, until my eyes glazed over,
that I saw how culture was beaten out in and between these vases, clocks
and candlesticks. With the fire beneath, the mantel was at the centre of
home life, negotiated, contested, gendered. I talked at length about how,
with Thatcher's popular capitalism and home-owning democracy, home and
family were placed in the centre of state policy. I made links between the
marginal 1930s households – the single young men and women in 'digs'

with landladies who might have lost their husbands and sweethearts in the First World War, and narrow lives of those who fell outside the central social space of 'home, family and self' in the later 20th century. Changing home and family practices were visible in the shifting geographies of home, now seen in the rise of the flatscreen and the sidelining, storing or digitising of memorabilia. At least, that is how I remember it.

A month or so later, I switched on the radio on my way to work, to hear my voice, weirdly changed by the recording, interweaved with my mantelpiece 'collage' (see Chapter 2), some original Mass Observation *Reports*, and recordings from a 1990s television series about celebrity mantelpieces. Artists and designers talked about the mantel being a window to your soul, about how you could tell who a person was simply by looking at it. I talked about my eyes glazing over at the sameness of 1930s mantel displays...it was the iPad of yesteryear...a new homeowner had marked his identity with his stone fireplace...

I drove on, gripping the wheel tightly in self-righteous indignation and howling self-doubt. Where were the politics, the complexity, the forgotten ones who had slipped through the gaps of 'our' home-owning mass consumer society? The mantelpiece had been put back firmly in its place as a conventional, aesthetic space which 'said' something about you, the individual, about your very soul. All the context of the interview words had gone, replaced by the ornament of music and well-known authorities on fine art and home interiors. It made for entertaining listening, as a nice package for the audience, who reciprocated in their droves on Twitter, with mantelpiece photos and comments. And I agreed with it – as a partial view. Was this what I had done with the interviews, snatched from the mouths of the participants to make up a nice academic book, framed by theories, histories and other views that had nothing to do with them? And was this what mantelpieces 'really' were; I had just spent far too long thinking about them? Were the politics of home and family too trivial, or was the scale I used simply too small to matter? Was my view of how social change (and continuity) were effected on the mantel unimportant, since we could read about that in the history books anyway?

That month, the same radio programme had been filled with coverage of the necessity for a new mass building programme for social [public] and affordable housing, due to desperate shortages. Vulnerable sections of society, such as those with special needs and, in particular, young people, would struggle to have decent homes (Clapham *et al.* 2012) by the end of the decade, and progressively fewer would be able to afford to climb the housing ladder. At the same time plans for a Right to Buy scheme for social housing tenants were hotly debated, as were apparent attempts by some urban councils to move their tenants to cities where rents were cheaper, away from their communities and families. The prime minister criticised the second- and third-generation workless poor who had children and lived on benefits in social housing, while hardworking young couples lived at home with their parents, saving to buy a house before marrying and raising a family. Of great concern also was the number of illegal immigrants – some failed asylum seekers – at large in the country, 'lost' by the authorities. Politicians and commentators battled to make their voices heard. A recent report by the Future Homes Commission (2012) stated that the majority of the population still wanted period features in their homes, although flexible living spaces and some generational changes in taste were noted. It was the wettest spring on record, so the central heating stayed on in houses across the country. The country spent millions on the Queen's Diamond Jubilee celebrations, and billions on the Olympic Games in London, which created (temporarily) a 'British identity', according to mass media. Happiness was still on the government agenda. The recession continued, and always, it rained.

Looking back

As I wrote in the Introduction, disorder, gaps and mess only make sense if there is order in between. And disorder is a strategy for ordering, as we saw in the clutter of David's mantelpiece and the use of Sian's 'little space' by her husband to keep the contents of his pockets safe (Chapter 6). Although the book assembles ideas, stories, histories and theories, this is a pretence of rhetorical completeness: that there is a 'whole' somewhere or other, outside of day-to-day practice. Bourdieu, writing about the agrarian calendar, noted the

> great temptation to amass and collate these different productions in order to construct a lacuna-free, contradiction-free whole, a sort of unwritten score of which all the calendars derived from informants are then regarded as imperfect, impoverished performances. The problem is that the calendar cannot be understood unless it is set down on paper, and that it is impossible to understand how it works unless one fully realises that it exists only on paper.
>
> (1977: 98)

Let us accept, for the moment, however, that a ' multitude of myopias limit the glimpse we get of our subject matter [. . .], and lurch along, seriously kidding ourselves that our rut has a forward direction'(Goffman 1983: 2).

Bourdieu, practised at the art of paradox, constructed an entire system of distinction practices (1986) which relied on an external, privileged observer and the dependence on some external far-off structure (Buchli 1999). In turn, I have used him, and that other great boundary-maker, Douglas, to make sense of this messy array of research materials. The point is that their lines of engagement were cultural practices. Similarly, the lines of beauty that some people make with their mantel displays are cultural, as are those cluttered endeavours, and bare traces of deprivation, like the thin firetops we saw in Chapter 2. They are not windows into the 'soul', unless the soul is a tidy housekeeper. I am joining current theoreticians who take Bourdieu as their conceptual 'origin', to press home the centrality of cultural practice to social theory, to modernity – and in particular, small cultural materials.

As we have seen, the relations between persons, things, times and places were not fixed. Adrian's clock was one of three wedding gifts; Alison's slate clock was constitutive of a personal aesthetic made from idealised images of home; Annette's mobile shelf removed her from her married past in RAF houses; Victoria aspired to a home with a mantelpiece of family photos; Karen has put her empty photo frame into a bedroom drawer; and Derek and Diane will not agree quite what a mantelpiece is. The fireplace and mantel themselves have authoritative, but doubtful histories, while their potential to colonise and be colonised with meanings across space and time indicate the flexibility of relations between narratives and things. However, these relations are contingent on power – the power to decide what gets told, or made visible, and what matters.

Objects could lose visibility, because the duration of their stay had made them disappear, become background. New or temporary things, or in particular, things that should not be there, might be visible – even spectacularly present – yet not verbally presented, since they were not of the particular order of 'tellable' goods. Yet these were often telling, in that objects such as the letter left forgotten and unposted on the mantelpiece, or the clutter – or even the dust – brought assumed concepts to the surface. These things are not fixed, inalienable or even deliberately placed: they are the happenstance, alien, displaced goods that, strangely, always have their place, on mantelpieces, shelf units and cabinets. This 'pollution' is allowed – by some and for some – even if it might, in the normal run of things, be unmentioned. A key point is that this is an everyday relation of power; who decides what belongs on the mantelpiece decides what and who 'counts' in the home. Second, the ability to 'tell' through narrative and to be able to relate memory accounts to things are valuable skills in constructing oneself as a 'tellable' person. Knowing how to do these articulations of persons and things, memories and narratives produces 'recognizable' identities (Butler 2004).

When domestic fires were ubiquitous, the practices of keeping them alight, of women maintaining them as part of housework duties, and of families gathering around them, were not just figurative devices, since they were rooted in everyday practice (Filbee 1980). Such practice was linked to symbolic meanings, as a metonym for the family, the house, the nation and nationhood (Chapter 1). Now, the fire, as a flame that has to be kept alight to heat the house, provide cooked food and hot water for cleaning clothes and bodies, hence, essential in performances of the civilised nation, household and body, has all but disappeared, and is certainly not necessary for these daily social reconstructions. Not to engage in these practices *then* was to dismember oneself from the social. All that remains of it now, in most cases, is the mantelpiece, which remains the centre point, as Adrian (among others) put it, of the main living room in some houses (Chapter 6). Others might have a shelf unit, top of a gas fire or a breakfast bar, but all of the houses I visited did have one thing in the main living room: the television. What does, or can, perform the same socially cohesive role as the fire has in the past, in this society? What can invoke the same ideas of nation, home and family? Some living rooms in Britain have mantelpieces, sometimes with fires underneath them that are used (although only one of the participants in this project used a coal fire occasionally). All had televisions in them.

The traditional distinction of the mantelpiece as a place for storage and display has undergone a syncresis, or elision, that is not altogether comfortable, the intersection being space for negotiation and conflict. The mantelpiece has been transposed to the modern living room, yet with the loss of the open coal/wood fire, something has been lost in translation: its everyday role in domestic practices. This perspective is now augmented by the suggestion that the mantelpiece is also a place of telescoped practice, in that previous practices, increasingly framed by cultural memory and imaginaries, rather than lived experience, are viewed 'at a distance' on the mantelpiece. Such compression is under more pressure since the entrance of the television (another type of viewing from afar). This tenant places the mantelpiece further into the margins of daily practices. A few years ago, it was fashionable to dress televisions up as 'period' furniture, or play DVDs of flickering flame (a short-lived Christmas trend). The latest move is to market electric fan fires that look like televisions (flatscreen or traditional box), with remote-controlled flames and/or heat. Is it reasonable to host a protruding, heavy, space-consuming 'piece of art', as Michael called it, in the centre of the reception room? Is it reasonable, then, to view the mantelpiece in its turn as metonym for hearth, and thus for nation, gods, home and family? Has its detachment, transposition and compression (literally, in the case of small modern mantelpieces) actually turned it into something else? Agnew stated that: 'Shelf life is by definition limited. Life on a mantel can last for ever' (2003: 16). But the mantelpiece is a shelf, an edge protruding into houses ancient and modern, a crossover of time periods that contests, challenges, comforts and constrains practices of identity and remembering beyond its physical bounds. For now, I will focus on a thread that seemed to interweave the diverse materials and modes of the study.

The angels of the hearth

In the Introduction, I attended to how Bachelard's *Poetics of Space* (1994) illuminated those affective dimensions of home that can get lost in social research, such as the studies mentioned above (Clapham *et al.* 2012; Future

Homes Commission 2012). However, as time went on, this book began to haunt me, because it was *still true*:

> From one object in a room to another, housewifely care weaves the ties that unite a very ancient past to a new epoch. The housewife awakens furniture that was asleep.
>
> (Bachelard 1994 [1958]: 68)

We have seen a conflation of symbolic meaning between mantelpieces and women, of women and home, women and ornaments as the keepers or repositories of memory, of family accounts, and within gift relations. We have also seen how the mantelpiece is a place of discomfort – an adult space, a visible space, a tangible place, which at the same time commemorates children, acts as a background for family life, and which is, in some ways, untouchable. This echoes Mauss's interpretation of the gift as a doubled entity – its German etymology is *poison* (1990 [1950]: 62). If we link this with the ancient notion of the poisoned chalice – a cup containing impure blood – then we can see why this normalised doubling of woman as both container and contained – in and of the home – should be contested. Like the notion of woman, keeper of the domestic interior, and kept within the interior, the linked notion of nostalgia – often confused with memory, biography and/or history – is characterised by paradox and ambiguity (Crowley 2001; Wright 2009). *Nostalgia* – literally, a sickness to return home – can be felt only by those not at home. However, the mantelpiece, as a nostalgic structure (Bourdieu 1977; Silverstein 2004), still looms large in both the geography and the collective imaginings of home. Sedimented deep into the geology of home, then, is a paradox – are we never 'at home'?

If we think back to the mass-observed mantelpieces of 1937, dust, decay and death were implicit presences. 'House work' and the constant cleaning and maintenance of the active fireplace were kept up by women: 'mother'; the 'char' (Chapter 2). Photographs of the dead were displayed, as a common practice. Change and decay were implicit in the ongoingness of practices around the mantelpiece: the broken vase, the slow clock, the movement of letters, collar studs and broken pen nibs. The contemporary fieldwork showed a past-orientation, in the metaphors – and practices – of 'memory' and 'mother' – containers of and contained within the notion of 'home' (Chapter 3). This conflation is, we have seen (Chapter 1), a construction of the 19th century – and of course, far more ancient than that, in Penelope staying at home weaving while Odysseus – one of the original home-sick *nostoi* – wanders heroically. Mass Observation, memory and other narrative accounts (Chapter 4) carry this attachment into the 20th and 21st centuries. Women continue to clean up, to manage, to remember. Their tidying traces ancient practice, their bodies the ghosts of long-dead women. They embody remembrance not only of the dead past, but also death to come – making it visible by holding it at bay, stopping the dust and the mess blocking the house up.

Similarly, the 'gift' as an ordering social relation has been a constant negotiator between hosts and guests, family and friends (Chapter 5). As I have shown, the often syncretised tropes of mother/memory/gift/home continue to be powerful invocations that are called upon when individuals are called to account. But in this syncresis, this compression, something has been squeezed out of place: fathers and futures. In the interview accounts, there was clearly a problem in the economies of domestic space, connected with compressions of new and old practices, most potently evoked by the relation between the mantelpiece and the television, and the gendered character of negotiation and conflict – in which children were silent witnesses (Chapter 6). They too are internalising this traditional way of 'knowing', a way of being that seems not to take into account the changes in the 20th century in gender relations, family and home practices. Further, this elision of home/family/memory/mother/gift diminishes the cultural and social space of those who do not fit into this condensed meaning of home (see Cohen and Taylor 1992; Chapman *et al.* 1999; Burns 2004; Desjarlais 2005; Gorman-Murray 2008: home-less, child-less, single, divorced and older people, non-heterosexual partners, young renters and other 'exotics' who do not fit into this compressed – enshrined – metaphor. Children are learning the same pattern of cultural categorisations, even though these do not 'fit' with 21st century practice. There is a need for House Work – on how houses and people who live or do not live in them practice 'home' – rather than this continuing 'domestication' of the body, which is imbricated within current social policy, despite numerous sociologies of home and family telling other stories.

This troubling 'stickiness' of gendered domesticity was to be the principal focus of the concluding chapter, as a critique of the 'modernity' agenda that has dominated social theory since the 1990s (for example, Giddens, 1991; Beck, 1992; Rose, 1998; Bauman, 2001; Beck and Beck-Gernsheim, 2002). However, a chance encounter which led to a film project with asylum seekers and refugees brought into focus a different horizon; rather, another world, which appeared just as I was bringing my home up to date, in that contemporary hybrid style of old/new. This has been a long decade of mantelpiece 'ethnography' in the sense that every day has involved decorating, seeing, reading, thinking, hearing and talking about them at work, at home and beyond, with visitors or as a visitor, with academics and acquaintances. I moved from the 1930s house with the mantelpiece I wrote about in the Introduction through several more to a Victorian terrace with five 'original feature' fireplaces. By this time, every visitor was asking me what my embarrassment of mantelpieces 'meant', until I posted a sign on the mantel in the main room stating, somewhat preciously, 'THIS IS NOT A MANTELPIECE.' As a visitor to other people's houses, I was usually asked the same question, and some friends became as self-conscious as I did about symmetry, dust, postcards and the meaning of things.

'Are we there yet?' Seeking home

It was with great relief that I moved to a modern(ish) house several years ago. I ripped out the orangey 1970s pine mantel from above the 'antique' French-style stove in the dining room and used it to prop up the hen run, where it is slowly rotting in the Welsh rain. However, the windowsills, book-shelves, garden walls and cupboard tops all seemed to fall naturally into a kind of mantelpiece order. We installed a modern woodburner with no mantelshelf in the sitting room. Years passed. Planning our new kitchen, the designer included a mantelpiece in the model he produced on a computer screen. I succumbed to the image of a granite slab, bolted into the wall above a (Chinese) slate hearth and cast iron stove. Imperishably solid materials, conjured in an instant on a screen, this new 'traditional' hearth trailed para-doxes. The old stove was taken from the drive, probably by sharp-eyed scrap merchants to be melted down into its original metal to meet global demand; its weight in iron now worth more than its form as an unfashionable heater. As Douglas argued, wanting 'purity ... hard and dead as a stone' is inimical to ambiguity, change, compromise (2002: 162–163). Yet this pure form of 'the kitchen hearth' is possible precisely because of the ease with which Chinese slate slides into British idiom, and computer-controlled blades slice stone to precise dimensions. The final product is the chimera of a taste for tradition, a dream of 'home', global markets and digital technology. And I will, once again, have somewhere to put the Christmas cards and the keys.

At around the same time as we were plotting this new shape to our home, designed to 'socialise' a previously inhospitable space, I was making a series of short films called *Making Wales, remembering home*. The project had aimed to produce films about home and identity – the materials and practices that make asylum seekers and refugees feel 'at home' in their accommodation. I was also interested in how they perceive Welsh identity and their possi-ble futures at home in Wales. In other words, I wanted to treat them as 'ordinary', within the same boundaries as other participants in the *Disman-tling Mantelpieces* study. At that time, word was spreading quickly about the alleged interest the 'authorities' had shown in a film about refugee women's housing in Cardiff. Many feared similar attention to my project might threaten their asylum claims or even refugee status. Somehow, the people who chose to take part were three men, classified as 'destitute' 'failed' asylum seekers, and one female refugee whose flat was provided by a social landlord. This final group challenged me to dig deeper into the 'common ground' of how connections between memory, identity and 'stuff', such as houses, photographs and mementoes remain deeply embedded in this apparently fluid, individualised globalised human world.

After spending some time going to the drop-in centres run by volunteers, talking with asylum seekers/refugees and doing some contextual filming, it was clear that this was not really what people wanted to talk about. At first, I thought their 'liveable' lives were produced through a kind of 'pure' relation of affect – in 'right now' interactions. Being listened to and exchanging stories of 'home' was very important, as was playing table tennis/football (for the young men) and sharing food at the drop-ins. Things do not matter, as 'Sabine', from Congo replied to my question about 'home' mementoes. When fleeing, 'You just run.' The concept of keeping memories of home and persons invested in display objects was unthinkable. For some, the asylum seeker and refugee drop-ins and the friends they meet are their home and family. So, display areas and things were not important, in terms of memory, and memory practices themselves deeply contrasted with those of other participants. The future, like the past, seemed hazy (Pannett 2011). Saying 'I haven't seen so and so for ages' might mean the week before, or a few months; nor would they make formal appointments to meet for the project. Either a vague time was arranged, or I called them just before I wanted to meet. At first, I thought people were not really concerned about time, or were confused, but this was because I was putting them into my time frame and calendar. It became clear that this ambiguity about time was a tactic for living. People disappear, so this time-fog stops the absence and presence of selves and friends becoming too pressing.

The films can be viewed online (Hurdley 2012); I will discuss two of them to illustrate how this project enlightened me. Mohammed is a young man from Afghanistan, whose claim for asylum has been rejected. As he was climbing the steps to the plane to fly back 'home', one of the security guards called him back. A high court injunction, taken out by the woman who runs the Cardiff Oasis drop-in centre he volunteers at, means he can stay – for the time being. Classed as 'destitute and with no state support', he stays with her family while he waits for another claim to be processed. We make the film there, where he shows me his belongings. At that time, he is staying in the elder daughter's room, while she is at university. During the Christmas holidays, he will move to the conservatory. He shows me his laptop, given by his host family, which he uses for English coursework and to stay in touch with friends. Then, a book of hymns in his language; a bible in Iranian, which he reads with the aid of a dictionary; his rugby hat: 'We all have one, my "family". But rugby...it looks like fighting!' He has a mock wrestle in the kitchen with his young host 'brother', and we drink tea.

On film, Mohammed will not tell the story of his escape from Afghanistan; he tells me that in an urgent low voice at the drop-in centre. It is horrifying, deadly, thrilling. After Christmas, a manager in an organisation supporting asylum seekers criticises Mohammed's film as 'poor quality'. The film is not the problem; it is Mohammed's 'story'. Because he has no 'mantelpiece objects', mementoes of home, his story will not move an audience. He has literally no thing from his 'home' which can conjure loss, belonging, memory or change, nor can he recount (on camera) his memory of fleeing: he is *too* lost. This illustration of the power of things in the telling of stories brings to the fore the paradoxical character of these two cultural materials. A thing without a story, like Becky's candle (that looked like a vase) has little value for 'doing' identity; it highlights the absence of narrative craft' (Chapter 7). Further, as Eleanor John, the head keeper of the Geffrye Museum, said (Chapter 8), memories are vital in authenticating an object, giving it meaning. But a story without a thing; this can have great value in legitimating a person. For example, the memory accounts in Chapter 3 relied on absence – of fireplaces, button boxes, damp and danger – in the performance of heroic, moral identities. Mohammed's story is so powerful, it cannot be told on film. Without this story, he will certainly be deported. If his story changes in a single detail, he will be deported. If the authorities decide the story is not true, he will be deported. If the story does not fit in to their categories of what counts as worthy of asylum, he will be deported. There is no place for memory lapse, for rhetorical flourishes or the contingencies of situated interaction. The 'biographic account' and the responses of the official audience are inflexible. The only belongings which would count towards Mohammed's performance of identity would be a passport, evidence of the threat in his homeland, and documents supporting his account. The horrible circle of accountability, however, means that Mohammed has none of these, due to the circumstances of his claim. The loss of these things both supports and undermines his claim to be 'who' he is.

Another participant, 'Joseph' (not his real name), from Eritrea, asks to be anonymised. I will never know how he came to be here; he wants to talk only of 'now'. We film him in silhouette against a window in the drop-in centre, behind him as he walks to college, and praying in church. He sleeps on a friend's sofa (unknown to the landlord) and is too frightened of discrimination to be seen on film; nor can we risk filming at his friend's. He says, 'I want to be a legal person.' Until then, he remains unseen, unheard, passing for someone he is not on the streets of Cardiff, unable, he says to get on with his life. Both say the drop-in centres and the friends are vital, as is the help they get – food, advice, support – from the people who work there. They wait in this limbo, belonging nowhere, moving between temporary beds, drop-ins, solicitors, college and church, unrecognised until they get their 'status'. The films are important to them, as they want 'us' to understand them, to be more welcoming. Another worker in the charitable support organisation is concerned that 'Joseph' is recognisable in the one moment he turns to smile at the camera; pixellation is not enough – I must blur the film entirely. All that the visual can evoke is a space where a person should be.

As I entered their world a little further, I then started to notice they had lots of 'stuff'; just not the 'museums... of domestic objects' I was looking for (Madge and Harrisson 1937). I simply did not have the 'habit of looking' (as Jun called it: Chapter 8) at this setting, this 'furnished frame' (Goffman 1986). The destitute asylum seekers seem stuck in an everlasting present, carrying everything that matters to them in bulging bags – the papers from the Home Office (central government department), solicitors and so on, their English class homework and their mobile phones. One man, hearing a ringing tone, pulled three phones out of his pocket. I learnt later that this is quite common. One phone is for 'back home', one for the solicitor and one for friends in Cardiff. Thus, somewhere around this world of presence and the ongoing moment are those other communications – with solicitors, the Home Office , friends in Cardiff and family back home. There is usually little or no credit on the phones (donated by well-wishers), and the greatest gift is a phone card. People wait to be communicated with – I am not yet sure whether this is with passivity, or the fury of someone eternally stuck in a waiting room. When someone gets their 'papers', there is great rejoicing, as the threshold to this 'home-coming' seems impassable. These papers are their most important possession. Like the ultimate mantelpiece objects, they materialise a present (and future) identity constructed through a biography that has been rubber-stamped as 'authentic' by the authorities.

The absences that surround the eternal present also take time to emerge, as terrible losses, of people, of memory, of home, whole worlds. There are no museums, unless absence is a kind of museum, made through silence or elusive histories. The only monument is the body that made it here. This moves home, family, past identities, far beyond absent presences, because that suggests a return; this is vacant, or vacated emptiness. It was only when I heard asylum seekers' stories of their other homes, and became aware of the silences, that I became more aware of the losses in other participants' memories. Unlike, for example, Andrew's account of his forebears' deliberate forgetting of war and loss (Chapter 3), Mohammed and 'Joseph' must not forget a single detail of trauma; 'genesis amnesia' is forbidden to them (Bourdieu 1977). Another refugee, 'Sami', could never forget, since the scars on his body were his memorabilia of torture; a body of proof to be recorded by experts to back up his claim. When seeking asylum, 'Sami' tells me that his memory of what had happened is perforated; events disappeared, or reappeared in different ways, so his story kept changing. This recognised post-traumatic condition, however, undermined his claim, until he 'got his story straight'. He was pressed between the survivor's twin, yet conflicting stresses: to forget and to remember. He carries his 'papers' close to his body, to show to anyone who asks – just in case.

Further, when a person is given refugee status, she must remember her story, to share with others, to remain one of the survivors who can give hope to others coming after – even giving them a temporary home, if they are destitute. Her past promises a good future for the rest; her present gives them a place to rest, and a common ground for sharing stories. Continual remembering is also necessary for her to belong, to be at home with others from her country. The audience for her story may become more limited; she no longer needs to be heard by so many in her plea to stay; the story can change once she has her 'papers' giving her a different identity: refugee. Therefore, she must negotiate this identity with that of becoming 'at home' in Britain, a constant process of moving between worlds. The ongoing conflicts in some countries, then, produce a different kind of remembering from that of, for example, holocaust survivors (Schwarz and Schuman 2005). As time progresses, refugees who came to Britain with no mementoes of home might buy replacement artefacts. For example, refugees from some African nations can find things in British shops, or, if possible, send for objects from their countries of origin. While not the same, these things are analogous, or stand in for the things they have lost (Pahl 2012), reconstituting 'home' and 'identity' as material, albeit with a sea-change. This is another loose thread I will pick up in forthcoming writing. For now, we will think about how these different demands on memory and identity reflect on the taken-for-granted 'thinkable' attachments between memory, identity, things-for-display and cultural practice discussed in earlier chapters. For example, let us return to Shyam, who recalls the 'sparkle' of the brass on her grandmother's mantelpiece: 'When you can have things, you don't appreciate – yeah, lovely memory, apart from the hard work.' Her account of her grandmother's mantelpiece, discussed in Chapter 3, dazzles the reader with its vividness, seemingly so different from Mohammed's story on film, so thin and quiet. Yet, on rereading it in juxtaposition with Mohammed's, the losses of that world, absent relatives, of taken-for-granted things, emerge.

Reflecting, then, on 'ordinary' accounts from middle-class women who spend a lot of time in interviews performing 'good', 'tasteful', 'classed' identities, we can see how they also do affective work when their worlds are collapsed. For example, Sian, who talks with disgust of the former 'taste-less' owners of her house (a policeman and his wife) and her careful restoration of (the appearance of) authenticity with 'real' fireplaces, suddenly loses possession of this 'proper' narrative when she talks about her husband coming in and 'dumping' the contents of his pockets on the bedroom mantelpiece – 'it's my little space and he just dumps his rubbish on it' (chapters 3 and 6). Her calm, tasteful construction of value just falls apart, and the relation changes from her/house/class to her/him/gender. I can only think of this turn as affective, and not just outside of the dominant narrative, but transformative of that 'thin line'. So, can we refigure 'valuable' persons as caught up in – not circuits of value – as this sounds contained, but shifting, unreliable networks that are just as precarious, in some ways, as those of asylum seekers, working class 'chavmums' and other 'marginal' persons who 'lack' (Lawler 2005; Skeggs and Wood 2009; Skeggs 2011)? Is it not peculiar how people with nothing and who do not 'matter' can do this, and the middle classes do too, and talk about it, but still have to have all the stuff? Clutter is the constant complaint of my participants; the demanding materiality of relations through gifts and doing identity through abundance is becoming more visibly a problem.

Sian is 'power-full' and 'valuable' when her narrative effects the network of taste/class, but, when she starts bringing into effect gender relations, which is utterly different from taste and absent in Bourdieu's (1986) systematic theory of culture, her world collapses (compare Becky and Rob's accounts in Chapter 7). Through the tale of her husband's disruption, her world changes, into one where her husband's domination has not only transformed space but also, inevitably, meaning and therefore symbolic value. Her only resource is affect, since her taste/class 'world' is no longer there. Of course, cultural, economic and educational capitals remain fixed as Sian's universal goods, for she always has massive capital resources to call on, constantly practised as 'home'. Further, the very fact that her husband is presented as disruptive mess means she still maintains herself as the rightful owner/maker of meaning and space. But at the same time, there is a terrible pressure in having to keep up that gendering of home as female domain, that by default occupies her time and attention, which could be elsewhere. Men *must* be kept out as value-less, messy, unhomely matter out of place. It is as if, once taste/class is cast out, and gender is dominant, home becomes a different problematic, a different value altogether – these two worlds/networks seemingly preclude each other, just as affect, feeling, sensing, cannot move Bourdieu's embodied *habitus*. However, this is only the case if we maintain modernity's effort at 'hideous purity' (Law, 1994: 4). By 'playing the game' (Bourdieu 1986), of women as homemakers, Sian makes the 'cut' which keeps her in possession of the mantel. The eternally conditional 'purity' of the mantelpiece keeps it as a hybrid space, a 'condensed network' (Strathern 1996: 523), slicing out those who cannot enter this circuit of value.

The politics of memory, of narrative, of things, home and identity – of how these move and are moved – can get lost through taking things for granted. This book has questioned how the collapse of boundaries between these very different artefacts produces a particular politics of telling. Therefore, the absence of 'proper' property in asylum seekers' worlds also turns to other worlds for different interpretations. However, another point must be made: the eye of the beholder's power to frame what is proper. I have deliberately used a mix of metaphors in the book; at various times, different figurative modes have been helpful in imagining different ways of thinking about the mantelpiece which, after all, is a figure so clichéd, it needs shaking up. One trope I have mentioned is Goffman's 'furnished frame' (1986). He used this figuratively, as a way of talking about the myths, habits and routines that produced symbolic interaction. In this book I have taken this metaphor literally: the mantelpiece is the furnished frame for the fire. I have also thought it through; thoroughly, perhaps obsessively, but this is what sociologists must do: '...to feel as if suddenly awakened in a house with which they had only supposed themselves to be familiar'

(Mills 1959: 8). In doing so, I dug down into the geology of home, to find stony conceptions that remain rigorously in place, despite the shifting surfaces of modernity. The ability to change one's story, to articulate memory and to have a number of identity and memory materials available for selecting or ignoring, as well as choosing not to choose, are monumentally powerful precursors to making and maintaining identity – as class, nation, gender, ethnicity. Savage proposes that middle-class narratives make class 'transparent' but actually effect the hiding of the true powers of class (2010). Paradoxically, by rendering such power opaque, we can see through its disguise.

The mantelpiece becomes more rapt with meaning as modernity moves on – if people trouble, or are troubled, to think about it. If not the mantel, and the things raised up by it, then it is 'home-made' cakes that matter, free-range eggs, 'ethnic' bracelets, conflict diamonds, donor eggs, pedigree dogs, granny's locket, electric cars, home fragrances, 'good' cholesterol, Kenyan Fairtrade flowers, Scottish raspberries, Welsh slate, Chinese coal, Californian oranges. The importance of the material intensifies, as the screen flattens, smoothens and cleanses (Kittler 1999 [1986]: 1, cited in Lury 2008). There is no texture of the past, or distinction, as all is there, both stored and immediately displayable. However, the Western home remains a site of common sociological ground. It is as if there is a disconnection between 'public' social policy and 'private' sociology. Both have invaded the space of home, but remain apart. In the 1990s, David Morgan wrote *Family Practices* (1996), transforming the contours of domestic social enquiry; anthropology and sociology came 'home' at around the same time (Jackson and Moores 1995; Allan and Crow, 1989; Cieraad 1999, Chapman and Hockey 1999; Miller 2001a). Since then, sociologies of identity have moved from family to intimacy and personal life as interpretations of relational identity deepen and widen (Carsten 2004; Smart 2007; Lawler 2008; Wetherell 2009), countering the dominance of non-empirical theorisations of 'individualisation'. But recognition remains marginal that the 'furniture' of home, of intimate, personal and/or family life, of what makes a person, is extraordinarily powerful in the politics of identity. It is framed by dominant public voices *as* a frame, mere ornament or incidental prop, a sideshow.

After I left the asylum seeker/refugee drop-in for the first time, I walked through Cardiff city centre in a strange daze. It was as if I were in a different world, looking through a membrane at all the others wandering down the street, rushing into the supermarket, out of clothes shops, talking on phones, to their children, sitting on benches eating burgers. Going there changed my world, and it has never changed back. The lengthy quote from Foucault's Introduction to *Order of Things* (1989 [1966]: xvi–xviii), which I had carried about in my head for years, suddenly made sense. Their world had become thinkable, the common ground on which I had skated about for years as a 'sociologist' had shifted, as I could see another surface, still on the edge, but visible. In the Introduction, we saw how social housing officers talked about how they judged their tenants – those workless poor – in ways they had never thought of, looking at the dust, mess and sparse décor of their homes, wraithish doppelgängers of wealthy minimalism. These lives were not recognised by the officers, although it might have been the only way in which the tenants could make their lives 'liveable' with the resources that were available to them (Butler 2004, Skeggs and Wood 2009; Wetherell 2009a; Skeggs 2012). Things matter; how do academics make them matter to those who make policy based on flat black text, simplified identity categories, performance politics and short official visits to 'the margins'?

'We' have always been at home

This late digression on asylum seekers trying to make a home unfolds the raw politics of identity. The Home Office decides whether one's identity, biography, memory, narrative, proof, social networks (in the shape of letters supporting one's claim) are true, unchanging, authentic, intelligible, recognisable. In short, if you are not a 'legal person' who counts, you will be brought to account, and cast out. Getting the ultimate gift of *status* (in Latin, literally, 'having been stood') is contingent upon this strangely passive-active standing, being 'stood for' by the mass of documents, recordings, interviews, people but always, in the end, 'standing for' oneself. The Home Office world is the only world; there is no ambiguity. Is home the same, and the various authorities within? The always growing body of sociological literature contends otherwise: there is no one statement of fact. However, the continuing status of women in the home, of memory as an important articulation of identity, and the attachment of persons to things are sticking points. It seems that property produces identity as material – fixing down the substantial person who matters. Practices, too, the 'doing' of genders, homes, identities, belonging and longings, are constant processes. This push and pull makes identity, memory and home relational, yet contingent still on the threads of 'identity', 'memory' 'home': attaching, fraying, repairing, unweaving, but always there.

Analogously, the British – or is it English? – deployment of tradition, the past and authenticity in the construction of nation is another nostalgic structuring that fixes meaning down. A recent book calls the [English] National Gallery *The Nation's Mantelpiece* (Conlin 2006), and the mantelpiece, in the making of home and homeland, is at once an anchor and a dead weight. Taking refuge in comfort leaves no way of imagining other futures that are not so deeply colonised by the past – however that is currently constructed. As we have seen, fluidity, contingency and multiple articulations are all productive of identity, but only by those who can negotiate these strategies, and using only those materials which are valuable, in the worlds where such strategies and values are mobilised.

The paradox is that asylum seekers practise – because they must – fluid contingent identities the supposedly powerful, choice-making neo-liberal individual pursues as the project of the self. Yet in order to become 'legitimate' persons in Britain, the asylum seekers must absolutely fix down their identities and memories, with the documents of identity and English language learning as their 'memory objects', and clearly-told narratives of how and why they came to Britain. Any 'slippage', interpretive ambiguity or gaps in memory risk rejection. They are caught between 'homeland', 'home' and 'Home Office'. 'Contingency' as a property of identity is meaningless; contingent how, and upon what, are the questions with which we must concern ourselves, and include ourselves.

Mol writes of 'a politics of who' and 'a politics of what', (2003: 184), discussed in Law's working paper *Making a Mess with Method* (2003):

> It is not just a matter of the politics of research (although this is important). It is also a matter of the politics of reality... So it is, for me, a point that is simultaneously a matter of method, politics, ethics and inspiration. Realities are not flat. They are not consistent, coherent and definite. Our research methods necessarily fail. Aporias are ubiquitous. But it is time to move on from the long rearguard action that insists that reality is definite and singular.
>
> (Law 2003: 11)

Drawing on Strathern's (2004 [1991]) work conceiving a fractal, multiple world which is not cut into 'parts' and 'wholes', but partial connections, Law contests both holism and relativism. Not only change, but constancy takes enormous effort, keeping multiple 'out-therenesses' in place, holding them apart, often negotiating/opposing others making other exclusions to keep their worlds in being. To have ended on the matter of gender would have been neat, but probably unethical, as it keeps the 'monsters' inside the house (Monguilod 2001): men, mess, children, unwanted gifts, modernity, futures and memories. These are *present absences*, which make seemingly uninvited appearances, just to keep them in mind – really, to *keep* them. A naughty child's toy is put on the mantel, or a husband's dumping of change is told; a friend's modern house is criticised, and the future is transformed into a return to the past. All these practices are 'world-making' (Law 2003; Mol 2003). They also 'keep' a certain 'outside' visible (Latimer and Munro keeping and dwelling). But what of the monsters that lurk beyond? This book has focused on the practices that make the world of 'the unacknowledged normality of the middle-class' (Savage 2003: 536). It is outrageous that women are still 'made' managers of the home, but a middle-class white woman's daily conflict with her family to keep the house tidy is, in the scale of vulnerability and warfare, minor. This politics of home, is indeed a quiet violence, since it sets up sociologically recognisable dichotomies of gender, public/private; child/adult and modernity/nostalgia which, although now nuanced by ambiguity and boundary-blurring, keeps that world in place. 'Middle-class': the world is bound up in that hyphen. The 'nostalgic structure' (Bourdieu 1977) of the mantelpiece is the paradox of modernity, a hybrid. Indeed, I would argue that hybridity is incorporated into this metonym for home, in its assemblages as well as its exclusions. Assemblage is a permitted hybridity, limiting it to this reduced purity, where mess is also encompassed. Where can we go from here?

Haunting Houses: *hiraeth*

Mantelpieces can be something different from a nostalgic structure. Recalling the shell case ornaments, remembrances of the First World War on 1930s mantelpieces (Chapter 2), let us evoke what those shell cases once told: a world at war. Like bullet holes in the Berlin wall, mantelpieces 'stand, significantly, somewhat outside of history as it is understood in terms of chronology' (Hetherington 2008). Drawing on the concept of 'kairos' as a prominent character of Walter Benjamin's work (2006 [1932–1934]; 1999), Hetherington conceives it as ' ... the disrupting event, the moment when something else is revealed ... ', for example the arcade, as 'a space out of time; it is of the past and yet resonates with the present in a way that challenges the chronological idea of progress that he sees as a dominant cultural expression within consumer societies' (Hetherington 2008: 278). The montage effect Benjamin creates in the arcades project makes an 'image-space', developing his redemptive view of the past in *Berlin Childhood Around 1900* (Benjamin 2006).

The mantelpiece too, holds within it the possibility of that 'image-space', rather than as a distanced view, making us voyeurs of a nostalgic structure, stopping the network of cultural forgetting in this habituated form of collective memory. *Hiraeth,* a Welsh way of longing, remembering, belonging, home, is not translatable. Deeply affective, rooted, inexpressible, it can be felt only in *doing.* Not nostalgia, nor memory or tradition, it is that something/somewhere else that haunts – if only we could all feel/do *hiraeth.*

The 'angels of the hearth' are ghosts we know haunt the home, but what of the others that are kept out? Vickery (2008) writes about superstitions concerning the fireplace as a vulnerable opening even in early modernity (Chapter 1). This perhaps continues in the reduced mode of Father Christmas/Saint Nicholas coming down the chimney, to eat and drink whatever culturally accepted offerings are left for him (even if there is no chimney!). However, there is now nothing so exotic, so explicit as a bundle of chicken skeletons in the hearth. Modernity might have swept these away, but the utter 'mundane invisibility' – what I have called *vacancy* – does not mean *the excluding* has become any more modern, just cut from the network, meaning the excluded have no power to shake the web of property and belonging. After Foucault, I can only press on with 'curiosity...a readiness to find our surroundings strange and singular' (1996 [1980]: 305), remembering that curiosity shares its genealogy with care and curate [from the Latin verb *curo*].

An Ending: the matter of *home*

Can the mantelpiece – its meanings and gaps – be disposed of to leave that 'bare fire' (after Thrift's concept of 'bare life', 2004)? Could it be that fire, that is, the heat of the hearth (Carsten 1997), rather than every moment accounted for in the accounting for self? For the mantelpiece is not just an assemblage of things, it is an assemblage of moments, of times and people and other places drawn into the network to make multiple stoppages, cuts in the network in four dimensions. 'The half-second interval is being trained up'; it takes only a moment to sit, look, and judge (Thrift 2004: 161). The middle ground has become a thin line; it is the interval in time/space between the mantel and the door or the sofa. It is the time it takes to look, or ask and be told a story, or note the china that 'people like us' do not display. How is that middle ground closed up, silently? Bourdieu wrote of the working classes making do with cheap substitutes that the 'dispossessing of the very intention of determining one's own ends is combined with a more insidious form of recognition of dispossession' (1986: 56). Here, I have been writing of the literally 'dispossessed', asylum seekers, to return to a more general point about property and belonging.

I am not sure that a 'bare life', or a 'bare fire' is possible; after all, even the 'heat of the hearth' is in a different mode – and we have to ask how a 'bare' life is possible, when 'naked taste' (Bourdieu 1986: 77) is so enclosed. Indeed, 'bare life at the margins is eclipsed' by a new, spectacular form of 'intimate citizenship', in which 'revealing of suffering has become a middle-class performance of virtue' in the apotheosis of the interview society and triumph of symbolic violence (Skeggs and Wood 2009: 63). A new politics of 'who' and 'what' can produce different gaps between 'them' and 'us' and what is 'proper' – rather than judging things as 'cheap substitutes' and what counts as cultural expertise. It is possible to rethink '...how people deploy the cultural means at hand to accomplish the kinds of "relational extension" that helps them feel at home' (Latimer and Munro 2009: 329). There is another 'common ground' of mediation here, rather than the thin line of white, homophilic middle-class recognition, or the performance of belonging through wedding invitations, clocks and trauma. There are 'other' homely practices that matter: the smell of cakes in the oven, warm 'naked' gas/electric flames in a reproduction fireplace; meeting in a YMCA gym to share stories; the hospitality of just listening: hearth talk, even if the hearth is missing. '... [D]welling is better understood today as that which *takes place* in terms of relations, rather than be defined in terms of a fixed abode'

(Latimer and Munro 2009: 328). These often intangible, or unspoken, sometimes profoundly sensorial worlds are now gaining academic attention (Puig 2009), although becoming mindful of them, and being able to articulate them in scholarly modes, are elusive research skills (Atkinson *et al.* 2007; Pink 2009; Mason and Davies 2009; Hurdley and Dicks 2011). It is time to come to our senses, to take possession of suffering, of loss and affect in a different mode of intimacy that is not cluttered up in circuits of middle-class 'ordinary' value. The social space is already there, if this 'stuff' can be cleared away.

Let us return to the discussion in the Introduction about the ' . . . weight of affective significance . . . [in] inherited jewellery or ornaments as memories of holidays, families, from friends' that Skeggs attributes to working-class persons (2011: 505). The affective dimension of things is also a clearly articulated relation of middle-class networks, as we have seen in this book, although it is not possible to quantify the 'value' of this dimension, or how expertise in 'telling' alters its visibility (consider Becky and Pete in Chapter 7). Perhaps this highlights the effect a sociologist's *habitus* has on the worlds we make explicit (Strathern 1992). This relation of affect offers a 'common ground' for the possessed and dispossessed to dwell, to belong. Further, I have criticised sight for its dominance in the hierarchy of senses, but it is not simply a distal sense. The ability to read, to hold books, laptops or iPads close up and know other intangible and/or imaginary worlds produces different ways of being in the world, opens possibilities. The mass-production of books changed worlds. The power to record in writing is vital to 'keeping' histories like Benjamin's which disrupt the line of chronology, brings the past close and palpable. Touch is not just with the fingers; seeing too is affective (Macdougall 2006). Puig has called for a removal of the distance of vision to have an engaged tangible materiality, adding to recent work in which she sees 'a manifestation of deepened attention to materiality and embodiment, an invitation to re-think relationality and its corporeal character, as well as a desire for concrete, *tangible*, engagement with worldly transformation' (2009: 298). This turn to the haptic, however, should not undermine the value of the optic. I too acknowledge that recognition and engagement with *all* the senses is important in sociological research, which is still struggling fully to understand how the visual adds to social worlds. However, building on arguments in previous work (Hurdley and Dicks 2011; Hurdley 2010), I suggest that there is value also in distance. This is not a pretence of being able to see the 'big picture', but mantelpieces offer closeness and distance. They are small enough to be 'thinkable', tangible and seeable, but also to show how this ability to move between positions is in the power of only some. Those who touch do so most often to cleanse and to re-order (although there is a world of difference between paid and unpaid labours); a few others can look inside or behind, to read communications from others on the hidden surfaces of cards and postcards.

Things can travel between people, and with people when they make homes elsewhere. Things are relations and dwelling. They have biographies, threading in with human biographies. As Gell comments, personhood is 'spread around in time and space' (1998: 223). Mantelpieces offer a 'perching', a stoppage for contemplating relations between persons, time, space and things, and distance can open worlds, as we saw in chapters 7 and 8. This 'perching' is different from keeping out or erasing 'others' in another 'stopping' mode: 'The large and powerful are able to delete the work of others in part because they are able, for a time, to freeze the networks of the social' (Law 1999: 95). Before concluding the book, I want to suggest, not Law's (1994) 'sociology of verbs', to contest the 'sociology of nouns' that keeps everything and everyone in its place (Morgan 2011), but a *sociology of gerunds*. These hybrid verb-nouns (or noun-verbs) – the reading, the writing, the thinking – stop us in our tracks, as sometimes we probably should, in the otherwise endless tumbling towards . . . what?

My great-aunt died today – Auntie Norah, six weeks short of her hundredth birthday, the 'aim' she had always articulated, before she forgot almost everything and everyone a few months ago. She gave me an ugly pottery couple, a porcelain pen holder that 'might be worth something', and invited me to choose books from her great collection before she went into residential care. She had kept a very few things and books, to make her room feel like home. I am not at home right now, but that ugly pottery couple has become 'worth something', as I know it was the one *she* really liked, which she wanted me to have. In her preparation for dying, she attached herself to that thing, and through it, to me. I can see her, and the ornament (currently not on show) in my mind's eye. The figure will go on to the mantelpiece when I return home, a small remembrance of her. As I make a space for it on the mantelpiece, I close the distance between the living and dying, just as Hannah has those moments of talk with her dad (Chapter 6), and Pete's dad's photo has his place in the 'living' room (Chapter 7). While many sociologists have focused on the distinction between the precarity of the have-nots, in contrast to the 'futures' of the haves, knowledge of death opens up our universal vulnerability. Auntie Norah brought me into her world when she passed her belongings to me; the unspoken between us was that death was closer to her than to me. Now I am left with those things, and a new clarity that dying is not so far off as I thought.

Grief transforms me, and my world, in ways that are hard to know yet, let alone narrate (Butler 2004a: 20). In their collection of empirical work on *the matter of death*, Jenny Hockey *et al.* contest the 'modernity' view of mortality, proposing ' . . . experiences of death as a site from which to *engage*, critically, with culture' rather than culture as 'that which we fling together to stave off the fragility of our embodied lives'. They suggest that the '*intersection* of living and dying' is prevalent for many families – not marginal or needing repair (2010a: 233). Fear, viewed by Bauman (2001a) as both an effect and necessary generative property of 'the consumer society', can be remade as vulnerability. Looking back at the book, I can see death, loss and grief as presences, not pushed aside but *kept*. 'Loss has made a tenuous "we" of us all . . . . each of us is constituted politically in part by virtue of the social vulnerability of our bodies – as a site of desire and physical vulnerability, as a site of publicity at once assertive and exposed' (Butler 2004a: 20). Joan Haran, writing about *Hope as Praxis*, concludes that:

> we cannot escape or evade our vulnerability but . . . we can recognize that the anxiety which this vulnerability provokes, and even rage experienced when we are harmed, could be redeployed wilfully and creatively to enroll antagonistic others into our utopian project.
>
> (Haran 2010)

Both the fireplace and its relic, the mantelpiece, offer a vulnerable opening into 'home', the house as a 'body *for* the body' (Gell 1998: 252). Hetherington called museumification 'a space of death' (2008: 290), but this making of domestic museums can produce another order of space and time. What we have seen of mantelpiece assemblages also suggests that a different tempo is possible here (Munro 2001), a chance to contemplate just where we are. Stillness is not a necessarily a weakness (Bissel and Fuller 2010). That space, the 'non-relational' that Hetherington (2011) sees in between 'seeing' and 'saying', where imaginaries can open up, is there, in the gap between the thing and the story, the sofa and the mantelpiece, the property-owning democracy and the dispossessed. Forgive the elisions here, but time is running out. Skeggs makes a distinction between middle-class 'futures' and 'precarity' for those who are outside 'circuits of value' (2011). If the circum-spections of contemporary power, seen in a nod, heard in non-committal assent, felt by the pat on the shoulder – but never affirming, always draw-ing (some of) us on and tying us in, can be undone, hope can enter the gap between future and precarity. Grief, woundability and mortality can keep us together. Rather than make worlds of matter and gentility, perhaps we could make worlds that matter, gentle places of loss and hope.

Epilogue: Encounter

> Today, he said, men had to learn to live without things. Things filled men with fear: the more things they had, the more they had to fear. Things had a way of riveting themselves on to the soul and then telling the soul what to do.
>
> (Chatwin 1987: 64)

Not long ago, I walked into the sitting room of a woman in early recovery from alcoholism. The house was rented from a family friend, and she hated it. The memories invested in it were brutal, shameful, angry. It felt cold, even though the sun was shining. I noticed, as I always do, the 'mantelshelf', a long wooden plank fixed into the wall above the television. It had a few very old photos of her son as a baby on it, and a small flower ornament. She showed me the most recent pictures of him, which she had not got round to displaying and so were lying on the coffee table. Her son was being cared for by her mother. There was no fridge, and we drank tea standing in the kitchen, made with milk left on the kitchen work surface. Dirty dishes stood in the sink; the washing machine was missing its door. In the corner of the sitting room was a pile of children's toys, scraps of furniture and clothing waiting to go to the dump, which she asked me to ignore.

We sat on the two sofas, which she disliked. She had swapped her nice ones with a friend, because she just did not want to live in that place. I looked around the room, as is the way when entering a 'new' house. It felt like the saddest story, because there was nothing to tell, and nothing to see, except the desire to leave. I wanted to get out too, feeling the past lie heavy in the cold sunlight. And the makeshift mantel was part of that story, of those memories waiting to be cast out, that were there only in the rubbish, the absence of stuff, and the cold. My friend's only way of making a home which could be part of her new, changing biography and future memories was to leave that place. This was more than cleansing memories of the past, it was about breaking free from that house to live a new future.

Memory, story, belonging: these three stand like a holy trinity around the stuff and sanctity of home; without them, how can one be, let alone do 'identity'? But what other work does this looking to the past to make the 'now' do? Where is the future, if it is not to be a reluctant keeper or refugee of too many pasts? And how can we not only write, but remake *home*?

Figure E.1

Figure E.2

Figure E.3

Appendix: Participants' Biographies

A version of this is available via Hurdley (2012), with photos – and photo-calendars for those who took part.

The three principal fieldwork sites were in Cardiff, or on its outskirts:

Radyr Gardens: a large modern 'executive' private housing development on the city outskirts, on the M4 motorway corridor, with excellent road links to London and west Wales.

Llandaff North: an established suburb, consisting principally of early 20th-century terraced houses near a local railway station. There is some social (public) housing, including a large estate and smaller developments of flats and houses. On the high ground above the railway line are large 1930s houses.

Cardiff Bay: this is the former dock area that has undergone extensive regeneration, including the demolition of traditional Victorian terraces, the construction of modern social public housing, and large gated private apartment blocks.

Participants in the second stage of fieldwork lived in different areas of Cardiff and Wales, and in other countries.

Adrian

Adrian is 40 years old and is a university science lecturer. He lives in Radyr Gardens with his wife, who is a doctor, and their three young children. They bought the house (with a mortgage) 'off plan' four years ago and had some input into the design, including kitchen and bathroom fittings. He considers himself 'British' and 'middle [class] now, working by upbringing'.

He thinks that the mantelpiece is different from other display spaces because it is in the 'central location in the main room', and that the mantelpiece in his childhood home was 'Similar to present one. Display but also with letters etc. A bit cluttered'. Other focal points include 'display cabinet, window sills, dressing table, office table and filing cabinet'.

Adrian made a photo-calendar.

Ailsa, Sasha and Emilia (second-stage participants)

This Scottish family relocated to New England ten years before our interview. They are well integrated into a wealthy middle-class American suburb. Ailsa, who is an artist in her forties with three daughters, is married to a Harvard professor. Her eldest daughter, Sasha (aged 18), also takes part in the interview. Sasha's younger sister, Emilia (aged 16) joins us towards the end of the conversation. For Sasha, who has been at boarding school in Scotland for two years, the fireplace is a 'comforting image' – the objects move to each house, it reminds her of 'mother', 'home': 'I can smell it almost.' We talk around photos of their own mantelpiece (which I later view when I visit), and photos of their friends and neighbours' fireplaces.

Alison

Alison is 49 years old and works as a civil servant in London. She is divorced and has no children. She bought a house (with a mortgage) 'off plan' in Radyr Gardens five years ago and had some input into the design, including kitchen and bathroom fittings and choosing a fireplace. She terms herself 'white' and 'middle class'.

The mantelpiece is different from other display spaces because, 'I change it more frequently; the clock is there; better for postcards and things not in frames.' Other display spaces are: 'sideboard in dining room & wall above it; to a lesser extent the dresser next to it'. She has no 'strong memories' of the mantelpiece in her childhood home: 'Vague recollection of parents' mantelpiece being sparse and functional – i.e. not used on a daily basis – merely a place for select ornaments'.

Alison made a photo-calendar.

Annette

Annette is 40 years old and works as a dentist. She lives with her partner in Radyr Gardens. She bought the house (with a mortgage) nearly four years ago 'off plan' and had some input into design features, including kitchen and bathroom fittings. She terms herself 'Caucasian' and 'working to middle [class]'.

She thinks her wooden display unit in the living room is different from other display spaces because: '1st impressions!! Sit looking at it every evening.' In the dining room is a 'similar shelf system (adds symmetry)'. Her childhood mantelpiece 'was always the first place to be dusted had a few ornaments on it and clock in the middle. Don't remember what else.'

Becky and Pete (second-stage participants)

Becky and Pete are in their early forties. They are tenants of a Cardiff Housing Association (HA), one of many not-for-profit organisations which now provide and manage affordable housing (also known as public housing). It is a small, century-old terraced house in the Canton district of Cardiff, in a street containing only five other HA properties. They will never be able to buy a house unless, as Becky says, they 'win the lottery'. Pete is long-term disabled and does not work, while Becky is a domestic cleaner, who fits her work around their teenage twins' school hours. Her wages supplement the government-funded financial support they receive. Their oldest daughter is in temporary accommodation, waiting for a secure tenure from the same HA.

Belinda

Belinda is 65 years old and a mature student. She lives in Radyr Gardens with her spouse, Frank, who is retired. They bought the house (with a mortgage) nearly four years ago. She considers herself to be 'British' and 'working [class]'.

Belinda distinguishes the shelf unit in the dining room as different from other display spaces because they 'put there things that don't have a permanent place (bills until paid, event tickets'. The bookcase in the living room is another 'focal point'. She has no memories of a mantelpiece from her childhood.

Frank took part briefly in the interview.

Bernie

Bernie is 68 years old and is a retired seaman rigger. He is long-term disabled, following a road accident in his youth. He lives alone in Cardiff Bay, in a house that he now owns outright, having been a local authority tenant. He and his parents were rehoused in this square of social (public) housing, following demolition of their terraced house and other original terraces in the area in 1989. He has lived in the area all his life, with his parents (until their deaths). He defines himself as 'Welsh' and 'working class'.

The china cabinet in the living room is soon to be replaced by a mantelpiece and gas fire from B&Q, if all goes to plan. Other 'focal points' are the walls in other rooms. 'The terraced house in Adelaide Street [now demolished] had fireplaces in every room including the bedrooms. The clocks seemed to be on every fireplace.'

It was very hard to understand the interview recording, due to his difficulties communicating verbally and background noise from the washing machine.

Bronwen

Bronwen is 25 years old and works as a research student. She lives in Llandaff North with her sister and a friend. They rent the terraced house from a family member and have lived there only a few months. She terms herself 'white' and 'middle class'.

The mantelpiece in the living room 'is central in the room, and is therefore a focal point'. Other 'focal points' are 'on bookshelves, walls, on top of drawers and dressing table, on coffee table'. 'Our mantelpiece at home was over a wood fire, and had a large mirror above it. It had a photo of my grandfather, and one of my parents' wedding day on it.'

Bronwen made a photo-calendar.

Christine

Christine is 60 years old and works as a housewife. She lives in Radyr Gardens with her husband, Harry, who is retired. They own their house outright and have lived there for two and a half years. She terms herself 'white' and 'middle [class]'.

As well as the mantelpiece, there are other focal points, such as 'all windowsills in house, display cabinet, small tables'.

Harry joined us for the latter part of the interview.

Christine took part in the photo-calendar.

Dan

Dan is 44 years old and works as an independent financial adviser. He lives in Radyr Gardens with his wife, Julia, a nurse, and their two children (aged 12 and 14). They bought their house (with a mortgage) 'off plan' six years ago and had some design input, including floor coverings. He terms himself 'middle class'.

The mantelpiece differs from the other focal point of the 'kitchen walls', in that there is 'very little change to what's on display even over years'. He remembers in his 'parents' house – plain mantelpiece with two bar fire'.

Julia and their 12-year-old daughter participated briefly in the interview.

Dan made a photo-calendar, using his digital camera.

Deb

Deb's story is in the *Epilogue*. Some months after I wrote this, she made a decision to enter a residential alcohol rehabilitation centre, a place she loves. Although fearful of returning home, she is looking forward to regaining residency of her son.

Derek and Diane

Diane is 63 years old and lives with her spouse, Derek, who is 66. They own their terraced house in Llandaff North outright and have lived there for 40 years. They removed the fireplaces because they were 'old-fashioned'. They term themselves 'British' and 'middle [class]'.

Derek selected the breakfast bar in the kitchen as the mantelpiece 'equivalent' and sees 'room dividers, TV corner unit' as other focal points. They remember mantelpieces in 'our parents' houses'. They both filled in parts of the questionnaire and took part in the interview.

Emma (second-stage participant)

Emma is a mature research student, aged 46. She defines herself as a black Kenyan woman, who spent much of her childhood in Malaysia. Married to a Belgian, with two adult children, she currently sees her family only on visits home to Nairobi. Our interview focused on how the Kenyan home has changed, with the move from villages to the town, from traditional household formations to small nuclear families, with concomitant shifts in domestic gender relations. Emma talks in depth about effects of colonialism, and how African ways of doing history, family and future have the potential to transform 'Western' practice. While Emma is not a named participant in the text, she greatly influenced my thinking on post-colonial/cosmopolitan worlds, and 'mini-museums of the future' was her vision for mantelpieces, which I use in Chapter 8. I plan a future paper focusing entirely on our interview, since Emma traced so many routes and roots.

Eric

Eric is 67 years old and lives in a terraced house in Llandaff North. He owns the house outright after living there for nearly 30 years and has a lodger. He terms himself 'Welsh' and 'lower middle [class]'.

He removed the fireplaces when the installation of central heating in 1975 'obviated' them. The piano top is different from other display spaces such as window sills, dining room wall and dressing table because 'It is central and more work-a-day.' He remembers his 'childhood home; a piano top, i.e. family photographs, a vase or two'.

Geoff

Geoff is 47 years old and works as an antiques dealer. He lives with his spouse and young child in a terraced house in Cardiff Bay, which they own with a mortgage. They have lived there for nine years and Geoff has done a lot of work to the house, but kept all six original fireplaces. Another focal point is the 'kitchen dresser', but the mantelpiece is different from other display spaces due to its 'permanence'.

Geoff took part in the photo-calendar.

Gina

Gina is 41 years old and works in Systems I.T. She lives with her spouse, who is a printer, and their three sons (16, 14 and 11 years old). They live in the pilot area, Whitchurch, in a 1930s semi-detached house. They have lived there for over 16 years and own it with a mortgage.

The shelf 'in the main sitting room' means more to her than the mantelpiece in the 'front room', 'simply because more time is spent there'. She recalls that her 'grand-parents had a huge fireplace with black lead and a double hob and a permanently blackened kettle on the coals. We toasted bread and chestnuts in the winter time.'

Gina's three sons took part briefly in the interview. I was invited to stay for supper.

Hannah

Hannah is 30 years old and works as an underwriter. She lives in a terraced house in Llandaff North with her husband, who works as a househusband and student, and their three pre-school children. They rent the house from a family member and have lived there for over two years. She terms herself 'White UK' and 'middle class'.

The mantelpiece differs from other display spaces because: 'The children can't reach it #1; as it's the furthest point from the door it's less cluttered than other surfaces (scary but true!)' Other focal points are the living room and kitchen walls. She remembers her grandparents' sideboard, 'which had 56 mahogany elephants in descending size order all down one side of the drawing room'.

Hannah's baby daughter was a non-speaking, but noisy participant in the interview! Hannah made a photo-calendar. When I return to interview her after the year-long study, I am invited to stay for supper: salmon, cooked in the dishwasher (it tasted good).

Harriet

Harriet is 35 years old and works as a policy information assistant. She lives in Llandaff North with her husband (a research scientist) and their sons, aged 9 and 7. They own their terraced house (with a mortgage) and have lived there for over four years. She terms herself 'white', her husband 'Indian' and their sons 'Anglo/Indian' and 'middle [class]'.

The mantelpiece differs from the 'dressing table', 'shelf in dining room' and other display spaces because: 'not sure – symmetry. It has a v. nice painting done by my great great grandfather which creates a focal point different to others'. Her memories are of the mantelpiece in her 'parents' house – symmetry, candlesticks – silver ornaments, photographs, paintings – similar to mine'.

Jane

Jane is 32 years old and is a student nurse. She has lived in the same terraced house in Llandaff North all her life, which she owns outright. It had been her mother's house, and Jane now lives there alone, following her mother's death some years ago (told at interview). She terms herself 'white' and 'working class'.

The mantelpiece is different from displays on the 'wall and shelves' because: 'It's the first thing a visitor may notice'.

Jane made a photo-calendar.

John and Charlotte

John is 70 years old and is retired. He lives in a modern detached house with his wife, Charlotte (also retired). At interview, I am told that he was a psychiatrist and Charlotte was a nurse. They own the house outright and have lived there for four years. John terms himself 'Brit.' and 'middle class'.

Other display spaces are 'top of bookcase' and 'windowsill'. The mantelpiece is different due to the 'fire'.

Charlotte participated in some of the interview.

John made a photo-calendar.

'Joseph', Mohammed, Ali, 'Sami', 'Sabine' and Elina (asylum seekers and refugees)

They are a few of the asylum seekers and refugees I met while working on the *Making Wales, Remembering Home* film project. 'Joseph', Mohammed, Elina and Ali made films with me, while Sami and Sabine's accounts are discussed in the Conclusion chapter. The films can be viewed through Hurdley (2012). 'Sami', in his forties, is a refugee from Turkey, who lives in Cardiff with his Polish girlfriend. 'Sabine', in her thirties, is a refugee from Congo, who lives with her young son. Elina, aged 48, is a refugee from Zimbabwe. They all live in Cardiff. 'Joseph', in his early twenties, from Eritrea, Mohammed, aged 19, from Afghanistan and Ali, aged 62, from Iran, were all classified as 'destitute' asylum seekers, since their claims had been refused. I met them all at the Oasis Cardiff drop-in centre and Cardiff Refugee and Asylum Seeker Welcome drop-in. At the time of this book going into production, Mohammed has finally been granted refugee status, and continues to volunteer at Oasis. Ali is still 'destitute' and volunteers at a charity shop. 'Joseph' has not been seen for a while at Oasis.

Jun (second-stage participant)

Jun is in his thirties. He is a lecturer in town planning, doing research in Cardiff. At the time of our interview, he is living in a flat in the city centre.

Karen

Karen is 28 years old and works as a PR consultant. She lives in a terraced house in Llandaff North, which she bought with a mortgage just over a year ago, and has one lodger. She terms herself 'white' and 'middle class'.

The mantelpiece is different from 'bookcase in lounge, set of shelves by phone' because: 'I guess more thought has gone into it and less cluttered than other areas as it is a focal point and "on display" '.

Karen made a photo-calendar.

Kate and David

Kate and David are both 56-year-old academics. They have lived in Cardiff for over 26 years, in a terraced house which they own (with a mortgage). Kate defines herself as 'Anglo' and 'RG1 (Prof & Managerial)'. David defines himself as 'White UK'.

David sees 'bookshelves (in several rooms)' and 'art-works on all walls' as other focal points, and recalls his parents' mantelpiece: 'Poole pottery vases; small brass ornaments; clock. All very neat & clean & orderly (not like mine).'

Kate considers 'bookcases' to be focal points, and writes that the difference between the mantelpiece and other display spaces is 'only that it is in the room where we work, and we work all the time'.

They filled in separate questionnaires and participated in separate interviews. Their selected mantelpiece was in their shared study. They were not from sample areas, but selected as 'exotic' informants.

Lok (second-stage participant)

Lok is in his late twenties and is a visiting researcher in town planning, living in student accommodation in Cardiff. He and his wife live alone in their Beijing apartment. This is common for many of his friends who have moved to the city, leaving their families in rural areas.

Matthew, Laura and Lydia (second-stage participants)

Matthew and his wife, Laura, have very recently moved to east Wales from South Africa. They define themselves as 'White South Africans', like Laura's mother, Lydia, who is visiting. Matthew is 44, and moved here to take up a post with the United Reform Church as a minister and training officer. Laura, aged 39, is a homeopath, and also works as a lay preacher. Lydia, originally from Zimbabwe (when it was Rhodesia) is retired.

Nick, Liz and Andrew

Nick is 39 years old and works as a manager. He lives in Radyr Gardens with his partner Liz (a teacher) and their four children, aged between 7 and 12. They bought their house (with a mortgage) 'off plan' nearly four years ago and had input into some design features, including kitchen and bathroom fittings. He writes that 'I don't feel it [class] is important now, at all. You are who you are.'

He would like a mantelpiece, and has chosen a shelf unit in the living room as his equivalent space. Other focal points are the wall and bedside table. The mantelpiece is different, because it is, 'personal, shared memories, family "things"'. His memory is: 'fireplace, focal point, reminds me of family values, childhood, security'.

Liz participates in the interview with Nick, until her father, Andrew comes in with his wife. They are visiting; gradually, Andrew takes over the interview, as the rest of the family disappears.

Nina (second-stage participant)

Nina defines herself as British Muslim woman of Pakistani ethnic origin, aged 28, married with two small children. They live with her husband's parents in Cardiff. She is a university social sciences researcher, doing a two-year project in Muslim family homes. I have therefore asked her to reflect both on her childhood home, and her conception of mantelpieces in Muslim households in Britain.

Nina's parents moved from Pakistan to Rochdale in the north of England, where her father progressed from being a mill-worker to a factory-owner. When Nina was born, the family lived in a 'working class Pakistani area' of the town. They later moved to a village which was in a 'mainly white area', where her parents still live.

Norah

Norah is 80 years old and lives alone (widowed) in a large semi-detached house on the Llandaff North/Whitchurch border. She owns it outright, having moved there 20 years ago, when she got married. At interview, she told me it had been her husband's house, where he lived with his first wife until her death. They worked for the Gas Board. She is 'middle [class]'.

As well as the mantelpiece in the drawing room, other focal points are 'mantelpieces in sitting room and dining room'. They are 'features – suitable to each room'. Her memory is that 'My maternal grandmother's mantelpiece was full of brass ornaments.'

Norah made a photo-calendar.

Phillip

Phillip is 56 years old and works as a manager. He and his partner Jo (who is in marketing) have lived in Radyr Gardens for over six years. They own their house (with a mortgage). He terms himself 'Welsh', and when asked about class writes, 'It depends how you define it. By upbringing working class, by current life style middle class.'

The mantelpiece differs from other display spaces such as 'windowsill in kitchen – on fridge in kitchen' because it is 'focal point of main living area'. His memory of a mantelpiece from his childhood is that: 'It was far more cluttered then the current one. It was functional – used to store anything that was small and used regularly.'

Jo took part at the beginning of the interview.

Phillip participated in the photo-calendar.

Ruth

Ruth is 53 and works as an insurance clerk. She has lived in a semi-detached 1930s house in Whitchurch for 23 years with her husband, who is retired.

She selects the piano top in the lounge as the mantelpiece equivalent, and although she writes in the questionnaire that she has no similar display spaces, we talk about several areas in the lounge at interview. Her memory of her childhood home is: 'I had a lovely fireplace when I lived at home, old-fashioned, black with a gold-leaf design. It was in the front room (the best room). When the chimney in the back living room was being swept, we would light a fire; it would seem special.'

Sharon

Sharon is 40 years old and a student. She lives in a terraced house in Cardiff Bay with her husband (HGV driver) and a teenage daughter. They have lived there just over two years and own it, with a mortgage. Since moving there, she has totally refurbished it. She defines herself as 'white' and 'working class'.

The mantelpiece is different because it is 'plaster moulded'. Another focal point is her dressing table, although at interview she takes me to photograph a shelf unit in the bedroom.

Sharon made a photo-calendar, but did not respond to the fortnightly email and a doorstep visit a few months into the project. The photographs are not available.

Sheila

Sheila is 56 and works as a receptionist. She has lived in a terraced cottage in Llandaff North, for three years, rented from an HA. She terms herself 'Welsh' and writes that she is 'middle [class], although following my divorce, house and financial state not up to usual standards'.

She would like a mantelpiece and chooses the top of the gas fire in the lounge as her equivalent space. Other focal points are 'coffee table (lounge), TV cabinet (lounge), shelf (lounge), bedroom'. Her memory is of her 'grandparents' home, photos, ornaments on sideboard and mantelpiece in sitting room and lounge'.

Shyam and Mike

Shyam is 74 years old and lives in Cardiff Bay with her husband. Both are retired and have lived for 46 years in their terraced house, which they own outright. They have changed most aspects of the interior décor during this time, including (as she tells me in the interview) refurbishment and replacement of some fireplaces. Shyam defines herself as 'Welsh/Arab' and her husband, Mike, as 'Jamaican', and as 'middle class'.

The mantelpiece is different from other spaces such as the 'cabinet/shelves' because it is the 'central point of room'. Her memory is: 'My grandmother's mantelpiece. Brass ornaments – candlesticks, button box, clock, animal models, actually you could hardly see the mantel for the amount of brass, all of which had to be "brassed" on Sat. morning.'

Mike takes part in the last few minutes of the interview.

Shyam made a photo-calendar, taking snapshots of mantelpieces in the three rooms downstairs.

Sian

Sian is 38 and works as a teacher. She lives with her spouse (an accountant) and their three children (11, 10 and 7 years old). They have lived for five years on the Llandaff North/Whitchurch border in their large semi-detached house, which they own with a mortgage. They are extending the house when I interview her. She defines herself as 'white' and 'middle [class]'.

The four mantelpieces in her house are different from other display spaces such as 'coffee tables, dressing tables, piano, dresser in kitchen, walls', because they are 'out of reach of children!'

The children were present during the interview and said a few words.

Sian made a photo-calendar, but did not respond to emails at the end of the project, so her photographs are not available.

Victoria and Luke

Victoria is 26 years old and is a community support worker. She has lived in a flat in Cardiff Bay for two years with her partner, Luke, who is a testing analyst. They rent the flat from a family member. Victoria defines herself as 'British-White' and 'middle class'.

The 'shelves in living room/dining room' have 'more space to put more things on it (on the mantelpiece-type place)' than other display spaces such as the 'bedside cabinet' and 'coffee table in centre of living room'. She writes that 'In my parents' home where I grew up they have a mantelpiece over an open fire where photos and cards are placed. Also had photos on top of the piano.'

Luke took part in the interview.

Bibliography

Adam B. (1995) *Timewatch: The Social Analysis of Time*. Cambridge: Polity Press.

Adkins L. (2004) 'Introduction: Feminism, Bourdieu and After'. *The Sociological Review* 52: 2: 1–18.

Agnew J-C. (2003) 'The Give-and-Take of Consumer Culture'. In S. Strasser (Ed.) *Commodifying Everything: Relationships of the Market*. London: Routledge: 11–39.

Ahmed S. (2004) 'Affective Economies'. *Social Text*, 22(2 79): 117–139.

Ali N., Kalra V.S., and Sayyid S. (Eds.) (2006) *A Postcolonial People: South Asians in Britain*. London: Hurst and Co.

Allan G. (1989) 'Introduction'. In G. Allan and G. Crow (Eds.), *Home and Family: Creating the Domestic Sphere*. Basingstoke: Palgrave: 1–23.

Allan G. and Crow G. (Eds.) (1989) *Home and Family: Creating the Domestic Sphere*. Basingstoke: Palgrave.

Amit V. (1999) 'Constructing the Field'. In V. Amit (Ed.) *Ethnographic Fieldwork in the Contemporary World*. London: Routledge: 1–18.

Anagnost A. (1997) *National Past-Times: Narrative, Representation and Power in Modern China*. Durham, NC: Duke University Press.

Appadurai A. (1981) 'The Past as a Scarce Resource'. *Man* 16: 201–219.

Appadurai A. (Ed.) (1986) *The Social Life of Things: Commodities in Cultural Perspective*. Cambridge: Cambridge University Press.

Appadurai A. (1986a) 'Introduction: Commodities and the Politics of Value'. In A. Appadurai (Ed.) *The Social Life of Things: Commodities in Cultural Perspective*. Cambridge: Cambridge University Press: 3–63.

Appadurai A. (1996) *Modernity at Large: Cultural Dimensions of Globalisation*. Minneapolis: University of Minnesota Press.

Ariès P. (1993) 'Introduction'. In R. Chartier, P. Ariès, G. Duby and A. Goldhammer (Eds.), *A History of Private Life*, iii, *Passions of the Renaissance* (Trans. A. Goldhammer). Cambridge, MA: Belknap Press of Harvard University Press: 3–8.

Armitage S. (1992) 'About His Person'. In *Kid*. London: Faber and Faber: 88. http://www.poemhunter.com/poem/about-his-person/ [accessed 15 October 12].

Armstrong J. R. (1979) *Traditional Buildings – Accessible to the Public*. Wakefield: EP Publishing Ltd.

Arnold D. (1998) 'The Country House: Form, Function and Meaning.' In D. Arnold (Ed.), *The Georgian Country House: Architecture, Landscape and Society*. Stroud: Sutton Publishing Ltd: 1–19.

Aslet C. and Powers A. (1985) *The National Trust Book of the English House*. Harmondsworth: Viking Penguin.

Atkinson W. (2012) 'Review Essay: "Where Now for Bourdieu-inspired Sociology?"'. *Sociology* 46: 167–173.

Atkinson P. (1990) *The Ethnographic Imagination: Textual Constructions of Reality*. London: Routledge.

Atkinson P. and Silverman D. (1997) 'Kundera's *Immortality*: The Interview Society and the Invention of Self'. *Qualitative Enquiry* 3: 304–325.

Atkinson P., Delamont S. and Housley W. (2007) *Contours of Culture: Complex Ethnography and the Ethnography of Complexity*. Lanham: AltaMira Press.

Attfield J. (1995) 'Inside Pram Town: A Case Study of Harlow House Interiors, 1951–61'. In S. Jackson and S. Moores (Eds.) *The Politics of Domestic Consumption: Critical Readings*. London: Prentice Hall: 290–300.

Attfield J. (1999) 'Bringing Modernity Home: Open Plan in the British Domestic Interior'. In I. Cieraad (Ed.) *At Home: An Anthropology of Domestic Space*. Syracuse: Syracuse University Press: 73–82.

Attfield J. (2000) *Wild Things: The Material Culture of Everyday Life*. Oxford: Berg.

Augé M. (1995) *Non-places: Introduction to an Anthropology of Supermodernity* [trans. J. Howe]. London: Verso.

Austen J. (2008 [1813]) *Pride and Prejudice*. UNC-North Carolina: Project Gutenberg: http://www.gutenberg.org/files/1342/1342-h/1342-h.htm [accessed 29 October 12].

Bachelard G. (1994) [1958]) *The Poetics of Space*. [Trans. M. Jolas]. Boston, MA: Beacon.

Bahloul J. (1999) 'The Memory House: Time and Place in Jewish Immigrant Culture in France'. In D. Birdwell-Pheasant and D. Lawrence-Zuniga (Eds.) *House Life: Space, Place and Family in Europe*. Oxford: Berg: 223–238.

Baldwin W. and Turk E. (2005) *Mantelpieces of the Old South: Lost Architecture in Southern Culture*. Charleston, SC: The History Press.

Banim M. and Guy A. (2001) 'Dis/Continued Selves: Why Do Women Keep Clothes They No Longer Wear?'. In A. Guy, E. Gree and M. Banim (Eds.) *Through the Wardrobe: Women's Relationships with their Clothes*. Oxford: Berg: 203–220.

Barfoot A. (1963) *Houses of the Ordinary People*. London: Batsford.

Barley M. (1986) *Houses and History*. London: Faber and Faber.

Barthes R. (2000 [1957]) *Mythologies*. [Trans. A. Lavers]. London: Vintage Classics.

Basit T.N. (1997) *Eastern Values, Western Milieu: Identities and Aspirations of Adolescent British Muslim Girls*. Aldershot: Ashgate.

Baudrillard J. (1996 [1968]) *The System of Objects*. [Trans. J. Benedict]. London: Verso.

Bauman Z. (2001) *The Individualised Society*. Cambridge: Polity Press.

Bauman Z. (2001a) 'Consuming Life'. *Journal of Consumer Culture* 1: 1: 9–29.

Beck U. (1992) *Risk Society*. London: Sage.

Beck U. and Beck-Gernsheim E. (2002) *Individualisation*. London: Sage.

Bede (731) *Historia Ecclesiastica Gentis Anglorum*: http://www.fordham.edu/halsall/basis/bede-book1.asp [accessed 20 February 2013].

Beecher C. and Beecher Stowe H. (1869) *The American Woman's Home, or, Principles of Domestic Science: Being a Guide to the Formation and Maintenance of Economical, Healthful, Beautiful, and Christian Homes*. New York, NY: J. B. Ford and Company: http://www.archive.org/details/americanwomansho00beecrich [accessed 5 October 10].

Belk R. (1993) 'Materialism and the Making of the Modern American Christmas.' In D. Miller (Ed.) *Unwrapping Christmas*. Oxford: Oxford University Press: 75–94.

Belk R.W. (1995) *Collecting in a Consumer Society*. London: Routledge.

Belk R. (1996) 'The Perfect Gift'. In C. Otnes and R. Beltramini (Eds.) *Gift Giving: A Research Anthology*. Bowling Green, OH: Bowling Green State University Popular Press: 59–84.

Benjamin W. (1999 [1927–40]) *The Arcades Project* [Ed. R. Tiedermann; Trans. H. Eiland and K. McLaughlin]. Cambridge, MA: Harvard University Press.

Benjamin W. (2006) *Berlin Childhood Around 1900*. Cambridge, MA: Harvard University Press.

Benjamin D. and Stea D. (1995) *The Home: Words, Interpretations, Meanings and Environments*. Avebury: Minnesota University Press.

Bennett A. (1980) *Enjoy*. London: Faber and Faber.

Bennett A. (2012) *People*. London: Faber and Faber.

Bennett T. (1995) *The Birth of the Museum: History, Theory, Politics*. London: Routledge.

Bennett T. (2002) 'Home and Everyday Life'. In T. Bennett and D. Watson (Eds.) *Understanding Everyday Life*. Oxford: Blackwell: 1–50.

Bennett T. (2003) 'The Invention of the Modern Cultural Fact: Towards a Critique of the Critique of Everyday Life'. In E. B. Silva and T. Bennett (Eds.) *Contemporary Culture and Everyday Life*. Durham, NC: Sociology Press.

Bennett T. (2005) 'The Historical Universal: The Role of Cultural Value in the Historical Sociology of Pierre Bourdieu'. *British Journal of Sociology* 56(1): 141–164.

Bennett T., Emmison M. and Frow J. (1999) *Accounting for Tastes: Australian Everyday Cultures*. Melbourne: Cambridge University Press.

Bennett T., Savage M., Silva E., Warde A., Gayo-Cal M. and Wright D. (2009) *Culture, Class, Distinction*. London: Routledge.

Bennett T. and Watson D. (Eds.) (2002) *Understanding Everyday Life*. Milton Keynes: Open University.

Bercovitch S. (1975) *The Puritan Origins of the American Self*. New Haven, CT and London: Yale University Press.

Berger J. (1972) *Ways of Seeing*. Harmondsworth: Penguin.

Berger P. and Kellner H. (1964) 'Marriage and the Construction of Reality: An Exercise in the Microsociology of Knowledge'. *Diogenes* 12: 1–24.

Berliner N. (2003) *Yin Yu Tang: The Architecture and Daily Life of a Chinese House*. North Clarendon, VT: Tuttle.

Berliner N. (2005) 'Sheltering the Past: The Preservation of China's Old Dwellings'. In R. Knapp and K-Y. Lo (Eds.) *House Home Family: Living and Being Chinese*. Honolulu, HI: University of Hawai'i Press: 205–220.

Bhatti M. (2006) 'When I'm in the Garden I Can Create My Own Paradise: Homes and Gardens in Later Life'. *The Sociological Review*, 54 (2): 318–341.

Billig M. (1995) *Banal Nationalism*. London: Sage.

Birdwell-Pheasant D. and Lawrence-Zuniga D. (Eds.) (1999) *House Life: Space, Place and Family in Europe*. Oxford: Berg.

Bissel D. and Fuller G. (Eds.) (2010) *Stillness in a Mobile World*. London: Routledge.

Bleyen J. (2010) 'The Materialities of Absence After Stillbirth: Historical Perspectives'. In J. Hockey, C. Komaromy, and K. Woodthorpe (Eds.) (2010) *The Matter of Death: Space, Place and Materiality*. Basingstoke: Palgrave Macmillan: 69–84.

Blunt A. and Varley A. (2004) 'Introduction: Geographies of Home'. *Cultural Geographies* 11: 3–6.

Blunt A. and Dowling R. (2006) *Home*. London: Routledge.

Boardman J. Griffin J. and Murray O. (1988) *The Oxford History of the Roman World*. Oxford: Oxford University Press.

Borges J.L. (1975 [1942]) 'The Analytical Language of John Wilkins'. In *Other Inquisitions* (Trans. R. Simms). Austin, TX: University of Texas Press.

Bourdieu P. (1977) *Outline of a Theory of Practice*. Cambridge: Cambridge University Press.

Bourdieu P. (1979) *Algeria 1960: The Disenchantment of the World, the Sense of Honour, the Kabyle House or the World Reversed*. Cambridge: Cambridge University Press.

Bourdieu P. (1986) *Distinction: A Social Critique of the Judgment of Taste* [Trans. R. Nice]. London: Routledge.

Bourdieu P. (1990) *In Other Words: Essays Towards a Reflexive Sociology*. Cambridge: Polity.

Bourdieu P. (1999) *Weight of the World: Social Suffering in Contemporary Society*. Cambridge: Polity.

Bournville Village Trust Research Publications (1941) *When We Build Again: A Study Based on Research into Conditions of Living and Working in Birmingham*. London: Allen and Unwin.

Bowden S. and Offer A. (1996) 'The Technological Revolution that Never Was'. In E. De Grazia with E. Furlough (Eds.) *The Sex of Things: Gender and Consumption in Historical Perspective*. Berkeley, CA: University of California Press.

Brah A. (1996) *Cartographies of Diaspora: Contesting Identities*. London: Routledge.

Bray F. (1997) *Technology and Gender: Fabrics of Power in Late Imperial China*. Berkeley CA: University of California Press.

Brett L. (1947) *The Things We See: Houses*. Harmondsworth: Penguin.

Brewer P. (2000) *From Fireplace to Cookstove: Technology and the Domestic Ideal in America*. Syracuse, NY: Syracuse University Press.

Brindley T. (1999) 'The Modern house in England: An Architecture of Exclusion'. In T. Chapman and J. Hockey (Eds.) *Ideal Homes?: Social Change and Domestic Life*. London: Routledge: 30–43.

Brink S. (1995) Home: The Term and the Concept from a Linguistic and Settlement-Historical Viewpoint. In D. Benjamin and D. Stea (Eds.) *The Home: Words, Interpretations, Meanings and Environments*. Avebury: Minnesota University Press: 17–25.

Brown J. (1988) 'Fine Arts and Fine People: The Japanese Taste in the American Home, 1886–1916'. In M. Motz and P. Browne (Eds.) *Making the American Home: Middle-Class Women and Domestic Material Culture 1840–1940*. Bowling Green, OH: Bowling Green State University Popular Press: 121–140.

Brunskill R.W. (1978) *Illustrated Handbook of Vernacular Architecture* (2nd Edn.). London: Faber and Faber.

Brunskill R.W. (1981) *Traditional Buildings of Britain: An Introduction to Vernacular Architecture'*. London: Victor Gollancz.

Buchli V. (1999) *An Archaeology of Socialism*. Oxford: Berg.

Buchli V. (Ed.) (2002) *The Material Culture Reader*. Oxford: Berg.

Bull M. and. Back L. (Eds.) (2003) *The Auditory Culture Reader*. Oxford: Berg.

Burns N. (2004) 'Negotiating Difference: Disabled People's Experiences of Housebuilders'. *Housing Studies*, 19(5): 765–780.

Busch A. (1999) *Geography of Home: Writings on Where We Live*. New York, NY: Princeton University Press.

Butler J. (1993) *Bodies that Matter: On the Discursive Limits of 'Sex'*. New York, NY: Routledge.

Butler J. (1999) *Gender Trouble: Feminism and the Subversion of Identity*. New York, NY: Routledge.

Butler J. (2004) *Undoing Gender*. New York, NY: Routledge.

Butler J. (2004a) *Precarious Life: The Powers of Mourning and Violence*. London: Verso: Ch. 2: 20–49.

Caddy F. (1874) *Household Organisation*. London: Chapman Hall.

Camesasca E. (1971) 'Anatomy of the House'. In E. Camesasca (Ed.), *History of the House*. London: Collins: 347–428.

Caplow T. (1984) 'Rule Enforcement without Visible Means: Christmas Giving in Middletown'. *American Journal of Sociology*, 89: 6: 1306–1323.

Carr E.H. (1964 [1961]) *What is History?* Harmondsworth: Penguin.

Carsten J. and Hugh-Jones S. (Eds.) (1995) *About the House: Levi-Strauss and Beyond*. Cambridge: Cambridge University Press.

Carsten J. (1997) *The Heat of the Hearth: The Process of Kinship in a Malay Fishing Community*. Oxford: Oxford University Press.

Carsten J. (2004) *After Kinship*. Cambridge: Cambridge University Press.

Carsten J. (2007) 'Connections and Disconnections of Memory and Kinship in Narratives of Adoption Reunions in Scotland'. In J. Carsten (Ed.) *Ghosts of Memory*. Oxford: Blackwell: 83–103.

Carsten J. (2007a) 'Introduction: Ghosts of Memory'. In J. Carsten (Ed.) *Ghosts of Memory*. Oxford: Blackwell: 1–35.

Casey E. (2008) *Women, Pleasure and the Gambling Experience*. Aldershot: Ashgate.

Casey E. and Martens L. (Eds.) (2007) *Gender and Consumption: Domestic Cultures and the Commercialization of Everyday Life*. Aldershot: Ashgate.

Cave L. (1981) *The Smaller English House: Its History and Development*. London: Hale.

Chapman D. (1955) *The Home and Social Status*. London: Routledge and Kegan Paul.

Chapman T. (1999a) 'Stage Sets for Ideal Lives: Images of Home in Contemporary Show Homes'. In T. Chapman and J. Hockey (Eds.) *Ideal Homes?: Social Change and Domestic Life*. London: Routledge: 44–58.

Chapman T. (1999) ' "You've Got Him Well Trained": The Negotiation of Roles in the Domestic Sphere'. In T. Chapman and J. Hockey (Eds.) *Ideal Homes?: Social Change and Domestic Life*. London: Routledge: 163–180.

Chapman T. and Hockey J. (1999a) 'The Ideal Home as It Is Imagined and as It Is Lived'. In T. Chapman and J. Hockey (Eds.) *Ideal Homes?: Social Change and Domestic Life*. London: Routledge: 1–14.

Chapman T. and Hockey J. (Eds.) (1999) *Ideal Homes?: Social Change and Domestic Life*. London: Routledge.

Chapman T., Hockey J. and Wood M. (1999) 'Daring to be Different?'. In T. Chapman and J. Hockey (Eds.) *Ideal Homes?: Social Change and Domestic Life*. London: Routledge: 194–209.

Charlton T. Myers L. and Sharpless R. (2006) *Handbook of Oral History*. Oxford: Altamira.

Chase S. (2011) 'Narrative Inquiry: Still a Field in the Making'. In N. Denzin and Y. Lincoln (Eds.) *The Sage Handbook of Qualitative Research*. London: Sage: 421–434.

Chatwin B. (1987) *Songlines*. Harmondsworth: Penguin.

Cheal D. (1987) ' "Showing Them You Love Them": Gift Giving and the Dialectic of Intimacy'. *Sociological Review*, 35(1): 150–169.

Cheal D. (1988) *The Gift Economy*. London: Routledge.

Chevalier S. (1999) 'The French Two-Home Project: Materialisation of Family Identity'. In I. Cieraad (Ed.) *At Home: An Anthropology of Domestic Space*. Syracuse: Syracuse University Press: 83–94.

Cieraad I. (1999) *At Home: An Anthropology of Domestic Space*. Syracuse: Syracuse University Press.

Cieraad I. (1999a) 'Introduction: Anthropology at Home'. In I. Cieraad (Ed.) *At Home: An Anthropology of Domestic Space*. Syracuse: Syracuse University Press: 1–12.

Cieraad I. (1999b) 'Dutch Windows: Female Virtue and Female Vice'. In I. Cieraad (Ed.) *At Home: An Anthropology of Domestic Space*. Syracuse: Syracuse University Press: 31–52.

Clapham D., Mackie P., Orford S., Buckley K., Thomas I., Atherton I. and McAnulty U. (2012) *Housing Options and Solutions for Young People in 2020*. Joseph Rowntree Foundation: http://www.jrf.org.uk/publications/housing-options-solutions-young-people [accessed 16 June 2012].

Clarke A. (2001) *Tupperware: The Promise of Plastic in 1950s America*. Washington, DC: Smithsonian.

Clarke A. (2009) 'The Contemporary Interior: Trajectories of Biography and Style'. In P. Sparke, A. Massey, T. Keeble and B. Martin (Eds.) *Designing the Modern Interior: From the Victorians to Today*. Oxford: Berg: 261–273.

Classen C. (Ed.) (2005) *The Book of Touch*. Oxford: Berg.

Classen C. (2005a) 'Touch in the Museum'. In C. Classen (Ed.) *The Book of Touch*. Oxford: Berg: 275–286.

Clifford J. (1997) *Routes, Travel and Translation in the Late 20th Century*. Cambridge, MA: Harvard University Press.

Cohen S. and Taylor L. (1992) *Escape Attempts: The Theory and Practice of Resistance to Everyday Life* (2nd Edn.). London: Routledge.

Cohen M. (2005) 'House United, House Divided: Myths and Realities, Then and Now'. In R. Knapp and K-Y Lo (Eds.) *House Home Family: Living and Being Chinese*. Honolulu: University of Hawai'i Press: 235–257.

Cohen D. (2006) *Household Gods: The British and Their Possessions*. New Haven, CT: Yale University Press.

Cole I. and Furbey R. (1994) *The Eclipse of Council Housing*. London: Routledge.

Conlin J. (2006) *The Nation's Mantelpiece: A History of the National Gallery*. London: Pallas Athene Arts.

Connerton P. (1989) *How Societies Remember*. Cambridge: Cambridge University Press.

Connerton P. (2009) *How Modernity Forgets*. Cambridge: Cambridge University Press.

Cook C. (1995 [1881]) *The House Beautiful: An Unabridged Reprint of the Classic Victorian Stylebook*. New York, NY: Dover: 110–128.

Coolen H. Kempen E. and Ozaki R. (2002) 'Experiences and Meanings of Dwellings'. *Housing, Theory and Society,* 19(2): 114–116.

Corrigan P. (1995) 'Gender and the Gift: The Case of the Family Clothing Economy'. In S. Jackson and S. Moores, *The Politics of Domestic Consumption: Critical Readings*. Hemel Hempstead: Prentice Hall/Harvester Wheatsheaf: 116–133.

Crain C. (2006) 'Surveillance Society: Mass Observation and the Meaning of Everyday Life'. *New Yorker* 11 September 2006: http://www.newyorker.com/archive/2006/09/11/060911crat_atlarge?currentPage= all#ixzz0Z4pLOQQ7 [accessed 7 December 2009].

Crang M. and Tolia-Kelly D. (2010) 'Nation, Race and Affect: Senses and Sensibilities at National Heritage sites'. *Environment and Planning A,* 42: 2315–2331.

Crewe L., Gregson N. and Metcalfe A. (2009) 'The Screen and the Drum: On form, Function, Fit and Failure in Contemporary Home Consumption'. *Design and Culture,* 1: 307–328.

Crompton R., Devine F., Savage M. and Scott J. (1991) *Renewing Class Analysis*. Oxford: Blackwell.

Crowley A. (2001) *The Invention of Comfort: Sensibilities and Design in Early Modern Britain and Early America*. Baltimore, MD: Johns Hopkins University Press.

Csikszentmihalyi M. and Rochberg-Halton E. (1981) *The Meaning of Things: Domestic Symbols and the Self*. Cambridge: Cambridge University Press.

Cullingford B. (2003) *Chimneys and Chimney Sweeps*. Princes Risborough: Shire books.

Czarniawska B. (1999) *Writing Management: Organisation Theory as a Literary Genre*. Oxford: Oxford University Press.

Czarniawska B. (2004) *Narratives in Social Science Research*. London: Sage.

Daniels I.M. (2001) 'The 'Untidy' Japanese House'. In D. Miller (Ed.), *Home Possessions: Material Culture behind Closed Doors*. Oxford: Berg: 201–229.

Darke J. and Gurney C. (2000) 'Putting Up? Gender, Hospitality and Performance'. In C. Lashley and A. Morrison (Eds.) *In Search of Hospitality: Theoretical Perspectives and Debates*. London: Butterworth-Heinemann: 77–99.

Darling E. (2009) ' "The Scene in Which the Daily Drama of Personal Life Takes Place": Towards the Modern Interior in Early 1930s Britain'. In P. Sparke, A. Massey,

T. Keeble and B. Martin (Eds.) *Designing the Modern Interior: from the Victorians to Today*. Oxford: Berg: 107–118.

Davidoff L. and Hall C. (1995) ' "My Own Fireside": The Creation of the Middle-Class Home'. In S. Jackson and S. Moores (Eds.) *The Politics of Domestic Consumption: Critical Readings*. Hemel Hempstead: Prentice Hall/Harvester Wheatsheaf: 277–289.

Davidoff L. and Hall C. (2002) *Family Fortunes: Men and Women of the English Middle-Class 1780–1850* (2nd Edn.). London: Routledge.

Day S. (2007) 'Threading Time in the Biographies of London Sex Workers' In J. Carsten (Ed.) *Ghosts of Memory*. Oxford: Blackwell: 172–193.

De Certeau M. (1984) *The Practice of Everyday Life* (trans. S. Rendall). Berkeley: University of California Press.

De Grazia V. with Furlough E. (1996) (Eds.) *The Sex of Things: Gender and Consumption in Historical Perspective*. Berkeley: University of California Press.

Denzin N. (1997) *Interpretive Ethnography: Ethnographic Practices*. London: Sage.

Denzin N. and Lincoln Y. (2011) 'Introduction: The Discipline and Practice of Qualitative Research'. In N. Denzin and Y. Lincoln (Eds.) *The Sage Handbook of Qualitative Research*. London: Sage: 1–20.

Desjarlais R. (2005) 'Movement, Stillness: On the Sensory world of a Shelter for the Homeless Mentally Ill'. In D. Howes (Ed.) *Empire of the Senses: The Sensual Culture Reader*. Oxford: Berg: 369–379.

Dewing D. (2008) *The Geffrye Museum of the Home*. London: Geffrye Museum.

Dicks B. (2000) *Heritage, Place and Community*. Cardiff: University of Wales Press.

Dittmar H. (1992) *The Social Psychology of Material Possessions: To Have Is To Be*. Hemel Hempstead: Harvester Wheatsheaf.

Doar B. (2005) 'Reconciling Tourism and Conservation: the Case of Historic Towns'. *China Heritage Newsletter* 2: http://www.chinaheritagenewsletter.org/articles.php?searchterm=002_historictowns.incandissue=002 [accessed 2 September 10].

Dolan J. A. (1999) ' "I've always Fancied Owning Me Own Lion": Ideological Motivations in External House Decoration by Recent Homeowners'. In I. Cieraad (Ed.) *At Home: An Anthropology of Domestic Space*. Syracuse: Syracuse University Press: 60–72.

Dong L. and Tian K. (2009) 'The Use of Western Brands in Asserting Chinese National Identity'. *Journal of Consumer Research*, 36: 504–523.

Douglas M. (2002 [1966]) *Purity and Danger: An Analysis of the Concepts of Pollution and Taboo*. London: Routledge and Kegan Paul.

Douglas M. (1986) *How Institutions Think*. London: Routledge.

Douglas M. (1973) 'Introduction'. In M. Douglas (Ed.) *Rules and Meanings: The Anthropology of Everyday Knowledge*. Harmondsworth: Penguin: 9–13.

Douglas M. (1993) 'The Idea of Home: A Kind of Space'. In A. Mack (Ed.) *Home: A Place in the World*. New York, NY: New York University Press.

Douglas M. (1986) *How Institutions Think*. Syracuse: Syracuse University Press.

Douglas M. and Isherwood B. (1996 [1979]) *The World of Goods: Towards an Anthropology of Consumption*. London: Routledge.

Dovey K. (1999) *Framing Places: Mediating Power in Built Form*. London: Routledge.

Downing A. (1969 [1850]) *The Architecture of Country Houses: Including Designs for Cottages, and Farm-Houses and Villas, With Remarks on Interiors, Furniture, and the Best Modes of Warming and Ventilating*. New York, NY: Dover Publications.

Drazin A. (2001) 'A Man will get Furnished: Wood and Domesticity in Urban Romania'. In D. Miller (Ed.) *Home Possessions: Material Culture Behind Closed Doors*. Oxford: Berg: 173–199.

Drobnick J. (Ed.) (2006) *The Smell Culture Reader*. Oxford: Berg.

Drummond J. (1971) 'From Saxon Hut to Tudor Manor'. In E. Camesasca (Ed.) *History of the House*. London: Collins: 99–103.

Duszat M. (2012) 'Foucault's Laughter. Enumeration, Rewriting, and the Construction of the Essayist in Borges's "The analytical language of John Wilkins"'. *Orbis Litterarum*, 67: 193–218.

Dwyer O. (2000) 'Interpreting the Civil Rights Movement: Place, Memory and Conflict. *Professional Geographer*, 52: 660–671.

Eade J. (Ed.) (1997) *Living the Global City: Globalisation as a Social Process*. London: Routledge.

Earle R. and Phillips C. (2009) 'Con-Viviality and Beyond: Identity Dynamics in a Young Men's Prison'. In M. Wetherell (Ed.) *Identity in the 21st Century: New Trends in Changing Times*. Basingstoke: Palgrave Macmillan: 120–138.

Eastlake C. (1969 [1868]) *Hints on Household Taste in Furniture, Upholstery and Other Details*. New York, NY: Dover.

Elias N. (2000 [1994] [Orig. German Edn. 1939]) *The Civilizing Process: Sociogenetic and Psychogenetic Investigations* (2nd Edn.) [Trans. E. Jephcott]. Oxford: Blackwell.

Edwards E. (2005) 'Grasping the Image: How Photographs are Handled'. In C. Classen (Ed.) *The Book of Touch*. Oxford: Berg: 421–425.

Evans D. (2012) 'Beyond the Throwaway Society: Ordinary Domestic Practice and a Sociological Approach to Household Food Waste'. *Sociology*, 26: 41–56.

Evans R. (1995) *Deng Xiaoping and the Making of Modern China* (2nd Edn.). Harmondsworth: Penguin.

Evans-Pritchard E.E. (1949) *The Sanusi of Cyrenaica*. Oxford: Oxford University Press.

Faure D. (2005) 'Between House and Home: The Family in South China'. In R. Knapp and K-Y. Lo (Eds.) (2005) *House Home Family: Living and Being Chinese*. Honolulu, HI: University of Hawai'i Press: 281–229.

Fazion M. and Snadon P. (2006) *The Domestic Architecture of Benjamin Henry Latrobe*. Baltimore, MA: Johns Hopkins University Press.

Featherstone M. (1987) 'Lifestyle and Consumer Culture', *Theory, Culture and Society*, 4(1): 55–70.

Featherstone M. (1991) *Consumer Culture and Postmodernism*. London: Sage.

Felski R. (1995) *The Gender of Modernity*. Cambridge, MA: Harvard University Press.

Felski R. (1999–2000) 'The Invention of Everyday Life'. *New Formations*, 39: 15–31.

Fernie E. (2002) *The Architecture of Norman England*. Oxford: Oxford University Press.

Filbee M. (1980) *A Woman's Place: An Illustrated History of Women at Home from the Roman Villa to the Victorian Town House*. London: London Book Club Associates/Ebury Press.

Finch J. (1997) 'Individuality and Adaptability in English kinship'. In M. Gullestad and M. Segalen (Eds.) *Family and Kinship in Europe*. London: Cassell: 129–145.

Fiske J. (1992) 'Cultural Studies and the Culture of Everyday Life'. In L. Grossberg, C. Nelson and P.A. Treichler (Eds.) *Cultural Studies*. London: Routledge.

Flath J. (2005) 'Reading the Text of the Home: Domestic Ritual Configuration Through Print'. In R. Knapp and K-Y. Lo (Eds.) (2005) *House Home Family: Living and Being Chinese*. Honolulu, HI: University of Hawai'i Press: 325–347.

Fletcher *Sir* B. (1989) *A History of Architecture* (Ed. J. Musgrove) (19th Edn.). London: Butterworths.

Flyvberg B. (2011) 'Case Study'. In N. Denzin and Y. Lincoln (Eds.) *The Sage Handbook of Qualitative Research*. London: Sage: 301–316.

Forty A. (1986) *Objects of Desire: Design and Society Since 1750*. London: Thames and Hudson.

Forty A. and Kuchler S. (Eds.) (2001) *The Art of Forgetting* Oxford: Berg.

Foster G. (2004) *American Houses: A Field Guide to the Architecture of the Home*. New York, NY: Houghton Mifflin.

Foucault M. (1989 [1966]) *The Order of Things*. London: Routledge.

Foucault M. (1977 [1975]), *Discipline and Punish: The Birth of the Prison* [Trans. A. Sheridan]. Harmondsworth: Penguin.

Foucault M. (1996 [1980]) 'The Masked Philosopher'. In S. Lotringer (Ed.) *Foucault Live (Interviews, 1961–1984)* [Trans. L. Hochroth and J. Johnston] (2nd Edn.). New York, NY: Semiotext(e): 305.

Future Homes Commission (2012) *The Way We Live Now*. Royal Institute of British Architects [RIBA] and Ipsos MORI: http://www.architecture.com/Files/RIBAHoldings/PolicyAndInternationalRelations/HomeWise/ThewaywelivenowRIBAIpsosMORIMay2012.pdf [accessed 23 October 12].

Gale S. (1949) *Modern Housing Estates*. London: Batsford.

Gardiner S. (1976) *Evolution of the House*. St Albans: Paladin.

Garfield S. (2009) 'We are at War: about the book': http://www.simongarfield.com/pages/books/we_are_at_war.htm [accessed 9 December 09].

Garfinkel H. (1988) 'Evidence for Locally Produced, Naturally Accountable Phenomena of Order, Logic, Reason, Meaning, Method etc. in and as of the Essential Quiddity of Immortal Ordinary Society (I of IV); An Announcement of Studies'. *Sociological Theory* 6(1): 103–109.

Garvey P. (2001) 'Organised Disorder: Moving Furniture in Norwegian Homes'. In D. Miller (Ed.) *Home Possessions: Material Culture Behind Closed Doors*. Oxford: Berg: 47–68.

Garvin J. (2002) *A Building History of Northern New England*. Lebanon, NH: University Press of New England.

Geffrye Museum (2012) http://www.geffrye-museum.org.uk/ [accessed 23 October 12].

Gell A. (1998) *Art and Agency: An Anthropological Theory*. Oxford: Oxford University Press.

Giddens A. (1984) *The Constitution of Society*. Cambridge: Polity Press.

Giddens A., (1991) *Modernity and Self-Identity*, Cambridge: Polity.

Giles J. (2004) *The Parlour and the Suburb*. Oxford: Berg.

Gilliat-Ray S. (2010) *Muslims in Britain: An Introduction*. Cambridge: Cambridge University Press.

Gilroy P. (1993) *The Black Atlantic: Modernity and Double Consciousness*. Harvard University Press.

Gilroy P. (2004) *After Empire: Melancholia or Convivial Culture?* London: Routledge.

Global Voices (2012) http://globalvoicesonline.org/2012/08/30/controversial-tibet-theme-park-project-is-launched/ [accessed 29 October 12].

Godbout J. (1998 [1992]) *The World of the Gift*. [Trans. D. Winkler]. Montreal and Kingston: McGill-Queen's University Press.

Goffman E. (1959) *The Presentation of Self in Everyday Life*. Harmondsworth: Penguin.

Goffman E. (1971) *Relations in Public*. New York, NY: Harper and Row.

Goffman E. (1983) 'The Interaction Order'. *American Sociological Review*, 48: 1–17.

Goffman E. (1986 [1974]) *Frame Analysis: An Essay on the Organisation of Experience*. Boston, MA: Northeastern University Press.

Gold J. and Ward S. (Eds.) (1994) *Place Promotion: The Use of Publicity and Marketing to Sell Towns and Regions*. Chichester: Wiley.

Gombrich E. (1995) *The Story of Art* [16th Revised Edn.]. London: Phaidon Press.

Goot M. (2008) 'Mass-Observation and Modern Public Opinion Research'. In W. Donsbach and M. Traugott (Eds.) *The SAGE Handbook of Public Opinion Research*. London: Sage: 93–103.

Gordon J. and McArthur J. (1986) 'Interior Decorating Advice as Popular Culture: Women's Views Concerning Wall and Window Treatments, 1870–1920'. *Journal of American Culture*, 9: 15–23.

Gorman-Murray A. (2008) 'Queering the Family Home: Narratives from Gay, Lesbian and Bisexual Youth Coming Out in Supportive Family Homes in Australia'. *Gender, Place and Culture*, 15: 31–44.

Gotch J. (1909) *The History of the English House*. London: Bracken Books.

Gow I. (2001) 'The Scottish Chimneypiece'. In M. Wood (Ed.) *The Hearth in Scotland*. Scottish Vernacular Buildings Working Group.

Gowans A. (1986) *The Comfortable House: North American Suburban Architecture 1890–1930*. Cambridge, MA: MIT Press.

Gregory F.M. (2003) *The Fabric or the Building?: Influences on Homeowner Investment*. Unpublished PhD thesis. Cardiff: Cardiff University.

Gregson N. and Crewe L. (2003) *Second-hand Cultures*. Oxford: Berg.

Gregson N. (2007) *Living with Things: Ridding, Accommodation, Dwelling*. Oxford: Sean Kingston Publishing.

Greensted M. (2010) *The Arts and Crafts Movement in Britain*. Oxford: Shire.

Gubrium J. and Holstein J. (2002) 'From the Individual Interview to the Interview Society'. In J. Gubrium and J. Holstein (Eds.) *Handbook of Interview Research: Context and Method*. London: Sage: 3–32.

Gullestad M. (1995) 'Home Decoration as Popular Culture: Constructing Homes, Genders and Classes in Norway'. In S. Jackson and S. Moores (Eds.) *The Politics of Domestic Consumption: Critical Readings*. Hemel Hempstead: Prentice Hall/Harvester Wheatsheaf: 321–335.

Hadsund P. (1993) 'The Tin Mercury Mirror: Its Manufacturing Technique and Deterioration Processes'. *Studies in Conservation*, 38(11): 3–16.

Hage G. (2008) 'Analysing Multiculturalism Today'. In T. Bennett and J. Frow (Eds.) *The Sage Handbook of Cultural Analysis*. London: Sage.

Halbwachs M. (1992 [1952]) *On Collective Memory* (Ed. and trans. L. Coser). Chicago: University of Chicago Press.

Haldrup M. and Larsen J. (2004) 'Material Cultures of Tourism'. *Leisure Studies*, 25: 275–89.

Hall C. (1979) 'The Early Foundation of Victorian Domestic Ideology'. In S. Burman (Ed.) *Fit Work for Women*. Canberra: Australian National University Press: 15–32.

Hall L. (2005) *Period House Fixtures and Fittings 1300–1900*. Newbury: Countryside Books.

Hall P. (1992) *Urban and Regional Planning* (3rd Edn.). London: Routledge.

Hall S. (1992) 'New Ethnicities'. In J. Donald and A. Rattansi (Eds.) *Race, Culture and Difference*. London: Sage.

Hallam J. and Hockey J. (2001) *Death, Memory and Material Culture*. Oxford: Berg.

Halle D. (1993) *Inside Culture: Art and Class in the American Home*. Chicago: University of Chicago Press.

Hanson J. (1998) *Decoding Homes and Houses*. Cambridge: Cambridge University Press.

Haran J. (2010) 'Redefining Hope as Praxis'. *Journal for Cultural Research*, 14(4): 393–408.

Haraway D. (1991) *Simians, Cyborgs and Women: The Reinvention of Nature*. London: Routledge.

Harrison W. (1577) 'Descriptions of Britain and England'. In *Holinshed's Chronicles*, http://www.english.ox.ac.uk/holinshed/ [accessed 27 February 2013].

Hartley L.P. (1953) *The Go-Between*. Harmondsworth: Penguin.

Harvey D. (1996) *Justice, Nature and the Geography of Difference*. Oxford: Blackwell.

Hayward G. (1975) 'Home as an Environmental and Psychological Concept'. *Landscape*, 20: 2–9.

Heath A, Curtice J. and Elgenius G. (2009) 'Individualisation and the Decline of Class Identity'. In M. Wetherell (Ed.) *Identity in the 21st Century: New Trends in Changing Times. Identity Studies in the Social Sciences*. Basingstoke: Palgrave Macmillan: 21–40.

Heidegger M. (2010 [1962]) 'Building Dwelling Thinking'. In *Basic Writings* (Trans. and Ed. D. Farrell) London: Routledge: 343–364.

Henderson A. (1964) *The Family House in England*. London: Phoenix House.

Hepeng J. (2004) 'The Three Represents Campaign: Reform the Party or Indoctrinate the Capitalists?' *Cato Journal*, 24(3): 275.

Hepworth M. (1999) 'Privacy, Security and Respectability: The Ideal Victorian Home'. In T. Chapman and J. Hockey (Eds.) *Ideal Homes?: Social Change and Domestic Life*. London: Routledge: 17–29.

Herman B. (2005) *Town House: Architecture and Material Life in the Early American City 1780–1830*. Chapel Hill, NC: University of North Carolina Press.

Hetherington K. (2003) 'Accountability and Disposal: Visual Impairment and the Museum'. *Museum and Society*, 1(2): 104–115.

Hetherington K. (2008) 'The Time of the Entrepreneurial City: Museum, Heritage and Kairos'. In A. Cronin and K. Hetherington (Ed.) *Consuming the Entrepreneurial City: Image, Memory, Spectacle*. London: Routledge.

Hetherington K. (2011) 'Foucault, the Museum and the Diagram'. *The Sociological Review*, 59: 457–475.

Hewison R. (1987) *The Heritage Industry: Britain in a Climate of Decline*. London: Methuen.

Higgins H. (2009) *The Grid Book*. Cambridge, MA: The MIT Press.

Highmore B. (2002) *Everyday Life and Cultural Theory: An Introduction*. London: Routledge.

Hillier B. and Hanson J. (1984) *The Social Logic of Space*. Cambridge: Cambridge University Press.

Hills N. (1985) *The English Fireplace: Its Architecture and the Working Fire* (2nd Edn.). London: Quiller Press Ltd.

Hinton J. (2010) *Nine Wartime Lives: Mass Observation and the Making of the Modern Self*. Oxford: Oxford University Press.

Hinton J. (2013) *The Mass Observers: A History, 1937–1949*. Oxford: Oxford University Press.

Ho P-P. (2005) 'Ancestral Halls: Family, Lineage and Ritual'. In R. Knapp and K-Y Lo (Eds.) *House Home Family: Living and Being Chinese*. Honolulu, HI: University of Hawai'i Press: 295–323.

Hobsbawm E. and Ranger T. (Eds.) (1983) *The Invention of Tradition*. Cambridge: Cambridge University Press.

Hochschild A.R. (1989) 'Economy of Gratitude'. In D. Franks and E. Doyle McCarthy (Eds.) *The Sociology of Emotions*. Greenwich, CT: JAI Press.

Hockey J. (1999) 'Houses of Doom'. In T. Chapman and J. Hockey (Eds.) *Ideal Homes?: Social Change and Domestic Life*. London: Routledge: 147–160.

Hockey J., Komaromy C. and Woodthorpe K. (Eds.) (2010) *The Matter of Death: Space, Place and Materiality*. Basingstoke: Palgrave Macmillan.

Hockey J, Komaromy C. and Woodthorpe K.(2010a) 'Recovering Presence'. In J. Hockey, C. Komaromy and K. Woodthorpe (Eds.) *The Matter of Death: Space, Place and Materiality*. Basingstoke: Palgrave Macmillan: 223–234.

Holstein J. and Gubrium J. (1995) *The Active Interview*. London: Sage.

House of Commons Library (1999) 'The Right to Buy'. *Research Paper*, 99: 36: http://www.parliament.uk/Templates/BriefingPapers/Pages/BPPdfDownload.aspx? bp-id=RP99-36 [accessed 27 February 2013].

Howes D. (Ed.) (2005) *Empire of the Senses: The Sensual Cultural Reader*. Oxford: Berg.

Howes D. (2005a) 'Introduction: Empires of the Senses'. In D. Howes (Ed.) *Empire of the Senses: The Sensual Culture Reader*. Oxford: Berg: 1–17.

Hsü, Immanuel C.Y. (2000). *The Rise of Modern China* (6th Edn.). New York, NY: Oxford University Press.

Hubble N. (2006) *Mass Observation and Everyday Life: Culture, History, Theory*. Basildon: Palgrave.

Hull L. (2006) *Britain's Medieval Castles*. Santa Barbara, CA: Praeger.

Hunt P. (1995) 'Gender and the Construction of Home Life'. In S. Jackson and S. Moores, *The Politics of Domestic Consumption: Critical Readings*. Hemel Hempstead: Prentice Hall/Harvester Wheatsheaf: 301–313.

Hurdley R. (2006) 'Dismantling Mantelpieces: Narrating Identities and Materialising Culture in the Home'. *Sociology*, 40(4): 717–733.

Hurdley R. (2006a) *Dismantling Mantelpieces: Consumption as Spectacle and Shaper of Self in the Home*. Unpublished PhD thesis: Cardiff University.

Hurdley (2007) 'Objecting Relations: The Problem of the Gift'. *The Sociological Review*, 55(1): 124–143.

Hurdley R. (2007a) 'Focal Points: Framing Material Culture and Visual Data'. *Qualitative Research*, 7(3): 355–374.

Hurdley R. (2010) 'In the Picture or Off the Wall?: Ethical Regulation, Research Habitus and Unpeopled Ethnography'. *Qualitative Inquiry* 16(6): 517–528.

Hurdley R. (2010a) *Identity in the 21st Century*. Book Review. In *The Sociological Review*, 58(4): 710–712.

Hurdley R. and Dicks B. (2011) 'In-between Practice: Working in the "Thirdspace" of Sensory and Multimodal Methodology'. *Qualitative Research*, 11(3): 277–292.

Hurdley R. (2012) Cardiff University Web Page: http://www.cardiff.ac.uk/socsi/ contactsandpeople/academicstaff/G-H/dr-rachel-hurdley-overview.html [accessed 23 October 12].

Hurdley R. (2013) 'Against Narrative: confronting Mass Observation as Collage, Fragment, Juxtaposition'. *Narrative Works Special Issue*, 3(2).

Hwangbo A.B. (2002) 'An Alternative Tradition in Architecture: Conceptions in Feng Shui and Its Continuous Tradition'. *Journal of Architectural and Planning Research*, 19(2): 110–130.

Jackson S. and Moores S. (Eds.) (1995) *The Politics of Domestic Consumption: Critical Readings*. Hemel Hempstead: Prentice Hall/Harvester Wheatsheaf.

Jarvis A. (1947) *The Things We See: Indoors and Out*. Harmondsworth: Penguin.

Jennings H. and Madge C, with Beachcroft T.O., Blackburn J., Empson W., Legg S. and Raine K. (1937) *May the Twelfth: Mass Observation Day Surveys*. London: Faber and Faber.

Jervis N. (2005) 'The Meaning of Jia: An Introduction'. In R. Knapp and K-Y. Lo (Eds.) (2005) *House Home Family: Living and Being Chinese*. Honolulu, HI: University of Hawai'i Press: 223–233.

Johnson M. (1993) *Housing Culture: Traditional Architecture in an English Landscape.* London: UCL Press.

Johnson M. (1999) 'Reconstructing Castles and Refashioning Identities in Renaissance England'. In S. Tarlow and S. West (Eds.) *The Familiar Past? Archaeologies of Later Historical Britain.* London: Routledge: 69–86.

Jones T. (1996) *Britain's Ethnic Minorities.* London: PSI.

Jun S-J. and Blundell Jones P. (2000) 'House Design by Surname in Feng Shui'. *Journal of Architecture,* 5(4): 355–367.

Kaufmann J-C. (2009) *Gripes: The Little Quarrels of Couples.* Cambridge: Polity Press.

Keane W. (2001) 'Money Is No Object'. In F.R. Myers (Ed.) *The Empire of Things.* Oxford: James Currey: 65–69.

Kemeny J. (1991) *Housing and Social Theory.* London: Routledge.

Kenyon J.R. (2005) *Medieval Fortifications.* New York, NY: Continuum International Publishing Group.

Kittler F. (1999 [1986]) *Gramophone, Film, Typewriter* (Trans. G. Winthrop Young and M. Wutz). Stanford: Stanford University Press.

Knapp R.G. (1999) *China's Living Houses: Folk Beliefs, Symbols, and Household Ornamentation.* Honolulu: University of Hawai'i Press.

Knapp R. (2005) 'China's Houses, Homes and Families'. In R. Knapp and K-Y. Lo (Eds.) *House Home Family: Living and Being Chinese.* Honolulu, HI: University of Hawai'i Press: 1–9.

Knapp R. (2005a) 'In Search of the Elusive Chinese House'. In R. Knapp and K-Y. Lo (Eds.) *House Home Family: Living and Being Chinese.* Honolulu, HI: University of Hawai'i Press: 37–71.

Knapp R. (2005b) 'Siting and Situating a Dwelling: *Fengshui,* House-Building Rituals, and Amulets'. In R. Knapp and K-Y. Lo (Eds.) *House Home Family: Living and Being Chinese.* Honolulu: University of Hawai'i Press: 99–137.

Knapp R. and Spence J. (2006) *Chinese Houses: The Architectural Heritage of a Nation.* North Clarendon, VT: Tuttle.

Kopytoff I. (1986) 'The Cultural Biography of Things: Commoditization as Process'. In A. Appadurai (Ed.) *The Social Life of Things: Commodities in Cultural Perspective.* Cambridge: Cambridge University Press: 64–91.

Kumar K. (2005). *The Making of English National Identity.* Cambridge: Cambridge University Press.

Kuson A. and King A. (2000) 'On Be(ij)ing in the World: "Postmodernism", "Globalization," and the Making of Transnational Space in China'. In A. Dirlik and X. Zhang (Eds.) *Postmodernism and China.* Durham, NC: Duke University Press: 41–67.

Kvale S. (1996) *Interviews: An Introduction to Qualitative Research Interviewing.* Thousand Oaks, CA: Sage.

Kwint M., Breward C. and Aynsley J. (Eds.) (1999) *Material Memories: Design and Evocation.* Oxford: Berg.

Kynaston D. (2009) *Family Britain, 1951–1957.* London: Bloomsbury.

Langlands R. (1999) 'Britishness or Englishness? The Historical Problem of National Identity in Britain.' *Nations and Nationalism,* 5(1): 53–69.

Lapidge M. (2001) *The Blackwell Encyclopaedia of Anglo-Saxon England.* Oxford: Blackwell.

Latimer J. (2001) 'All-Consuming Passions: Materials and Subjectivity in the Age of Enhancement'. In N. Lee and R. Munro (Eds.) *The Consumption of Mass.* Oxford: Blackwell: 158–173.

Latimer J. (2004) 'Commanding Materials: Re-legitimating Authority in the Context of Multi-disciplinary Work'. *Sociology*, 38(4): 757–775.

Latimer J. and Munro R. (2009) 'Relational Extension, the Idea of Home, and Otherness'. *Space and Culture*, 12: 317–331.

Latimer J. and Skeggs B. (2011) 'The Politics of Imagination: Keeping Open *and* Critical'. *The Sociological Review*, 59(3): 393–410.

Latour B. (1993) *We Have Never Been Modern*. Cambridge, MA: Harvard University Press.

Latour B. (1998) 'How to be Iconophilic in Art, Science, and Religion?'. In Jones C. (Ed.) *Picturing Science, Producing Art*. London: Routledge: 418–441.

Latour B. (2004) 'Why Has Critique Run Out of Steam? From Matters of Fact to Matters of Concern'. *Critical Inquiry*, 30: 225–248.

Latour B. (2005) *Reassembling the Social: An Introduction to Actor-Network-Theory*. Oxford: Blackwell.

Law J. (1994) *Organising Modernity*. Oxford: Blackwell.

Law J. (1999) 'After ANT: Complexity, Naming and Topology.' In J. Law and J. Hassard (Eds.) *Actor Network Theory and After*. Oxford: Blackwell: 1–14.

Law J. (2002) 'On Hidden Heterogeneities: Complexity, Formalism, and Aircraft Design'. In J. Law and A. Mol (Eds.) *Complexities: Social Studies of Knowledge Practices*. Durham, NC: Duke University: 116–141.

Law J. (2003) 'Making a Mess with Method'. Online paper by the Centre for Science Studies, Lancaster University: http://www.lancs.ac.uk/fass/sociology/papers/law-making-a-mess-with-method.pdf [accessed 19 October 12].

Law J. (2004) *After Method: Mess in Social Science Research*. London: Routledge.

Law J. (2007) 'Making a Mess with Method'. In W. Outhwaite and S. Turner (Eds.) *The Sage Handbook of Social Science Methodology*. London: Sage: 595–606.

Law J. (2008) 'Actor-Network Theory and Material Semiotics'. In B.S. Turner (Ed.) *The New Blackwell Companion to Social Theory*. Oxford: Blackwell: 141–158.

Law J. and Mol A-M. (Eds.) (2002) *Complexities: Social Studies of Knowledge Practices*. Durham, NC: Duke University.

Lawler S. (2005) 'Disgusted Subjects: The Making of Middle-Class Identities'. *The Sociological Review*, 53: 429–446.

Lawler S. (2008) *Identity; Sociological Perspectives*. Cambridge: Polity.

Leal O.F. (1995) 'Popular Taste and Erudite Repertoire: The Place and Space of Television in Brazil'. In S. Jackson and S. Moores (Eds.) *The Politics of Domestic Consumption: Critical Readings*. Hemel Hempstead: Prentice Hall/Harvester Wheatsheaf: 314–320.

Leece S. and Freeman M. (2006) *China Style*. North Clarendon, VT: Tuttle.

Lefebvre H. (1991 [1974]) *The Production of Space* [trans. D. Nicholson Smith]. Oxford: Blackwell.

Levi M. (1989) *Of Rule and Revenue*. Berkeley, CA: University of California Press.

Lewis C. and Short C. (1879) *Freund's Latin Dictionary*. Oxford: Clarendon.

Lim S. and Corrie C. (2006) *Chinese Style: Living in Beauty and Prosperity*. Layton, UT: Gibbs Smith.

Liu H. (2005) *The Transnational History of a Chinese Family: Immigrant Letters, Family Business, and Reverse Migration*. Piscataway, NJ: Rutgers University Press.

Lladró (2012) www.lladro.com [Accessed 21 September 12].

Lo K-Y. (2005) 'Traditional Chinese Architecture and Furniture: A Cultural Interpretation'. In R. Knapp and K-Y. Lo (Eds.) *House Home Family: Living and Being Chinese*. Honolulu, HI: University of Hawai'i Press: 161–203.

Long H. (1993) *The Edwardian House*. Manchester: Manchester University Press.

Long H. (2002) *Victorian Houses and Their Details: The Role of Publications in Their Building and Detail.* Oxford: Architectural Press: 71–96.

Loukaki A. (1997) 'Whose *Genius Loci?*: Contrasting /interpretations of the "Sacred Rock of the Athenian Acropolis"'. *Annals of the Association of American Geographers,* 87(2): 306–329.

Low S. and Lawrence-Zuniga D. (Eds.) (2003) *The Anthropology of Space and Place: Locating Culture.* Oxford: Blackwell Publishers.

Lowenthal D., Feeley-Harnik G., Harvey P. and Kuchler S. (1996) 'The Past is a Foreign Country'. In T. Ingold (Ed.) *Key Debates in Anthropology.* London: Routledge: 199–248.

Lury C. (2008) 'Cultural Technologies'. In T. Bennett and J. Frow (Eds.) *The Sage Handbook of Cultural Analysis.* London: Sage: 570–586.

Macdonald S. (Ed.) (1998) *The Politics of Display.* London: Routledge.

Macdonald S. (2002) 'On "Old Things": The Fetishization of Past Everyday Life. In N. Rapport (Ed.) *British Subjects: An Anthropology of Britain.* Oxford: Berg: 89–106.

Macdonald S. (2007) 'Changing Cultures, Changing Rooms: Fashioning Identities and Anthropological Research'. In D. Bryceson, J. Okely and J. Webber (Eds.) *Fashioning Identities and Weaving Networks: Gender and Ethnicity in a Cross-Cultural Context.* New York, NY: Berghahn: 21–37.

MacDougall D. (2006) *The Corporeal Image: Film, Ethnography and the Senses.* Princeton, NJ: Princeton University Press.

Mackintosh M. (1979) 'Domestic Labour and the Household'. In S. Burman (Ed.) *Fit Work for Women.* Canberra: Australian National University Press: 173–191.

Madge C. and Harrison T.H. (1937) *Mass Observation.* London: Frederick Muller Ltd.

Madge C. and Harrisson T.H. (1938) *First Year's Work.* London: Lindsay Drummond.

Madigan R. and Munro M. (1999) '"The More We Are Together": Domestic space, Gender and Privacy'. In T. Chapman and J. Hockey (Eds.) *Ideal Homes?: Social Change and Domestic Life.* London: Routledge: 61–72.

Maleuvre D. (1999) *Museum Memories: History, Technology, Art.* Stanford: Stanford University Press.

Mallett S. (2004) 'Understanding Home: A Critical Review of the Literature'. *Sociological Review,* 52(1): 62–89.

Malpass P. and Murie A. (1999) *Housing Policy and Practice* (5th Edn.). Basingstoke: Palgrave Macmillan.

Marcoux J-S. (2001) 'The Refurbishment of Memory'. In D. Miller (Ed.) *Home Possessions: Material Culture behind Closed Doors.* Oxford: Berg: 69–86.

Marcus C.C. (1995) *House as a Mirror of Self: Exploring the Deeper Meaning of Home.* Berkeley: Conari Press.

Mason J. (2004) 'Personal Narratives, Relational Selves: Residential Histories in the Living and Telling'. *Sociological Review,* 52(2): 162–176.

Mason J. and Davies K. (2009) 'Coming to Our Senses? A Critical Approach to Sensory Methodology'. *Qualitative Research,* 9(5): 587–603.

Mass Observation (1937) *Mantelpiece Reports.* Sussex: Mass Observation Archive.

Mass Observation (1943) *An Enquiry into People's Homes.* London: Murray.

Mass Observation (1983) *Mantelpiece Reports.* Sussex: Sussex University.

Mass Observation (2006) *Your Home.* Sussex: Mass Observation Archive.

Mass Observation (2012) www.massobs.org [accessed 31 October 12].

Matrix (1984) *Making Space: Women and the Man-Made Environment.* London: Pluto.

Matthews K. (1999) 'Familiarity and Contempt: The Archaeology of the "Modern". In S. Tarlow and S. West (Eds.) *The Familiar Past? Archaeologies of Later Historical Britain.* London: Routledge: 155–179.

Mauss M. (1990 [1950]) *The Gift: The Form and Reason for Exchange in Archaic Societies* [Trans. W. D. Halls]. London: Norton.

McCrone D. (2008) 'Culture and Nation'. In T. Bennett and J. Frow (Eds.) *The Sage Handbook of Cultural Analysis*. London: Sage: 317–337.

McCracken G. (1991) *Culture and Consumption: New Approaches to the Symbolic Character of Consumer Goods and Activities*. Bloomington, IN: Indiana University Press.

McCracken G. (2005) 'Homeyness: A Cultural Account of One Constellation of Consumer Goods and Meanings'. *Culture and Consumption II: Markets, Meanings, and Brand Management*. Bloomington, IN: Indiana University Press: 22–47.

McVeigh T. (2009) '30 Years on, the Right-to-Buy Revolution that Still Divides Britain's Housing Estates'. *The Observer*, 6 December 2009: http://www.guardian.co.uk/society/2009/dec/06/right-to-buy-housing-thatcher [accessed 8 February 2010].

Melchior-Bonnet S. (2002 [1994]) *The Mirror. A History* (Trans. K. Jewett). London: Routledge.

Meldrum T. (1999) 'Domestic Service, Privacy and the 18th Century Metropolitan Household'. *Urban History*, 26: 27–39.

Mick D.G. (1996) 'Self Gifts'. In C. Otnes and R. Beltramini (Eds.) *Gift Giving: A Research Anthology*. Bowling Green, OH: Bowling Green State University Popular Press: 99–120.

Miller D. (1987) *Material Culture and Mass Consumption*. Oxford: Blackwell.

Miller D. (1988) 'Appropriating the State on the Council Estate'. *Man*, 23: 353–372.

Miller D. (Ed.) (1993) *Unwrapping Christmas*. Oxford: Oxford University Press.

Miller D. (Ed.) (1995) *Acknowledging Consumption: A Review of New Studies*. London: Routledge.

Miller D. (1998) *A Theory of Shopping*. Cambridge: Cambridge University Press.

Miller D. (Ed.) (2001a) *Home Possessions: Material Culture Behind Closed Doors*. Oxford: Berg.

Miller D. (2001b) 'Possessions'. In D. Miller (Ed.) *Home Possessions: Material Culture Behind Closed Doors*. Oxford: Berg: 107–122.

Miller D. (2001c) 'Inalienable Gifts and Alienable Commodities'. In F.R. Myers (Ed.) *The Empire of Things*. Oxford: James Currey: 91–115.

Miller D. (2002) 'Accommodating'. In C. Painter (Ed.) *Contemporary Art and the Home*. Oxford: Berg: 115–130.

Miller D. (2008) *The Comfort of Things*. Cambridge: Polity.

Miller J. (1995) *Period Fireplaces*. London: Mitchell Beazley.

Mills C.W. (1959) *The Sociological Imagination*. New York, NY: Oxford University Press.

Mo Y. (2003 [1988]) *Red Sorghum* [Trans. H. Goldblatt]. London: Arrow.

Modood T., Berthoud R., Lakey J., Nazroo J., Smith P., Virdee S. and Beishon S. (1997) *Ethnic Minorities in Britain: Diversity and Disadvantage*. London: PSI.

Mol A-M. (2003) 'The Body Multiple: Ontology in Medical Practice. Durham, NC: Duke University Press.

Mol A-M. and Law J. (2002) 'Complexities: An Introduction'. In J. Law and A-M. Mol (Eds.) *Complexities: Social Studies of Knowledge Practices*. Durham, NC: Duke University: 1–22.

Monguilod C. (2001) 'Ordering Others and Othering Orders'. In N. Lee and R. Munro (Eds.) *The Consumption of Mass*. Oxford: Blackwell: 189–204.

Morgan D. (1996) *Family Connections: An Introduction to Family Studies*. Cambridge: Polity.

Morgan D. (2011) *Rethinking Family Practices*. Basingstoke: Palgrave Macmillan.

Morgan J. (2005) *Domestic Cult in the Classical Greek House*. Unpublished Doctoral Thesis, Cardiff: Cardiff University.

Morgan J. (2007) 'Space and the Notion of a Final Frontier: Searching for Cult Boundaries in the Classical Athenian Home'. *Kernos*, 20: 113–129.

Morley D. (1995) The Gendered Framework of Family Viewing'. In S. Jackson and S. Moores (Eds.) *The Politics of Domestic Consumption: Critical Readings*. Hemel Hempstead: Prentice Hall/Harvester Wheatsheaf: 173–185.

Morley D. (2000) *Home Territories: Media, Mobility and Identity*. London: Routledge.

Morley J. (under review) 'Mass Observing the Great War in 1940'. In Mass Observation 2012 Conference Collection.

Mumford L. (1961) *The City in History*. Harmondsworth: Penguin.

Munro R. (2001) 'The Disposal of the Body: Upending Postmodernism'. *Ephemera*, 1: 108–30.

Munro R. (1999) 'Disposal of the X Gap: The Production and Consumption of Accounting Research and Practical Accounting Systems'. *Advances in Public Interest Accounting*, 7: 139–159.

Munro R. (2001) 'The Waiting of Mass: Endless Displacement and the Death of Community'. In N. Lee and R. Munro (Eds.) *The Consumption of Mass*. Oxford: Blackwell: 114–128.

Munro R. (2004) 'Punctualizing Identity: Time and the Demanding Relation'. *Sociology*, 38: 2: 293–311.

Munro R. (2005) Partial Organisation: Marilyn Strathern and the Elicitation of Relations'. In C. Jones and R. Munro (Eds.) *Contemporary Organisation Theory*. Oxford: Blackwell.

Muthesius H. (1979) *The English House* [Trans. J. Seligman]. London: Crosby Lockwood Staples.

Myers F.R. (2001) 'Introduction: The Empire of Things'. In F.R. Myers (Ed.) *The Empire of Things*. Oxford: James Currey: 3–61.

Newton C. and Putnam T. (Eds.) (1990) *Household Choices*. London: Futures Publications.

Nissenbaum S. (1997) *The Battle for Christmas*. New York, NY: Vintage.

Office for National Statistics [ONS] (2011) 'Family Spending, 2011 Edition': http://www.ons.gov.uk/ons/rel/family-spending/family-spending/family-spending-2011-edition/sum-consumer-durables-nugget.html [12 May 2012].

Nora P. (1989) 'Between Memory and History'. *Les Lieux de Memoires'* (Trans. M. Roudebush). *Representations*, 26: 7–24.

Oliver P. (1975) *Shelter, Sign and Symbol*. London: Barrie and Jenkins.

Oliver P., Davis I. and Bentley I. (1981) *Dunroamin: The Suburban Semi and Its Enemies*. London: Barrie and Jenkins.

Oliver P. (2003) *Dwellings: The Vernacular House Worldwide*. London: Phaidon.

Osaki R. (2003) 'The "Front" and "Back" Regions of the English House: Changing Values and Lifestyles'. *Journal of Housing and the Built Environment*, 18: 105 – 127.

Packard V. (1957) *The Hidden Persuaders*. New York, NY: Random House.

Pahl K. and Pollard A. (2010) 'The Case of the Disappearing Object: Narratives and Artefacts in Homes and a Museum Exhibition from Pakistani Heritage Families in South Yorkshire'. *Museum and Society*, 8(1): 1–17.

Pahl K. and Rowsell J. (2010) *Artifactual Literacy: Every Object Tells a Story*. New York, NY: Teachers College Press.

Pahl K. (2012) 'Every Object Tells a Story: Intergenerational Stories and Objects in the Homes of Pakistani-heritage Families in South Yorkshire, UK'. *Home Cultures*, 9: 3: 303–327

Pannett L. (2011) *Making a Livable Life in Manchester: Doing Justice to People Seeking Asylum.* Manchester University: unpublished PhD thesis.

Parisinou E. (2007) 'Space in Early Greek Domestic Architecture'. In R. Westgate, N.R.E. Fisher and J. Whitley (Eds.) *Building Communities: House, Settlement and Society in the Aegean and Beyond.* British School at Athens 15. London: British School at Athens: 213–223.

Parissien S. (1995) *The Georgian Group Book of the Georgian House.* London: Aurum Press: 155–165.

Parrott F. (2010) 'Bringing Home the Dead: Photographic Objects, Family Imaginaries and Moral Remains'. In M. Billie, F. Hastrup and T. Sorenson (Eds.) *An Anthropology of Absence: Materialisations of Transcendence and Loss.* New York, NY: Springer Press.

Peabody Essex Museum (2012): http://www.pem.org/sites/yinyutang/ [accessed 23 Jan 2013]

Peck H.T. (1898) (Ed.) *Harpers Dictionary of Classical Antiquities:* http://www.perseus.tufts.edu/cgi-bin/ptext?doc= Perseus:text:1999.04.0062 [accessed 25 May 2009].

Pennell S. (1999) 'The Material Culture of Food in Early Modern England c. 1650–1750'. In S. Tarlow and S. West (Eds.) *The Familiar Past? Archaeologies of Later Historical Britain.* London: Routledge: 35–50.

Perring D. (2002) *The Roman House in Britain.* London: Routledge.

Perseus (2012): http://www.perseus.tufts.edu [accessed 21 Jan 2013].

Peterson F. (2000) 'Anglo-American Wooden Frame Houses in the Midwest, 1830–1900: Origins of Balloon Frame Construction'. In S. McMurry and A. Adams (Eds.) *Power, People, Places: Perspective Vernacular Architecture, Vol. 8.* Knoxville, TN: University of Tennessee Press.

Petridou E. (2001) 'The Taste of Home'. In D. Miller (Ed.) *Home Possessions: Material Culture Behind Closed Doors.* Oxford: Berg: 87–104.

Pevsner N. (1963 [1943]) *An Outline of European Architecture* (7th Edn.). Harmondsworth: Penguin.

Phillips D. (1997) *Exhibiting Authenticity.* Manchester: Manchester University Press.

Phillips D. (2006) 'Parallel Lives? Challenging Discourses of British Muslim Self-segregation'. *Environment and Planning D. Society and Space,* 24: 25–40.

Phoenix A. (2010) 'Ethnicities'. In M. Wetherell and C. Mohanty (Eds.) *The Sage Handbook of Identities.* London: Sage: 297–320.

Pink S. (2004) *Home Truths: Gender, Domestic Objects and Everyday Life.* Oxford: Berg.

Pink S. (2009) *Doing Sensory Ethnography.* London: Sage.

Plummer K. (2001) 'The Call of Life Stories in Ethnographic Research'. In P. Atkinson, A. Coffey, S. Delamont and J. Lofland (Eds.) *Handbook of Ethnography.* London: Sage: 395–406.

Pomeranz K. (2002). 'Political Economy and Ecology on the Eve of Industrialisation: Europe, China and the Global Conjuncture'. *American Historical Review,* 107(2): 425.

Pow C-P. and Kong L. (2007) 'Marketing the Chinese Dream Home: Gated Communities and Representations of the Good Life in (Post-)Socialist Shanghai'. *Urban Geography,* 28(2): 129–159.

Prizeman J. (1975) *Your House: The Outside View.* London: Quiller Press.

Puig de la Bellacasa M. (2009) 'Touching Technologies, Touching Visions: The Reclaiming of Sensorial Experience and the Politics of Speculative Thinking'. *Subjectivity,* 28: 297–315.

Puig de la Bellacasa M. (2012) 'Nothing Comes Without Its World: Thinking with Care'. *The Sociological Review,* 60: 197–216.

Purbrick L. (2007) *The Wedding Present: Domestic Life Beyond Consumption*. Aldershot: Ashgate.

Putnam T. (2002) 'Mantelpiece Arrangement in the Modern British House'. In G. Ecker, C. Breger and S. Scholz (Eds.) *Dinge – Medien der Aneignung Grenzen der Verfügnung (Things – Media of the Appropriation, Borders of the Order)*. Königstein/Taunus: Ulrike Helmer Verlag: 44–59.

Putnam T. and Newton C. (Eds.) (1990) *Household Choices*. London: Futures Publications.

Puwar N. (2004) *Space Invaders*. Oxford: Berg.

Quennell M. and Quennell C. (1937) *A History of Everyday Things in England* (3rd Edn.) London: Batsford.

Rapoport A. (1969) *House Form and Culture*. Englewood Cliffs: Prentice Hall.

Rapaport A. (1995) 'A Critical Look at the Concept "Home"'. In D. Benjamin and D. Stea (Eds.) *The Home: Words, Interpretations, Meanings and Environments*. Avebury: Minnesota University Press: 25–52.

Rapport N. (Ed.) (2002) *British Subjects: An Anthropology of Britain*. Oxford: Berg.

Ravetz A. and Turkington R. (1995) *The Place of Home: English Domestic Environments 1914–2000*. London: Spon.

Reay D. (1998) *Class Work: Mother's Involvement*. London: University College Press London.

Reay D., Hollingworth S., Williams K., Crozier G., Jamieson F., James D. and Beedell P. (2007) 'A Darker Shade of Pale?' Whiteness, the Middle-classes and Multi-Ethnic Inner City Schooling'. *Sociology*, 41: 1041–1060.

Reed C. (Ed.) (1996) *Not at Home: The Suppression of Domesticity in Modern Art and Architecture*. London: Thames and Hudson.

Reed-Danahay D. (2001) 'Autobiography, Intimacy and Ethnography'. In P. Atkinson, A. Coffey, S. Delamont, J. Lofland and L. Lofland (Eds.) *The Handbook of Ethnography*. London: Sage: 407–425.

Reiger K. (1985) *The Disenchantment of the Home: Modernising the Australian Family 1880–1940*. Melbourne: Oxford University Press.

Reinberger M. (2003) *Utility and Beauty. Robert Wellford and Composition Ornament in America*. Newark, DE: University of Delaware Press.

Ricoeur P. (2006) *Memory, History, Forgetting*. Chicago: University of Chicago Press.

Rogaly B. and Taylor B. (2009) *Moving Histories of Class and Community*. Basingstoke: Palgrave Macmillan.

Rose G. and Tolia-Kelly D. (Eds.) (2012) *Visuality/Materiality: Images, Objects and Practices*. Farnham: Ashgate.

Rose N. (1998) *Inventing Ourselves: Psychology, Power and Personhood*. Cambridge: Cambridge University Press.

Rosselin C. (1999) 'The Ins and Outs of the Hall: A Parisian Example'. In I. Cieraad (Ed.) *At Home: An Anthropology of Domestic Space*. Syracuse: Syracuse University Press: 53–59.

Rowlands M. (2002) 'Heritage and Cultural Property'. In V. Buchli (Ed.) *The Material Culture Reader*. Oxford and New York, NY: Berg: 105–133.

Rumford (1796) *Of Chimney fFire-places: Essay IV*: http://www.rumford.com/chimneyfireplaces1.html [accessed 5 October 2010].

Rybczynski W. (1986) *Home: A Short History of an Idea*. London: Pocket Books.

Said E. (2003 [1978]) *Orientalism: Western Conceptions of the Orient* (2nd Edn.). Harmondsworth: Penguin.

Samuel R. (1994) *Theatres of Memory: Past and Present in Contemporary Culture*. London: Verso.

Saumarez Smith C. (2000) *The Rise of Design: Design and the Domestic Interior in 18th Century England*. London: Pimlico.

Saunders P. and Williams P. (1988) 'The Constitution of Home: Towards a Research Agenda'. *Housing Studies*, 3(2): 81–93.

Saunders P. (2002) 'Memory and Conflict'. In V. Buchli (Ed.) *The Material Culture Reader*. Oxford and New York, NY: Berg: 175–201.

Savage M. (2003) 'Review Article: A New Class Paradigm?' *British Journal of Sociology of Education*, 24(4): 535–541.

Savage M. (2007) 'Changing Social Class Identities in Post-War Britain: Perspectives from Mass-Observation'. *Sociological Research Online*, 12: 3: www.socresonline.org.uk/12/3/6.html [accessed 4 March 2010].

Savage M. (2008) 'Affluence and Social Change in the Making of Technocratic Middle-Class Identities: Britain, 1939–55'. *Contemporary British History*, 22(4): 457–476.

Savage M. (2010) *Identities and Social Change in Britain Since 1940: The Politics of Method*. Oxford: Oxford University Press.

Savage M. (2010a) 'Using Archived Qualitative Data to Study Socio-cultural Change'. In J. Mason and A. Dale (Eds.) *Social Researching: New Perspectives on Methods*. London: Sage.

Savage M., Wright D. and Gayo-Cal M. (2010) 'Cosmopolitan Nationalism and the Cultural Reach of the White British'. *Nations and Nationalism* 16: 598–615.

Schama S. (1996) *Landscape and Memory*. New York, NY: Vintage.

Scholz S. (2002) 'Andere Interieurs: James Agees Innenraume'. In G. Ecker, C. Breger and S. Scholz (Eds.) *Dinge – Medien der Aneignung Grenzen der Verfügung [Things – Media of the Appropriation, Borders of the Order]*. Königstein/Taunus: Ulrike Helmer Verlag: 60–64.

Schwarz B. and Schuman H. (2005) 'History, Commemoration and Belief: Abraham Lincoln in American Memory, 1945–2001'. *American Sociological Review*, 70(2): 183–203.

Scott S. (2009) *Making Sense of Everyday Life*. Cambridge: Polity.

Scourfield J., Taylor C., Moore G. and Gilliat-Ray S. (2012) 'The Intergenerational Transmission of Islam: Evidence from the Citizenship Survey.' *Sociology*, 46(1): 91–108.

Sear F. (1992) *Roman Architecture*. New York, NY: Cornell University Press.

Sheridan D. (1993) 'Writing the Archive: Mass-Observation as Autobiography'. *Sociology*, 27(1): 27–40.

Sheridan D., Street B. and Bloome D. (2000) *Writing Ourselves: Mass-Observation and Literacy Practices*. Cresskill, NJ: Hampton Press.

Silverstein P. (2004) 'Of Rooting and Uprooting: Kabyle Habitus, Domesticity and Structural Nostalgia'. *Ethnography*, 5(4): 553–578.

Simmel G. (1978) *The Philosophy of Money* [Trans. Bottomore T. and Frisby D.]. London: Routledge and Kegan Paul.

Sixsmith J. (1986) 'The Meaning of Home: An Exploratory Study of Environmental Experience'. *Journal of Environmental Psychology*, 6(4): 281–296.

Skeggs B. (1997) *Formations of Class and Gender*. London: Sage.

Skeggs B. (2004) *Class, Self, Culture*. London: Routledge.

Skeggs B. and Wood H. (2009) 'The Moral Economy of Person Production: The Class Relations of Self-Performance on Reality Television'. *Sociological Review*, 57(4): 626–644.

Skeggs B. (2010) 'Class, Culture and Morality: Legacies and Logics in the Space for Identification'. In M. Wetherell and C. Mohanty (Eds.) *The Sage Handbook of Identities*. London: Sage.

Skeggs B. (2011) 'Imagining Personhood Differently: Person Value and Autonomist Working-Class Value Practices'. *The Sociological Review*, 59(3): 496–513.

Skeggs B. (2012) 'Feeling Class: Affect and Culture in the Making of Class Relations'. In G. Ritzer (Ed.) *International Encyclopaedia of Sociology*. Oxford: Blackwell.

Skey M. (2012) *National Belonging and Everyday Life*. Basingstoke: Palgrave Macmillan.

Smart C. (2007) *Personal Life*. Cambridge: Cambridge University Press.

Sparke P. (1995) *As Long as It's Pink: The Sexual Politics of Taste*. London: Pandora.

Spence J. (1999) *The Search for Modern China* (2nd Edn.). New York, NY: W.W. Norton and Co.

St Fagans (2012) St Fagans National History Museum, Wales/Sain Ffagan Amgueddfa Werin Cymru: http://www.museumwales.ac.uk/en/stfagans/ [accessed 20 October 12].

Stange M. (2002) ' "A Strain of Constructive Artistry" – Zum Verhaltnis von *Gender* Und Interieur '. In G. Ecker, C. Breger and S. Scholz (Eds.) *Dinge – Medien der Aneignung, Grenzen der Verfügnung (Things – Media of the Appropriation, Borders of the Order)*. Kőnigstein/Taunus: Ulrike Helmer Verlag: 65–69.

Stanley L. (2001) 'Mass-Observation's Fieldwork Methods'. In P. Atkinson, A. Coffey, S. Delamont and J. Lofland (Eds.) *Handbook of Ethnography*. London: Sage: 92–108.

Stanley N. (1998) *Being Ourselves for You: The Global Display of Cultures*. London: Middlesex University Press.

Steedman C. (1982) *The Tidy House*. London: Virago.

Steinhardt N. (2005) 'The House: An Introduction'. In R. Knapp and K-Y Lo (Eds.) *House Home Family: Living and Being Chinese*. Honolulu, HI: University of Hawai'i Press: 13–35.

Stevenson G. (2003) *The 1930s Home*. Princes Risborough: Shire Publications.

Stoller P. (1997) *Sensuous Scholarship*. Philadelphia: University of Pennsylvania Press.

Strathern M. (1988) *The Gender of the Gift*. Berkeley, CA: University of California Press.

Strathern M. (1992) *After Nature: English Kinship in the Late 20th Century*. Cambridge: Cambridge University Press.

Strathern M. (1995) *The Relation: Issues in Complexity and Scale*. Cambridge: Prickly Pear Press.

Strathern M. (1996) 'Cutting the Network.' *The Journal of the Royal Anthropological Institute*, 2(3): 517–535.

Strathern M. (1999) *Property, Substance and Effect: Anthropological Essays in Persons and Thing*. Cambridge: Athlone Press.

Strathern M. (2004 [1991]) *Partial Connections*. Walnut Creek, CA: Altamira.

Tarlow S. and West S. (Eds.) (1999) *The Familiar Past? Archaeologies of Later Historical Britain*. London: Routledge.

Taschen A. and Guntli R. (2006) *China Style: Exteriors, Interiors, Details*. Cologne: Taschen.

Taussig M. (1999) *Defacement: Public Secrecy and the Labor of the Negative*. Stanford: Stanford University Press.

Taylor L. (1999) 'Re-entering the West Room: On the Power of Domestic Spaces'. In D. Birdwell-Pheasant and D. Lawrence-Zuniga (Eds.) *House Life: Space, Place and Family in Europe*. Oxford: Berg: 223–238.

Taylor R.L. (1982) 'Proposition and Praxis: The Dilemma of Neo-Confucian Syncresis'. *Philosophy of East and West*, 32(2): 187.

Thomas R.S. (2003 [1988]) 'The Other'. In *Selected Poems*. Harmondsworth: Penguin.

Thomas S. (2007) *Romanticism and Visuality: Fragments, History, Spectacle*. London: Routledge.

Thrift N. (2004) 'Bare life'. In H. Thomas and J. Ahmed (Eds.) *Cultural Bodies: Ethnography and Theory*. Oxford: Blackwell: 145–169.

Tilley C. (2001) 'Ethnography and Material Culture.' In P. Atkinson, A. Coffey, S. Delamont, J. Lofland and L. Lofland (Eds.) *Handbook of Ethnography*. London: Sage: 258–272.

Tolia-Kelly D. (2004) 'Locating Processes of Identification: Studying the Precipitates of Re-memory Through Artefacts in the British Asian Home'. *Transactions of the Institute of British Geographers*, 29: 314–329.

Tolia-Kelly D. (2006) 'Mobility/Stability: British Asian Cultures of "Landscape and Englishness" '. *Environment and Planning A*, 38: 341–358.

Tolia-Kelly D. (2010) *Landscape, Race and Memory: Material Ecologies of Citizenship*. Farnham: Ashgate.

Tosh J. (1999) *A Man's Place: Masculinity and the Middle-Class Home in Victorian England*. London and New Haven, CT: Yale University Press.

Tsakirgis B. (2007) 'Fire and Smoke: Hearths, Braziers and Chimneys in the Greek House'. In R. Westgate, N.R.E. Fisher and J. Whitley (Eds.) *Building Communities: House, Settlement and Society in the Aegean and Beyond*. British School at Athens 15. London: British School at Athens: 425–431.

Turkle S. (2007) *Evocative Objects*. Cambridge, MA: MIT Press.

UNESCO (2012) http://whc.unesco.org/en/list [accessed 25 October 12].

Upton C. (2005) *Living Back-to-Back*. Andover: Phillimore and co.

Urry J. (1990) *The Tourist Gaze: Leisure and Travel in Contemporary Societies*. London: Sage.

Utley J., Shorrock L. and Bown J. (2003) *Domestic Energy Fact File: England, Scotland, Wales and Northern Ireland*. Department for Environment, Food and Rural Affairs. [WWW], http://www.defra.gov.uk//environment/energy/research/domestic/index.htm [Accessed 20 February 2006].

Valentine G. and Sporton D. (2009) 'The Subjectivities of Young Somalis: The Impact of Processes of Disidentification and Disavowal'. In M. Wetherell (Ed.) *Identity in the 21st Century: New Trends in Changing Times. Identity Studies in the Social Sciences*. Basingstoke: Palgrave Macmillan: 157–174.

Veblen T. (1953 [1899]) *The Theory of the Leisure Class*. New York, NY: Mentor.

Vickery A. (2008) 'An Englishman's Home Is His Castle? Thresholds, Boundaries and Privacies in the 18th Century London House'. *Past and Present*, 199: 147–73: http://past.oxfordjournals.org/content/199/1/147.full [accessed 29 September 2010].

Waring A. (1947) *Approach to Better Housing*. London: Leonard Hill Ltd.

Weiner A. (1985) 'Inalienable Wealth'. *American Ethnologist*, 12(2): 210–227.

Wells K.(2012) 'Melancholic Memorialisation: The Ethical Demands of Grievable Lives'. In G. Rose and D. Tolia-Kelly (Eds.) *Visuality/Materiality: Images, Objects and Practices*. Farnham: Kent: 153–170.

Werbner P. (1990) *The Migration Process*. Oxford: Berg.

Werbner P. (1996) 'The Enigma of Christmas: Symbolic Violence, Compliant Subjects and the Flow of English kinship'. In S. Edgell, K. Hetherington and A Warde (Eds.) *Consumption Matters*. Oxford: Blackwell: 135–162.

Werbner P. (2004) 'Theorising Complex Diasporas: Purity and Hybridity in the South Asian Public Sphere in Britain'. *Journal of Ethnic and Migration Studies*, 30(5): 895–911.

Westgate R. (2007) 'House and Society in Classical and Hellenistic Crete: A Case Study of Regional Variation'. *American Journal of Archaeology*, 111: 423–457.

Westgate R. (2012) Personal email communication.

Weston C. (2002) 'A Window on the Past?: Viewing the Welsh Vernacular Interior c1800–1900'. Paper delivered at the Design History Society Annual Conference 'Situated Knowledges', Aberystwyth, Wales.

Wetherell M. (Ed.) (2009) *Identity in the 21st Century: New Trends in Changing Times*. Basingstoke: Palgrave Macmillan.

Wetherell M. (2009a) 'Negotiating Liveable Lives: Intelligibility and Identity in Contemporary Britain'. In M. Wetherell (Ed.) *Identity in the 21st Century: New Trends in Changing Times. Identity Studies in the Social Sciences*. Basingstoke: Palgrave Macmillan: 1–20.

Wetherell M. and Mohanty C. (Eds.) (2010) *The Sage Handbook of Identities*. London: Sage.

Wetherell M. (2012) *Affect and Emotion: A New Social Science Understanding*. London: Sage.

Whitman W. (2008 [1855]) *Leaves of Grass*. UNC-North Carolina: Project Gutenberg: http://www.gutenberg.org/ebooks/1322 [accessed 15 October 12].

Wicks R. (2003) 'Literary Truth as Dreamlike Expression in Foucault's and Borges's "Chinese Encyclopaedia"'. *Philosophy and Literature*, 27(1): 80–97.

Wilhide E. (1994) *The Fireplace: A Guide to Period Style for the Heart of the Home*. London: Little, Brown and Company.

Wilkins J. (1668) *An Essay towards a Real Character and a Philosophical Language*. London (publisher unknown).

Williams R. (1977) *Marxism and Literature*. Oxford: Oxford University Press.

Wood M. (1965) *The English Medieval House*. London: Phoenix.

Woodward I. (2001) 'Domestic Objects and the Taste Epiphany: A Resource for Consumption Methodology'. *Journal of Material Culture*, 6(2): 115–316.

Woolf V. (1929) *A Room of One's Own*. London: Harcourt.

Wright P. (2009) *On Living in an Old Country: The National Past in Contemporary Britain*. Oxford: Oxford University Press.

Wu F.L. (2004) 'Transplanting Cityscapes: The use of Imagined Globalisation in Housing Commodification in Beijing'. *AREA*, 36: 227–234.

Xenophon (1923 [362B.C.]) *Oeconomicus* [Trans. E. C. Marchant]. London: Heinemann LOEB.

Yan Y. (1997) 'The Triumph of Conjugality: Structural Transformation of Family Relations in a Chinese Village'. *Ethnology*, 36(3): 191–212.

Yan Y. (2005) 'Making Room for Intimacy: Domestic space and Conjugal Privacy in Rural North China. In R. Knapp and K-Y. Lo (Eds.) (2005) *House Home Family: Living and Being Chinese*. Honolulu, HI: University of Hawai'i Press: 373–395.

Yeh D. (2009) *Beyond (British) – Chineseness: The Politics and Poetics of Art and Migration in Multi-ethnic Contexts*. London: unpublished PhD thesis, University of East London.

Zelizer V. (1994) *The Social Meaning of Money*. New York, NY: Basic Books.

Index

Printed and bound in Great Britain by
CPI Antony Rowe, Chippenham and Eastbourne